Dwelling Portably

formerly named Message Post
POB 190, Philomath OR 97370
April 2000 $1 per issue   Add 50¢ to check/mo under $6

Stick makes cord handle more comfortable.
     Without it, the cord digs painfully
into my hand. The stick must be LONG or
the cord will slip off.
     The cord may be on several light objects
bundled together as a hand-~~~~~~ or on a
pail. I often find pails
to which I attach cords.
remove wire handles (easy
and replace with cord for
quiet. Julie Summers, OR

Plastic bottles make good
     Lighter weight than cases ~~~~ ~~~~
     Some lotion bottles are ideal size. I cut off enough of
the top to BARELY fit the glasses in (so they don't fall out).
Or, if too wide, I put a rubber band around it. Julie, 1996

Steel bread boxes are rodent-proof food-storage containers.
     I often find them in thrift stores. Bruce of BC, May 99

All-metal ammunition boxes good for storing electrical gear.
     Look for ones with good gaskets, and levers that pry the
lids closed tightly. Put gear inside with a drying agent.
The contents are relatively safe from water, animals, fire if
not intense, and EMP from a nuke weapon (or close lightning
strike?) because the metal shields contents. Paul Doerr, 1991

Wear gloves when handling watch batteries.
     Touching them with bare fingers may put sweat on them
which can gradually discharge them and shorten their lives.
     I prefer lithium watch batteries. They still work in
sub-zero cold where other batteries conk out. I had a cheap
Casio wrist watch with a 5-year lithium battery. Bruce of BC

Cheap, light way to sharpen blades; even stainless.
     Buy a variety pack of silicon carbide sandpaper
(five 5x11" sheets < $5). Place paper FLAT on (eg)
wood block. Stroke blade against grit, just like
with a sharpening stone. Don't press too hard or
the grit will quickly wear out. (Silicon carbide is
very hard but BRITTLE.) Use coarse grits (eg, 80)
for removing much metal; then fine grits (over 200)
for honing. The finer the grit, the keener the edge.
(Cutting oil did not help, and it unglued the paper.)
     For convenience, glue sandpaper to one end of a
wood block. Use remainder of block as handle. If
stuck on with rubber cement, worn-out sheets easily
replaced. Silicon carbide is so labeled on package
or sheets. Usually black. Greg DeLoach, ME 040, June

sand-
paper

handle

← 2" →

Before you use force, remember of course:
Always steer clear, of all that is dear:
Your eyes and your nose, your thumbs and your toes;
Your forehead and chin, your thighs and your shin.
     Make sure all your body parts are clear before applying
force with any tool, especially sharp ones such as needles,
awls, knives, saws. Ask yourself where the tool will go if

your stroke is longer than expected or the tool slips off your material or goes all the way thru. Especially when using awl, knife or screwdriver to pierce with, assume it will go thru the material and beyond. Make sure it will go harmlessly into space, or a work surface - NOT into your palm or thigh ! A lacing needle, or awl used to tighten a knot, will keep going the way you are pulling if lace breaks or awl slips. Pull in a safe direction, or brace elbows to limit stroke. Julie (?)

For one year I lived in a cellar in Toronto.
My friend was opening a small cafe, so I asked him to let me occupy 150 ft^2 of the basement. A small south-facing window opening to a sidewalk grate, let in some light and provided an emergency exit. I cleaned out some junk, then put up a simple 2x4 wall with locking door. I sound-insulated the wall and ceiling so I could practice on my sax - and not hear footsteps overhead. I spray-painted the walls with white latex, and put some found carpet on floor. (City folks throw out good stuff.)
I used the cafe's washroom, but urinated into wide-mouth bottles and sometimes just poured into the floor drain (to city sewer). For showering I used another bathroom, above the cafe, though sometimes I went to a public swimming pool.
I prepared simple meals on an alcohol camping stove, and had a small bar frig. Eventually I made a deal with the cafe and swapped dish washing and clean up for food.
I set up a small desk for writing, and could play my horn, listen to music, or watch a small TV. Rent: $75/mo. The building owner was pleased: my work had improved the basement.
I was renovating a school bus to live in (see May97 DP). When done, and agreed year over, I moved. Fred, Ont., March 99

Advantages of various kinds of insulating boards.
Caution: the half-inch thick aluminum-faced insulating board (in Aug99 DP), is a type of fiberglass. When cut or rubbed, it releases particles which are harmful to breathe. Also, when wet, its insulating value is almost zero.
Another rigid insulation available is blue board. Designed for underground use, it is impervious to water (it even floats). It is a type of styrofoam, so particles are not harmful. I am familiar with 1" and 2" thicknesses. Laura LaBree, WA 981, Oct

(Comment:) Unlike styrofoam, fiberglass does not melt, or burn and emit toxic fumes. That may be why it's much used in home construction (building codes). But no reason to use it where fire unlikely or where occupants can easily escape. B & H

Duct tape and first-aid tape can be re-rolled.
I carry duct tape in my fanny pack for expedient repairs of tents, packs, shoes, bikes, etc. But an economy roll is big and heavy. So I re-roll some onto (eg) a stick. Julie, 1996

How many window layers ? More not always better.
The more layers (spaced $\frac{1}{2}$" to 1" apart), the greater the insulation but the less light passed. Also, the less condensation on inner surface. But condensation not always bad.
Most winters we have two layers and, with two occupants (and no heater), our 10-ft-D $4\frac{1}{2}$-ft-high inner shelter is usually 60 to 65°F (and hotter when sunny or cooking). So far, this winter has been mild, so we've had only one layer. Result, 5° cooler, and more condensation (which collects in a trough and has to be sponged up every two days). But clothes dry faster, and mold stopped growing on the typewriter case. Bert

More on winter shelters.

May99 DP had tips on site selection & prep, window direction, floors, entry.

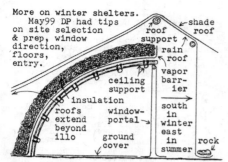

Here I'll discuss the shelter itself.

Though I've necessarily drawn a particular shape, what is best will depend on site, use, builder, and materials. A partially underground structure, with roof flush with the ground surface (such as in May95 DP), will be more sheltered from wind, less visible, and warmer during cold spells (because of heat from more earth surface exposed). However, digging may be impractical: ground frozen, solid rock, weak soil (sand), no drainage (swamp), or too little time.

To minimize transport, use mostly materials abundant nearby.

Though a single part may do more than one thing, I'll discuss: ceiling support, vapor barrier, insulation, and roofs.

Ceiling support might be branches interwoven or tied together to form a partial dome. Most branches are curved, and may be more available than straight poles. Conifers (eg, cedar, fir) are more durable than most broad-leaf trees. If sheltered, may last ten+ years. Mid-age dougfirs may have dead lower branches still sound. Drawback: pitchy.

However, for a dug-out, straight poles are easier to use. Lay across hole with ends extending at least a foot beyond. A small shelter might not need frame. Vapor barrier might be strong enough.

The vapor barrier keeps moisture (of breathing and cooking) out of insulation. Otherwise, during cold, vapor condenses: adds weight (danger!), lessens insulation, and eventually drips on occupants. Common polyethylene plastic is fine unless more strength is needed for (eg) a ceiling with no frame, or wide gaps. If you dislike buying plastic (which causes more to be made), look in furniture store dumpsters for shipment wrappers. (Stores generally love people to take them; else they quickly fill dumpster. The store may have more inside: ask.) If plastic holey, overlap wrappers.

For insulation, use anything fluffy or foamy that is ABUNDANT nearby. (But, fiberglass hazardous.) Bubble plastic passes light, but I've not found much. I find thin white foam (pads shipments). Too weak and squishy for mattress, but okay for insulation if nothing heavy will rest on it. To reduce amount needed, sheets might be spaced apart with (eg) dfir cones or styrofoam chips. If chips abundant, use to loosely fill plastic produce bags, then nestle bags together. (If loose, chips can blow.) Or suspend a few sheets of plastic ½" to 1" apart. (See Apr92 DP) Remember: stilled air is what insulates; not the solid material.

April 2000

Natural insulations: moss, leaves, hay. Gathering and hauling laborious, but can be done gradually after shelter is erected. If below freezing, snow can help insulate but needs other insulation under it; else shelter will remain cold and will gradually melt the snow.

In a dry climate, the roof might rest directly on the insulation. Otherwise I'd suspend it above; else puddles may form and compress insulation, or seep through small holes. In illo, the rain roof, which might be a big clear plastic tarp, is supported by poles or ropes (which are fastened to trees or braced-poles at the side - not shown).

The site may include trees or bushes with live branches extending over the shelter. If not, and if the shelter will be left up during sunny seasons, a shade roof will protect the rain-roof plastic from sun; and reduce visibility. Any dark cloth will do. Acrylic resists both sun and rain. (Some, in partial shade, has lasted us 20 years.) B & H

Rustic Retreats: build-it-yourself guide.

David and Jeanie Stiles provide brief instructions and diagrams for 26 diverse structures including: bowers, huts, small houses, cart, and cabin raft. Diagrams are generally clear and well-chosen for conveying much info briefly.

Tools, safety and joints get 7 pages. "Without electric power, the most difficult job: ... boring holes." Battery-powered drill suggested. "The most important hand tool is a crosscut saw with Teflon coating or a stainless steel blade and ten teeth per inch." If it binds, "spray the blade with silicone sliding compound or rub it with soap." 25 tools listed in order of usefulness.

"Thousands of accidents on ladders every year." Make sure legs are level and stable (but not mentioned: side-bracing tall ladder with cords). Never climb to top or above spot it leans on.

Nails "must be used perpendicular to the expected force. Use only galvanized nails and, if necessary, drill a pilot hole to avoid splitting." "Screws have 3 times the holding power of nails. Bolts are the best fastener because they provide a permanent clamping force...."

I question some of their joints. One they call "strong", I call "less weak". And, to attach a beam part way up a post, they recommend notching both members, which is extra work, and weakens them. I say, better to simply fasten beam to post (which they call "weak"), and add brace piece below, thusly:

Windows, doors and roofs get 11 p. Some roofs are encumbered with chimneys, turrets and sky-lights, which are complex and prone to leak. I say, better to put them thru a wall, beneath a roof with a big overhang.

For a handcart "capable of moving up to 500 pounds" they specify used 26" bicycle wheels. I say: too weak sideways, especially on rough ground at a construction site. 20" BMX wheels stronger.

Seven different huts get 30 p. Most are as complex as small houses. Simplest is a bent-pole hut covered with plastic and then "camouflaged with twigs, branches, or whatever is handy"; and a

3

lean-to thatched with boughs. "A very crude lean-to can be built in less than an hour using only an axe. However, one that will last more than one season and repel rain may take 2 or 3 days."

"Primitive native shelters": wigwam (3p), tipi (6p), yurt (6p), and stacked log hogan (4p). Canvas covered, except hogan which needs MANY logs.

Tree huts get 12 pages. A few of 15 guidelines: "Never design your tree hut first and then try to find a tree that fits. Let the tree suggest to you what the design should be." "Make safety your first consideration." "Allow for flexibility in the joints so the tree can grow and move with the wind." "You can nail or screw into large trees without causing much damage." Eek! ANY metal put into tree may cause you to be cursed when, long after hut is gone and tree dead and down and being cut up, someone's saw hits a forgotten nail !

This book inspires thinking about a wide variety of shelter shapes and construction techniques, though not always the most simple and reliable.

Bibliography describes 23 books, 2 periodicals, 6 catalogs (Campmor, Bean, Defender (marine), Silvo Hardware, Woodcraft, Harbor Freight Tools).

1998, 159p.8x11 (much white space), many diagrams, 2 color photos, $20 + shipping?, ISBN 1-58017-035-8. Storey Books, Schoolhouse Rd, Pownal VT 05261. Has 11 other home do-it-yourself books. 1-800-441-5700; www.storey.com   (B&H)

Making Bentwood Trellises, Arbors, Gates.

Also from Storey, Jim Long's book is about decorative structures. But the techniques can also (eg) form a shading over-roof at a semi-permanent camp-site.

"Bentwood projects ... can be made from a vast variety of woods. The main requirement: use green, flexible limbs for the arched parts." Cut "no more than 24 hours before you begin.... Wood loses flexibility quickly." Not fully restored by soaking. Before you cut, decide on a design and list the arch pieces needed.

Jim discusses good and bad traits of 29 eastern trees, including toxicity and invasiveness, in 15 p. Most rot in 2 or 3 years, except: bald cypress (Taxodium distichum), but hard to find and often short and stocky; eastern red cedar (Juniperus virginiana), but sap slightly sticky and needles mildly irritating; and osage orange (Madura pomifera). Not mentioned but we have used: western red cedar (Thuja plicata). It has relatives elsewhere (also called arborvitae).

"Settlers moving west in early 1800s took osage orange cuttings" and planted them "in rows spaced every 3 ft, then allowed to grow together into a dense hedge that was cut every 3 or 4 years... Impossible for cattle or people to penetrate hedge due to the tough, dense limbs and the short thorns along them."

"As the wood dries it will lose its flexibility, so don't try to reshape.... Joints that are wired will need to be retightened after shrinkage occurs."

Jim also tells (in 4p.) how to form a living arbor by training live saplings/ bushes/vines. That takes much longer as they must grow, but endures. Of the ten plants suggested, hemlock (Tsuga) and holly (Ilex) have foliage year-around.
April 2000

Designs for 22 bentwood and 9 other trellises, 6 gates, 13 fences, 4 arbors get 96 p. Jim then suggests vines for climbing them, and, finally, devotes 10 p. to recipes for teas and cakes to ingest while admiring your handiwork !

1998, 158p.8x9 (much white space), 14 color photos, many diagrams. $20 + shipping? ISBN 1-58017-051-X. (addr to left)

Report on Ero tent and a moss hut.

Last autumn we were temporarily in an area where we had little equipment and didn't want to build anything elaborate.

Holly had found a small dome tent in a dumpster; in good shape except poles missing and hole melted in netting. The floor showed no wear, indicating little use. Made in China for Ero Industries, Morton Grove IL 60053; sold by FredMeyer. 60x92x38"; floor 4.5oz reinforced polyeth, walls 1.7oz nylon taffetta. Much like the Taiwan-made Stansport (see May 96 & 97 DPs) except the door zipper was less convenient ($\perp$ instead of $\cap$ routing).

One problem: the top was net, with a fly (hooked-on tarp) suspended above, giving much ventilation whether wanted or not. (Done so someone can't asphyxiate self with candle, causing lawsuit?)

I salvaged slender branches from a fallen cedar and, by lashing two together with thin ends overlapping, made poles long enough to erect tent - with difficulty: I had to add side bracing cords to stabilize. (Maybe branches were less stiff than original poles.)

But the tent alone with its unstoppable ventilation, gave little warmth. Okay at night when huddled under sleeping bags. But not for frosty early mornings when we wanted to do things inside while waiting for outside to warm up.

An old moss-covered maple had fallen nearby. That inspired me to build a moss hut around the tent. I did not trust the tent to support the moss (it barely held up itself !). So, over the tent, I made a squat tipi-like frame (from little alders in need of thinning), and layed moss on that. I had to repeatedly chink thin areas and sags. (I used MUCH moss.)

To reduce ventilation, and keep our breath moisture out of the moss, I covered the tent with plastic; except the door on which I hung several burlap bags which we raised to enter. When we wanted light inside, we replaced the burlap with plastic. To keep dew and rain off the moss, another tarp went over it, extending to the ground on 3 sides, but tied out in front to form an antiway in which we could remove rain wear and keep water and pee containers.

After ALL THAT, we were comfortable. One cold mid-Oct dawn, outside measured 29°F, inside 60°. Quite dry after moss added. (With tent alone, condensation on walls trickled down into our foam pads, becoming wet spots.) Minor gripes: moss fragments fell on us and bed when we went in or out; tent walls sagged. YKK Winnebago plastic zippers all worked at first, but outer one soon failed.

Despite having a level site and all items within 200 yds, project took ± 30 hours. Worthwhile for a two-month stay? Probably not. But educational. Bert

Our backyard tent rotted in the sun !!!

We set up a smaller tent, but keep it covered during day. Phyllis, CA 921

Free parking for live-in vehicles ?

Many community parks allow free camping, usually boondocking (no piped water or power), but sometimes with limited hookups. Some fed lands allow boondocking, but usually charge.

My husband and I spent $3 total for camping fees during our first 3 years on the road as full-time RVers. That was for one night in a NM park on the Mex border. Coleen Sykora
(from Workers On Wheels #24)

(Comments:) My impression: communities that offer free camp sites are generally in long-depressed areas (eg, Great Plains) where chambers of commerce try desparately to attract retirees or anyone who will spend money. (Years ago, DP got a brochure from a highway assoc in s.Nebraska listing free camping there.)

In western Oregon, though there may be possibilites we do not know about (not having a motor vehicle, we are not keenly attentive), the only campgrounds we know of close to cities are not free. (And we've heard of people ticketed for sleeping in vehicles parked on streets.) Farther out, there are many graveled logging roads, negotiable by most pickups and vans, and some sedans. (But I'd not take a motorhome.) Many of the roads, espec close to cities, have locked gates (more now than 20 years ago) and are posted against motor vehicles (though motorcycles often bypass gates): often good for hikers and bicyclists. Most gravel roads are occasionally patrolled by police or timber-company security (depending on whose land: some areas are a checkboard). There are many dead-end spurs where one can park away from the main road. B & H, OR 973

Protecting a trailer against thieves and vandals.

Replying to Angela in Nov99 DP: many things can be done to make a trailer safer. Most cost less than $50 and are sold by building supply stores. Old trailers are less-easily made safe than mid-1970s and later, because built differently.

First: install an interlocking hinge protector. This keeps door from being jacked open, or pried open with crowbar; because the hinge locks from the hinges, not the door handle.

Next: add lock guards that go over door next to handles. Door knobs and dead-bolt locks also worth adding or changing.

Also good: reinforce door frame with 2x4s nailed into the wall. This helps prevent jacking a door open. (A burglar can use a car jack to force apart the frames on each side of a door. After half an inch, the door will just swing open.)

Windows, too, need attention; especially any near ground level. Bolt on Plexiglas, Lexan or other coverings that are difficult to break. If caulked, they also add insulation.

Home security systems can be bought and easily installed, and you can subscribe to a monitored alarm system. There are other possibilities, but these will get you started.

Remember: even a fort will not keep burglars out if the occupants don't do their part. Lock your doors, get to know your neighbors, and tell them what you would like them to do if they see anyone but you go into your trailer.

If someone is strongly determined to get in, they will. But with some thought and a little work, you can make breaking-in too difficult to tempt a casual thief. Steven Cleveland,
TN 377, Dec

(Comment:) Instruct your neighbors CAREFULLY. If (eg) a friend arrives before you do and enters with your permission, you don't want someone over-reacting and calling the police !!
April 2000

Be wary of distant job offers, especially at campgrounds.
        If seeking work, I'd only go to areas where I wanted to
spend time whether or not I found jobs. Then, while there,
I'd check out what was available. If I found a camping
facility I thought I'd like, I'd stay there a few days to get a
feel of the place and to learn what work they might need.
        I've heard many horror stories about people who accepted
far-away jobs and spent much time and money traveling to them,
and then were unhappy. Coleen Sykora (from Workers on Wheels)

For quick earning with little expense, consider cab driving.
        I can almost always get a job immediately, anywhere in
the country. Drivers often quit, and cab owners are anxious
to keep their equipment rolling.
        After 6 months, a driver will usually start to 'burn out'
and not put in as many hours. That's okay: if you've worked
hard and not spent much, you'll have enough money to move on.
        I just quit the best deal I ever had: 38% of meter plus
owner paid gas. I did so much business I couldn't handle the
stress. But I now have enough to live modestly for two years.
        I usually lease a 24-hour (single shift) cab and sleep in
it, bathing at public facilities. Generally, if one is
working hard, the owner gives you a lot of leeway.
        You will need a valid drivers license with good record,
and a sense of direction and ability to rapidly learn your way
around. Cab driving is a good way to scout a new area, and
gain information and interesting experiences.
        I buy a map and (if available) a cab-drivers handbook.
The handbook tells the city's numbering system, and the map
shows lakes, rivers, railroads which break up the system.
        Alas, driving is becoming increasingly competitive and,
in big cities, regulated. Also, some cities are dangerous,
even if one knows the streets well. I advise: small towns,
or working-class suburbs adjacent to big cities. Depressed
areas are actually good places to make money as many people
there can't afford cars. You'd be surprised how many people I
take to welfare offices. Waitresses and bartenders often tip
well, because THEY depend on tips. Las Vegas is, by universal
acclaim, the best place to earn big bucks. As with anything,
ask the old timers - which will be easier after one has
'hacked' a few times. Kurt Wettstein, IL 606, March 99

Are freight trains more dangerous than highway vehicles ?
        (Responding to Laura's report in Nov99 DP:) One of my
uncles worked many years as an engineer (train driver). He
told about folks trying to hop freights. Of how they were
injured trying to get on, and of hassles by railroad security.
Ever since, I've stayed far away from moving trains.
        Hopping may be a thrill for some folks. But I'm content
to walk, hitch, or get rides other ways. You are correct that
known hobo camp-sites become targets of police. Steven, TN377
                                                        Dec
(Comment:) Someone in Hobos From Hell (review in May96 DP)
thought railroads were safer than highways, at least for going
long distances. Though getting on and off a moving train is
risky, while on,you are relatively safe, provided you (eg)
avoid cargo that might shift and crush you ! Yes, railroad
security can be nasty. But so can highway police. These days
with ANY mode of travel, do it only if you have a STRONG
reason to, and KNOW what you are doing !!!
        To anyone considering hopping, I strongly recommend the
Hobos From Hell books (review, at least) for safety tips. B&H
                        April 2000

I spent summer in the police states of Florida and Louisiana.
The Florida Marine Patrol stopped my slow boat on a slow
day. After I was interrogated and my boat searched, and cited
for no life preserver on board, I was "free" to go if I would
wear a state-loaned life jacket. (I wonder how the REAL natives
(Creek, Apalach, Seminole) survived for centuries without life
jackets in their canoes !) Which is the least policed of the
50 police states ? I want to move somewhere and be left alone.
I've been living car-free for almost a year. Jimmy, TN 374,Jan

Be wary of "welfare agencies", especially if you have kids.
A family consisting of mother, father, and two children
age 4 and 6, had been living in their van, going from day job
to day job. A local church announced a food bank for needy
folks. But, when the family asked for food, the church turned
them in to police. The children were taken into custody by
child "protection services" and the parents were arrested for
"child endangerment." The parents are now out of jail and
trying to get their kids back, so far to no avail. Steven,
                                                    TN 377, Dec
Pluma Beyer (who edits/publishes Green Pathfinder) lives
in a 12x12 ft cottage she built. The cottage has electricity,
stove, sink, and running cold water; but no frig. Hot water
is obtained by heating on the stove.
After giving birth, Pluma's sister was staying with Pluma.
Social workers visited, supposedly to make sure the baby was
well cared for. They pretended to be friendly, and left. Two
hours later they returned with police, snatched "the two-day-
old baby from the arms of its mother who was successfully
breast-feeding,it", and took it to foster care. They cited
the baby's temporary surroundings. Several months and one
court hearing later, the baby had not been returned. Pluma
reports, "I am astonished at how social workers lie." TN 376

(Comments:) Social workers have an incentive to lie ! In May
97 DP, Tom Van Doren in Idaho reported: "State social services
get $4000 from the government for every child they put into a
foster home. They keep 75%, and are not responsible for what
it is spent on." Also in May97, Michael Sunanda reported on
kids snatched from people he knew. And we've read many horror
stories elsewhere. Tips for avoiding trouble in Dec96 DP.
Though most portable dwellers less jeopardized than rooted
folk (either hard to find or quick to move), best avoid roads
and public places (except maybe summer when many kids about).

After any suspicious encounter, promptly move on.
Local news item: A 15-year-old boy was playing basket-
ball. Needing to pee, to save time he went into bushes. An
8-year-old girl saw him and told her mother who called police.
They arrested him, charging child abuse. He was convicted of
exposing himself and is now in a juvenile prison with a sex
crime permanently on his record. Steven Cleveland, TN 377, Dec

(Comments:) If the boy had immediately left the scene, he
probably would have been well away by the time the police
arrived. (But maybe he didn't know he'd been spotted.)
When we visit cities, we often use bushes, not only to
pee, but for jug showers, and to temporarily stash and later
retrieve big items we don't want to lug around: all activities
a law-n-order fiend might consider offensive or suspicious. Of
course, we use (eg) undeveloped park areas where few people go.
But accidents happen. If spotted, we quickly leave the area.
                        April 2000

How to live during tough times ?

Recently, many readers have asked this or similar questions. Some say the USA (USSA?) is now a police state. And police are not the only threat.

Is a portable dwelling safer than a house or apartment ? That depends on particulars, as there are many options.

During our 20-odd years dwelling portably, Holly and I have had very few scary encounters; and no arrests or fines, serious injuries or illnesses, or major property losses. Because we did things right? Or mostly luck? Anyhow, for what they're worth, our suggestions.

Minimize travel on roads. Besides bringing hassles, vehicles destroy more years of life and health than does any other menace. (Cancers mostly kill those who have already lived long.)

Recreate near home. Instead of big, far-away gatherings, seek local picnics, etc. For distant fellowship, maybe hold many the same day and link by radio.

If you must travel on roads, ride-share with careful drivers. Keep windows clear (no stickers or danglies) and all lights working. Carry spare bulbs for promptly replacing any burn-outs.

For rest stops, park away from public roads. If bicycling, you might go into some bushes. If motoring, pull into a shopping-center parking lot (where cops seldom hassle unless complaint.) *5/99p3

For long stays, seek private land where you can park (with permission) out of sight of roads and neighbors.

When employed, try to find shelter close to work. Some companies allow employees to park overnight or camp on their lot, and use water and electricity. (Advantages to employer: workers are more available for unexpected rush over-time jobs, and their presence deters burglars.) When choosing a job, pay attention, not to the supposed pay rate, but to how much you can CLEAR after all living costs are paid. *6/88p7

Though a motor vehicle is sometimes useful, ownership is a costly nuisance. If you must have, pick a common one that won't attract attention and that has parts widely available. *5/96p11

Backpackable dwellings are much easier to hide. *5/95p9-12, 5/94p10-11. But, if remote, will re-supply be a problem? Think about various ways to. *5/96p3

Don't expect to find one dwellingway that combines all the advantages of several different ways. Eg, as roomy as a house or big dome, mobile as a 4WD, portable and low-cost as a small tent, and secure as a dug-out. You must choose. However, contrary to beliefs of folks whose only camp-out was an ordeal, physical comfort is quite easily obtained, though may require learning how. *9/84.

Regardless of dwellingway, generally be quiet and unobtrusive. Do anything noisy either in a remote TEMPORARY spot and leave immediately, or in a sound-proof chamber. (Underground? *9/86p5)

Store at least 6 months food. 6 YEARS is better if you expect to remain in the same area. *9/85p1, 6/88p3. But hide in several places to protect from thieves both private and official. (Now law: when an emergency is declared in an area, anyone caught with more than six-months food is eligible for 15 years in prison, REGARDLESS of when purchased!)
April 2000

Cut costs. Expensive possessions and activities not only attract robbers, but take much of your life to pay for.

Don't train for jobs or start businesses that need licenses.

Get your dwellingway in good shape before having children. Have kids only if you(all) can care for them full-time. (Sticking them in schools forces them into a clash of values between other kids and you, that will likely make them AND YOU miserable.) Keep school-age kids unseen during school hours. *12/96

Don't give up hope. Police states don't last forever. (The 70-year USSR lasted unusually long.) Unless reformed, they eventually bring themselves down by fouling their economy or environment, and alienating supporters. Ordinary people can hasten change by avoiding taxes and fines, and spending less. Eg, a boycott of recreational travel would not only save lives and reduce pollution, but cut the profits of oil companies, auto makers, airlines, and giant resorts - and THOSE folks will get atten-tion if they tell the cops: "lay off" ! Bert & Holly, Oregon 973, January
* DP issue and page with more on topic.

Safety for a woman or child alone.
Best be hard to find. But maybe your camp is temporary and you don't want to spend much time hiding it.

To deter two-legged predators, you might simulate being with other people whose return you expect at any moment. Eg, when a second sleeping bag is not needed for warmth, lay it out to suggest an additional bed. And, beside it, put sweater, jeans, and boots much larger than yours. (If big enough to wear over yours, they'd also give extra warmth.)

Against four-footers I suggest, first a spear, which can be just a sharpened pole of a tough wood (test), light enough to move fast. Jab, DON'T throw. (If you throw, it's GONE!) Also see Nov99 and May95 DPs. Holly & Bert.

Be wary of big, dead, high limbs.
Even a small branch can kill or maim if it falls far enough to gather speed. A hard-hat or helmet can save your head from light blows but not heavy ones.

Though limbs and whole trees often fall during winter storms, they also fall on warm summer days when carpenter ants, termites, and fungi are active.

Be alert for breaking sounds above: you may have time to dodge. Also be aware, if you grab or bump a tall slim tree that bends, it may knock something loose high up.

Best not camp near big trees. If you must, choose the base of a straight live conifer (eg, fir, pine) with many large limbs near ground that may intercept branches falling from higher up. Even a plastic tarp adds some protection. (Though weak, it will stretch and absorb energy.) Camp on SIDE (not top or bottom) of narrow valley. (Less wind.)
(B&H)

Choosing pack frames for comfort.
In summer 1999 Outdoor Explorer, Mike Randolph, though writing for rec hikers, gives some advice good for all.

If you hike mostly on trails or easy terrain, choose an external frame with "a high pack bag, which enables the wearer to stand up straight and helps the frame ... transfer the weight onto hips." Also, "inexpensive, and cool in hot weather because the frame keeps the pack bag away from your back." "If, however, you scramble up mtns and need lots of flexibility," pick an internal frame.

Mike prefers bags with drawstring closures. "Zippers eventually wear out."

Not addressed: how easily can pack bag be removed when frame is used for hauling (eg) pails and boxes, and how well does it endure such use? Extra-strong "freighter" frames are made.

To stow map, compass, sunglasses, etc, Mike favors a pack bag with many external pockets. But they won't help when the pack bag isn't on. I prefer pouches on the waist belt. Or, on a smooth trail, I sometimes wear a small knapsack in front as well as an external frame in back. I can access knapsack's contents without removing anything. Also, the weight in front improves my balance. Drawback: I can't easily see my feet and where they step. To keep the knapsack's straps from slipping off, I put it on first, with the frame's straps over.

For comfort, seek a frame with "hip belt that hugs the sides of your pelvis without creating any gaps. When you have the pack on and it's loaded down, the angle of the hip belt is not right if the belt is tighter at bottom than at top." "Firm foam preferable...."

Shoulder straps should "meet your (shoulders) at a comfortable angle."

"Be wary of stores that carry only one style of frame, and of zealous salespeople who recommend a type of pack before asking the magic question: 'what kind of hiking do you plan on doing?'"

But the proof is in the wearing. "If possible, borrow a friend's pack, fill it up, and take it for a test hike."

Almost any frame will eventually cause sore spots. Not mentioned: if with others, swap loads occasionally, so weight bears on different spots. Or, if carrying in stages, taking one load part way and then going back for the next, use two+ different frames, alternating.

Also not mentioned: building your own. Plans for a simple triangular frame of branches in LLL. Merits, besides being buildable when needed: potentially light-er; easily folds for rides or storage. But loading for comfort takes longer, espec with big hard items like pails.

Polyprop clothing preferred to wool.
(Re March & Sept 84 DPs): I've used polypropelene Boy Scouting, and it kept me dry and warm where wool did not. I make sure new boys' parents get it for them. Steven Cleveland, TN 377, July

Good wicking helps prevent blisters.
California College of Podiatric Med study: runners in cotton socks got twice as many blisters, three times as big, as those wearing acrylic. Dampness blamed: not wicked away as well by cotton as by acrylic or wool. Julie Summers, 1990

Vapor barriers, sweat - and odors.
Stephenson (see p.5) sews vapor barrier liners into sleeping bags, and sells vb undershirts ($25-$30 + ship). He challenges readers: "do a test. (If) you are wearing an undershirt, one or two insulating shirts, and a warm jacket: replace the undershirt with a vb shirt.

(Lacking a proper one, use a plastic bag with holes cut for head and arms.) Don't put the jacket back on and you will notice you are as warm as before.... The vb shirt reduces loss of humidity and thus reduces evaporative cooling at your skin...." I'm now trying that and, yes, I need one less sweater. But I put on the plastic bag, not next to my skin, but over my undershirt, because yrs ago:

I was bivying in a city and had only one thin sleeping bag. So I used a big plastic bag as a liner. It was not comfortable next to my skin, clinging to me when I turned over. But it did add warmth. However, after 2 days, despite daily washing of feet and arm pits (but not liner), my whole body and the liner got stinky - much like feet can smell.

Stephenson claims, a vapor barrier reduces odors because of "quick sensing and thus avoidance of sweating, plus blocking of air circulation that causes sweat to turn rancid." But I found, ABSENCE of circulation was what caused odor build up. (Feet stink; not hands.)

(Later.) I've now worn the plastic bag during 7 days, with the same upper-body garments. Only arm pits washed. No unusual odors. Maybe the cloth between skin and plastic allows enough circulation. (However, bag's neck and arm holes enlarged, compromising test.)

I plan to repeat sleeping-bag test, but with a cloth liner INSIDE plastic.

Stephenson's vapor barrier is not a smooth plastic but a "flannel-like soft fabric". Assuming no clinging, perhaps it alone allows enough air circulation. Stephenson claims: "easy to clean with a wipe of a damp cloth (soap or detergent okay if needed)." B & H, February

More about ticks. (Also see May99 DP)
If wearing clothes, smooth fabrics, such as windbreakers, are better than knits. Harder for ticks to grab onto.

If wearing long pants, tuck into socks, so that any ticks that get on feet must crawl up the outside of pants and might be spotted before reaching skin. But ticks may grab on elsewhere.

Any clothes should be light colored, for easier spotting of dark ticks.

If you cut your fingernails short, and seldom carry POINTED tweezers, you might leave parts of a few nails long enough to use as tweezers. Grab tick as close to your skin as possible.

Permethrin "repels 82% to 100% of ticks", but is toxic and absorbed thru skin. If used, apply only to clothes and let dry before wearing. Ditto DEET. An early DP tip: wear cat flea collars on boot ankles. But won't stop ticks above.

Larval ticks feed on mice. To de-infest an area, scatter tubes of cotton balls dipped in insecticide. (Eg, Damminix) Mice use cotton to make nests.

A former lyme patient says: few MDs can/will diagnose or cure lyme (which requires high doses of antibiotics for months). For lyme specialists, plus treatment info (latest only on internet: some librarians can help): www.Lyme.org

The map, from Yale U of Med, shows "lyme risk" by county in ne. Only other mod-risk county: Mendocino CA. But a county may be "low risk" either because ticks few or not infected, OR because humans are seldom outside. Within an

April 2000

area, risk depends on habitat, espec mouse numbers. A backyard or park may be more hazardous than a remote mtn. H & B, Jan

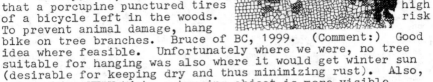

moderate
risk →

low
risk ↙

high
risk

Store bicycle off ground ?

In May98 DP, Bert reported that a porcupine punctured tires of a bicycle left in the woods. To prevent animal damage, hang bike on tree branches. Bruce of BC, 1999. (Comment:) Good idea where feasible. Unfortunately where we were, no tree suitable for hanging was also where it would get winter sun (desirable for keeping dry and thus minimizing rust). Also, unless hung VERY high, a hanging object is more visible.

Many years we've left bikes over winter in woods, protected only by tarps, with no damage. We were hoping to stay lucky. That winter we didn't. Bert & Holly, OR 973

Folding bicycles are handy but expensive.

In Nov 1998 I bought Car-I-Bike's "Urban" 5-speed at Cruiser Bob's in Oceanside CA for $270. Under 30 pounds with a factory kickstand. No problems so far.

I found the Urban takes about the same effort as a full-size bike. Maybe a bit more on hills. I pulled a trailer shopping, but not up any serious hills. (But a trailer is no fun on hills even with a full-size bike.) I would not use it for loaded touring (only 5 speeds), but I did a comfortable 80 miles in one day out of Seattle with a daypack.

It's best feature: when folded, there is room for it almost anywhere, so I can take it with me to use at a camp-site, in town, wherever. Cruiser Bob says, you can stuff it in a bag and carry it on a bus. I also test rode a Dahon but found it way too flexible. Ken Gilbert, WA 982, Nov

Bicycles with 20" wheels have some advantages for adults.

They fit easily inside trunk, shell or van. Though not as compact as folders, they cost much less. Often found at yard sales. Tires and tubes are cheaper than for 26" wheels. Spokes are shorter and much stronger. BMX one-speeds are built for abuse. But extra-long seat post needed. Ken, Nov

Small bike handy, not speedy.

I'd had trouble fitting a full-size bike into some vehicles. So, when I saw a 20" "kiddy" bike free at a yard sale, I took it. It lacked a seat but was otherwise okay and seemed sturdily built.

Fortunately, I had a seat and a LONG seat post among my parts collection. The post's diameter was a little too small, but with a shim of drink-can aluminum, it fit passably. When I raised the seat high enough, only the recommended-minimum 2" was within the bike's frame. But the bike's sissy bar, when positioned high and angled forward, reached the (regular,

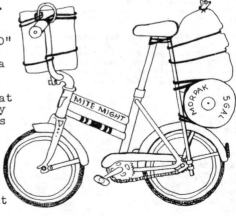

MITE MIGHT

MORPAK 5 GAL

April 2000

not banana) seat, to which I lashed it as added support.

Unfortunately, with the shim and the lashed sissy bar, the seat won't easily lower for transport. But the high-rise handlebars swivel down after loosening one nut, and that alone allows the bike to fit in some small cars.

The sissy bar plus the sturdy rear fender provides a fairly good rack, to which I lash a load with rubber straps. And the dip of the high-rise handlebars is just right for holding a 5-gal pannier (see May97 DP), which I attach to rings I lashed to the handlebar near the hand grips.

I don't ride fast on this bike. It has only one (low) speed; and, with the short wheel base, small wheels, and high me, a pot hole could literally throw me for a loop. Also, the short cranks give little leverage for climbing hills. But, otherwise, it handles nicely.

If getting a 20" bike, remember, it won't be a bargain at any price if you must buy expensive parts to make it usable. Seat posts are costly at bike shops. On one full-size bike, I used a wooden branch as seat post, but don't yet know how well it will hold up. Julie Summers, November

Crab trap easily made from salvaged items.

Find: hoop (eg, bike rim, bike tire stuffed to stiffen it, flexible branch bent round and lashed to self); fishing net (in trash cans near fishing boats); 2 or 3 pound weight; rope; bait (eg, fish heads or guts). Tie: piece of netting to hoop, weight to center of net, and rope to hoop in 3 or 4 places. Place bait on net. Lower to bottom of water. Wait. After crabs have found bait, pull up. Herbert Diaz, CA 956, 1996

Improvising a fishing reel.

Fasten a weight (a spark plug is easy to tie to) to one end of the fishing line (often  found in trash cans on fishing piers, sometimes WITH HOOKS (be careful !). Attach hooks to the line near the weight. Bait is easy to find. (Many people throw away left-overs.)

Tie the other end of the line around the neck of a jar, bottle or drink can that has smooth parallel sides. Then, starting at the neck end, wind the line around the bottle, trying not to overlap turns except for the first few. (You want the line to easily slip off the bottle.)

Hold the neck of the bottle firmly in one hand. With the other, throw the weight to where you hope the fish are. Most fish are one or two pounds and can be easily pulled in with a 6 or 20 pound line. Herbert Diaz, CA 956, 1996

Discarded music strings usable as snare wire.

In a musical-instrument-store dumpster, I found brass or bronze guitar strings, in good condition. Bruce of BC, 1999

Don't get scalded by steam from a hot pot.

It's no fun anywhere, but in the back-country away from medical help, it's worse. When lifting the lid, first raise the FAR side while keeping the NEAR side resting on the pot, so the lid will deflect steam away from you. Also, do not peer in immediately. Let initial blast dissipate. Julie

A better reminder than a string around my finger:

A clothes-pin dangling from my hair onto my forehead. When an easily-burned food is cooking, the clothes-pin reminds me to check, even if I'm doing other things. Julie Summers

April 2000

Be careful when selecting and instructing companions.
   Bert asked what led to my recapture after I successfully
escaped in Texas (eluding pursuing dogs, described in autumn
97 DP) and traveled to Tennessee.
   I was with a friend and his wife. I was confident she
knew my situation and understood that she should not talk
about me. But she told some of her friends that I had escaped
and they told others, etc, and the story reached the police !
   Lessons: If you can possibly do something by yourself,
do it alone even though it may be more work. The fewer people
who know about your business, the better. Never assume
another person sees the situation as you do: "everyone is
logical unto himself." While there is nothing wrong with
traveling or dwelling in two-somes or more-somes, make sure
every member of your party knows all the do's and don'ts -
even the obvious. Lance Brown, Texas, August

Social workers DO often lie.
   (In response to the report in April 2000 DP), Pluma is
right. It has been my experience that social workers would
rather tell lies - to justify their jobs and their seizure of
children, than to tell the truth and risk being reprimanded
or told by a judge they were wrong to take a child.
   Supposedly, the goals of the social workers and judges is
re-unite the child with its birth parents. In actuality, with
institutionalized foster care, very few parents ever get their
children back unless they go through all kinds of hoops.
   The social workers have way too much power and authority.
And, as Pluma found out, attorneys and the law are stacked
against unconventional child rearing. Steven Cleveland,
                                      TN 377, Feb
How do "wild" families deal with education/socialization ?
   An unconventional lifestyle that children are born into
and grow up with, is not exciting and idealistic to them, as
it was to their parents. For the children it is just routine,
and, often, something to be rebelled against. That was the
main reason for the demise of the Kibbutz movement in Israel.
You touched on some of this in DP. (In Aug-Nov 99 with part 2
of "a naturist park with portable dwellings" ?)
   I also understand people's need to keep their family's
business (and their family) "on the D-L" because of hassles
from the Kulturpolitzei. Alan, NY 140, April

I like the Spyder clip-on knives.
   Military guys call them "tick" knives. There are various
styles. My favorite is the Endura, fully serrated. These
knives are light, rugged and easily accessible because of the
clip. When new, they are almost too sharp. I purposely broke
the tip off mine so I would not have to be so careful: I use
the knife to eat with. I've had one since late 1980s. Eugene

Dwelling Portably   Aug/Dec 2000

I am interested in living on a house boat.
Or in an old summer house. Maybe on Hog Island or
Prudence Island across from Newport. As a first step, I
bought an air boat and pump.
The article about welfare and families with children (in
April 2000 DP) is true. Churches often squeal on people.
Churches treat me badly, perhaps because I am big and smart
and have Indian in me. Social workers steal. They prey on
the weak and retarded. They pressure you to put their name on
your bank account so they can withdraw funds - leaving you no
money for food. One social worker told me she can get me on
SSI - IF I pay her and her lawyer. (Have you heard about
this ?) People shouldn't depend on welfare or SSI if they
want to live free.
I live communally. We collect aluminum cans (5¢) and
deposit bottles, trash-pick used clothes and stuff, sell and
hustle at flea markets, barter, borrow, gamble, get free food
at churches, and buy price-reduced bread, fruit and vegies.
I often cook spaghetti and beans. Elaine, Rhode Island, July

I am still living on a boat.
My fifth winter without space heating. John, WA 981, Oct

A dairy goat, plus foraging, can nourish.
In Jan 91 MP(DP), Anne Callaway wrote: "Dairy goats are
not very portable, we've found. To set up their pen and house
and feeding, was almost as much work as moving the whole rest
of our camp.... Powdered milk is much less hassle."
Maybe that's true - IF you don't count the hassle of
going to town to buy powdered milk, and the hassle of getting
a job to earn the money. Also, if you ignore the environmental and social damages inflicted by commercial milk
producers, dehydrators and transporters - and the war-making
paid for by those industries' taxes.
"Goat walking is one of the few ways that a group of
people can live without making war on life", says Jim Corbett
in Goatwalking, Viking, 1991, a book I highly recommend. Jim
tells how to select the proper goat and train her for range
milking, and how to supplement her milk with foraging. "With
a daily supply of three or more quarts of milk, you won't need
to worry about protein and calories; but sources of vitamin
C, iron, copper, manganese, and fiber must be added."
Goats are one way to survive the collapse of society.
After your food reserves are eaten, goats will still feed you.
Bear, Idaho 832, May
(Comments:) Goats are the only domesticated animals (we know
of) that might be able to move through the steep and brushy
woods where we usually live. But I wonder how much milk a
goat could produce here. Good browsing/grazing areas are
small and scattered. (In your May99 DP article you cautioned:
a goat producing milk could not also carry loads. Would
traversing very rough terrain, even without a load, be a no no
?) I also wonder about winter. Even in western Oregon, where
farm animals can graze almost year around (snow infrequent),
they also receive hay. Does your goat find enough winter
browse in Idaho ? (You bought feed for a pack llama.)
Another advantage of goats over cows or horses: their
hoof prints are almost identical to a deer's, and thus won't
arouse curiosity (but might attract a deer hunter). But is
noise a problem ? Can you train goats to remain silent ? Or
do you surgically mute them ? Holly and Bert, July

(Reply:) Quoting Corbett: "Quick-witted, social and educable, with a capacious, high-speed digestive system, a thorn-chewing mouth, cliff-climbing hooves, and a relatively undiscriminating appetite for low-grade roughage, goats thrive on a wider range of plants and in more varied terrain than any other large herbivorous mammal.... Because goats will readily admit human beings into herd membership, they can be managed and moved without fences, corrals, hobbles, tethers...." Not necessary to move pen, house and feed, as Anne did.

"In canyonlands or other rough country, goats are at home on cliff faces where humans can follow only with difficulty."

You CAN pack females. But better to pack neutered males so females' energy all goes into milk production. During winter here in cold snowy Idaho, I do feed hay - because ranchers will still trade me hay for dead pine trees (fence material). And I still buy food for myself in stores. But with the goats as partners, I'm prepared for the day when I can no longer get either hay or groceries. Goats milk more in summer than winter, and if dependent solely on wild browse in winter, might not milk much if at all. But during summer, I make and store cheese. Corbett tells how. I've found solar drying is the best way to preserve - learned from an old Nat Geo article on Mongolian nomads (fellow goat herders).

A happy, secure goat is very quiet. I have bells on mine to help keep track of them. Bells also serve as night-time alarms: if anything chases them, I'm awakened by the clanging - a consideration here where wolves hunt at night. Some goat packers say Nubians are noisy and don't want them. But I milk a Nubian whose milk is rich and sweet. She cries a bit just prior to milk time, to hurry me. If a goat is scared, trapped, or separated from its herd, it will make noise. But I could NEVER see a reason to surgically mute them.

A goat's track is similar but not identical to a deer's - a herder must learn the difference to track lost goats.

When I camp the goats share my tarp shelter. They are trained to stay off my bed and to pee outside. A squirt gun will teach a goat its bounds: they don't like water. However, if herd/herder bond strong, they can be trained to wade creeks.

Bear, ID 832, August

(Comment:) I believe Anne was living in urban/suburban areas. Without a pen, keeping goats from ranging onto neighbors' land and eating gardens or rousing dogs, might be difficult. B & H

Yes, there is a law authorizing confiscation of food.

Though, to find it, you must wade through reams of legalese. It is part of the anti-hoarding/profiteering act. It applies only after an area has been declared a disaster zone. To date it has been enforced: in flooded parts of the Mississippi Valley several years ago; in San Francisco after the earthquake; and even here in Lenoir City when we had our tornado. The law reads: anyone with over 6 months of food in their home is a hoarder regardless of when the food was bought or put up. Your food can be confiscated. You may also be fined and imprisoned. The law was passed in reaction to a group in Houston who, after a tropical storm, bought up all the ice and resold it for $10 a bag. Bureaucrats said they feared that, after a disaster, some rich man might buy up all the food in an area. Class-action suits have been launched against enforcers of the law including the Federal Emergency Management Agency, and are still being fought through the courts. Steve Cleveland, Tennessee 377, July

December 2000

Dwelling Portably

formerly named Message Post
POB 190, Philomath OR 97370
Add 50¢ to check/mo under $6

April 2001 $1 per issue

More about tents used in the California Sierras.

The North Face tent was a tadpole model, two-person, 4½ lbs. It is great for long pack trips where weight is a concern. I took it along on an 80-mile round trip into John Muir Wilderness Area, to Puppet Lake and back. My hiking partner liked it very much (and bought one after we got back). North Face uses what they call a no-hitch pitch system on many of their tents. The poles stay together on the tent, making it easy and fast to set up. That is nice if the weather worsens and you need to set up camp fast - which I've done many times with this tent. Cost about $100 in 1996.

The Eureka was a geo-desic #4 dome tent that sleeps four. Large and roomy, and totally wind and waterproof when closed, it is designed mainly for bad weather. It is not easily set up in wind by one person; it really needs two. It is sturdy: I spent several days and nights in it during a storm that dumped 3 feet of snow. The tent handled that fine.

John Atkins, CA 960, July

(Addendum:) Campmor's New Year 2001 catalog lists no "Tadpole". North Face "Slickrock", free-standing, "3-season", floor 4½x7½, center ht 3½', 4½ lbs, $240. Eureka "K-2 Extreme", "geodesic design", "4-season", floor 7½x9', center ht 3½', 10 lbs, $300 on sale. (Prices plus shipping.) Bert

Report on tents, based on 30 years experience.

All tents, are a compromise between comfort, weight, and cost. I've lived in a tipi (comfortable but heavy); an 8x10' canvas wall tent (more portable than tipi and comfort comparable; but need a stove if you want a fire inside); a yurt for a few days (very comfortable, but need a stove, and difficult to move); many nylon dome tents (light weight, but can't have a fire inside, and sun rays destroy in a year or two).

These days, when not in my wagon, I use a plastic-tarp lean-to, an army-surplus bug net over my bed, and a fire in front of the lean-to with a pile of rocks behind the fire as a heat reflector. As I age, I become more and more a minimalist.

I'm spending the winter 50 miles from the nearest town, on the edge of the Frank Church wilderness area - the largest and least explored in the U.S. outside of Alaska. I'm training two horses to pull my wagon, But I hesitate to take it on highways. I just need to be mobile on forest roads. I plan to spend next summer exploring hot springs. Bear, ID 832, May

I camp on an island in Maine.

I live there 7 months a year in a large green tent. The tent sets on a poly tarp that covers a thick mat of twigs and leaves. That keeps the tent's inside drier, I hope. (The site is wet.)

I use 4 big plastic containers to store food, tools, clothes, and

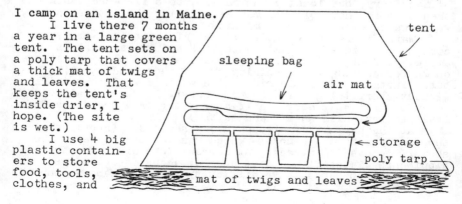

tent

sleeping bag

air mat

← storage

poly tarp

mat of twigs and leaves

books. On top of them, an air mattress and sleeping bag
provide comfortable seating and sleeping.
  I work on and in boats, which enables me to spend five
months a year in the caribe/tropics. There I use a 6x4' kid
tent and a 3x6' air mat. Total cost: $38 at a big box store.
With a nice floral bedsheet I thrifted, I sleep well. Off the
ground, I found no need for a sleeping bag. David, February

(Comments:) Is the air mattress in Maine just a hollow shell?
Or does it also contain foam ? The latter provides more
insulation. In May98 DP, Double Dorji, who had used a stack
of three Thermarest pads for ten years, reported favorably.
  Does your tent include a fly (tarp) suspended over it ?
Or a liner within ? We've found they add warmth and dryness.
  I wonder if your containers are the long/wide squat
"totes" we sometimes see on sale at hardware stores. How well
do they close ? How durable ? (We've been using 4-gal plastic
pails, which are okay, but not as stable a foundation, and
more tedious to open if accessing many things.) Bert & Holly

I lived aboard a sailboat for seven years.
  Back in the 1970s, my husband then and I spent months at
a time living in the Bahama islands. We found little to
forage on land. But fish was free for the taking. We learned
to salt dry fish. I ground wheat kernels for bread, and we
supplemented with brown rice and freeze-dried and canned foods.
Fresh foods on the islands were and are very expensive.
  It was a grand adventure but, like anything else, not
entirely "free". You must maintain the boat, and purchase
maps and other needed supplies. You can certainly get by
without such accessories as self-steerers, but some gadgets do
make things easier. Depends on your values and budget.
  Many tricks made life easier. Eg, rain catchers on
canopies can supply fresh water for drinking and, when plentiful, other uses. But I remember drought periods when, after
bathing only in salt water for weeks, I would have adored a
fresh-water shower.
  From what I hear, living aboard and cruising is more
difficult now, and not as safe, but can be done. Read up
first. And do it only if you've already spent much time on a
boat, because you will need courage and expertise. Lynn,
                                                OR 970, Dec
Frequent showers cool comfort while working hard in heat.
  A few years ago, Bert and I helped with a hay harvest in
interior Oregon during 90-degree temperatures, racing rain
forecast for the next day. The hay had been cut and bailed
by machinery, but loading the bails onto a flat-bed truck and
then into the hay loft was manual. During the hottest hours,
we showered every 15 or 20 minutes.
  Water there was plentiful. But if showering merely to
cool, or to rinse off dust (without soaping), a quart is
ample. I feel better drinking moderately and pouring water
on me for cooling, than gulping huge amounts and sweating it
out. Furthermore, I can rinse with water I would not drink
without sterilizing. (To quench thirst, I prefer plain water
to sweet drinks. Then, a half hour after drinking, I may eat
fruit to replenish sugars and salts.)
  At the haying, I introduced jug showers. (Previously
the family had used a hose - which was out of the way.) To
shower, remove jug's cap. The narrow mouth plus appropriate
tipping regulates flow. Some people, accustomed to piped
showers or tub baths, have difficulty at first maneuvering the
                        April 2001

jug and getting the flow where they want it. However, with practice, the motions become automatic. If a full jug is too heavy, use several partially full. (For more about simple showers/baths, see esp LLL Packet or Set, and DPs: June87 p.1, Mar89p.1 (now in Dec88), Jan91p.3&8, May93p.1, May97p.7, May98p.8, Aug 00p.1)

During the hay harvest, everyone worked nude but for shoes, gloves (for grabbing bails by their twine), and (during mid day) sun protection. Except: a near-teen girl who drove the truck, wore clothes, maybe to avoid skin-to-seat contact. (As I recall, she showered nude a few times, though usually she just wet her head.) A neighbor's house was within binocular-viewing distance, but no one seemed concerned.

Being nude not only exposes more skin for cooling, but makes showering easier. No need to remove clothes - or get them wet and have them bind. (Wet shorts or slacks are especially uncomfortable.)

Also, when warm, nudity is more healthful. Men's genitals need to stay cooler than their bodies: that's why they hang out. Pants and undies not only promote genital cancers, but cause more birth defects due to mutations of sperm than do all nuclear activities combined (we read in a fallout-shelter book). And, for women, bras are now thought to be the main cause of breast cancer. Bras constrict lymph flow, interfering with excretion of toxins. "Breast cancer is epidemic only in cultures where bras are worn. Where there are no bras there is little breast cancer, despite high' levels of toxins in the environment and a poor diet." (from Naturally, summer 1996)

To protect head, neck and shoulders from sun, Bert and I wore bill caps with short capes attached. They were not too satisfactory; when hoisting bails, the cape often flopped to one side, uncovering a shoulder. Other people wore wide-brim hats. Holly & Bert, OR 973, 97& 01

Free city has hot summers; mild winters.

Slab City spreads across the desert a few miles east of Salton Sea near the foot of Chocolate Mountains in southeast California. Within ill-defined borders, squatters live in vehicles ranging from $300,000 mobile palaces to junkers that can't budge - and in tents.

Thousands dwell there from October thru April. A hundred or so remain year around. Summer temperatures can exceed 110° day after day. Frequent baths or showers help cope with the heat.

Most residents are seniors living on pensions. But there are younger people, too - some too broke to live elsewhere. One extended family of 30 including kids, living in old trailers, now shun highways after being told to pay $1500 for insurance and smog device.

Most residents live individually. But there are a few organized groups, RV clubs mostly, including one composed of ±200 singles. Residents communicate on CB channel 23.

The main street is a flea market with diverse merchandise. Many of the conversations are in Spanish.

Slab City got its name from concrete slabs poured in 1942 as foundations for army buildings. They are treasured as level and comparatively-dust-free camp-sites. There's still an aerial gunnary range nearby that disturbs the quiet.

The county would like to regulate Slab City and charge fees; claiming the squatters benefit from (eg) fire protection while paying no taxes. (But they do pay taxes indirectly when they buy from area businesses.) However, the state owns the 640 acres and, last we heard (early 2000), the governments had not gotten their graft together.

Residents haul in their own water from a freshwater spring near the salty Salton. They also haul out their own wastes, and generate their own electricity if any. Many RVs, large and small, have one or more photovoltaic panels. (From Out West 1995(?); Time 17Aug98; Double Dorji; Phyllis Hordin.)

Travels and troubles with a motorhome.

In March 1997, I departed my Asheville NC home, driving a recently-purchased 1981 motorhome. With me was my dog and cat, and a little money from the sale of my house. I had read much (though not yet learned of DP) and talked with people about how to travel economically. My goal was to backpack and hike a lot. I was perhaps as well-informed as someone can be who has not actually done this. But, as I learned, you have to actually do something to learn what you really need to know - and you usually learn the hard way !

I learned that older motorhomes require tremendous upkeep - my small capital did not last long. Perhaps most important I learned: "What you own and what you owe, owns you." I knew this about houses. But only after I was out there on my own, did I realize that my 23-foot RV was owning me just as much as my house had. I wanted to go places off the beaten path, but worried that my vehicle might not be able to - or might, but break down and maroon me with no money for repairs. Chronic worry does not add up to a fun time.

By spring 2000 I'd run out of money, having had horrendous mechanical troubles. My replacement engine warranty turned out to be worthless, because a warranty is only as good as whoever gives it. After that new engine imploded, I should have stopped, found a place to park, and gone to work. But I was in the middle of nowhere with an RV full of stuff I'd collected. And, by then, seemed like I'd replaced every dang part. So I replaced the engine AGAIN, which cost my remaining funds. Next ? I got two flat tires at once. I had to call someone to send me money. Fortunately I knew someone who did, else I might still be sitting there in an immobilized vehicle. But I did not like having to ask. At nearly 60 years of age, I do not have indulgent parents willing to foot the bill.

After that, I thought I had already experienced the worst that could happen. WRONG ! Flat broke, I arrived in Beaverton OR one cold night, parked my vehicle, and went to sleep. I was awakened by my dog barking frantically and licking my face. I could not breathe - I was seconds from dying of smoke inhalation - the furnace had set the motorhome on fire ! The dog and I managed to tumble out the door just as
April 2001

flames engulfed the interior. I could not get back in to save my cat or anything I owned.

The fire department arrived. My dog and I watched as they tried to extinguish the fire. Hopeless! The RV burned to the axles, destroying everything I owned except the sweat pants and T shirt I was wearing. No shoes.

After receiving a small insurance settlement, I rented an apartment and bought work clothes. Presently I have an (ugh) real job while living in an (ugh) real apartment in a Portland suburb. Not thrilling, but it is how I will finance my next adventure and replace some of my losses. I bought a Toyota pickup and had installed a small canopy - which is beginning to look like a camper's den. Slowly I am replacing camping equipment so, when I do take off I will have a good-quality tent and other gear, and not be huddled under a leaky tarp somewhere - which isn't fun for me. For a while, I will have to satisfy myself with short trips, but that's okay. Before going to bed, I read books about hiking - and dream.

Advice to those preparing for mobility: Go as small and light as you possibly can. (Read Travels With Charlie and Blue Highways for inspiration.) Even if you have mechanical skills (I didn't), replacing tires and other parts can be very costly. Don't set off in an unreliable vehicle: be in the best possible shape mechanically, and have a reserve for maintenance and the inevitable repairs. OR be prepared to work when you need replenish your coffers - which may be easier said than done. (I met a delightful young couple living out of their van who needed jobs but had no "interview clothes" nor money for even a brief stint at local hostel.)

Everyone's situation is different, so figure out, IN ADVANCE, what the worst-case scenario FOR YOU might be - because that may happen. If you have (eg) $2000, will you travel on the first thousand and then look for work while you still have a thousand in reserve? Or will you keep going until you spend it all? If the latter, are you willing to accept whatever happens? If so, I hope all you have is a backpack. If you are able to live comfortably that way, WONDERFUL, because you can nearly always get by if you don't have stuff that needs money to operate. Lynn, Oregon 970, November

How to keep pickup-bed contents drier?

My pickup has a bed liner. And the canopy was installed with a felt liner that is supposed to help. It probably does, but not enough: everything kept in there is continually damp. I don't look forward to camping in or living out of this space. What have others done - other than move to Arizona? Lynn, OR, Jan

(Reply:) We've not had a pickup. Maybe readers who have, will advise. Meanwhile, tips based on other shelter experience.

Any heat source that does not add moisture, will help dry. Eg, if you often park where a household electric extension cord will reach, a small incandescent bulb (60 watts, Hank Schultz said he used; in Mar89 DP) may warm your canopy space enough to dry it. Place bulb inside canopy, but NOT touching anything it might scorch or melt.

If the canopy has a window, park the pickup so the window faces the sun. (That will work better in Arizona.)

Unless the felt liner is quite thick ($\frac{1}{2}$" or more?), it won't provide much insulation. If there is a narrow air space ($\frac{1}{2}$" to 1" optimum) between liner and shell, that will help insulate. If the space is much wider than $\frac{1}{2}$", placing additional insulation between liner and shell should help. Eg, the white flexible shipping foam often found in furniture-store dumpsters.

IMPORTANT. The liner should have a vapor barrier on its inside surface. (Ordinary felt doesn't.) Else moisture will diffuse through the liner, condense on the shell when outside is cold, eventually wet the liner, and won't be easily removed by ventilation.

If you haven't already, you might try living in that space for a few days to learn the effect. Our experience with well-insulated shelters (but on the ground or sunken; we've not been on a platform above ground), has been that, especially during mild cloudy/rainy weather, our presence reduces dampness, despite the moisture emitted by our breathing, cooking, bathing. Ie, our body heat dries the shelter more than our moisture dampens it. To achieve this, the shelter needs enough ventilation to let moist air out, but not so much that most heat is lost. Try varying amount of ventilation. Bert & Holly

Selecting a portable dwelling area.

This is for people with backpackable or improvised dwellings. (Those who live in or beside motor vehicles have different capabilities and problems.)

Where will you obtain supplies? Even if you are able to live entirely by foraging/fishing/hunting/trapping, or by grazing a dairy goat or by cultivating small plots, you may learn that (eg) patrolling your trap line, day after day in all weather, though interesting at first, eventually ceases to be fun. Also, a high-protein diet (likely during winter when plant calories are scarce) may cause long-term health problems. If near a coast, subsisting mostly on shell fish may be easy - but risky. Filter feeders accumulate toxic heavy metals, even in unpolluted waters. (All oceans contain some.)

Unless you will dwell where you grew up and, luckily, are already well accepted by the natives, I suggest locating within easy hiking or bicycling (or kayaking?) range of a city or urban cluster that has at least 25,000 people within its trade area. In small towns (except some resort and highway communities), someone unfamiliar will arouse curiosity, especially if they show up repeatedly. Also, a city has more stores, usually including a wholesale grocer or co-op or feed store that sells 50#/25# bags of grains.

Some people locate far from any city, hoping that fewer folk will traipse through the woods and possibly blunder into them. In our experience, the important distance, is not to a city, but to the nearest settlement or road. A spot only a few miles from a city, but with those few miles roadless and rough, will probably be less frequented than a spot far from cities but close to roads April 2001

or rural residents. This assumes contemporary economic conditions when (eg) avid hunters, many of whom would rather drive than hike, often drive far to reach grounds not recently hunted. If gasoline become very expensive or scarce, driving distance may matter more.

For us, an ideal city would have no outlying farms or diffuse suburbs. Ie, where the shops and houses end, the wilderness begins. Western Oregon cities do have outliers, but also some sizable forests or brush areas fairly close.

For chosing a site WITHIN an area, see especially DPs: May99p.5; May95p11& 12; May94p.10; Sept86p.1.

How will you earn money to buy supplies ? Cities are where most of the money is. Even people who work in woods mostly commute from towns and cities, and are hired by companies with personnel offices in cities. So, a city may be your best bet. Earn money as fast as possible and live economically while earning it. (Many people become addicted to (eg) costly foods or housing and spend money as fast as they earn it, dooming themselves to perpetual wage-slavery.) Try to sleep close to work. Maybe your employer will let you sack out on the premises. Spend spare time at no/low cost activities such as catching up on reading at libraries.

How will you transport supplies without a car.? Some suggestions in May96 DP, p.3. Unless you have a sizable group, a 4-wheel vehicle will probably be more trouble to store, maintain, insure, and license, than it is worth for occasional hauling.? If you must use a vehicle, generally cheaper to borrow or hire than to own. Or possibly buy the cheapest heap you think will go the distance, do the haul, then promptly dispose of it. Bert & Holly, January

Scooter test report.
Inspired by DP's discussion (Dec 00), I borrowed a scooter for a test ride. Sturdy (steel?) construction; 25(?) lbs; wheels about 7" diameter, 2" wide. Two hand brakes. Plus one foot brake actuated by pushing down on the rear fender with one foot. Not foldable, but easier than a bicycle to fit into a small hatchback car. In good condition.

I was able to get on and go, and feel in control and stable immediately. I rode about 2 miles one way on a paved road that had mild rises and dips, somewhat more up than down. I did not know legalities, but felt more at ease riding on the left side so that I could see any oncoming traffic and get off the road for it. Then I rode ¼ mile on smooth gravel, which the scooter handled well.

I had better balance when pushing with my right leg, but was able to trade off. My muscles tired much quicker than they do on a bicycle. Because I was using muscles I don't use much when bicycling or walking ? Wearing a heavy knapsack didn't help. But even when I removed it (for the gravel test), my legs continued to tire quickly.

On the level, I needed a series of 4 pushes to build up enough speed for a glide, and then got about a 4-second glide. I did not seem to go much if any faster than walking. (This puzzles me because, when I walk, skateboarders and roller-bladers outdistance me.) Downhill

(not very steep or long), scooting was faster than walking but maybe not as fast as bicycling. Uphill I walked. This test lessened my interest in scooters. Anna Li, OR 973, January

Cheap push-scooters are made in China.
They do not impress me. Like Paul said, their small wheels easily catch in holes, cracks and ruts, and trip the riders. Some kid scooters I've seen up close, had poor welds or were too heavy. Bruce of BC, January

At home on the roam.
Before traveling in town or country, by foot or bike or auto, I go over this check list and select items to take. (Seldom if ever do I take everything on the list.) It has evolved over many years because, while traveling, I note usefulness of items I do have, and note other items I would LIKE to have had.

I try to be as well prepared as possible within limits of weight and bulk and costs, vis-a-vis likelyhood of needing. (I can't be ready for every contingency. Sometimes I just have to improvise as best I can.) The more multipurpose an item, the better. Eg, bar soap may be used for body, clothes, hair (and shaving); and as deodorant.

I offer this list as a guide to help others make their OWN lists, which they should tailor to THEIR individual needs.

CLOTHING. Rain: waterproof jacket with hood (or poncho; better on bike but not thru brush); pants; mitten covers; plastic bags (to protect items in knapsack, and as shoe-liners). Sun: bill cap with skirt; light-weight long-sleeve shirt. Rocks/thorns: shoes/boots. Cold: socks; mittens; dicky; sweaters; cap; vapor-barrier shirt; sweat pants; wind breaker; insulated vest or hooded jacket. (Extra clothes are cheap insurance.) Bugs: head net. Prudes: tee shirts (double astowels); pants/shorts.

SHELTER: clear plastic rain tarp with tie-out cords already on; bug bar; sleeping bag; pad; sheet; (tee shirt stuffed with extra clothes form pillow); twine; rubber straps (from innertubes).

TOOLS: knife, small saw; clippers; pliers; trowel; work gloves; knapsack or packframe; compass; hand lens; mirror; binoculars; watch; air thermometer; duct tape (small roll off big roll); small scissors; mouse trap; fishing line/hooks.

NOURISHMENT: canteen (used plastic drink bottle); water treatment (iodine crystals and water in small bottle); food (more than when sedentary); vitamin C; berry-picking jug (gallon plastic wide-mouth with shoulder strap, can be packed with food, also used to wash clothes); assorted plastic bags; pot, or foil as improvised pan; wire for use as a fire-proof pot hanger.

FIRE: flame maker (butane lighter/ matches/ magnesium/ large flat plastic lens); wax (for igniting damp kindling).

ILLUMINATION: flashlight; spare cells; candle. (Can usually find jug or can to make lantern to shield candle from wind. If not, use berry jug.)

GROOMING: bar soap; safety pins; sewing kit; comb; nail clippers; menstral sponge (and date of last menses).

INFORMATION: field guides to plants; other reading material; maps; pencils/
April 2001

pens; paper; crayon/felt marker (for hitching and other signs); stamped envelope (to notify someone if delayed); money (including phone coins).

BICYCLING: sun/wind glasses; helmet; panniers; pump; tube-patching kit (with an UNopened cement; or self-stick patches); adjustable wrench; 3 tire irons (or spoons); screw driver (on knife); heavy plastic scrap (to line tire if big hole - inaddition to duct tape); spare tube (stays tied on bike); spare brake pads; lube oil (motor oil in reused small plastic bottle); rags; generator light (attached to bike); black plastic for covering parked bike.

MEDICAL: sun screen; chap stick; toothbrush; floss; adhesive tape (to make band-aids, etc); foam (to pad blisters - see LLL paper); tweezers (for thorns and ticks); snake bite kit if in rattler country. Additional kit for long trip: medical thermometer; oral antibiotics; large gauze bandages; sutures and/or butterfly bandages; sterile scapel; povidone-iodine; elastic bandage; more tape. (I don't include aspirin or other pain killers. Seldom do I want them, and they soon deteriorate and become harmful.)
Julia Summers, OR 973, 1991 and 2000

Poison oak (and ivy) update.
Leaves are thornless and in groups of three (except on poison sumac, which grows in the East). Leaves' shapes and colors vary; often shiny. Grows as a bush in the open, as a climbing vine in woods, and as low undergrowth hard to spot among other plants.

Poison oak has no leaves during winter, but twigs are distinctive (here at least): light brown (most other shrubs have green or dark brown twigs); dull texture (most twigs shiny); branch alternately (leaves on maples and most honeysuckles branch opposite); tips about 1/8" thick (most tips thinner).

Merely brushing against the plant supposedly won't cause rash IF foliage not damaged. The toxin is sequestered in resin canals within stems and leaves (else it would react with the plant's own tissue) and released only when plant parts are crushed or broken. Or burnt - the smoke is harmful to breathe.

The toxin takes 20 minutes (say some) or an hour (say others) to penetrate skin deeply enough to cause rash. To remove, some say, wash with soap and cold water as soon as possible. (Hot water may spread toxin.) Others say, wash IMMEDIATELY with anything moist. If no soap, gently rub repeatedly with lots of plain water, damp dirt, pee, or crushed leaves. (But careful: don't use poison oak !) Sandra Baker (review in May82 DP) rubbed on DRY dirt to hopefully absorb the toxin.

Tecnu, sold specially for removing toxin, is effective but no more so than washing with soap and water, according to dermatologist Dr Scott Serrill (in Albany Democrat-Herald 9July2000).

If you can't wash soon enough, Dr Eric Weiss (in Men's Journal 6/99) says gasoline (? !) or paint thinner will dissolve the toxin and halt a rash up to 6 hours after contact. Rub on with a clean rag, then wash off.

Avoid contact with contaminated clothes until they can be washed.

If a rash forms, it will remain until new skin grows, in about 20 days. After the toxin is washed off, scratching will not spread the rash.

Trying to develop immunity by eating a little, or buying toxin-containing pills, is dangerous. Better for any damage to be on your OUTSIDE than INSIDE.
H & B

Plants of the Pacific Northwest Coast: WA, OR, BC, AK. Andy MacKinnon and Jim Pojar, editors, with 8 other writers including ethnobotanist Nancy Turner. 539 pgs 8x5, ±20 oz; 1100 color photos. 1000+ line drawings and silhouettes.

Each entry describes one or more related species and includes a range map. Usually two entries per page. Many entries include uses for food, medicine, and construction. Many plant names are explained. Has index for common and scientific names, but none for uses. My only other gripe: some species' families are not mentioned. Regardless, this is THE BEST field guide I've seen - and at a reasonable price. Sample entry:

COOLEY'S HEDGE-NETTLE ● Stachys cooleyae.

GENERAL: Perennial from rhizomes; stems erect, leafy, mostly unbranched, square in cross-section, bristly-hairy on the angles, 70-150 cm tall.

LEAVES: Opposite, deltoid or heart-egg-shaped, long-hairy on both sides, stalked, coarsely blunt-toothed, 6-15 cm long.

FLOWERS: Deep red-purple, hairy, 23-40 mm long, stalkless; sepals united in a tube, the lower lip 3 lobed; 4 stamens; 4-lobed ovary; several to many in open terminal clusters.

FRUITS: 4 nutlets.

ECOLOGY: moist roadsides, clearings, thickets and open woods; common at low elevations.

NOTES: Taxonomists are not unanimous about the distinction between Cooley's and Mexican hedge-nettle. In fact, Calder and Taylor (1968) maintain they are all Stachys cooleyae in our region. ● The odour given off by hedge-nettles when bruised is pungent, fishy, and rather unpleasant (tho they are of the mint family). ● The reddish-purple deep-throated flowers are attractive to hummingbirds. ● The Saanich made a spring tonic by steeping the crushed rhizomes in hot water. The Green River and Puyallup people used the plant for healing boils. The Quiliute made a steam bath to cure rheumatism by putting the leaves in an alder tub with hot rocks, sitting in the tub, and covering themselves with an elkskin or bearskin. ● The Haida of the Queen Charlotte Islands apparently used to chew the young stems of this plant, sucking out the juice and discarding the fibre. The Quinault sucked the nectar from the purple flowers. Other northwest coast groups did not consider it edible. ● This "nettle", which often grows along hedge rows, was first described from Nanaimo on July 18, 1891 by Grace Cooley, a professor from New Jersey. Stachys means 'a spike' (as an ear of grain) and refers to the inflorescence. (Despite sharing the common name "nettle", Stachys is not closely related to Urtica (stinging nettle). Unlike Stachys, Urtica is not in the mint family.)
April 2001

A few tidbits from other entries:

"Nettle" comes from Indo-European ne meaning to spin or sew, "reflecting the widespread use of nettle (Urtica) as a source of thread."

"Nightshade" came by error. "An old herbal describes the narcotic Atropa belladonna as a solatrum, or soothing painkiller. In translation this was mistaken for the words solem atrum, meaning black sun or eclipse."

Self-heal (Prunella vulgaris) has long been used by aboriginies and Europeans alike, for healing purposes. "Prunella is from the German die Braune or 'quinsy'" (inflamed tonsils), which the plant was used to treat.

The leaves of wintergreens (Pyrolas) "contain acids that are effective in the treatment of skin eruptions..." Oil of wintergreen does not come from Pyrolas, but from another member of the heath family, false wintergreen (Gaultheria procumbens), a salal relative.

Birch resin contains zylitol, a disinfectant now sold as a natural tooth cleaner. It also contains terpenes, and "Athabaskan Indians were reported to chew birch gum much as Andean people chew coca leaves." The sap is used to make syrup, soft drinks, beer, and wine.

Some say "the red huckleberry (Vaccinium parvifolium) was created by Asin, the monster-of-the-woods, and that those who ate the berries lost their reason and were carried off to the woods." However, "They were popular and were eaten fresh by all coastal aboriginal groups within range of the plant."

The Saanich dried leaves of vanillaleaf (Achlys triphylla) "and hung them in houses to keep" flies/mosquitos away.

"Several species of Polygonum were called 'smartweed' or 'arsmart' in the old days, because of the irritating effect of the leaves. It is not clear why species in this genus were used medicinally on the human hindquarters, but they were, for everything from poultices for external bleeding to treating piles and itchy skin diseases."

Before the flowers matured, the peeled sweet young stalks and leaf stems of cow parsnip (Heracleum lanatum) were eaten by many aboriginal groups. But care should be taken to not confuse it with violently poisonous water-hemlock or poison-hemlock. However, cow parsnip contains furanocoumarins, which can cause rashes and persistent blisters after handling the plant and then exposing your skin to sunlight. Giant cow parsnip (H. mantegazzianum), known from Strait of Georgia area, is apparently more phototoxic than H. lanatum.

The central pith of fireweed (Epilobium augustifolium) was eaten by the Haida and other aborigines. French Canadian voyageurs ate the plant as a pot herb. "The leaves are rich in vitamin C; can also be used to make a tea."

1994; Lone Pine Publishing, 1901 Raymond Ave SW, #C, Renton WA 98055. 800-518-3541. $20+$3 p&h in 2000. (Canada: 206, 10426-81 Ave, Edmonton AB T6E 1X5. 800-661-9017. $27+?p&h). Revu by Julia Summers

Store-bought herbs seldom effective.
They may have been grown in poor soil, sprayed with pesticide, picked at the wrong time, heated, or left in the sun too long (which destroys active ingredients). Much better to get fresh herbs and process yourself. Evidence shows that raw foods and herbs raise immunity levels and prevent (eg) cancer.

We are surrounded by natural healers that are free. Many tree saps are better than expensive wound lotions. (If sap too thick, dissolve in booze.) I use aloe vera and comfrey on burns. Cayenne peppers increase circulation, and have been successfully used on many diseases. Lobelia tinctures, if made from good seeds with booze (eg, vodka) and vinegar, have knocked out pneumonia.

To judge potency, smell the herb. If no smell, not effective. Al Fry, ID 836, 1998?

Garlic oil cures my earaches.
It is cheap and effective. I extract a few drops from fresh garlic cloves and put in the painful ear, repeating if pain persists. Bruce of BC, 2000

Homemade ear-drops for "swimmer's ear".
Mix equal amounts of rubbing alcohol and white vinegar, lie on your side, and put a few drops in the ear. This creates an acid environment that eliminates the bacteria which cause the irritation. G.S.Stevens (from Men's Journal 6/99)

Garlic treats various infections.
Stevens says, for a cold or sore throat, sip garlic soup. For a cut or scrape, mash a fresh clove and rub on, then cover with a bandage.

Honey, too, has antimicrobial properties.
Apply to wounds, burns, abrasions.

I clean my teeth with a twig.
For removing incrustations, a plain twig plus much rubbing works about as well as anything, I've found. (Pumice, toothpaste, or baking soda don't seem to help much.) I reshape the tip various ways, using a knife, as needed to fit between my teeth.

Use only twigs from bushes/trees you know are not poisonous. (A few woods are very toxic. Eg, oleander, which grows in southern Calif and much of South.) Bert

Root fillings now thought harmful.
George Meinig, DDS, a root-canal pioneer, changed his mind after seeing much evidence that root fillings often cause serious infections of heart, lung, joints, kidneys, stomach, eyes, and other organs. To warn, he wrote Root Canal Coverup in 1993, updated 96. (226 pages, $20 + p&h, Bion Publishing, 323 E. Matilija 110-151, Ojai CA 93023.)

Teeth are not solid. They contain tiny tubules. Body fluids normally flow from blood vessels in a tooth's root outward through the tubules, nourishing the tooth. Filling the root blocks this flow. Then, normally-aerobic mouth bacteria that get into tubules, turn anerobic and produce dire toxins. Neither immune-system cells from the blood nor antibiotics injected into the blood, can reach those bacteria to kill them. But the toxins (being very tiny molecules) reach the blood and travel to other body parts where they may cause "degenerative diseases".

Not everyone is so affected. Some have immune systems able to cope with the toxins, at least until they suffer. April 2001

What kinds of pails are best for what ?
Storing food ?   Shedding water ?   Sealing air-tight ?
Bruce of BC
(Reply:)   For unsheltered storage, we prefer round 5-gallon
pails with rubber gaskets on lids, and NO pouring spouts
(which might crack and leak).   Check that rims and lids are
in good condition, with no breaks, and no cuts taller than
needed to open. (Some food-handlers slash ruthlessly)   Those
pails sometimes seal air tight, but don't depend on it.
For extra protection, we may put a small tarp over each
pail, with a clump of dry paper, moss, bark, or leaves
between lid and tarp, to bow up the tarp so puddles don't
form and leak through any punctures in the tarp. (We do NOT
suspend a tarp ABOVE a group of pails.   Rodent residence !)
For storage within a shelter, we prefer 4-gal squarish
pails because they fit closer together.   Also for transport
because, on pack frame, their weight is closer to our backs,
or, in knapsack, the flat surface is more comfortable.   H&B

How can I get pickle-smell out of a plastic pail ?
I found a neat pail with a tight lid that formerly
contained pickles.   Lynn, Oregon 970, January

(Reply:)   I don't know of any quick way.   The smell of our
pickle pails SLOWLY lessens with time and use storing books
or clothes.   The stored items pick up the odor but lose it
when exposed to air or (with clothes) washed.
Storing water in a container, with occasional changes,
seems to help.   Eg, a former peppermint-shampoo jug we've
used for rain-water storage for ten (?) years, is now ALMOST
ODORLESS.   Because the water picks up the smell/taste, we put
in such jugs only water for washing.
, With some onion barrels, we tried: scrubbing with hot
detergent solution;   setting open several days in hot sun;
stuffing with crumpled newspapers and leaving in for a few
weeks.   None helped much.   Holly & Bert, Oregon 973

Tips for getting food free or cheaply.
Fast-food outlets often discard large amounts of unbought
still-good food each night when closing.   Find out the closing
time of one close by, and politely ask the manager if they
have any cooked left-overs they are about to dump.   Usually
the manager will be glad to put unsold food to good use and
let you have it free or for a dramatically reduced price.
The owners or managers of some independently-owned
restaurants will swap meals for dishwashing, cooking (unless
local laws require handler's permit), or other needed services.
I have used both these approaches when I didn't have
money, or simply wanted to save money.   Jane Johnson, NY 100,
Dec
(Comment:)   I have seen left-overs set on top of dumpsters
for people to take.   Perhaps worth checking if going by an
outlet already closed.   But keep in mind that most prepared
foods spoil quickly, especially those containing meat, milk,
eggs, or concoctions that include them (eg, mayonaise).
For dumpster diving tips, including tales of some
fabulous hauls, see Lazlo Borbely's article in Dec97 DP.   H&B

Your eating choices intrigue me.   I'd like more details.
Especially your avoiding canned foods, yet using a stove
only once a day.   I eat from cans little compared to most
Americans but I do like canned peaches and tomatos.   Laura,
April 2001   WA 981, Oct 99

(Reply:) We preferably eat fresh foods, mostly wild, when available. We try to obtain a variety but aren't fanatic. Eg, during blackberry season, we may eat only berries all day until evening meal. And during spring, if near a good patch, nettles are our chief cooked green vegetable. During winter, we eat mostly stored grains and beans, various kinds, sometimes sprouted, cooked once a day for the evening dinner with the remainder consumed the next day. Cooked starches keep at least 24 hours if cool (under 60°?) we've found. Dry unoiled popcorn keeps much longer. (We don't have a frig.) Holly & Bert

Holey pot becomes portable fire pit.
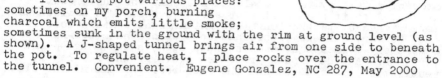

I found a big old pot with holes in its bottom. I set it on rocks to let air through the holes. With a grill set on top to hold a pan, it works well for cooking.

I use the pot various places: sometimes on my porch, burning charcoal which emits little smoke; sometimes sunk in the ground with the rim at ground level (as shown). A J-shaped tunnel brings air from one side to beneath the pot. To regulate heat, I place rocks over the entrance to the tunnel. Convenient. Eugene Gonzalez, NC 287, May 2000

(Comments:) The sunken arrangement is somewhat like the Dakota Hole, shown in May94 DP (and 94 Summary-Index). Advantages I see of using a pot as hole liner, instead of building a fire directly in the hole: keeps the sides of hole from slumping into the fire (especially a problem if soil sandy/gravely); less fire hazard, especially if the soil contains old roots, because the fire does not directly contact the soil.

Advantages of an air tunnel narrower than the fire hole: may be easier to form; easier to partially block off air flow. Advantage of two symmetric holes (as in May94 DP): air hole and fire hole can be interchanged if wind reverses direction. For most air flow, put air entrance up wind and (if ground slopes) downhill from fire hole. Bert & Holly, OR 973

"Stinger" water heaters are used in prison here.
To heat water for soups, teas, coffee. They are safe if you don't spill water on yourself or put your finger in the water while the power is on. A meal can be cooked by putting food in two plastic bags, one inside the other, and submerging in a 5-gal bucket of water heated with stingers. (To make a stinger, see Dec97 DP.) They are also made commercially: 200, 300, 500-watt sizes. Herbert Diaz, CA 939, July

Why we have no telephone.
A friend gave us a phone that hooks to a car battery and an antenna. But it seems to be a party line. Without lifting the phone, we hear others talking. When we tried to use it, there was so much static we couldn't hear well. And the bill shocked us: must have charged us for all calls crossing it.

We had a phone in our car, but too much static here. We had to drive a half mile for it to clear up.

Some visitors have come with cell phones that worked fine. But they need to be plugged in all night. We can't: no electricity on this plateau. Betsy and Jim Frazier, Widow's Mite Mission, AZ 860, June (from Another Look Unlmt.)

(Puzzle:) Near a valley camp, many vehicles went up a logging road, then soon back down. (Explanation:) They went up to get cell-phone reception. B&H   April 2001

Dwelling Portably

formerly named   Message Post
POB 190,   Philomath OR 97370

Sept 2001 $1 per issue   Add 50¢ to check/mo under $6

Living underground with secret entrance and rooms.
I am seeking info about that. Joseph, IL 606, March

I'd like to live COMPLETELY underground; so well hidden
that someone could walk across my home and not spot it.
Have you heard any more about the underground home on
Nantucket Island ? Al, New Mexico 880, May

(Reply:) A 4Dec98 AP clip, reprinted in Living Free #111,
told a little more. "There is a skylight, and a small
entrance hidden under dead branches." "The dwelling is heated
with a small stone stove." Discovery was by a hunter who
"found a stovepipe sticking slightly above the ground." A
stovepipe is easy to conceal, so I assume the hunter was
attracted to it by smelling or seeing smoke. (The builder was
interviewed by the Boston Globe which might contain more info)
So far, our experience has been with sunken-but-not-
completely-buried base-camp set-ups such as the Snugiup in
May95 DP. A wide window protrudes above ground for light,
ventilation and access, and the over-roof is some mix of cloth
and woven branches - not dirt.
Someone might get within ten yards of such a structure
without spotting it, but could not walk across it. Natural
obstructions, perhaps added to with dead conifer branches and
maybe live briars and brambles, discourage anyone from getting
close. One time a mushroom hunter came within ten yards of
ours, apparently without spotting it. But an experienced
searcher looking for hidden camps, who got that close, might.
  Living completely underground seems more difficult. If
you do much more than sleep in a buried chamber, you will need
artificial lighting. For an electric light, a photovoltaic
panel that recharges batteries may be as difficult to conceal
as is a window. A gas lantern will produce fumes. B & H,

More about Wendy's earth-sheltered home in Vermont.
The only portions that protrude above the earth are the
greenhouse and the peak of the addition. The addition has a
metal roof; the rest of the house a sod roof.
You asked (in DecOO DP) if I hid my house from inspectors.
NOPE. My town only requires building permits, not inspections.
But every time the town re-does its property-tax list, we get
checked out. For ten acres plus the house
and outbuildings, I pay about $600/year
tax. That is cheap for Vermont.
Folks who believe they can't
legally build a house for less
than $100,000, might be
pleasantly surprised here.
I know people who started
very small and added on,
or built cheaply. My
daughter is building
a 16x24' cabin.
The materials and
roofing come to
$2000. Totally
furnished and
insulated,
it should

sod roof

addition

green-
house

earth

earth

not cost more than $5000.

My inexpensive house provides space for books and sewing stuff, and starting garden plants in spring, yet leaves time and money for travel south during winter. Wendy, VT 056, Apr

(Comments:) Much thanks for the further information.

I'd be very reluctant to spend even $5000 for something a government controls, because, if I do, I'm on their hook. Some year, the tax accessor may say, eg: "The rules have changed." Now you must install a flush toilet with septic system." That may cost a few thousand more. And, I must either obey, or lose the $5000 and considerable time I've already invested. If I obey, then I invest even more, and am even more on their hook next time they demand something. That makes me a slave !

But maybe $5000 is small enough to you that you don't feel hooked, and could walk away without major regrets if demands became excessive.

Holly and I invest quite a few hours and a few dollars in a base camp - which we could lose if a hostile found it (though no one has). So, the basic issue: how much is someone willing to risk - or how much abuse will they take ?

Because I am in earthquake country, I do not want a sod roof or anything heavy above me. (But a thin mat of branches, berry vines, moss, and fallen leaves is okay.) You are probably far enough from the Mississippi Valley to survive the next big quake there. (See below.)

Holly and I have many books and sewing items, most of which are stashed in pails here and there. They may be safer from rot and rodents (and inspectors) than if in a house, but not as accessible - and keeping track of what-is-where is a chore. So, our way, and any way, has its pros and cons. B & H

Potentially the greatest natural disaster of modern times.

The Mississippi Valley Seismic Zone consists of at least six fault systems that dwarf those in California. Because of their size and resonant rock, an earthquake could devastate large areas of MO, KY, TN, MS, AR, IN, IL. Moderate damage could extend to OH, LA, VA, NC, SC. A series of 8-plus size quakes in 1811-12 were so strong that church bells in Boston were shaken hard enough to ring. Though that quake affected a thinly populated area, a similar event today would kill and injure millions. Most seismologists expect one or more such quakes this century. (from Peter Hernon's book, "8.4", review
by LiveFree(IL)

More people can be housed in existing buildings.

There are many large houses here, built when families were bigger, with unused rooms that could be rented out. Also, ordinances could be expanded to allow owners of single-family homes to add an apartment within or attached to their house or garage. Legalizing such accessory units provides a quick and effective way to add affordable housing. The Seattle region needs tens of thousands of them. Doug Kelbaugh (much condensed from Seattle Times, 20Apr97; sent by Roger Knights)

(Comments:) Bill Kaysing made a similar proposal in Oct94 DP. I am glad that idea finally got into big media.

But, though helpful temporarily, seems better long-term to minimize occupancy of heavy buildings, at least in regions known to suffer severe earthquakes. Instead, turn a house into a resource centre time-shared by several families. Use its plumbing, washer, freezer, stove, etc; but sleep in tents.
September 2001

More idiotic temporary housing by a government agency.

The state of Washington is getting into the labor-camp business, spending an estimated $1.2 million to house about 750 cherry workers in state-purchased tents on public land.

The new plan is to erect at least three camps with as many as 50 tents at each camp. Each tent sleeps up to six workers on cots. The camps would be set up in succession, following the harvest around the state, with no one camp operating more than 21 days. Growers would pay a fee of $15 to $20 per worker per night. Workers also would pay $3 each per night to use the camps, or $10 for a family.

The state plans to hire a 24-hour staff for the camps, which would have trailers with showers, toilets, and cooking facilities. Water would be trucked in and sewerage trucked out. State prisoners would move and set up the tents.

An official called the program "an experiment" to determine whether growers and pickers would use centrally-located camps. Pickers tend to shun housing far from the orchards because they are expected at work as early as 5 am.

Every year, about 38,000 migrant workers, picking every-thing from berries to tree fruit, are homeless for the harvests. The cherry industry is most affected because of its brief, labor-intensive harvest. Many workers have been sleeping on riverbanks, in their cars, or in woods. Lynda Mape (from Seattle Times, 10Apr00)

The state's first emergency tent camp for migrant cherry pickers opened Monday - just as the cherry season was coming to an end. It will be open for 21 days. The cost of 50 military-style tents was $800,000 - about $16,000 per tent. The per-unit cost will be spread over a number of seasons IF the state can find what it has yet to find: a permanent place to put the camp. (from Seattle PostIntelligencer, 16July00)

Saga of Chicago's Mad Housers.

The homeless are everywhere, and because there are so many, they often gather together to create communities. These "shanty-towns" are beginning to appear in major cities. They are usually hidden, but those who look carefully will find them - on vacant lots, in old factory areas, along river edges, by railroad tracks, and under viaducts.

While searching for potential sites, I came across many wintertime camps. A carpenter by trade, I marveled at the ingenuity of some constructions. People built with whatever they could scrounge: construction debris, milk crates, discarded furniture, old carpet. It is wonderful how society's cast-offs are turned into good habitations.

But many people, lacking decent tools and materials, have difficulty constructing even modest shelters. That is why Mad Housers became involved. The Mad Housers built ultra-low-cost houses and gave them away. The houses were small (6x8x8'), had no electricity or running water, and were not up to code.

By late spring, 18 were spread along railroad tracks, creating a new village in the heart of Chicago dubbed "Tranquility City" by its residents. Soon the huts were transformed by proud owners from raw spaces into homes. They painted walls, put up shelves, cleaned up yards, and planned to plant gardens. As word spread, the residents were encour-aged by (eg) railroad workers who tossed bags of food and clothing from passing trains. The media, sensing a good story, started to tell the tale of Tranquility City.

But, as media coverage grew, city officials became alarmed. They did not want a third-world city growing within

September 2001

sight of sleek Loop office towers. Inspectors showed up and
summarily declared the houses unsafe. We hoped that media
coverage would protect the houses: dramatic images of
residents standing with folded arms before oncoming bulldozers
would not be welcomed by politicians. But the city did not
use bulldozers. Instead, city officials promised to give the
18 residents public-housing apartments if they would vacate
their houses. One by one, the residents accepted.
    Of course, officialdom's favors to those few, delayed
public-housing availability to others, and did nothing for the
thousands of homeless still on the streets.
    The city argues that it provides shelters for the
homeless. But city shelters are a poor solution at best.
Many homeless prefer the streets to the strict regimen of city
shelters; especially those who have jobs that conflict with
shelters' hours. **ALL** hut residents I spoke with, found the
huts a better solution than the city's shelters.
    Thereafter, Mad-Houser-built houses were put in
inconspicuous places and their locations were kept secret.
Tor Faegre, IL 602 (who reported in Jan00 that Mad Housers are
no longer active but may be revived (from Heartland Journal;
                                                  winter 93)
I welcome info on turning a cold shoulder to the system.
    I'm a squatter, though right now I'm sleeping in the
belly of the beast. Squat for life - live free. Randy,
                                      TX 782, March
Napping in city parks and airport terminals.
    Many urban residents use public parks to read, picnic,
play ball - and to nap on blankets on the grass. So can
backpackers and travelers, discretely, during the day or
early evening. (At night, either parks are closed or sleeping
is illegal.) However, obvious camping gear, such as tents or
sleeping bags, will probably bring hassles.
    Many travelers sleep in airport lounges while waiting for
ongoing flights. If you have typical air-travel gear, you are
less likely to get hassled. Jane Johnson, NY 100, December

(Comments:) In Feb90 DP, Cowboy, a homeless-resource-person
in Los Angeles, wrote: "At night I walk the streets with my
notebook. I sleep in the daytime in the park with a big
cowboy hat over my head to keep the sun out of my eyes." I
wonder if many urban nomads tend toward night activities
because sleeping spots are more available during days.
    Backpacks, too, may bring hassles. In Abapa Freer,
someone reported seeing police hassle a man with a backpack
who was sleeping on a park bench in Eugene. And, many years
ago, while waiting for a bus beside a park in downtown San
Diego, Holly and I saw police arrive and begin hassling people
with packs. (We left promptly - before the police got to us.)
I expect a big suitcase would have the same effect.
    In a park there may be bushes which, though not big
enough to sleep in, are adequate for hiding a backpack and
other items not carried by most park users. The main risk:
a busybody might see you hide your things and tattle. B & H

Places to park a car while napping.
    Several friends of mine have successfully used train and
bus parking lots. Station officials and police realize that
people may sleep for hours in a car waiting to pick up a
friend or relative. Jane Johnson, NY 100, January

I lived in a van for two months and may do it again soon.
    Jen, CA 941, December   Sept 2001

Effective treatment of chronic lyme was not obtained in U.S.

Despite spending $26,000 and 25 years going to 110 MDs.

Finally, Michael traveled to a Mexican pharmacy across from Douglas AZ. For $390, he bought enough Claforan I.V. to "break" the disease (though he needed follow-up drugs for several years to kill remnant Borrelia and prevent relapse).

Treatment of third-stage lyme is complex, requiring a special diet and oral antibiotics to thin out the Borrelia before taking intravenous drugs. Otherwise, (eg) Claforan I.V. may kill so many Borrelia so suddenly that their die-off neurotoxins paralyze the heart. Allergy tests are also needed. (Claforan is chemically similar to penicillin.)

The only reliable treatment info Michael found: "Rutgers University Co-op Extension Paper on Lyme's Disease", ten documents available at www.lymenet.org . H & B

More about Mexican-border medical services.

I asked the Chamber of Commerce in Douglas AZ which Mex pharmacies had English-speaking pharmacists, and which clinics could install catheters. In 24 hours they obtained that info.

The Mexican pharmacy required a few days to obtain the large amounts of medicines I needed. Each of three 10-gram bottles of Claforan I.V. cost $130. (Cost in the U.S.: about twice as much IF you could buy it. You can't, but if you could, professional administrations would be required, costing tens of thousands.) In Mexico, catheters cost about $8 each, installed. For twice as much, the clinic will administer the dose with a doctor or nurse present. If taking high doses once a week, clinic administration is probably preferable to doing it yourself without equipment such as a bottle stand. But if dosing every few hours, as I was, clinic administration would be inconvenient and expensive.

Regardless of who administers, best do it in Mexico. Otherwise you must carry medicines across the border. I did - and DEA special agents stuck dirty knives into factory-sealed packages of sterile medicines. (The regular border guards, polite and efficient, occasionally delayed me a few minutes while checking the drugs against a list.) Michael in Oregon,
Oct 00

More about seeking services in Mexico.

I have lived in Mexicali part-time for the past 5 years, while working on a documentary project and pursuing business interests. When I first came I could hobble along in Spanish. Now, after a total of about 4 months there, I am fluent: I can read a newspaper, listen to the radio, and have discussions beyond the "Where's the bathroom?" level. I have an ability with languages, but, more importnat, when in Mexico I hang with Mexicans, not Americans. For a while I had a Mexican novia (sweetheart). A so-called "sleeping dictionary" helps.

Be aware that I'm an extremist: few of your readers would adopt my lifestyle just to save a few bucks on a crown. When I first arrived, I lived in a 10x10' tin shack among the bar-girls and pingos that hang out in the old downtown area. The latter thought of me as prey until I disabused two of them of that notion. Those folk were the subjects of my photographic work. And who is more believable - some timid camera-toter who goes home every night to a hotel room, or someone who lives where the action is ?

If you are hanging with the locals, one of them would probably help you find decent medical or dental care at affordable prices. That is not as good as being able to speak and negotiate for yourself, but it's better than being limited
September 2001

to English-speaking practitioners, especially if you have little money. Even if you lack local friends, resourcefulness helps. If you can gesture, speak a few words, and count enough to negotiate, then why not give it a try ? Stay in control, just as I hope you would in the U.S.: shop around, get a second opinion, and remember that you are the customer.

My little successes include getting a crown for my novia for less than she could find it for, and renting a 1000-square-foot bodega (cellar) for $100 U.S. per month and converting it to living quarters. The same landlord later rented me a hacienda (estate) for $100/month just to keep it occupied.

But let's be practical. If you're only after inexpensive medical or dental care, then seek out an English-speaker. You will pay only a little more - and much less than in the U.S.

But if your interests run deeper, then settle in and enjoy life in Mexico. Michael Trend, Nevada 891, May

My daughter and I plan a road trip to Montana this summer.
Heather, who dropped out of school in second grade and was an unschooler for ten years, will be working for the Student Conservation Association at Glacier National Park. I went to college for forestry at University of Montana in Missoula, and want to see what it's like out there now. Heather and I have camped out in southern U.S. and Mexico most winters. Now we will have a chance to camp up north. Wendy, VT 056, April

I live in Belgium, run a distro, and assist anarchistic groups.
Dwelling portably seems interesting. But isn't an address a problem ? Here, you have to have an ID card, and tramping is against the law. Peter, Bruges, Belgium, May

(Comment:) Belgium sounds horrid. (France is too, last I heard, requiring registering with police if you move or are away from home overnight.) But how much are the laws enforced? Is it really any worse than the U.S. ? Bert & Holly

Expedient backpack.
With a little twine, you can transform ordinary pants into a pack. You can do the same with a long-sleeve shirt. (Sent by John Atkins)

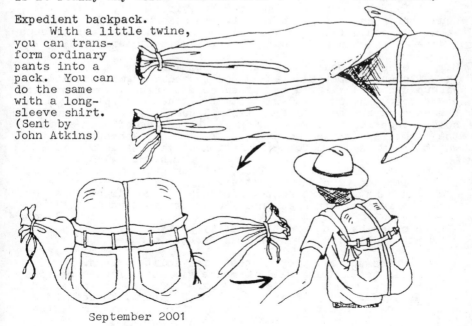

September 2001

For water I now use a large MSR Dromedary bag.
     It holds 2 or 3 gallons. To heat water, it can be hung
in the sun like a Solar Shower bag, but is much stronger. It
has heavy-duty grommets for easy carryng or hanging.
     To water plants, I added a 3-foot length of 3/8 or 1/2
inch clear vinyl tubing on the nozzle end (just pokes on
easily), and attached straps to the bag so I can wear it on my
back. I hold the tube in my hand to direct the flow. Eugene,
                                                NC 287, May

Catching menstral flow - or puddling through.
     Commercial tampons and pads are costly, and contain
ingredients questionable for health. Cloth pads are a nuisance
to wash. Moss may have dirt/grit in it, and sheds.
     I tried making paper pads, with newsprint inside and brown
paper from food bags outside (so the newsprint doesn't contact
me), but they weren't very absorbant nor comfortable.
     At times I have used clean rags and discarded after use.
But I don't always have a surplus. Nor do I like keeping used
rags around until they are dry enough to burn.
     I bought sea sponges at an art supply store, cut tampon-
size pieces, and attached strings. But insertion was uncomfortable (as are tampons that lack Tampax-type inserters).
     Finally, I sewed together two of the largest sea sponges,
forming a 7x4x1" chunk, and used that as a pad, held in place
by panties. Depending on flow, I rinse the sponge once or
twice a day. (I seldom have a heavy flow.) Sea sponges seem
amazingly absorbent and, unlike fabric, rinse easily in a few
changes of water. Then I squeeze out as much water as possible
(wringing would tear them). Unfortunately, drying requires 24
hours or more. If used wet, a sponge absorbs my flow, but
dampens what I'm sitting on. I could buy more sponges and use
them in rotation, but they're expensive. Sea sponges aren't
very durable: mine started tearing after only a few months.
I reinforced by sewing back and forth and all around.
(I should have done that before using.)
     Polyurethane foam is supposedly quite inert, so I cut a
chunk off a cushion and tried it. It absorbed my flow, but
wasn't as comfortable as the sea sponge - and more apt to cause
a sore at the top of my butt cleft. Julie Summers, 1999

Simple electric heater also circulates air.
     (In Apr 01 DP, Lynn asked how to reduce dampness within a
pickup canopy.) If you are often able to plug into commercial
electricity, mount a 100-watt light fixture on a plywood base.
Remove tops and bottoms from two #10 cans (2# coffee), and
solder together to form a chimney. Place the chimney around
the light fixture and mount it 2 or 3 inches above the plywood,
which provides a gap for circulation as the heated air rises.
                                      D.L.Smith, FL 322, May
(Comments:) If you lack solder, you can punch holes near the
cans' rims and wire them together.
     The cans will get hotter and induce more air circulation
if their insides are blackened (to absorb instead of reflect
                                                        light.)
I have never had the lid blow off my potty pail.
     But, when warm, it does leak enough to have an odor.
                                                Bill Fargo
If honeybees scarce, provide nests for solitary bees.
     Their pollinating will increase yields of fruits/berries,
wild or tame. In a fir block ± 4x6x24", drill thru-holes of
various sizes, 1/8 to 5/16", spaced 1/2" apart. To seal holes,
mount a board on back, using screws. Once a year remove board
and clean holes. Paul Doerr, CA 945   Sept 2001

Dwelling Portably

formerly named   Message Post
POB 190,   Philomath OR 97370
Add 50¢ to check/mo under $6

March 2002 $1 per issue

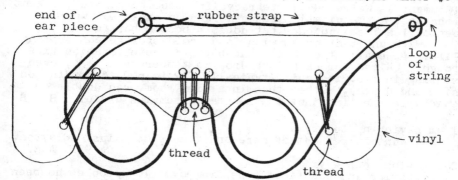

Eye guard made from vinyl bottle.

The biggest threat in the woods and brambles we frequent,
has not been animals (neither 8 legged (spiders), 6 legged
(insects), 4 legged, 2 legged, or no legged (rattlesnakes)),
but branches that can poke eyes. Ordinary sunglasses are not
adequate, because often my head is bowed, watching where I am
stepping, which allows twigs to intrude above my glasses.
Safety glasses I've seen were little better. They included
side guards but nothing above the frames.

I cut plastic from a 2-liter drink bottle, bored holes in
it with an awl (or strong needle, or a nail or wire sharpened
to a fine point), and sewed it on using strong thread.

Made several years ago and worn whenever I hike, the
guard has endured well. Minor problems: the vinyl, though
clear initially, was soon clouded by abrasive dirt wiped off,
slightly reducing peripheral vision; and it has a bit too
much curl and touches my forehead - irritating if worn many
hours. When I make another, I will use flatter plastic.

To help hold glasses on when moving through brush, or in
a gale, I melted small holes in the tips of the ear pieces
(using a fine nail or big pin, held with pliers, heated with a
candle), tied string (or several strands of thread) through
each hole to form loops an inch or so long, and then tied a
light rubber strap (cut from bike inner tube) between the
loops. (Easier than tying the strap directly to the ear
pieces.) The strap goes around the back of my head.   Bert

In summer 2003 we will travel the country.

We are searching for the perfect place to start a punk
farm. We are seeking new friends all over, to help make our
journey a little easier and more exciting. Christopher and
                                  Danielle, PA 180, Oct
(Comment:) I wonder if there is any good (forget "perfect")
place to start a farm of any kind. Especially if you lack
experience and money. Land that is cheap to buy will generally
be far from jobs. But you will probably need jobs, not only to
pay property taxes and other overhead expenses, but to pay for
the vehicle you will need to commute a long distance to a city
where you can find jobs ! Result: more expense, more stress,
more danger (driving), more pollution, more resource consumption, less free time, and maybe even less fresh foods (because
of less time to garden) than if you lived in a small or middle-
size city. Christine of Slug & Lettuce, who searched a few
years ago, concluded that rural living was a snare and delusion.

We use a non-prescription tetracycline for infections.
    Fish-Cycline: a hundred 250mg capsules, under $10.
                                    D. Smith, FL 322, August
(Comment:) We've read: tetracycline becomes harmful if kept
long past its expiration date (marked on package), whereas
penicillan loses potency but doesn't become harmful.
    With antibiotics as with food, cold storage can prolong
life. Generally the colder the better: deterioration rate is
roughly halved for each 10°F drop in temperature. So, even
storing in a buried pail (typically 50° to 60°, depending on
site and depth), rather than in a warm room, can double or
quadruple the time that the substance remains useful. H & B

I am saving up to buy a van.
    I want to get out of here and take some trips. Clayton,
                                    CA 932, Aug.
Car Living Your Way:
    Stories and practical tips from over 100 people who been
down the road. This is A.Jane Heim's second car-living book.
(Her first was reviewed in Apr 00 DP.) It includes items from
her first book and from DP (with many DP writers mentioned),
but also much that is new.
    "I am happy with my Ford Explorer ... which is going
strong at 200,000 miles. The seats fold down in back and I
can stretch out. The windows are tinted. And snow is not
going to stop me with four-wheel drive."
    "The main problem I had with the (Dodge) van, and heard
of others having too, was that fumes from the engine would
quite often enter inside. I worked hard at sealing things up,
to no avail....· So, while not nearly as stealthy as a van,
I think that a pickup with camper is probably preferable."
    "... In Mexico, have a car that is not cosmetically
perfect on the outside. Don't get too fancy, whether it be
your car or the way you dress. You are less likely to be
molested or robbed.... Make sure the car has had good
maintenance and is a make for which parts are readily
available. I prefer a Dodge or Ford because the engines and
running gear are so interchangeable from year to year."
    "For added privacy, most states allow solar film on the
side windows only. A night-driving hazard on front and back."
    "I cook on an alcohol stove (non pressurized), light
mostly with candles", and shower with "a 2-gal pump-up garden
sprayer.... No solar panels on the roof to be smashed by hail,
or water lines to freeze in a cold spell, or propane tanks to
explode if in a crash. Funny that nearly every RV has a
propane stove and frig, but if you use propane on a boat you
can't get insurance because of explosion danger."
    Phil Johnson's 1973 Dodge Dart Swinger "is well planned
and well organized." While visiting his sister, though her
half-million-dollar home was "full of all kinds of material
goods,... she was always coming out to my car to borrow
important things she couldn't find in her house - stamps,
sewing kit, markers."
    "Don't stay in single-business parking lots. A strip
mall is better - everyone assumes you are associated with one
of the other stores." "Truck stops are nearly always one-
nighters. I never met anyone that made (one of) them a
regular living spot," because that would not be tolerated.
    "... Police are generally fearful of strangers (as are
the residents they serve), so it was better if I spent my
                        March 2002

nights in locations that were outside town limits, or in parking lots that had late-night business activities, or on properties that belonged to someone I knew. Because I was a member of the local Junior Chamber of Commerce, I got permission to park on their property with the understanding that I would act as an informal watchman. A small-town park was right next to it, so I had a public bathroom to use. There I stayed for a year or so."

At bed time, "Joyce suggests getting in your car and staying there.... Use a bottle for a call of nature so you do not have to go out in the middle of the night."

"There is a law against 'residing' in a National Forest. You are supposed to be vacationing. After talking with forest rangers, I understand this rule is hard to enforce." "In Colorado, anyone caught sleeping more than 14 days in a 30 day period faces up to a $5000 fine or 6 months in jail. This is to discourage resort workers in Steamboat Springs from living in Routt NF, 'taking prime spots away from tourists'."

Wherever she went, including a party at an elite country club, Jane found people who lived in their cars at times - including some who had plenty of money but did not like motels.

Each August, a high official attends hot-rod expositions in Reno, during which the city's population doubles, crowding facilities. Instead of paying $100 a night for a hotel room, he lives in his hot rod - but uses hotel pools free. "I always take a white towel (that) looks like a hotel towel. In the early morning, I get out of my car in my bathing suit, walk in, put down my towel, and jump into the pool. You can't do this at the same hotel each day; you've got to change hotels. In the afternoon I take my blankets and pillow and go to one of the public parks to nap.... I sleep by day and cruise by night.... You can't appear to be a vagrant. You walk with an air about you as if you own the place. You have clean clothes. You have an appearance of professionalism and quality about you. I never get hassled in the public parks...."

"I was a starving homeless person with two adorable sons, aged 6 and 8. We lived in various Disney World hotel parking lots, and found ways to crash the parks and restaurants daily. A bit nerve-wracking for me but a riot for the boys. They enjoyed car living so much they tried to persuade me to revert to this lifestyle a year or two later."

"... I've noticed a number of trucking families that live on the road. Mom and dad take turns driving, and the kids ride and play in the sleeper." Most are owner-operators contracted to household-goods movers. "Household-goods loads are light so you can have a really big sleeper." Also, "the delivery schedules tend to be less demanding so you won't have to run 30 or 60 hours straight.... The kids are pre-school age, or they are 'homeschooled' on the road...."

"At least 10,000 hippies live in or around the New South Wales (Australia) town of Nimbin. Most live in the 62 communes surrounding the village, but others live in tepees, tents, vans, campers.... 'It is a very tolerant, accepting community. That means we've also got junkies, alcoholics, mad people.' Tourists have discovered this 'colorful spectacle'. Their money presents a Faustian dilemma to townsfolk whose lifestyle is founded on eschewing materialism."

Lists, with some descriptions: 40 products and resources; 77 books; 28 periodicals; 29 media articles or shows. Index. 257 pages 6x9. 2001. ISBN 0-9649573-3-7. $22 + $4 shipped first class. A.J.Heim, Touchstone Adventures, POB 177-dp, PawPaw IL 61353. (Review by Holly & Bert)

March 2002

Home-made fly paste did not catch flies.

A house I sat had many flies in the kitchen. Not wanting to swat (tedious; messy; nik-naks in the way) nor spray, I got a formula for fly stickum. (A reference librarian found it in a Readers Digest book, "Back To Basics: How to Learn and Enjoy Traditional American Skills".) Mix one egg yolk, tablespoon molasses, tablespoon black pepper. I dabbed onto 3 jar tops, and set on window sills. Result: in a week, one dead fly (and it might have died of other causes and fallen in: I also killed flies by trapping between a sheet of paper and window. Through the paper I could see where the fly was. I tried to press hard enough to disable without squashing, but sometimes squashed.) Julie Summers, Oregon 974, December 2000

To stay healthy, get plenty of rest and sleep.

According to Science News 14July01, a century ago American adults averaged 9 hours sleep daily; today they average less than 7. Sleep-short people may use insulin less efficiently and become diabetic. (I've read elsewhere) if rest/sleep not enough, toxic wastes that form in cells during activities, do not get cleared out. Also, to get going and keep going, sleep-deprived people take drugs. Coffee, the most popular drug, contains caffeine and other potent chemicals, plus tars formed by roasting. Whether or not very harmful directly, coffee harms indirectly by suppressing urges to sleep or rest. And coffee no longer suffices: stronger drugs are sought. Most are legal, but that doesn't mean they are harmless.

Like rest, exercise is beneficial in moderation. But an excess can harm. People who (eg) win marathons seem super-fit, but may hurt their health long-term (I've read).

Sad, the number of fairly young people (40s, 30s, even 20s) who suffer heart attacks or cancers. Caused by longer work hours (with two jobs now needed to pay for the same life-style that one job paid for in 1970) and a more frantic work pace ? Or by more pollution ? (And, the more hours worked, generally the more exposure.) Likely, multiple causes.

Some medical spokespeople claim that Americans are living longer than ever. But they are talking about life expectancy AT BIRTH. Intensive care enables more premature and defective babies to live. But ADULT life expectancy ? There was a big gain from 1800 to 1900, due to learning more about infectious diseases, leading to better hygiene; and a lesser gain from 1900 to 1960, due to developing more antibiotics. But since ?

(To understand how statistics can mislead, imagine a place where half the babies die soon after birth and the other half all live to age 80. Average life expectancy: 40 years. Then, baby care improves, only 1/4 die, and the others live to age 80. Average life expectancy: 60 years. Finally, only 1/8 of babies die. Average life expectancy, 70 years. Obviously better for mothers, and for babies who would other-wise die. But people who survive infancy live no longer.)

Many forms of portable dwelling, because they require less work to pay for, allow more rest, less pollution, better nutrition, and more compatable exercisings. Thus they can improve and prolong health. Holly & Bert, OR 973, November

Drinking enough water greatly reduces cancer risks:

(breast 79%, colon 45%, bladder 50%), and eases 80% of joint and back pains. A 2% dehydration (barely enough for thirst) impairs short-term memory. 75% of Americans are chronically dehydrated. I should drink a gallon a day (16 8oz cups) at my weight (210 lbs). author unknown (from recycle bin)
March 2002

Dwelling Portably

or Shared, Mobile, Improvised
Underground, Hidden, Floating

June 2002 $1 per issue   POB 190-d, Philomath OR 97370

Copper wire: the best thing since rubber straps.
     I wrote an LLL paper, "How to Hold Your World Together",
about the many uses of rubber straps (cut from discarded innertubes). But sunlight or oil deteriorates them. Eg, lashings
on my home-made bike racks rot in a few years. Covering with
duct tape extends their life, but costs money and extra time.
     I found a good alternative: copper electrical wire. Much
gets discarded when buildings are remodeled. I prefer
strands 1/16 to 1/8 inch thick. (The fine wire within the cords
of discarded appliances is too flexible for most structures.)
Copper wire is more flexible than steel wire, enabling tighter
joints. Aluminum is lighter but too weak for most of my uses.
     Most wire I've found has an outer plastic casing with
several separately-coated wires inside. To remove the casing,
I prefer a knife with a straight cutting edge that comes to a
point (versus a curved cutting edge). I may leave the coatings
on the individual wires. They are less likely than bare wire
to mar the bicycle's paint.
     In addition to lashing things together, I've used copper
wire (both with and without the plastic coating) to make guards
on thrift-store kitchen knives. That facilitates strapping one
into a sheath I wear on my belt when hiking. (A guard also
keeps hand from sliding onto the blade if jabbing.) I also made
a magnifier holder (described in Oct90 DP): two thicknesses of
1/8" wire bent easily yet is stiff enough to hold shape once
bent. Wire may also be formed into a small "cage" to hold a
pretty pebble - to be worn as a pendant. Julie Summers, Dec

Steel wire is good for making pot handles.
     Sometimes we find a pot, free at a
dump or cheap at a thrift store, from
which the handle has broken off without rupturing the pot. A pot lacking
handle is desirable for cooking with
solar heat using a clear shroud, or
on a well-controlled flame (eg, gas
stove) using an insulative shroud.
(A long side handle would get in way
of shroud.) Drawback: need pot holders or thick cloth to move hot pot.

     However, if wanted, a handle can be formed from stiff wire
such as coat hangers. Various types of handles are possible.
Here I've shown a swing handle (bail), which is useful if
hanging the pot over a fire. Wrap wire around pot and twist a
little to hold it on. Form "ears" (small side handles).
Another piece of wire becomes the handle. Fasten it to the
ears, loosely enough so that it can swing down close to the rim
for storage or if using a shroud. Holly & Bert, OR 973, Jan

We live on our boat three and a half months a year.
     We are very comfortable, as it contains everything we need.
We cook with propane and have a gas frig. A diesel generator
powers lights and VHF radios, and tools my husband needs for
boat work. We dig for clams on nearby beaches, set crab and
prawn traps, and jig up a flounder or cod or halibut at times.
(We have sports fishing licenses.) We also fish commercially,
but the seasons are very short now and fenced in with miles of
red tape and extra expenses. I'm 65 and my husband 75, so we
probably won't play that game much longer. My husband also has
two ex-seine boats he is turning into live-aboards. Eleanore, BC

More about nomadic dairy goats.

Answering questions asked by Kurt. Yes, a doe needs to be bred and have kids to produce milk. She can then be milked for two years before she needs to be bred again.

I sell my kids to the local Mexican farm laborers. I have a problem with Kurt's (and many other meat eaters') attitude. If he eats meat bought from Safeway, someone kills those meals for him. The animals live in pens up to their knees in shit, are injected with growth hormones and antibiotics, and never experience kindness or love. Why is it okay to eat them, but not eat an animal you raise in a kind manner, slaughter without fear or trauma, and process without polluting the environment ?

Holly's suggestion to buy a milking doe and trade her in, is one answer. But she still has kids, some of which will be eaten by someone.

Any dairy breed will fit into a nomadic lifestyle. Avoid individuals who are very high producers. Some goats milk up to 3 gallons a day and those mostly have poor udder attachments - and too much weight to carry around. Choose goats who milk 3 or 4 quarts per day. Good feet and leg joints are important in any animal who is expected to walk to its food rather than having its food carried to it. Males make good pets or pack animals but must be neutered at one month of age so they don't become smelly and ornery. Bucks are ornery only if mistreated.

I don't know if grazing goats on public land is legal. I move camp every few days, which keeps the impact on the land low, keeps fresh food in front of your animals, and keeps you ahead of slow-acting federal employees. Bear, Idaho 832, Dec

Giant biting flies trapped and killed by tarp set-up.

One summer we were camped on a cattle ranch infested by inch-long biting flies. Most summers we live in light-weight minimal shelters - often just an insect net under a plastic tarp. But that summer we were still in a winter shelter, not having had a reason to move. (With ventilation, it was cool.)

Attracted by our odors, the flies came toward the front of our shelter and flew in under a clear plastic over-tarp. A net curtain prevented them from entering the shelter itself. Smart as they are (compared to other flies), the big flies got confused by the clear plastic. Encountering it and feeling trapped, they flew toward the sun which was behind the shelter. That brought them between the over-tarp and the dark-colored insulated roof - which the sun made HOT. In front, the over-tarp was a few inches above the roof. But, toward the back, the tarp rested on the roof. Struggling toward the light, the flies wedged themselves between tarp and roof. Hundreds exhausted and solar-cooked themselves - quite by accident. (We had not arranged roof and tarp in hopes of catching flies.)

I've thought about fabricating a biting-fly trap that could mount on the exhaust vent of a shelter. It would be a boon, not only to portable dwellers, but to people raising animals. (Anything like that already manufactured ?)

The stinky-jar traps, containing rotting meat as bait, catch many dung flies and yellow jackets, and some carrion beetles (which are beneficial and should not be caught), but few if any biting flies and mosquitos. Bert & Holly, 2000

Dwelling Portably   June 2002

Suggestions for preventing and treating animal bites.
    Most victims are small children. The vast majority are
bitten by pets: their own, or friends' or neighbors'. Most
others are bitten by "cute" wild animals they try to feed or
pet. To help prevent, don't keep pets, don't take small kids
to visit people who do, and don't otherwise encourage contact
with animals - at least until your kids are mature enough (8 or
10 ?) to clearly understand that an animal is not a toy or an
oddly-shaped human, but is a very different creature with its
own perceptions and urges. If a small child wants a pet,
provide something inanimate that's soft and cuddly. And shun
movies/videos/shows/books that portray animals unrealistically.
    If bitten, wash wound immediately and thoroughly with
plenty of water and soap. Generally leave open. (Don't suture)
If infection develops, it will probably do so within 12 hours.
If it does, take oral antibiotics (eg amoxicillin/clavulatate -
if not allergic). Keep wound elevated. Severe pain may mean
that teeth penetrated a bone, joint, or tendon. (Cat bites
often do.) If much pain, or if any swelling or inflamation does
not lessen within 24 hours, or if animal seemed rabid, seek
further advice (desirable in any case). (15July01 Patient Care,
                                         in p.o. recycle bin)
When is treatment for rabies advisable ?
    Rabies is a disease of mammals, mainly bats and carnivores
such as raccoons, skunks, foxes. It's almost never found in
squirrels, other rodents, rabbits. In U.S., wild animals are
more likely rabid than are dogs or cats, many of which receive
protective vaccinations. Rabies is extremely rare in humans.
But if someone exposed waits until symptoms develop before
obtaining treatment, the disease can't be halted and death sure.
    The rabies virus penetrates any mucous membrane (need not
be broken), or broken skin. The virus is fragile and can be
washed away with soap and water and inactivated. However, if it
has penetrated, death can be prevented only by administering
rabies vaccine plus rabies immunoglobulin.
    Who should get them ? Consider type of contact and local
prevalence. Eg, when rabies has been reported in area wildlife,
someone bitten by a raccoon should undergo treatment. On the
other hand, transmission is very unlikely when a squirrel
scratches the pants of a park visitor and does not break the
skin. Cases between these extremes pose problems. Abnormal
behavior of an animal is a warning sign. But the only sure way
to know, is to study tissue from its brain. If the animal can't
captured and observed or autopsied, the decision is anguishing.
During the past 20 years, no untreated bite victims developed
rabies from doubtful exposure. But a Texan bitten by a bat,
who rejected treatment, developed rabies.
    Some victims reject treatment because of cost: $1000 to
$2000. (How much in Mexico ?) Others hesitate because they've
heard that injections are painful and cause severe effects.
This was once true, but not of treatment available in U.S. the
past 20 years. Laurie Lewis & consultants (from Patient Care)
                                         15July01)
(Addendum:) I read elsewhere that people who enter bat-occupied
caves or buildings, sometimes get rabies without being bitten.
By getting bat saliva or urine into eyes, nose, mouth, or into
a pre-existing scratch ? Encouraging bats to nest nearby might
not be wise. As insect eaters, birds may be safer. Humans are
less closely related to birds than bats and share fewer diseases.
    Dwelling Portably   June 2002

Tuberculosis a threat in crowded, poorly ventilated buildings.
Between 11/00 and 11/01, 17 active and 53 latent cases were
discovered at a Lane County (Eugene) homeless shelter. Of the
17, 16 were male, 16 U.S. born, 14 white non-Hispanic. Ages 23
to 59, median 48. None HIV (AIDS) positive. Microbes identical;
evidence that infections happened at the shelter.
Since a 1994 TB outbreak, skin tests have been required of
shelter residents and, if positive, other tests, and treatment.
The shelter has beds for 250 transient men, 90 men doing work
for the shelter, 60 women, and 11 staff.
In Oregon as a whole, TB has declined, from a high of 50
cases per 100,000 population in early 1950s, to 4 per 100,000
in late 1990s. (from CD Summary, 18Dec01)

(Comments:) This accents the importance of providing your own
shelter and not depending on institutions - and the evil of
officials who outlaw and police who hassle people sleeping in
cars or parks. TB, still very common and a major killer world-
wide, is only one of many diseases that spread anywhere that
people are close and enclosed. The most common may be flu.

No matter how nomadic I am, before preparing food I clean up.
I wash hands and work surfaces with soap and water, scrub
my nails, rinse with a drop of bleach, and then lemon juice if
available. Lemon juice can kill most hepatitus, I'm told, which
is why clams and oysters on half-shells come with lemon wedges.
For most of my life I've had extremely limited cooking and
sanitary facilities. I learned the hard way not to be dirty.
Never let trash or dirty dishes sit around after a meal. Lisa

Wild Child: Girlhoods in the Counterculture.
This book is by women whose early years were unorthodox.
Editor Chelsea Cain says: "Hippie kids grew up the products of
a great experiment. As with any scene, there were good parents,
and bad parents, and everyone's experience was not the same.
But these parents were all trying something different....
"How successful were the hippies at insulating themselves
from the mainstream culture, and what influences could they
not escape ? What aspects of the counterculture have their
children embraced as adults, and what have they rejected ?..."
Most if not all the authors are writers/editors/performers
quite well known in literary circles - which may be how the
editor found them. They now live in cities and have
conventional dwellingways. Thus they are not representative
of ALL women who had unusual beginnings.
Some tell only about their earliest years. Others also
describe growing to maturity. One says nothing about her past,
but promises her baby an American Dream childhood. Some
provide cryptic poems or prose (which I've ignored). Some
recall their girlhoods fondly. But most are put-down-ish.
Several dwelled in vehicles or other unusual abodes when they
were children; others had conventional homes with some
"hippie" trappings. Most or all attended public schools at
times. Childhoods full of snubs and taunts from other kids,
may explain why most grew to reject their parents' ways.
(The following excerpts are heavily edited to shorten.)
"Fear of a Bagged Lunch." I was born on the kitchen
table in a tiny cabin in rural PA. A midwife and my dad
composed the entire birthing team. It was a glorious moment
for my parents, that October day in 1972. They were both 25
and growing most of their food, raising goats, and making
dairy products. I slept with my parents until I was 5, drank
goat milk, and peed in an outhouse. Photos of me show a
naked girl-child, smudged with dirt and smiling like crazy.
June 2002

When I was a year and a half, my parents loaded everything we owned, which wasn't much, into a green 1952 Chevy truck and moved across country. My dad had built a miniature house on the back of the truck, and into this they packed our meagre belongings, our two dogs, and our goat....

Everything we possessed had been made by my parents or bought second hand. When I wanted something we couldn't afford (which was often) my parents would do their best to build or sew it. In third grade, I lusted after pin-striped jeans - and my mother valiently sewed me stiff, ill-fitting pink denim jeans (which fell off during a ferocious game of Red Rover). We lived my parents' hippie dream in various New Age communities: in WA Skagit Valley and, later, Sedona AZ.

When I was six, we traveled across the country again, this time to Ithica NY. I entered an "alternative" school. When I expressed an aversion to math, my first-grade teacher replied that I didn't have to do it if I didn't want to. Years later, my 7th grade teacher would wonder why I still didn't know my multiplication tables. (So what ? Calculators were cheap by then. Or, if high tech was taboo, slide rules.)

My isolation intensified when we moved to Beantown WI. My parents had two folk-musician friends there and wanted to start a band. We were a complete anomaly: my mom still made most of our clothes, and a wood stove was our only source of heat. My parents were pagan, and our "bible" was a combination of I-Ching, Tarot cards, and Seth channelings. Obscure lifestyles or any sort of difference can seem threatening in a small town - and we were misjudged accordingly. People saw my parents and immediately assumed (incorrectly) that we did drugs.

At school, my bagged lunches amused the hot-lunch kids. They had never seen home-made wheat bread, blue corn chips, tofu, natural licorice. And so again and again - the pointing finger, the gaping mouth and the inevitable comment, "What IS that ?" I tried to defend my family's organic choices. But my words were wasted - because the food looked different, which made it weird, which made ME weird.

In high school, my friends rebelled by stealing their parents' cigarettes, skipping class, and getting stoned at lunch. I rebelled by becoming a cheer leader and class president. Thankfully my parents were patient enough to let this wild stage run its course, as I pranced through my teen years in disguise - my bangs curled high and immobilized with hair spray, my lips glimmering with shell-pink lipstick, my jeans rolled tight to my legs, my Keds whiter than white.

My friends went to college and became vegetarians. I went and became a meat eater. The natural foods craze held no sense of independence or contained rebellion for me. I felt more insurgent satisfaction from eating a hamburger or a slice of chocolate cake. So even now, as an adult who enjoys eating healthy foods and is surrounded by a community that sanctions rather than punishing this choice, I am still guilty of occasional secret trips to fast-food restaurants. Rain Grimes

"Seeing Belize." I was 7 and Shelly my sister was 5 when, in 1974, we spent five months in the village of San Antonio. My mother had been there before, during the summer that Shelly and I spent with our father. Her older brother was doing research on Mayan agriculture and she'd helped construct and plant his experimental raised-bed system.

Little is conventional about my mother. We'd stayed in a Canadian commune, a Greenwich Village apartment, a tree house, a teepee, and a white Dodge van. My mother thought nothing of taking us out of school to go to Belize for the winter.

June 2002

Our house in Belize had an old-fashioned palm roof that let in the breeze. On hot days the school teacher's wife, whose new house had cement-block walls and a tin roof, would come over, sit on the steps with us, and list the drawbacks of a tin roof: hot in sun; noisy in rain. Our roof never leaked, even during the rainy season when mud washed through the streets in waves and people ran about with cardboard pieces over their heads.

Nearly everyone in San Antonio kept pigs. In the morning we'd see blood on their ears where vampire bats had fed during the night; everyone slept with windows closed. Many pigs ran loose, rooting through garbage and corn husks along the street and getting into people's gardens. At night and in the heat of day, they slept under our house, the only one on stilts. We could hear them snuffle and grunt below us.

Shelly and I came in one day and found our cousin lying face down on the floor. He'd found a knothole and was peeing through it. We were thrilled: the path to the outhouse was overgrown and I had seen snakes there. Why go there when we could pee through the floor ? Our mother put a stop to it.

The muddy green Rio Hondo was slow moving, with trees and vines draped over its banks. We bathed in it near our house. Shelly and I were the only kids with bathing suits: other girls wore old cotton dresses; the boys swam in shorts.

We ate rice and beans - for breakfast, lunch, dinner. Sometimes there was an egg; sometimes a friend brought a fish from the river. Shelly and I craved anything that wasn't rice and beans. Sometimes, as a treat, our mother bought us corn-flakes. We ate them in handfuls without milk, and could empty a box in half an hour. Shelly also liked sweetened condensed milk, which she drank directly from the can.

We walked to school, barefoot but with neatly combed hair. Kindergarten, first and second grades met in a whitewashed room with the same teacher. The day began with the ringing of a huge bell in the school yard. We found our places at the low wooden desks, then stood together to recite the Lord's Prayer and to sing the national anthem: "Oh Land of the Gods by the Carib Sea, our tran-quil haven of dem-o-cra-cy."

English is the official language of Belize, and though everyone in the village spoke Spanish or Mayan at home, school was taught in English. It's an English slightly different. "Don't vex me now", the teacher said when a student misbehaved. In the U.S. I'd struggled hopelessly over phonic worksheets; but in Belize, because of my English, I was the star pupil. It was in Belize that I finally learned to read. The texts were Dick and Jane primers, yellow and cracked. In Belize, Dick and Jane read like fantasy. Spot, their pet, did not resemble the lean mangy dogs who fought and copulated in the dusty streets.

The price of cane had shot up and all the young men and some of the old men had switched from farming corn to cane. They worked land that they carved out of the jungle and leased from the government for a few pennies per hectare. The cut cane went to a sugar refinery in nearby Orange Walk. After my uncle and his family returned to MN for the spring semester, my mom worked in the cane fields. She was the only woman who did, except for an occasional wife or daughter who helped out for an afternoon. She got up before dawn and waited by the general store with the other workers for a cane truck to come by. She loaded, standing on a board over the back wheel of the truck and passing great bundles over her head. Sometimes there'd be ants swarming on the cane. She made maybe six dollars a week ($\pm$ $25 in 2002 dollars ?). Now, when I ask her why she did it, she shrugs. "I wanted to make some money, and see what it's like."

No one in San Antonio had much money. Two families were

June 2002

rich enough to own generators. One of them had a TV. They watched it religiously in spite of the picture being barely visible.

Our house had two rooms, furnished almost entirely with hammocks. From the start I loved the feeling of being suspended and at the same time held tight. At night we lit brittle, dark-green mosquito coils under our hammocks. They burned for about 8 hours with a strong, unpleasant smoke.

Nostalgia is a funny thing. Those months in Belize were among the most vivid in my life, and I remember them with an ache of longing. But, at the time, it was a world too raw, too strong for me. And when, the following year, my mother announced that we were returning to Belize, I shook my eight-year-old head and refused to go. Carin Clevidence

Seal Press, Seattle; 1999, 186p.5x7, $16 cover price. (Revu
by Anna Li)

How can hammocks be made comfortable for sleeping ?

Bruce of BC wrote: "Homeless people spend lots of time in all types of weather, including damp rainy weather. I am sure they would sometimes appreciate a hammock to keep their bodies elevated off of damp or insect-ridden ground."

In past DPs, several people said they had tried sleeping in hammocks but found them uncomfortable. Others mention using hammocks, but did not tell how they achieved comfort.

In Sept83 MP(DP), Judy Brueske told how she rigged a hammock from an old floor-to-ceiling curtain (fairly easy to find at yard sales or dumpsters). She advised: "The difference between a crummy hammock and a luxury job is not so much in the materials used, as in the DIMENSIONS (she's 5'3" and uses cloth 8x8') and in the ANGLE at which you hang it"(she hangs it deep, with lots of slack). She doesn't use spreaders. She didn't say whether she usually sleeps in it, or merely lounges in it briefly.

Duration affects comfort. Eg, on sunny days, city people lounge on the grass in parks during lunch breaks with only a towel under them. But I doubt that'd be comfy for all night.

Bruce sent instructions (from Earth Garden magazine) and a list of twine sources. I said that Judy's method seemed "much easier than making or cheaper than buying a knitted hammock...."

Bruce replied: "Can anyone, including convicts or disabled, really make their own hammocks from bedsheets ? (Also), a knitted hammock may have many advantages compared to a hole-less type."

Availability of materials varies. Sometimes we find old drapes; sometimes lots of discarded hay twine.

Julie Summers replied (to what I'd said): "A knitted hammock may be lighter than a cloth hammock, and dry faster. But I doubt it is cooler. A few years ago, I lounged several hours in a big knitted hammock with about one-inch mesh. I needed cushions under me. Otherwise the cords dug into me uncomfortably."

I wonder if hammock comfort depends on preferred sleeping positions. I sleep mostly on my sides, only briefly on my back. Bert sleeps mostly on sides-toward-front, sometimes on sides or sides-toward-back; seldom on back. Conventional hammocks may be most comfy for people who prefer sleeping on their backs.

I think I read that tropic peoples who routinely sleep in hammocks, make them WIDE - and lay in them cross-ways.

Seems to me, a hammock's main advantage: no need to clear and level ground, which might be rocky, hard, frozen, snow covered - or a swamp with no dry ground. Main disadvantage: need trees suitable for suspending. Advice needed from people who spend most of their sleeping hours in hammocks. Holly & Bert

We are grounded here in San Jose for a month.

We were vehicularly nomadic but I lost my license. Rent prices alone are enough cause to live portably. Joshua, November
June 2002

Dwelling Portably
or Shared, Mobile, Improvised
Underground, Hidden, Floating
September 2002 $1 per issue   POB 190-d, Philomath OR 97370

Ways to cut twine when you lack a knife.

At a county fair where I was selling my crafts,
I went to the hay storage to look for twine. Two
young girls came to fetch hay for their animals.
They did not want a whole bail, but lacked a knife
to cut the bail's twine. Resourcefully, one girl
picked up a loose piece of the same twine,
and, using it like a wire saw, she pulled
it back and forth across a spot on the
bail's twine, severing it in a few
seconds. Anna Li, Oregon 973, November

(Addendum:) A way I've used: Find a rock
with a sharp edge. (Or, if only rounded rocks,
to make a sharp edge, break a rock by hitting it with a bigger
rock.) Lay cord over edge and pound it with another rock.   Bert

Selecting and lashing poles to build structures.

I use small diameter poles, seldom more than four inches
thick. Thicker poles are too heavy to handle easily without
complex rigs or several helpers. I avoid long unsupported
spans that would need thick poles. Eg, with four-inch poles,
I want supports not more than seven feet apart.

Because we like sun, and DON'T like to be under big trees
that could fall on us, we usually live in areas that have been
clear-cut within the past 10 to 20 years, or in rocky areas
where trees are stunted. Consequently, poles must be carried
from neighboring areas that have older trees - another reason
to use light-weight poles. I look for groves, maybe 25 to 40
years old, that include some tall spindly trees which are dying
because of shade by bigger trees. I prefer trees that have
died within the past year and not yet rotted (sign: some
needles hang on but have turned brown), or that will die within
the next few years (live foliage only at top, and bigger trees
within a few feet). This avoids conflicts with whoever is
growing the trees commercially. Also, such trees no longer
have branches along most of their height, minimizing trimming.

I prefer conifers (eg, doug-fir, hemlock, spruce, pine,
cedar) for durability. However, they exude pitch, so, for
inside structures that will stay dry (rot less) and may be
touched frequently, I use broad-leaf trees such as maples. For
posts that touch or penetrate the ground, I use cedar if I want
the structure to last much longer than a year.

Though removing bark will reduce weight and may increase
durability (bark may shelter boring insects), I seldom remove
it except from interior wood where flaking bark would annoy.

If a tree still has strong branches,
I do not immediately cut them off
flush with the trunk. Instead,
I leave stubs a few inches long
which could facilitate fastening
or hanging things. Later, I trim
off stubs not needed, or in the way.

To lash together two poles
that cross each other, I wrap the
twine quite a few turns over and
under, pulling each turn tight. Then I
wrap around those turns to further tighten
them. (Some call this a "square" lash. But
it will be square only if the poles are

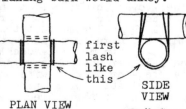

first
lash
like
this

SIDE VIEW

PLAN VIEW

then
like
this

the same diameter and cross at right angles. Better name: parallel lash, because, in plan view, turns are parallel to poles.)

To join poles that must swivel, such as a tripod whose legs come together for carrying, I lash as shown here. (Called a "sheer" lash.)

The poles are usually green or moist and will shrink as they dry. If the joint must stay tight, I add a tightening wrap of rubber straps (cut from discarded innertubes). Light ruins the rubber in a year or two. If I want longer life, I then wrap the joint with strips of black plastic, quite a few layers, tying frequently as I wrap. Light gradually ruins the plastic, but the inner layers will last many years. (What would endure both light and rot ? Cedar bark ?)

For twine I usually use synthetic hay cord. We find it discarded where hay has been fed and along rural roads. It does not rot and it endures partial sun for several years. If limited to natural materials, I'd try vines. Some are very strong while alive, but weaken in a year or so. Vines can't take knots. Use several clove hitches ?

We've not sought great durability. Though we might return to the same site seasonally for a few years, we'll eventually stop using it because of too much shade if for no other reason.

I dis-recommend nailing. Weak; apt to split poles unless drilled; noisy.

(For more about fastening poles, and for calculating diameters needed with various loads and spans, Vonulife 1973 recommended, (DP sells for $2.) esp if building something heavy enough to injure if it collapses. VL is 30 years old, but the techniques probably haven't changed in millenia.) Bert

Five tents tested in windy mountains.

All were advertised as "expedition" models. Three were big, heavy-duty geodesics, weighing 8 to 10¼ pounds, capable of sleeping 3 people. The North Face VE-25 and Walrus Eclypse did well; the Moss Olympic failed.

To save weight, some "four-season" tents are designed to flex: yield to the wind and spring back. In 1981 four of us "were holed up in a VE-24 (VE-25 sans vestibule) on Tibet's Xixapangma. Brutal winds crushed the tent and its occupants into the floor with every gust. When winds subsided, tent popped back up. That went on for days."

But the Moss: "A gust of 50 to 55 mph hit. The windward sidewall folded nearly in half; the ridgepole bowed under; then one of the leeward poles snapped in two. Its broken edge punctured the vestibule which then ripped." Not repairable in those strong winds.

Two light-weight (3 pound, two person) tents did well:

The Stephenson Warmlite survives high winds and snow loads by not resisting. "If you leave the tent alone in a heavy snowfall, it'll just sag in the middle until the load hits the ground. Nothing breaks or rips, it just yields." One drawback of the R2: screened vents small. "With all vents open and one person sleeping inside, on a dry dirt platform in a low-moisture area, condensation was considerable, especially on the single-layer door. I'd hate to be stuck inside on a hot day in mosquito areas." (2SR has screened windows.)

The Chouinard Pyramid achieves lightness by having no rain fly, bug screens, floor. Good as emergency shelter in summer thunderstorms. Four people can squeeze inside. "You won't be comfortable but you won't get wet." The shape isn't roomy "but with most of the surface close to ground, it's very stable in high winds. The beefy, single center pole shivers and sways with the wind, but it doesn't break or let the tent collapse." Eric Perlman (from Backpacker 3/88; sent by Bruce of BC)

(Comment:) These models may no longer be made, but may show up at yard sales or outdoor-club swap meets. If the Moss is cheap because of its poor rep, it may be a good buy for gentler use.

Further report on a small dome tent.

We bought a Stansport #723 over ten years ago ($30 on sale). We've used it only during summers - a few months total so far. We protect it from sun either by setting up where shady, or by covering with cloth (or, at one gathering, with cardboard). Between uses, we remove poles and store fabric in a plastic pail. It has so far endured our gentle, infrequent uses. Problems (also see May96,97,98 DPs):

Scary chemical stink (fire retardant?) dissipated after several years.

Light-color fly (built-in top tarp) admitted some light but was difficult to conceal. We painted it with dark drab green exterior latex housepaint thinned with water. That may also slow sun harm but adds weight.

Leakage, esp near bottom. At first we blamed lack of seam sealing. But applying a sealant (which maker didn't furnish) did not help much. During rains, seepage wets anything that contacts tent. The fabric is fine-weave nylon (not ripstop) and is not coated. Even when no rain, lower sides dampened by condensation. (Inside top stays dry, thanks to insulative space between tent top and fly.) If more than dew or brief drizzle expected, we suspend a 10x12½' piece of clear plastic above (NOT touching) tent (with extra length in front). But that adds to set-up time, and the tie-out cords encumber movement around the tent.

I wonder if all single-wall self-supporting tents have a wet problem. If the built-in fly is small, it does not shield the whole tent. If it is big, extra poles or other complications are needed to support it.

Sept 2002

This summer the Stansport has supported, not only itself, but also a heavy, sometimes-wet cotton drape layed over it as sun screen. It hasn't experienced snow load or strong wind.

We like the Stansport better than the Ero (report in May99 DP). Stansport ventilates through a net layer that is part of the door and can be closed by a separate zipper when not wanted, whereas Ero ventilates through a net ceiling that can't be closed.

I don't like either tent's zipper configuration (∩ on Stansport; ⊥ on Ero) because it must be kept zipped to exclude flying insects, requiring an unzip for every access of things outside. I think I'd prefer a ∪ zipper, so the door will drape closed and need zipping only if there is much wind or many crawling insects. Bert, October

Dome tent versus bug net plus tarp.

Advantages of a small self-supporting dome tent: quicker set up; no tie-out cords to encumber movement around it; somewhat warmer IF vent can be closed; better protection from rain and from crawling insects, esp when windy; blocks view of any prudes.

Advantages of an insect net plus a clear plastic over-tarp: admits more light; less weight; no hard/sharp poles to transport - and replace if they break; easier egress (if no floor); much simpler to fabricate if making it yourself (for how to, see May96 DP). Set-up can be quickened by rigging net and tarp together, but won't be as quick as a good dome tent.

With either, I recommend a plastic ground tarp, to keep tent bottom or mattress cleaner. If tent, the tarp should not extend beyond its sides; or if over-tarp, the ground tarp should end well inboard of its sides (else it will collect rain). Bert & Holly, Jan

How to keep mattresses drier.

If using porous padding such as open-cell foam, leaves, straw, or boughs; put two-thirds of layers under the tent floor but on top of the ground tarp; and only one third tween you and the tent floor. Or, if no floor, use two tarps under you: one on the ground, and one between layers of padding two-thirds of the way up.

This will keep water vapor (from breathing and sweating) from diffusing all the way down through the padding and reaching a temperature near ground cool enough to condense the vapor.

If using closed-cell foam, or open-cell entirely sealed within plastic, condensation may not be a problem. B&H

More reports about plastic tote bins.

A few years ago, I was given four 21-gal Rubbermaid bins. I first used them to store grain. They worked fine.

Last winter, I used one as a water trough for the horses. It worked fine until it got very cold - maybe 20° below. The plastic got brittle and could no longer endure being kicked

and bitten by the colts. I repaired a big crack in the bottom by melting it together with a spoon heated red hot.

When traveling last summer (see Mar 02 DP), I used two bins as panniers (pack baskets) on one of my horses by rigging a sling out of old car seat belts. The bins held folding shovel, axe, horseshoeing tools, etc (hard, heavy objects). They got smashed into trees, and once dropped 3 feet when the horse snagged her saddle on a low tree and broke a cinch. They withstood all that. Bear, ID 832, Jan

Rig for mounting barrels on horses.

A "pivot point" lets barrels hang straight whether going uphill or down; whereas ordinary pack boxes tilt. And on "a deep trail where ordinary boxes would drag", the barrels rock up out of the way. Designed and sold by Ken Wegner of K&S Saddlery in Spinaway WA (s of Tacoma), the rigs are made of nylon seatbelt strapping and brass.

As barrels, Ken suggests Rubbermaid garbage cans. They are "soft enough that if you run into a tree, they bend and come back out. And if you do destroy one, you just buy another for $10." Kathy Peth (from Cascade Horseman, May01; sent by Anna)

Choosing a bicycle to carry luggage.

If a bike hauls weight other than its rider, tire cross-section is very important. A tire is a rim protector. It is also a suspension part. Luggage is dead weight; unlike a rider it has no hands or legs to act as springs. At every bump, it pushes down hard. A 125-pound rider with 30 pounds of luggage is harder on a bike than a 200 lb rider with 10 lbs of luggage.

The tire's air pocket is what protects wheels and cushions bumps. So if you carry non-rider weight, get the fattest tire that fits the frame. A tire narrower than 28x1½ or 26x1.25 is likely to damage the wheel.

Also important, if using panniers, is length of chainstay - the tube that connects rear axle and pedal crank. Mountain, hybrid and most cyclo-cross bikes are long enough. Most recent road bikes, which are racing designs (even those falsely touted as "sport touring") are too short. 16½" from bottom bracket center to rear axle, is minimum for heels to clear panniers.

Almost all mountain bikes work well for hauling as long as the rider is comfortable with the hand positions that flat handlebars allow. Mtn bikes have rigid flames that won't flex much when carrying extra weight, and rims wide enough for a tire that will support the loaded bike and cushion rider well. (If riding on pavement, non-knobby tires roll easier and quieter than knobbies.) Some racks are made for attaching to shock forks. Mtn bikes with frames 14" or less often need customizing and special hardware to mount a rear rack. As on any bike, threaded holes in the frame's rear dropouts (where the wheel clamps in) are necessary for rack attachment. (Desirable but not necessary. I've lashed a rack's struts to the chain stays and seat stays with rubber straps. See (eg) May99 DP.)

Hybrid bikes fit 32c to 45c tires that will support weight and absorb shocks. Most hybrids have rack and fender eyelets and some have shock forks. Don't attach front racks to bikes that have rigid aluminum forks.

Most so-called road bikes made since 1990 lack room for tires wider than 700x25c, and have short chainstays and non-steel forks. Frame strength isn't a problem but wheel strength may be. I wouldn't pack luggage on wheels with less than 32 spokes, esp with a 700x25c tire. David Feldman (from Oregon Cycling, 8/01)

In-line skates for transportation ?

I had hoped that skating would be faster than walking, for mobility in a city to which I ride in a vehicle that can't easily accomodate a bicycle.

I bought a pair at a yard sale for $10. At thrift stores I bought wrist, elbow and knee protectors: $3 total. I wore my bike helmet ($2 at a thrift store previously). To protect my tailbone (and neck - they're connected), I put foam in my underpants. After a few falls I also wore a piece 1½x15x 17" over my butt, outside my clothes, crudely tied to waist and legs.

I'd watched a video, Let's Roll, 5 months before. It was encouraging and covered some basics, but not how to fall - a VITAL skill ! I read 5 books about skating. The best was Inline, William Nealy, 1998, 201p., Menasha Ridge Press, AL (with hilarious cartoons). It had the most about falling. Next best, and more concise: In-line Skater's Start-up, Doug Werner, 1995, 159p., Tracks Pub, Chula Vista CA.

I kept a record. After 24 hours total on skates during several weeks, I don't fall often, esp if not trying anything fancy. But I don't do well on rough surfaces. I tried skating on a typical asphalt highway and could not - my skate would stick and I would have to catch myself from falling forward. Part of the problem: the highway was narrow and busy, confining me to the right edge (in OR the legal side for skaters, who are considered "vehicles" by police). On a surface equally rough but with almost no traffic, I was able to skate with difficulty - because I could zigzag more. I had to exert much force to get any momentum; and I continually feared the skate sticking and tumbling me before I could catch myself.

On smoother streets I was able to skate easier. A patch of ultra-smooth concrete was a dream - I felt graceful. But smooth surfaces are few. (And when I went back to asphalt, it seemed more difficult than before.)

Timing myself on 1/8 mile of fairly smooth asphalt with a slight grade:

both up grade and down, my skating speed was about the same as a brisk walk (6 mph ?) and only a few seconds faster downhill than up. Bicycling quite fast, upgrade was 2½ times faster than walking or skating; downgrade 3 times faster. Walking and bicycling took less energy than skating. I skated 10 minutes while wearing a 10-lb knapsack. No problem. But I don't think I'd feel steady with much more, at my present skill level.

On smooth concrete when wet, I had no control - and doubt anyone would. One book said: when it starts raining, take off your skates. Another said skating was possible.

For now I've given up skates for transportation, but plan to practice more and will report. I hope more-experienced skaters will too. Anna Li

Winter wanderings in a pickup camper.

Two weeks ago I was in Vermont, huddled by the wood-stove as below-zero temperatures froze the garden solid. Now, my daughter and I are in Florida at the Ortona Lock and Dam on the Okeechobee Waterway near Ft Myers. On one side is a cattle pasture dotted with cabbage palms and spreading oaks. On the other side is the lock. As we watch, watercraft cue up and go thru: immense barges, yachts, canoes. My daughter has been out there in her 17' sea kayak she built last summer. With her are manatees, otters, an alligator.

We are seldom bored. My daughter has her roller blades and kayak. We swim in pools, keys, and the ocean. We have snorkeling equipment we use in the keys or in (eg) Salt, Alexander and Juniper Springs in Ocala NF. We write in our journals and work on articles. We read things brought from home and trade while on the road. We stop at libraries; sometimes score a temporary card, sometimes borrow one; or just sit and read. (When short of cash, stick your hand between cushions. We often find something.)

We have a 1989 Chevy Cheyenne half-ton truck with a beat-up camper on it. Driving from VT to FL costs about $150 for gas. We camp free in parking lots of Wal-marts, Kmarts, and truck stops.

National Forests now charge for sites that used to be free: $4 per night; or $40 for a year's pass. Big Cypress Preserve has free campgrounds.

When we get to an area, to learn of local events, we pick up the free weekly paper, a daily paper, and any interesting tourist info at the chamber of commerce. Often there are discount coupons for attractions. We also converse with folks and learn even more that way: Sometimes we are invited to homes or churches, or told about off-the-beaten-path opportunities. Other snowbirds or full-time RVers are also good info sources.

During summers I grow and sell vegetables in Vermont. The season is short, leaving winters free for travel to warmer places. At home I make fruit leathers, dry fruits and veggies, and save up garlic, onions, shallots, potatos, carrots and squash from my garden. We take with us enough food for months. We eat the fresh and heavy stuff first. As we travel we glean just-picked fields, and get food from campgrounds and folks we visit. This campground has all the oranges, grapefruits, kumquats you can pick. Heather has eaten two gallons of kumquats in three days ! Don't overlook dumpster diving. We get much perfectly good food that way. Marines practice in our favorite national park, and in two weeks we got over 500 pounds of MRE's (meals ready to eat - canned in plastic/foil pouches) from dumpsters. Check after weekends. We've snagged still-frozen cases of food and cans not opened - left by Boy Scouts. (WHY didn't they take them home ? Waste !)

I bought our camper for $300 years ago. On our first trip to Arizona, we had to rebuild the overhang, which almost broke off enroute. A couple of years later we faced reality and cut most of the overhang, leaving only a foot. The camper is 8 ft long, barely fitting in the truck bed with the tailgate closing up behind it. The tailgate folds down to become our back porch. The camper has a built-in stove/oven and a propane furnace.

We now have staggered bunks, with storage under each. I keep a leather seat cushion on a porta-potty so it doubles as a seat. We sit on that and the lower bed and use a wooden tray table between us for eating and playing cards. Three big cupboards hold food and utensils. Next to the stove is a counter with the dishpan. A 5-gallon water jug sets on the floor. We have totes of clothes, toiletries, candles, medicines and other items. Under the bed is a HUGE food storage container, two ice chests, a pressure clothes washer, and a footlocker of books. Up front, between us on the seat, is a storage organizer containing snacks, wet-naps, maps, and other stuff needed while driving. Heather's kayak goes on the roof and her backpacking tent at the foot of her bed. Wendy Martin, VT 056, 2000

(Comments:) Wow. What fabulous food finds ! (Holly and I have scored freebes but never such huge amounts.)

Re porta-potties. I might want one if I often entertained guests accustomed to flush toilets. But I've heard a pp can be a nuisance to empty and an expense for chemicals. In the woods we bury. In a city, if no toilet handy, we wrap well and dispose of as garbage. (No worse than disposable diapers.) May96 DP tells how to defecate simply, almost anywhere. B&H, OR 973, Febr

Wild Child: Girls In Counterculture. (These book exerpts much shortened.)
"Our Mail Truck Days." In 1969 my father was arrested for an anti-war protest and sentenced to two years in prison. He had become increasingly focused on political work, and his arrest meant my mother had no help caring for me. She was furious at him and fury made her feel free.

She met Jim who had embraced the counterculture but not on political terms. They soon made plans to head across the country in Jim's truck. A platform bed stretched across the width of the van, and a hinged half-moon table folded down from the wall and perched on one leg. We ate sitting cross-legged on the mattress. The walls were lined with bookshelves, fitted with bungee cords to hold the volumes in place. On a shelf behind the cab was our kitchen: a two-burner propane stove, a tiny cutting board, and a ten-gallon water jug. Jim covered the metal floors with Persian rugs and hung a few ornaments on the wall. Jim bought a small wood stove and bolted it to the floor near the back wall. The smokestack jutted out the side of the truck, the hole weather-sealed with a tin pie plate. A friend wired in a stereo system, and mother sewed heavy denim curtains that velcroed to the window frames for privacy at night. The engine on those snub-nosed trucks bulged into the cab and was housed by a metal shell. Jim covered it with a piece of thick foam, which would be my bed.

In spring 1970, we packed essential belongings and set out on a year-long journey. Thrills of travel sustained me for a while, but I was a difficult age (4) to be rootless. I played with other kids for a day at a campground or city park; then we drove on. After a day on the road, mother tucked me in on my foam bed, warmed from below by engine heat. Lisa Michaels

"Water Baby". In late May 1970, my parents successfully crossed the Canadian border. They had driven all day, anxious to reach the British Columbia island of Sointula. Mom was 7 months pregnant with me, her first of two children. They were traveling in a GM panel truck, altered with a blowtorch to create plexiglass skylights above where their heads rested on the sleeping platform. Underneath it lay all their possessions.

Sointula was founded by Finnish immigrants in late 1800s who started a commune before communes were cool. Altho their dream faded, it has never been entirely forgotten. Then along came hippies to start a new way of living. They were mostly city folks and had no idea how to relate to the locals or even that they should.

Mom said she didn't know what hard work was until they left the city. Photos usually show her bending over a baby, or dishes, or a row of weeding in the garden. Sometimes she is singing with a band on the front porch.

Mom's parents were excited about the coming birth, but knew nothing of the "home" part. Mom thought it best to spare them anxiety and suggested they come a week or two after my due date. But, as a well-grounded hippie child, I came when I was ready. Altho I did not arrive in June, my grandparents did. Grandma took one look around the ten-by-ten-foot room (a converted sauna) and KNEW: the eye drops and gauze, the Whole Earth Catalog with birth section earmarked, the Basic Guide For Midwives open on the kitchen table, the piles of fresh linen and buckets for extra water.

Dad delivered me; grandma coached him. When mom's afterbirth didn't come out right away, dad was afraid to push her belly too hard and hurt her. Grand ma told him he better, and he did.

Growing up on Sointula was in many ways grand. There were no locked doors and I had the whole forest, beach and ocean for a playground. Zoe Eakle

(Though these excerpts are positive, most authors rejected alternative lifestyles. Comments in June 02 DP.)

Editor, Chelsea Cain; Seal Press, Seattle, 1999, $16 cover price, 186p. 5x7. (Review by Anna Li)

Health advice: 2000 BC to 2000 AD.

2000 BC: Here, eat this herb.

1000 AD: That herb is heathen. Here, say this prayer.

1850 AD: That prayer is superstition. Here, drink this potion.

1950 AD: That potion is ineffective. Here, take this antibiotic.

2000 AD: That antibiotic no longer works. Here, eat this herb.

(from Nutrition Today, 3/01)

Why We Get Sick. (A Darwinian View)

This book explains why our bodies function - or fail. It is especially insightful for portable dwellers who selectively adopt prehistoric ways enhanced with contemporary tools. Though Randolph Nesse MD and George Williams PhD don't offer much HOW-to, they prompt readers to think about WHAT-to and, especially, what NOT-to.

Why do we have seeming "flaws, frailties, makeshifts? Why do we crave the very foods that are bad for us ?

"Evolution does no sensible planning." It proceeds by slightly modifying what it already has. This results in some trouble-prone arrangements. Eg, in vertebrates, food and air tubes intersect, allowing choking. And optic nerves pass in front of sensors, shading them. (Whereas in squids' eyes, nerves pass behind sensors.)

Because of humans' big brains, fetal heads fit through pelvises only with difficulty. "This explains why human babies have to be born at such an early and vulnerable stage of development, compared to ape babies."

Every major structural change brings problems. "Walking upright enables us to carry food and babies," but because of inadequate adaptations, predisposes us to (eg) back pain, gut blockages, hernias, vericose veins, swollen feet.

"Sitting for hours at a time on chairs or benches in classrooms is unnatural. Nothing of the sort was ever demanded of Stone Age children."

Hunter-gatherers must be able to spot distant edibles and threats. Arctic natives "were seldom nearsighted when first contacted by Europeans. But when their children began attending school, 25% became myopic" - the same percent as among Americans. Why ? Eyeball growth is controlled, not by genes alone, but also by neural feedback. If often looking too close to focus, the brain prompts the eyeball to grow longer. To prevent myopia, the authors suggest using very big print in childrens' books. (I doubt that would help much, because books must be held close to turn pages easily. Simpler: wear reading glasses)

Sudden infant death syndrome is up to ten times higher in cultures where babies sleep apart from their parents instead of in the same bed.

In the Stone Age, "you were born into a nomadic band of 40 to 100. It was a stable social group." You knew everyone in the band and their genetic and marital connections. "Some you loved deeply and they loved you in return. If there were some you did not love, at least you knew what to expect from them, and you knew what everyone expected of you. If you occasionally saw strangers, it was probably at a trading site, and you knew what to expect of them too.

"Despite great variation, social systems were constrained by economics and demography... Groups that had to gather their food from within walking distance, remained small. No chief could control enough food, wealth, or people to build pyramids or cathedrals.

"Natural selection clearly favors being kind to close relatives because of their shared genes. It also favors being known to keep promises and not cheat members of one's group or habitual trading partners in other groups. There was, however, never any individual advantage to altruism beyond these local associations. Global human rights is a new idea never favored by evolution during the Stone Age....

"Individuals may be viewed as vessels created by genes for the replication of genes, to be discarded when the genes are through with them.

"Natural selection has no mandate to make people happy, and our long-range interests are often well served by aversions." Eg, nausea and food aversions during pregnancy evolved to impose dietary restrictions on the mother, thereby lessening fetal exposure to toxins when most vulnerable (first few months). The fetus is a minor nutritional burden then, so a healthy woman can afford to eat less. She usually prefers bland foods "without the strong odors and flavors of toxic compounds....

"Women who have no pregnancy nausea are more likely to miscarry or bear

Sept 2002

defective children" because they are more apt to eat harmful foods. Unwisely, many doctors attempt to alleviate symptoms. "Pregnant women should be extremely wary of all drugs, both therapeutic and recreational....

"Colds bring many symptoms children dislike: runny nose, headache, fever, malaise. Acetaminophen (eg Tylenol) can reduce or eliminate some of these symptoms." Traditional physicians are likely to recommend it.

"Fever is unpleasant but useful. It is an adaptation shaped by natural selection to fight infections." In one study, children with chicken pox who were given acetaminophen, averaged about a day longer to recover than those who took sugar pills. (More important: did they also incur more complications such as pneumonia ?)

Why aren't we normally hotter ? "Fever has costs as well as benefits. Even a moderate fever (103^0) depletes nutrient reserves 20% faster."

Taking (eg) aspirin for a fever is not ALWAYS bad. "Each condition needs to be studied separately and each case considered individually."

Malaise, too, helps us. By deterring unessential activity, it favors immune defenses and tissue repair.

Distinguishing defenses from defects can be vital. Totally block a cough "and you may die of pneumonia."

By 1970s, iron lack was proven to inhibit infections. "But even now, only 11% of physicians and 6% of pharmacists know that iron supplements may" worsen infections.

"The majority of kidney stones are composed of calcium oxalate." For years, doctors told such patients to reduce calcium intake. However, a study shows that low-calcium diets INCREASE kidney stones. "Calcium binds oxalate in the gut so that it cannot be absorbed." If too little calcium is eaten, some oxalate is left free.

Why such medical ignorance ? One cause: "pervasive neglect of evolutionary science at all educational levels," due to religious opposition.

"The body is a bundle of careful compromises. Stronger stomach acid helps digestion and kills bacteria but aggrevates ulcers."

Microbes are "sophisticated opponents. We have evolved defenses to counter their threats. They have evolved ways to overcome defenses or even to use them to their benefit."

Pathogens can evolve rapidly, because of their fast reproduction and vast numbers. How they change will depend on conditions. They may not become more benign. "A rhinovirus (cold) that does not stimulate abundant secretion of mucus and sneezing is unlikely to reach new hosts." If more than one Shigella strain is in a host, "the one that most effectively converts the host's resources to its own use will disperse the most progeny before the host dies....

"If disperal depends not only on a

host's survival but also on its mobility, any damage to the host is especially harmful to the pathogen. If you are so sick from a cold that you stay home in bed, you are unlikely to come into contact with many people that your virus can infect...."

Fatal diseases lurk in hospitals. "People who are acutely ill, do not move around much, but hospital personnel and equipment move rapidly." Pathogens are spread by inadequately cleaned hands, thermometers, eating utensils. "Diseases may rapidly become more virilent" because the pathogens don't need mobile hosts.

"Mosquito-borne infections are generally mild in the mosquito and severe in the vertebrate. This is to be expected because any harm to the mosquito would make it less likely to bite another vertebrate." But (eg) malaria does not need a mobile vertebrate. In fact, experiments with mice and rabbits show: "a prostrate host is more vulnerable to mosquitos."

In the Stone Age, most ills were caused by worms, and by protozoa born by (eg) bugs. Most bacterial and viral infections require rates of personal contact only possible in dense populations.

Our bodies evolved during millions of years for lives spent in small groups hunting and gathering. "Those conditions ended a few thousand years ago (for most people) but evolution has not had time since then to adapt us to" present conditions.

"Life on a primitive farm or third-world village may be as abnormal" as are offices, classrooms, fast-foods.

"During almost all of human evolution, it was adaptive to conserve energy by being as lazy as circumstances permitted." Energy was a scarce resource and could not be wasted.

This book refers to Timothy John's "With Bitter Herbs They Shall Eat It" (reviewed in May93 DP). "Our dietary problems result from a mismatch between tastes evolved for Stone Age conditions and their likely effects today. Fat, sugar, and salt were in short supply through nearly all of our evolutionary history.... In the Stone Age it was adaptive to pick the sweetest fruit available. What happens when people with this adaptation live in a world full of chocolate eclairs ?

"When every household had to make its own wine ... in small vessels and with primitive equipment, it was not likely that anyone would have enough for heavy daily consumption...."

"Paradoxically, the increased food production made possible by herding and agriculture, resulted in nutritional shortages...." About 1500 years ago, some tribes "abandoned hunter-gatherer lifestyles and started growing corn and beans." Compared to earlier skeletons," the farmers are on average less robust and show B-vitamin lack.

"There is great wisdom in our innate tendency to follow the seemingly

Sept 2002

arbitrary dictates of culture. The rituals of many societies require that corn be processed with alkali before it is eaten." Though Stone Agers did not know that doing so balanced the amino acids and freed niacin, they or their ancestors observed that eaters of unprocessed corn more often got pellegra. (But many contemporary rituals were crafted by governments/ churches/corporations, not to help US but to help THEM. Beware !)

"Nectar is an elaborate cocktail of sugars and dilute poisons." It evolved as an optimal trade-off between the flower's need to repel the wrong visitors and attract the right ones.

"Toxin molecules in sufficiently low concentration will be quickly taken up by receptors" on liver cells and rapidly detoxified by enzymes. "If we overload our body with so many toxic molecules that all processing sites are occupied, the excess circulates through the body, doing damage...

"There is no such thing as a diet without toxins. The diets of all our ancestors, like those of today, were compromises between costs and benefits.

"Human diets expanded after fire was domesticated" because heat detoxifies many of the most potent poisons.

Artificial pesticides are a special hazard because some "are extremely different chemically from those with which we are adapted to cope.

"Since the invention of agriculture, we have been selectively breeding plants to overcome their evolved defenses. Most wild species of potato are highly toxic, as you might expect, given that they are an otherwise unprotected, concentrated source of nourishment. A new variety of disease-resistant potato was recently introduced that did not need (artificial) pesticide protection, but it had to be withdrawn from the market when it was found to make people ill. Sure enough, the symptoms were caused by the same natural toxins that" had been bred out.

"Toxin manufacture (by a plant) requires materials and energy, and the toxins may be dangerous to the plant. In general, a plant can have high toxin levels or rapid growth but not both. Rapidly growing plant tissues are usually better food than stable or slowly growing structures." Spring's first leaves are relished by bugs.

"It takes such elaborate processing to turn acorns into human food that we wonder if the tannin may be too much even for squirrels. (8% kills rats.) Perhaps it leaches out when acorns are buried. If so, the squirrels are processing as well as hiding food.

"The Pomo indians of CA mixed unprocessed acorn meal with a certain kind of red clay to make bread. The clay bound enough tannin to make the bread palatable. Other groups boiled acorns to extract the tannin. Our enzyme systems can apparently cope with low concentrations of tannin, and many like its taste in tea and wine."

Domestic animals and plants were bred to be tender, non-toxic, easily processed. "The mainstay foods of the Stone Age would seem to us inedible or too demanding of time and effort. Many wild fruits, even when fully ripe, are sour to our tastes, and other plant products are bitter or have strong odors." (I disagree. Many wild berries are as sweet as most domestic fruits, and nettles and some other wild greens are as tasty as garden greens - though not as seductive as candied cherries or pumpkin pie !) Random House, 1994, 289p, $13 cover price. (review by H&B)

Should I taste unknown green plants ?
Many people, including me, taste leaves or fruits WITHOUT swallowing. I chew a tiny piece and hold in my mouth a minute or so. If it tastes bad or burns/numbs/stings, I spit out and keep spitting. But suppose it tastes bland - or nice. Then what ?

Some people swallow a tiny portion. If no bad effects within 24 hrs, they may eat somewhat more. And so on.

Ray Vizgirdas, in Wilderness Way v5n2, condemns this. He points out that water hemlock (Cicuta) smells and tastes good to many people, yet a piece of root "the size of a marble may kill you within a half hour." Some other plants' poisons are cumulative and thus can't be assayed by sampling. And most of the toxins in lupines "are excreted by the kidneys. One must eat a lethal dose at one time to die." Ray advises, eat only plants you've positively identified as edible.

Except for fruits, I agree, partly because most plant parts won't provide enough energy to sustain me if I'm famished. Leaves contain vitamins but few calories (and I'll probably be able to identify before developing a vitamin deficiency). Most roots are tough to dig. Most wild seeds are tiny and difficult to separate out.

However, with an unknown plant, although I don't SWALLOW it, I may TASTE it - to reduce the number of plants I must identify. Most plants taste awful to me. So, tasting saves me much time otherwise spent keying.

As for fruits, in this area at least, the only wild fruits that taste good to me are edible. (I deliberately tasted a baneberry, one of the few poisonous berries, and didn't like it) And fruits are rich in sugars which provide energy, and vitamin C which humans need frequently. Holly & Bert

Water: easy out-flow abets in-flow.
Chronic dehydration (body too dry) is believed to be a major cause of cancer, joint pains, memory and vision loss, over-eating, and lack of pep; perhaps because removal of toxins (which all body tissues produce during normal activities) is slowed.

70% of Americans are chronically dehydrated, I've read. One cause: a weak sense of thirst (which is not felt until 2% dehydrated - I suppose

Sept 2002

because dehydration was seldom a problem for primate ancestors who usually got enough moisture from their food: mostly shoots and fruits rich in water, and healthier than often-contaminated streams and ponds). But, in present society, the biggest cause may be: not wanting work, play, or sleep interrupted by trips to toilets.

To minimize inconvenience, keep pee jugs/bowls handy. When inside, I have one within a few feet. Even when we sit a house, I use a pee jug, to save me time as well as saving the owners water and electricity. For men, liquid detergent bottles have good-size openings and are not easily mistaken for water/juice jugs. For women, 64-oz plastic bowls are low enough to squat over and wide enough to reliably intercept flow. Use tight-fitting lid.

Pee frequently. Letting urine set long in you, may harm bladder.

To decide how much to drink, I do not rely on thirst alone. If I feel irritation when I pee, or if I've not had an urge for many hours, or if my pee looks dark, I drink more.

Water is best drunk between meals: at least 2 hours after and 1/4 hour before eating. (If drunk with meals, it dilutes digestive secretions.)

Sweet fruits or drinks may not relieve thirst and might increase it. On one hot 60-mile bike trip, we took scant water, thinking we'd pass some. We didn't. We ate many blackberries, which lessened thirst but did not provide enough moisture. When we did reach water, we drank MUCH (slowly) - but that night I hallucinated.

According to MDs Clark Cobb and Rahul Khosla in 7/01 Patient Care; "During heavy exercise in a hot environment, most people should drink 16 to 32 ounces (2 to 4 glasses) of cool water each hour. Water is just as good if not better than sport drinks. Do not take salt tablets." (If needing salt, will likely crave salty foods.)

Cold, too, increases water needs, because cool air becomes drying when warmed by lungs. High altitude further increases water needs because of more breathing in the thin air. B&H, March

Buying at wholesale grocers.

Though Bert and I sometimes buy (eg) ramon noodles on sale at retail stores, most of our food purchases are at wholesalers. In western Oregon, we have recently payed about 25¢ a pound for oatmeal and popcorn and under 20¢ for red wheat, buying 50-pound bags. Brown rice was over 30¢ and (we've read) is more pesticided than other grains, so we now eat less. Recently, lentils were much cheaper (±30¢/pound) than other beans, and they cook faster, so we bought hundreds of pounds. Prices vary, depending on harvests.

Whereas, if noodles on sale are $1 for ten 3-ounce packets, that is 53¢ a pound. Not really a bargain. Also, when we get to cities, we are usually too busy to want to chase sales.

A decade ago, we were able to buy 50-pound bags of organic red wheat at a local co-op for under 25¢/pound. But now, the co-op not only marks up more, but no longer stocks extra bags - because they "need" the space for more shelves of (eg) "organic" cookies and candies. (Sad story. They began as a small, simple, funky, volunteer-run shop selling basic foods and some locally-grown produce - but now differ from Safeway mainly in hype. That seems the fate of any organization that grows big enough to need a full-time employee or a professional manager - because one yuppy who buys pricy processed junk, profits them more than do 10 customers like us.) If you want organic grains and local sellers are pricy, consider buying from THEIR source - if your group has enough storage for a truckload.

Most grains we buy are grown else-where: eg, popcorn in IA and wheat in MT. People in central U.S. can likely buy for less than we do - esp if they can buy direct from growers. (Weather here is chancy for grains. Some feed-store corn (±10¢/lb) included moldy kernels. A nuisance to pick out.)

Most sizable cities have wholesale grocers. I look for ones (also called institutional grocers) that cater to restaurants, bakeries, schools, etc, because they have the big bags. (Some sell cases of small packages to retail stores - which are not bargains.)

A few wholesalers, pressured by retailers who fear losing trade, say they don't sell "to the public". I ignore that - and briskly walk in like I'm a business person who's been there before, know where I'm going, and do not have much time. (Don't pause and ask.) If questioned, I might say I have (eg) a popcorn stand at the fair, or am a cook at Camp Cukinuki. Seldom am I refused - they want my money. Of course, I pay cash - and carry.

Bert and I together spend ± $400 a year for food. (Total expenses ± $600 a year; not including DP which costs and earns under $1000/year.) H & B

Solar pre-cooking can save fuel.

Here and in much of North America, sunshine is often too brief (because of morning clouds, or hills or trees) to rely on solar alone. However, on most summer days and some days year around, water can be heated to 170°F or hotter. That will greatly reduce fuel needed to finish cooking, esp if (eg) rice soaks in the water while it is heating: very worthwhile if using (eg) propane or alcohol that must be bought and backpacked. 170 is also more than hot enough to kill disease organisms in drinking water. (163 is supposedly hot enough, but thermometer might not be accurate.)

Time needed to get water hot can be shortened by keeping the water inside overnight (if your shelter is insulated) or under a pile of leaves or (eg) extra clothes. Bert & Holly, March

Solar cooker easy to pack and store.

This reflector-type cooker is esp for portable dwellers at mid latitudes (most of N.Amer). Its main advantage over similar designs: folds to 8½x11: small enough to fit into a 5 gal pail: important where its materials will rot or lose shine unless sheltered.

Covered with 12-inch-wide aluminum foil (standard size); little scrap. Accomodates pot up to 10" diameter.

I built ours out of non-corrugated cardboard from recycle bins. (Stiff pieces best.) Hinges and reinforcements of Tyvek, a super-strong paper (from used "Express Mail" envelopes). White glue. About 6½ feet of foil. Total cost under 25¢. Tools: pencil, ruler, sizzors, knife, clean flat surface at least 2½x3 feet.

The cooker consists of eight 8½x11 panels hinged together. (If bigger sheets available, less gluing needed.)

CONSTRUCTION. (Read through to "use" before starting.) Cut bottom side panels as shown on right, leaving tabs. Cut slots in back side panels. I reinforced tabs and slots and fold lines by gluing Tyvek onto cardboard. For best adhesion, apply glue to blank sides (if one side has printing).

Cut a Tyvek piece 7x9", fold into a shape 9" long with "feet" 1" wide and glue to (what will be) non-reflective side of top panel.

Cut foil slightly larger than the cardboard. (Eg, 9½x12" to cover an 8½x11 panel) On top of the LEAST shiny side of the foil, put a panel (or multi-

back left panel

KEY
——————— cut
— — — — hinge or fold
- - - - - guide line
(don't cut or fold)
all dimensions in inches

slots

top panel

tube for holding support stick

back left panel | back center panel | back right panel

bottom left panel | bottom center panel | bottom right panel

KEY
——————— cut
— — hinge or fold

front panel

tab

bottom left panel

SCALE IN INCHES

panel section), centering so the foil extends about ½" beyond all edges. (Except: I trimmed off foil that would cover tabs.) Fold foil up over the edges of the panel. (I did not glue foil to cardboard. I did sticky-tape to non-reflective sides in a few spots to help hold.)

Place panels, reflective sides down, about ¼" apart (to allow fold-up room). To hinge panels together, cut 18 pieces of Tyvek about 2x4" (2 for each 8½" join; 3 for each 11" join). Before gluing on, trim off folded-over foil that would otherwise be covered by Tyvek (so the Tyvek will glue to the cardboard, not the foil). Don't put glue on the hinge/fold lines.

Though not essential, a 2x3-foot piece of flat material (eg, plywood), to be a platform the cooker sets on, will faciliate turning the cooker (because the cooker and the props that adjust it can all set on the platform and turn with it).

September 2002

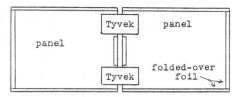

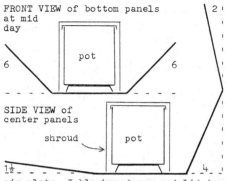

FRONT VIEW of bottom panels at mid day

SIDE VIEW of center panels

shroud

USE. I cook or heat water in a spot sunny for several hours. Place platform level and non-tipsy. Or, if no platform, level and smooth ground.

Connect each bottom side panel to a back panel by folding in edges of tab, pushing tab through slot, and then partly unfolding tab. If sun is quite high: eg, near mid day from April until mid Sept near 45° latitude (eg, near Portland, Minneapolis, Montreal, Milan, AlmaAta, Vladivostock, Christchurch), I put each tab into the third slot from the bottom. During the same period near 35° latitude (eg,near Santa Barbara, Albuquerque, Memphis, Charlotte, Algiers, Beirut, Tokyo, Capetown, Sidney, Buenos Aires), I'd use the second slot. At latitudes 25° or less (eg, Miami, Honolulu, Calcutta), I'd use the first slot. If at 55° or higher (eg, Prince George, Edmonton, Edinburgh, Copenhagen, Moscow), or late in day or season (sun low in sky) I'd use the fourth slot. Ie, the lower the sun, the higher the slot.

Set the cooker's bottom center panel on the platform. Hold up the top panel by inserting into the tube a 2-foot-long stick. Place (eg) rocks against the bottom of stick.

I set an uncolored glass dish, 5"D, 1" high, upside down, on the bottom center panel, and set pot on dish - to insulate pot from panel. Or, 3 small clear glasses or jars. Last choice: chunks of bark (will block a lil sun).

Don't use a pot that has a long side handle. (It would get in way of a shroud). For the greatest heat, the pot and lid should be dull black.

Turn cooker and adjust panels to reflect most sun onto pot. Slant the back panels by placing objects under the back side panels, or against the non-reflective side of the back center panel. Adjust top panel by moving the stick that holds it up. Raise front panel by setting something under it, or lower it by raising the platform.

The shroud should be enough larger than pot to provide a narrow air space (½" to 1") between them for insulation. A transparent jar or pail will be most convenient. Next best: oven bag. If using an ordinary plastic bag, try to keep it from touching the hot pot. The bag may be kept extended by inserting a few bent, limber twigs.

TESTS. On 6 days of late summer at 43° latitude 600 ft altitude, I heated 8 cups of water. I used a slightly rusty "tin" can, 6¼Dx7" (8 cups filled it 5" deep) because I happened to have a transparent plastic jar that fit it well as shroud. Lid made from aluminum pie plate. I blackened can and lid in a fire. (Black adhered to can, not lid)

I adjusted cooker once an hour but left tabs in third slots all day. At 1:30 (sun highest), as shown above. Early and late in day, I set center back panel steeper, top panel less steep, front panel horizontal or below.

During all tests the water got hot enough long enough to cook almost anything. (I didn't cook because can had soldered (lead?) seam, and because the tests were too long.)

The last test, Sept 8, got hottest despite lower sun, because sky had no clouds. Strong breeze in early PM. At 9:00, when sun rose above trees, test began: air 55°F, water 49°. 11:30,162°. 12:00, 177° (now steaming). 12:30,187°. 1:30 (local solar noon), 202°, air 87°. 3:00, 208° (hottest). 6:00, 195°, air 66°, sun going behind trees, test end. A cup of water evaporated. Its cooling effect prevented boiling. (A pressure cooker would have gotten hotter.)

On Sept 2, when sky mostly/partly cloudy until 3:30, water 170° at 2:00, max 197° at 4:00. 185° or hotter for 3 hours. (Plenty hot enough to cook - typical simmer 182° on a gas stove.)

COMPARISON. A decade ago, we built a window-box-type cooker out of cardboard, insulated with crumpled newspaper. We cooked with it almost every day during July and early Aug. We had no candy thermometer to measure temperatures. As I recall, it got steamy hot though not audibly boiling. It needed adjusting less often than does our reflector cooker; and had few parts to adjust. But it required a high sun (or else tilting the whole box, which would complicate pot support). Biggest problem: VERY BULKY - much too big to fit in any container we had. Sheltered only by wrapping in plastic, moisture and mice ruined it in one winter.

COMMENTS. Some may wonder why we want to solar cook, living as we do where wood is plentiful. Solar is safer: no chance of starting forest fire or of producing smoke (which can cause alarm and attract hassles, even from a safe wood stove). Also, with solar, less chance of scorching food. Also, we might be able to cook inside, where we definitely don't want smoke !

September 2002   B&H

Dwelling Portably

May 2003 $1 per issue

or Shared, Mobile, Improvised
Underground, Hidden, Floating
POB 190-d, Philomath OR 97370

Update on Rubbermaid storage bins used as horse packs.

A horse fell on one, cracking it along a corner. Also, the lids are cracking; maybe sunlight has weakened the plastic. However, they were free, and I got two summers use as packs, and can still use them to store 'junk' at my base camp.

I spent most of the summer training horses on a light wagon, but did manage a three-week trip into the wilderness to visit hot springs. Bear, ID 832, Oct

Cook stove made from one-gallon paint can.

I read about this on the internet and made one to use on a recent camping trip. I punched a 4x2" hole near the bottom as the main air inlet, and many small holes (nail size) on the opposite side near the top. At first I did not have enough holes: the fire almost died when I put a pot on top. So I gave the stove a "face" by cutting "eye" and "ear" holes. I dubbed it "Fire Monster". Use a large nail and light hammer. After punching the holes, hammer out the dents.

Feed fuel mostly through the top, but small pieces can go through the eye/ear holes. I put leaves/paper in first, then pine cones and small pieces of wood, then anything burnable that fits. As a starter perhaps a candle stub. Light it through the mouth. As an air blower, I used a piece of bamboo with a ¼" hole in the fire end. Blowing into the 2" end creates a strong air stream that gets a fire going quickly. I kept the fire end damp so it wouldn't burn easily. Don't cook food on the first fire, and stand back while the old paint burns off.

Careful ! I burned my fingers trying to reposition the stove. Leave the bail handle on and use a stick to move the stove. For stability I put stones in the bottom.

To slow the fire, turn the face away from the wind. I was able to slow it enough to simmer. But the stove seems best for boiling. Fred Spek, Ontario M6J, Sept

I use propane for heating and cooking.

A small refillable one-gallon bulk tank (much smaller/ lighter/handier than the standard 20# 5-gallon tank) lasts me for months. U-haul locations fill propane tanks and have no minimum (this is rare). I pick slack times.

My stove is a one-burner designed for the disposable bottles. But I use a "Mr Heater" 90° elbow/adaptor and leave it attached to the tank between refills. It is very stable for cooking. For heating, it will warm my tent or pickup shell in a minute or two, even in freezing temperatures. So, in the evening, I turn it on and off several times. In the morning, I stick one arm out of my bag, turn the propane on full so I can hear it, light a 'strike anywhere' match, and get a small 'poof' as the stove lights. (Takes practice to not get a big poof !) In a minute or so my space is warm and I get up. (I have never gone back to sleep after lighting the stove. Fumes could be deadly. Ken, WA 982

Benefits of foraging and gardening.

I lived on 45 acres once. Though there was a pond, cattails, rose hips, and many blackberries, I could not gather enough wild food to feed my family. I had to buy, and plant.

Hunting/gathering takes ALL your time. That is why horticulture was developed.

This week I put in early garden stuff: spinach, onions, peas, lettuce. I have a row of broad-leaf dandelion and winter cress. Those greens are full of vitamins. Indoors I've started the cabbage family and tomatoes, peppers, squash. I buy seed for 10¢ a package at Walgreens. For a few kinds I have to pay more at specialty stores. But, all in all, my garden pays. A bonus: people stop by, look over the fence, and comment. We share what we have and what we know. Suzanne, OH 451, Mar 02

(Comments:) Interesting that you are cultivating dandelions. Edible weeds are hardier than domestic vegies and seem a better bet for nomadic gardeners. They taste about as good and have more vitamins than do most domestics, though fewer calories than (eg) potatos. I've read that some "weeds" were formerly cultivated. Did they lose status because they were EASY to grow ?!

If growing weeds, best to encourage those native to the area. A few years ago we were given some amaranth seeds gathered from garden weeds. We planted. They sprouted but soon died. Wrong soil ? Not enough sun ? Too dry ? Most garden weeds here are from eastern N. America and need summer rains or else irrigation, as do the domestic vegies.

Foraging does not fully feed us, even during summer. Plenty of vitamins but little fat. However, we do forage most of our fruit and vegies; which are expensive to buy, heavy to transport (mostly water), and difficult to store (without great loss of nutrients). We buy mostly grains and other edible seeds; which are cheap in bulk, light weight per calories, and easy to store.

We've known people who bought or built rural "homesteads", thinking they could grow all their food. But, though they did produce some, they also had to buy food - in most cases more than we do, because of lack of time due to needing jobs to pay the taxes, and pay for the cars needed to commute !

Some anthropologists say that early hunter-gatherers had MORE leisure than did horticulturalists; perhaps because the latter were more easily preyed upon through taxes and conscriptions by lords or through robberies by raiders. Agriculture displaced hunting/gathering, not because it took less time, but because it took less land. A problem for contemporary foragers: most of the lusher areas are now occupied by farms and cities. Holly & Bert, OR 973, February

Living lightly in the Chicago area.

I manage to scavenge most of my food. I am leery of food straight out of garbage cans. I spend much time cutting off the better portions and discarding the rest. I douse with tumeric or curry, esp if drying. Tumeric kills viruses and bacteria and arrests rotting. It apparently kills bugs.

I also salvage most clothing and much else. I never walk the streets when I can walk the alleys. Anything that won't fit into a sealed locker or foot-locker should probably not be taken. I've made money selling salvagings: eg, $5000 on two boxes of signed first-edition books that someone left in an alley. To learn value, I check references in libraries.

My experience being homeless in Chicago. The cops don't need you - and they expect the same. Ie, if you don't look well heeled, your safety is not their concern. Cops generally won't bother you if you are minding your own business. But they do take a dim view of exercising your 2nd amendment rights - including knives over 3 inches. At first I was somewhat worried, sleeping day time in parks on the near-west/ northwest side. But no one bothered me. After 20 years experience, I've learned to avoid groups of homeless as they draw the wrong kind of attention. Aggressive beggars and drug addicts are slowly closing down one of Chicago's best services: showers in the Public Park District.

   I just walk in like I belong there and bathe myself and and my clothing (which I leave on) with a bar of laundry soap. Okay for hair, too. After wringing my clothes, during summer I put them in a mesh bag to dry naturally. During winter I carry them in a plastic bag to a laudromat and use the driers. When I was driving a cab, I'd put them on newspapers below the dash board, open the windows, and turn the heat on full blast. Fashion concerns aside, one needs only one change of clothes.

   Backpacks don't seem a problem, but I carry an innocuous book bag. Sleeping bags or bed rolls do seem to draw attention. Walking railroad tracks is an excellent way to travel. Northern tier railroad personnel seem almost nostalgic about hobos. Under land-grant laws, railroads have virtual sovereignty over their right-of-ways and stations. Trespass involves city police only if they are called in. However, not all police know this. My only hassles have been by drinkers.

   As I tend to work a circuit, I have a series of places where I deposit my finds. Bridges and overpasses provide my roofs and windbreaks during inclement weather. One problem: the heavy pesticide spraying, esp in the South. Of course, I gather and plant far off the right of way. I don't even sleep in areas that have been sprayed. Goats and other animals should not forage in those areas. Kurt, IL 606, March 02

Encounters bear with cub while hiking.
   I heard sounds of claws scratching on a tree. I followed the sounds toward their source. I spotted a small cub approx 25 feet up in a slim jackpine. I was 20 or 30 yards away. I immediately turned and started running away (mistake) down into a gully that emptied onto a railroad track. I glanced back and saw the mother black bear trotting toward me.

   As I ran, I took off a small daypack and dropped it on the ground. It contained donuts and baked buns (my snack for the day). I thought the bear might smell them and stop. When I got to the railroad and riverbank, I felt safer. Much of the ground there is covered with big boulders which bears have difficulty traversing. I waited two hours before going back and retrieving my daypack. It was still where I had dropped it and the food inside was untouched. Apparently the bear had stopped after advancing only a few yards in my direction. I guess she felt I wasn't much of a threat (and she wasn't very hungry). Over time, I've read many reports of bear attacks and maulings of innocent hikers and campers.

   I often see black bear scat and even tracks in this area. But bears haven't molested the small amounts of dry foods and tinned foods I leave at ground level. One rule: I NEVER cook or eat meat or fish at my base camps. Those odors are much more attractive to bears than are odors of (eg) beans or rice.
                                                    Bruce of BC
Food I put out for my cats attracted rats.
   Also ants. A factory near where I put it, said not to. I now feed my cats on an abandoned lot I cleaned up. I planted some seeds there. It is beautiful outside. Elaine,

Long-tolerated hut dwellers finally hassled.

For 12 years, Thelma Cabellero and Besh Serdahely have lived in a home-made hut built amongst the branches of a sprawling oak tree halfway up San Bruno Mountain south of San Francisco. The hut masterfully blends tree branches with building materials salvaged from dumpsters. The roof is a patchwork of plastic panels held together with cords and clips.

The couple met and fell in love at a S.F. homeless shelter in the late 1980s and set up a home in some bushes by the Caltrain tracks before discovering their present site....

San Bruno Mountain Watch, an environmental group that has fought commercial development, want Thelma and Besh to stay. "They have always been good stewarts. Because of their efforts Owl Canyon has no invasion of broom, fennel, hemlock."

Their home looks out on San Francisco Bay, freeways, power lines, and other apparatus they don't need. Thelma said, "We have the trees and the sunshine and the sky."

Occasionally the couple hike into town for supplies; mostly beans and bread. Other times they snip away at the non-native plants, tend their compost heap, haul water from a nearby spring, and relax by reading cast-off books, playing Monopoly and working crossword puzzles. Steve Rubenstein (from San Francisco Chronicle 4Sep02; sent by Herbert Diaz)

Lynnwood criticized for ban on living in cars.

Lynnwood's code-enforcement officer, Peter Van Guisen, said the law, approved last month, was passed to prevent transients from living in cars they park in front of parks or homes, often using the shrubbery as bathrooms. Car camping has especially been a problem, Van Guisen said, at Gold Park, a wooded, city-owned lot at Highway 99 and 200th St SW, across from the Labor Ready temp agency, a magnet for the homeless. The lot is also adjacent to condominiums whose residents, Van Guisen said, complain they often can't walk through the park without stumbling across makeshift camps.

The ordinance prescribes jail terms of up to 90 days or fines of up to $1000 for people caught living in their cars. It particularly targets people who have "camping paraphernalia" including tarps, sleeping bags, cooking gear in their cars.

Laws like these irk "homeless" advocates who say that Lynnwood is just passing its problems on to Seattle and other cities. Seattle's city council proposed a similar ordinance a few years ago but dropped it under pressure from activists.

Some cities, including Seattle, ticket cars that have been parked in the same place longer than a specified time. However, car dwellers get around those laws by moving frequently. Catherine Tarpley (from 5/7/01 Seattle Times)

(Comments:) Many vacationers carry "camping paraphernalia" in their vehicles because they plan to stop at (eg) National Park campgrounds. They may be more threatened by laws such as Lynnwood's than are poor car dwellers. Because, these days, most police are, first and foremost, revenue sources. So, regardless of a law's intent or their formal instructions, police are encouraged to issue citations to people who can and will pay fines, rather than to people who are likely to end up in jail, costing the city government money.

I wonder if homeless advocacy groups could form potent alliances with travelers' organizations such as AAA. AAA lists towns where police operate speed traps, and urges motorists to avoid them. Laws that prohibit sleeping in vehicles are much worse than speed traps. Such laws not only

rob; they ENDANGER by discouraging sleepy drivers from
stopping and napping.

Seattle officials agree to stop hassling tent city.

Tent-city residents now have the right to put their 100-
person encampment nearly anywhere - a big back yard, church
property, commercial parking lot - so long as (eg) their camps
are at least 20 feet from a neighboring lot and hidden from
view by an 8-foot-tall buffer. Tent city may stay in one spot
for up to 3 months. Neighborhoods cannot veto. Only one tent
city is allowed. Tent-city residents are elated that officials
have stopped insisting that tents are substandard housing.

Tent city, which has moved 27 times in its two-year
history, has spent much of the past year in church parking
lots. Those lots became havens from the threat of city fines
after city officials acknowledged that federal law may be
viewed as allowing churches to ignore land-use codes by
insisting that welcoming the homeless is part of ministering
to the poor and integral to their religions.

(Summary of events. Parts were reported in 9/01 DP)
March 00. A tent city with 20 residents begins on
undeveloped land in Seattle, with tolerance by owner.

Jan 01. Now numbering 100, tent city leaves El Centro de
la Raza after a 6-month stay. Officials had ordered El Centro
to eject tent city. El Centro refused. Officials threatened
to fine El Centro, and rejected its application for a permit.

Apr 01. Officials decide to not fine a Ballard church
for hosting tent city, citing fed court rulings.

Sept 01. King County Superior Court Judge Thomas Majhan
rules that the city was wrong to refuse a permit to El Centro.
The judge said, the military, scouts, and disaster-relief
groups all have histories of establishing safe tent cities.
City officials appealed, but rather than risk losing, which
could throw housing laws into doubt, they conceded.

March 02. Tent-city and Seattle officials sign agreement.
How tent-city residents beat the system, is a story of
persistence, pushiness, good legal advice, and alliances with
churches that made hosting tent city part of their ministry -
and backing city officials into a morally-difficult corner.

That tent-city residents have won anything, is close to
a miracle. They are out of work or under employed. They are
construction workers, often injured, without training to do
something else. They have some money, but not two months
rent. They are hiding from husbands who beat them. They are
mentally ill. They are divorced. They didn't get that job on
a fishing boat that they came to Seattle hoping for.

Gary Gibson, a tent city resident 10 months, says the
group has succeeded because of its record as a quiet, safe
neighbor. Anyone who comes in drunk or disorderly is expelled.

Seattle deputy major Tom Byers said, "My feels are
profoundly mixed. Is it a victory to win the right to sleep
in a tent in the rain ?" City Council President Peter Stein-
brueck, has begun to see things differently. "Why is a tent
settlement worse than a mat on a floor in the basement of a
church ? Talk to the folks who are there. They're happier.
There's self determination. There's strength in that...."

But some other city council members are expected to try
to outlaw tent city, at least on non-church sites, by
requiring plumbing and other facilities that tent city could
not provide. How the council will vote is not known.

Complaints of homeless advocates regarding Seattle's
officially-approved shelters: too few for the thousands who

need shelter; no private spaces for couples to sleep together;
no segregation of potentially dangerous residents; requiring
residents to be in by 10 pm and out by 6:30 am, which prevents
night employment, and forces people with nowhere to go onto
streets in cold and wet weather. Beth Kaiman (much shortened
from 14 & 28 March 02 Seattle Times, sent by Roger Knights).

(Comments:) Officials and media, whether sympathetic or
hostile, blatantly ignore an embarrassing fact: the main cause
of homelessness is the lack of low-cost housing - which is
POLITICALLY CREATED by the myriad zoning laws and building
regulations that greatly increase costs of legal structures.
    Instead of changing their policies, officials campaign for
more tax money to provide government-managed housing. But most
anything a government does, it does clumsily at exorbitant cost
(eg, those WA state camps for migrant harvesters, reported in
9/01 DP). So the result is a token project that benefits only
a few people who are able/willing to jump through all the
hoops - and then spend ten years on a waiting list. But, hey,
such projects provide some high-pay jobs for administrators !

When the homeless move in next door.
    The three months that tent city spent on the hill beside
Lake City Christian Church, tested the depth of convictions of
its neighbors. One took a homeless woman to dinner, while
another itched to call the cops. One said she would welcome
another tent city, while her neighbor began locking her car in
her driveway. Kathern Carlstrom lives closest to the former
site. Like many, she was bothered that the church did not
notify neighbors before the tents went up. But she told me how
polite the tent city residents were. They even cleaned up
around the bus stop, and two men did some edging on a steep
hill in front of her property. "I look out now and miss their
tents., I hope their weeks here allow some of them to move up."
    But another neighbor, Virginia Arnoux, said: "I am glad
they are gone." Though she is a church goer, taught to help
those in need, she said that a friend who works with the homeless told her that "tent-city people don't want jobs and don't
want to help themselves." Nicole Brodeur (Seattle Times 7/8/01

(Comments:) The many campers near that temp-work agency in
Lynnwood (p.13) refutes the claim that tent dwellers don't want
jobs. But probably, most don't want to work 40 or more hours
a week steady - and have rent take most of their earnings !
    Those house-dwellers who hope the "homeless" will "move
up" (ie, get high-pay jobs so they can afford houses) seem
unaware that, if the homeless do, they will bid up housing
prices even higher - causing some present house renters to find
THEMSELVES homeless. Anyone who has a house (or apartment), is
benefitted by people living in tents, cars, bush huts, etc -
because those people are not competing for that house. Likewise
anyone who has a high-paying job, is benefitted by people who
live economically, because they are not competing for that job.

Survey of urban campers who live in Vancouver.
    The city has become home to hundreds who sleep on beaches,
in doorways, under bridges, in cars, and in dozens of other
mostly-hidden places. "Urban campers are most readily found
near densely populated areas, fast-food outlets, laundromats,
and liquor stores - the same areas that appeal to many single
people", says Judy Graves, who has spent several years doing
walkabouts at night with teams of people to count urban campers.
"The shelterless do not distribute themselves evenly across the
city. They look for alcoves, bushes, trees, landscaping,
underground parking lots, unlocked public buildings, and wash-

rooms." Some sleep on porches or garages in Kitsilano, with the home-owner's permission. Many said they lived outside because they had no income, and they either didn't qualify for welfare or had given up applying for it.

However, Graves found much fewer urban campers in Vancouver than in Toronto. In Vancouver "we have to really search to find many people sleeping out." Whereas "in Toronto, as we knelt on the pavement talking with one person, we could always see the next 2 or 3 we would be talking with. In most blocks there were 3 steam grates, and someone slept on every steam grate. In shop doorways, as many as 8 under-age youth slept closely side by side." Graves thought the difference may be due to BC building more "social"(subsidized) housing.

At least two-thirds of those that Graves and companions found, had severe addictions to alcohol or other drugs. Frances (from 22June02 Vancouver Sun, sent by Bruce of BC)

(Comments:) The difference between cities might be due to topography and climate. North of Vancouver are extensive forests. Whereas a land-use map shows mostly farms around Toronto. Also, Toronto has much colder winters. In January, a steam grate may seem better than a tent in the bush.

As for the two-thirds that supposedly have severe addictions. Addicts are more easily found, because they are likely to fall asleep on the nearest bench or lawn, instead preparing a hide-out. So any such survey will be biased. (The article failed to mention that.)

Though Holly and I camp mostly in remote forests, over the years we have also spent quite some time in/near cities. As far as I know, our camps were never found. Partly luck, I suppose. But also because we spent time and effort finding and preparing good sites, and because we went further into the brush or out of town (not wanting liquor or fast foods). B & H

Where can I build a small cabin without getting hassled ?
Preferably some place where I can obtain work. I've found plenty of info on HOW to build, but none on WHERE to build. I just want a base to work from during summers.

Do you live on vacant land ? Doesn't that bring hassles? If you know anyone who has built not to code and gotten away with it, please let me know what county. How is Sonoma co. ? Shane, CA 922, 1998. (I replied immediately, and put reply in a Network Supplement, but not DP, hoping for more info.)

(Reply:) For non-hidden dwellings that are not to code, I read a few years ago: the most tolerant county in CA was Humboldt (Arcata, Eureka). I don't know if it still is.

You say you have plenty of info on HOW to build. Even more important is WHAT to build. A conventional cabin is tall and has an unnatural shape (difficult to conceal) and needs truckloads of materials that are nailed together (difficult to haul in and assemble without attracting attention). Bert

Many people live in tents and vehicles on Prudence Island.
Also in abandoned houses. The island is across from Newport and Portsmouth. Ferry round trip, $5. I plan to go there this summer. Elaine, Rhode Island 029, April 02

How do you stay warm during winter ?
My tent (small dome) is okay in summer but was often too cold the one time I tried camping during winter. Eve, CA 950

(Reply:) We build small, low, WELL INSULATED shelters. Sept Some designs in 5/95, 4/92, 9/85, 5/99 DPs. However, best to form the shelter to the site, rather than trying to find or reshape a site to accomodate a particular design. B & H

Dwelling Portably

or Shared, Mobile, Improvised
Underground, Hidden, Floating

Dec 2003 $1 per issue   POB 190-d, Philomath OR 97370

While living in Portland, I have been eating free food.
        In season: Je-Jy cherries; Jy-Ag-Sp blackberries; Jy-Ag
plums; Sp-Oc-Nv-Dc apples. Also, some charities put out free
bread (past pull date; stores/bakeries donate) each week. You
just go and get what you want. Zalia, OR 972, December 2002

(Addendum:) Here (100 miles south) our free fruit this year:
My-Je salmonberries (but seldom got filled); Je-Jy redberries
(Vaccinium parvafolium, shaped like blueberries, tarter but
much tastier if sweetened); Jy black-cap raspberries; Ag-Sp
blackberries. No apples (in abandoned orchards) this year,
due to hard freeze while blooming. Fortunately we dried quite
a few redberries. So, most mornings this winter, I make a
little redberry-ade by soaking the berries in water a few
hours, adding vit C powder and a SMALL amount of sugar. I do
not know if natural vit C survived the drying, but the berries
add bioflavenoids which enhance vit C. Holly & Bert, Dec 03

In Iceland I discovered a wonderful light-weight trek food.
        Dried paper fish, white fillets. At first they feel like
paper in your mouth. But they puff up with saliva - and are
darned good. They supposedly taste better with margarine, but
I don't approve of margarine so I didn't try. Icelandic
cowboys carry them easily in pockets. Lisa Falour, France, 03

When boiling pasta by the sea, try using salt water.
        If the water is clean, it imparts an enjoyable sea-salt
taste. And salt water cooks foods faster. Drew Feuer, July 03

(Comment:) Also, it has a better balance of minerals than does
refined salt. Eg, potassium and lithium, as well as sodium.
But also wee amounts of toxic heavy metals. Holly, Oregon

Ramen noodles need not be cooked to be tasty.
        I was on a bike trip and didn't want to cook. So I got
HOT water from a campground bathroom, mixed it with noodles,
waited, checked, waited. After 20 minutes the noodles were
ready to eat. Since then I've never cooked ramen noodles.
        Soy protein (TVP) mixed with ramen noodles provides a good
ready meal, tasty and nutritious. TVP takes on the flavor of
whatever you add it to. 37% protein. $2 to $3 per pound.
        I get hot water from store bathrooms, convenience-store
coffee/tea counters (where I ask first), and by solar-heating
water in a GREEN 2-liter plastic soda bottle. I also use the
bottle for showers. Zalia, traveling, March 03

Gatorade bottles, used as canteens, never leak.
        I used to buy "camping" bottles. But they always leaked.
Then, in 1998, I took a Gatorade bottle on a bus trip. Though
it got bashed and sat on, it never leaked. Since then I have
used them everywhere. They also store dry foods well. Zalia

Bottles form low-drag float.
        Many objects float.
This float's advantage:
streamlined: often desirable
where water flows or a boat moves.
        Collect three empty smooth-sided plastic bottles the same
size. The straighter their sides, the better. Two need caps.
(If lacking, close by wrapping ends with pieces of plastic held

on by rubber bands.) From the third bottle, cut off the top and bottom. (The top can be used as funnel to fill jugs. The bottom as bowl.) Slit lengthwise the cylindrical middle piece. Bore or punch small holes in it. Place the two whole jugs together, bottom to bottom. Fit the cut piece around them to hold them in line. To keep them from slipping apart, tie a string between their necks and to the holes in the cut piece. Two-liter bottles will float up to 4 pounds without much drag.

One use: fishing if lacking a casting rod, or where over-head branches prevent casting. If you plan to stand in mid stream, tie a cord to the float's upstream end. If you will be on the bank, tie a long slender pole. The pole can be longer and more flexible than an ordinary fishing pole because the float supports the far end. To the float's downstream end, tie your hook. Bert, Oregon, September 2003

Floating island built from 250,000 plastic bottles.

Richie Sowa, a skilled carpenter, 49, left his native England 6 years ago. Soon after, on Mexico's Yucatan peninsula, he began gathering thousands of bottles, putting them in sacks made of strong fish netting, and weaving the sacks tightly together. Local kids helped collect bottles.

Now 65 by 54 feet, the island holds a 4-room house, sand beaches, and lush vegetation including palm trees. The house's roof collects rain for fresh water; and holds a photo-voltaic panel for electricity, and what looks like a parabolic-reflector solar cooker. The 5-foot-thick foundation of bottles is topped by a bamboo and plywood floor holding, in places, a two-foot-thick layer of soil. Richie plans to grow his food.

The island gets bigger as Richie adds bottle-filled sacks to the edges. He is also thickening the layer of bottles to float the island higher above the waves. "I scuba dive so I can check the underside regularly." The island has survived two hurricanes. He seeks a woman to share it with. It is presently moored 40 yards from the mainland, off Puerto Aventuras.

Local authorities gave permission to build, to encourage awareness of trash reuses. Richie hopes his feat will inspire others. "This proves you can use the garbage from consumer overspill to create land for people to live simple lives in great surroundings." Richie, who earns money as musician and artist, sometimes takes tourists to his island and their donations help cover costs. Chris Pritchard (from National Enquirer 5Nov02 and Sun 8Oct02; sent by Roger Knights)

(Comments:) I think the plastic bottles (designed to withstand acid drinks) and the fish netting (designed to withstand sea water) may have a long life, sheltered from sun. But I wonder about the bamboo and plywood. I also wonder if the island, which weighs 60 tons, can withstand towing in open ocean to a new site; in case officials change their minds or impose taxes and restrictions that Richie finds unacceptable. B & H

More about Prudence and Hog Islands near Providence.

On the back side of Prudence Island are blue berries, pear and apple trees, and rocky Indian Springs. Hog Island is next to Prudence. The ferry won't stop there because the dock isn't safe. Some squatters had trouble with the summer-home people. A man washed up dead. One must be careful and self sufficient. I tell homeless people how to make tents, heat water and cook on tin-can stoves, shower using jugs, and live in boats and cars. Many are rough and dirty. Elaine, RI, 02

Cleaning and fueling Coleman Pressure Lamps

Many vans and RVs have Coleman lamps. Upkeep can be cheaper and easier than most people suppose. Coleman-made replacement mantles cost half as much in Mexico.

Premium unleaded gasoline works as lamp fuel at less than half the price of name-brand white gas. Only it doesn't burn as clean. After a couple months of nightly use, unburned gunk may block fuel flow through generator (the tube between the mantles). Symptoms: balky fire-up; higher pump pressure needed to maintain brightness; dim. Instead of an expensive replacement, clean generator. That can solve many problems.

You need pliers, a knife, and two small wrenches.

Loosen the two generator-securing nuts all the way, and remove generator from lamp.

From the tube bottom, slide out cleaning needle rod.

With knife, scrape carbon deposit from all around rod until brass is shiny. Careful: needle wire tip breaks easily.

Remove top orifice piece from tube: screw out with pliers.

Now, to burn gunk out of tube, with pliers center tube over a stove burner or set into campfire coals. Remove it as soon as yellow flames stop shooting out its ends (in ± 2 min).

After it cools, re-assemble all parts, being very careful to center cleaning wire when re-inserting it into tube center, so it doesn't hook on to the capillary spring inside.

Light up and see the difference. Bridgey, UT, May 02

Candles versus LED lights with batteries recharged by sun.

At first I used candles at night. But I found problems: fire hazards of open flame and tipping over; uses up oxygen (and emits toxic fumes); often flickers; most candles don't burn right because wicks too thin for wax; heavy to carry along; costs $5 to $6 PER MONTH - thats $60 to $72 per year.

So 3 years ago I changed to LEDs, fed by NiMh AA's ($8 for four 1600-mah at Walmart), recharged by a small 5-watt 12-volt photovoltaic (PV) panel ($20 used). The AAs also power a tape player and cell phone. I use a yellow LED most: for reading and writing; most chores; bicycle front light. I use a white LED for area lighting and some chores.

Total weight less than a few candles. Total investment $78, and no more costs until my NiMhs need replacing in a few years. (NiCds I tried got bad 'memory' in 6-18 months.) Zalia

(Comments: $60+ a year for candles ? Wow ! Do you stay up late most nights ? Back when we used only candles (and wax lamps) we may have burned them 2 hours average per winter night for 5 months a year. (Very seldom during summer: we usually go to sleep when dark.) Buying at yard sales and thrift stores, as I recall we spent only a few dollars a year average. We bought paraffin (home-jam-canners use) as well as candles. Most candles were remains of decorative craft gifts. They did not burn well: wax broad, so flame melts a crater and then flickers - and illuminates only ceiling. But wax usable in lamps (see Sep84p.4, Oct93p.1, Sep04p.1 DPs). Recently, by luck, Holly found a few pounds of warped or broken candles in a thrift-store dumpster. She also bought 2 pound-packs at Dollar Tree: each $1 for ten candles 6x$\frac{3}{4}$".

Flames seem to flicker mostly if deep in narrow jars or craters. Our shallow wax-lamps ($1\frac{1}{2}$x$\frac{1}{2}$") seldom flicker.

For the past 7 years we've also used LEDs and rechargable batteries: a winter-base-camp system with PV, and two flashlights (one home-made from $3 LED). Many problems (see May97 p.4&5; Dec97p.8&9; May98p.11&12; Oct98p.3; Nov99p.8; Mar02p.11 DPs). Connections corrode; need cleaning often. Much testing.

Dwelling Portably

or Shared, Mobile, Improvised
Underground, Hidden, Floating
POB 190-d, Philomath OR 97370

April 2004 $1 per issue

There are many alternative ways to move things.
        Once, while working on a tug boat, the marine engineer
asked me to help carry a heavy, greasy, irregularly-shaped
chunk of machinery. I assumed we would both just grab hold and
struggle away. But the engineer, being of Philippino descent,
knew a better way. Wisely, he found a 2-by-4 and lashed its
middle to the machinery. Then we each took hold of an end of
the 2-by-4. That made our task much easier, and kept us clean.
        Different cultures have different ways. Some people often
carry objects on their heads. Some drag them. Some use
stretchers. All those ways work. There are backpacks, and big
messenger bags. There are one-wheel wheelbarrows often used in
rural environments, and two-wheel hand carts commonly used for
deliveries and salvaging in cities.
        Some of the old photographs of Chinese laborers building
railroads in the West, illustrate ingenious ways of moving
stuff around. Noticing how different cultures do things, can
help us develop more techniques; enabling us to better solve
a wider variety of problems. Drew Luna Feuer, NY 120, July 03

Auto seat belts make excellent pack-frame straps.
        They are easy to scrounge (eg, at auto salvage yards ?).
        I put them on several frames I made from hardwood slats
bolted together, like shown in Jaeger's book, Wildwood Wisdom
(reviewed in May93 DP p.7). For packing heavy, hard, irregularly shaped objects, they are easier to use than are many
aluminum pack frames. Al Fry, Idaho 836, 2001 ?

Simple water pre-filter easy to make.
        Loosely drape 9 layers of white
cotton flannel (or, in an emergency,
T-shirts) over a pail. Tie cord or
elastic strap tightly around the rim of
pail to hold cloth in place. Pour
water into the cloth. Let it drip
through. This removes particles
larger than 5 microns (1/200 millimeter)
in diameter. Once a week, wash the
cloth with soap. Rinse well. Zalia, Feb 03

water — strap — cloth — filtered water — pail

(Comments:) This is for removing sediments from water prior to
sterilizing with iodine or chlorine. If not removed, the
iodine may mostly react with the sediments instead of killing
any microbes. I don't believe this will reliably remove
microbes; certainly not viruses (see May 03 DP p.2).
        Some sediments will settle out of water in a day or so.
Others (especially organic sediments) will not settle.
        If boiling water, first removing sediments is not
necessary for sterilization, but may improve taste or reduce
the amount of chemical contaminants.
        Zalia designed several variants. The above is the
simplest to build; but not the easiest to use if filtering
much water (because the cloth must be removed to extract the
filtered water). Other variants: a pail with a faucet near
its bottom; a short length of big-diameter pipe with a catch
basin under it. Holly & Bert, OR 973, February 04

Some local thrift stores have an end-of-month sale.
        Clothes are only $1. I stock up then. Zalia, OR 972

A kerchief is a very versatile garment.

Uses include: water filter for removing mud and insects; nose/mouth air filter; washcloth; towel; carrying bag; dew collector (drape over bush at night); neckerchief; hat for shade; woman's bathing-suit top (need two); bandage; splint holder. Can you think of 5 more uses ? (Sent by John Atkins)

(Comment:) A spare T-shirt has the same uses and is better for some (carrying bag, shade hat, towel) as well as providing a change of clothes. But it is slightly bulkier and heavier.

A moving vehicle, plus bucket, can serve as washing machine.

I use this method when on a boat or when traveling in a vehicle. The vibration and rocking provides agitation. All you need is a bucket with a tight-fitting lid, water, soap, and a way to secure the bucket so it doesn't tip over or slide about. I just tie the bucket in place on my truck's bed or boat's deck. In a few hours, the grime will be removed.

However, when on the road, I may splurge on a laudromat if I have many dirty clothes and am spending a few hours in some small town where I can do a load for a dollar.

Soap is usually available in the bathrooms of fast-food restaurants and truck stops. If the dispenser is empty, check cabinets/cupboards. Drew Luna Feuer, NY 120, July 2003

(Comments:) Vehicle-as-agitator was mentioned in an early DP. But NOT mentioned was how to RINSE. In my experience, wringing between rinses is much of the work when hand laundering. In the woods, if doing multiple pail loads, or doing other activities at the same time, I may hang the clothes and let them drip for an hour or so, instead of wringing. In a vehicle, I couldn't do that. Also, if the clothes are rinsed in 3 changes of water, and each rinse goes for a few hours between stops of the vehicle, washing AND RINSING would be practical only on a long trip. So, enroute laundromats are attractive. But on a boat voyage ? Probably plenty of time - and lots of water - and no mid-ocean laundromats !

If using a laundromat, check their trash for discarded detergent containers. We sometimes find cardboard boxes that had gotten damp on the bottom, with much detergent stuck inside. And any liquid detergent bottles that have not already been rinsed, can thereby yield a fair amount. Bert & Holly

What is more economical when driving up a long hill ?

Run the engine fast and use a low gear ? Or lug the engine in high gear ? Many trucks have a vacuum gauge, and it's a rule of thumb that high manifold vacuum, which occurs during high-rpm part-throttle running, means better economy. Low-vacuum readings mean high fuel consumption.

Engines generally consume least fuel at or near their torque peak. For most big V8 truck engines, this is around 2500 rpm. So trying to stay somewhere between 2000 and 3000 rpm is a good target. But both carburetors and fuel injection will richen the mixture at wide-open throttle (WOT) to prevent engine knock and keep temperatures down. So, for most fuel-efficiency on long up-grades, use the highest gear you can pull with the engine around 2500 rpm that doesn't require WOT. (From Popular Mechanics, Apr 2000, sent by Roger Knights)

I have a small pick-up with a camper shell.

St Louis summers are hot and buggy; winters are cold. I am a 44-year-old nurse working in a small urban hospital. I don't want to rely on my grown children. I need $10 worth of your best advice for urban survival. Maureen, MO 631, 2002

Wintering in the West on wheels.
    Travel rigs should be small and light to not guzzle gas.
There are hundreds of small Toyota-powered mid-1970s Chinooks
around that are ideal. Few are worn out, because motorhomes
tend to be driven less than are cars and trucks. Police seldom
bother them, unlike the psychedelic-painted vans of the 1960s
and 70s. Toyota makes engines that last and last. Dual wheels
have just been a pain for me. They cut mileage and pick up
more nails. If needed for more weight, a larger tire is better.
    Baja Mexico has much shoreline. While there I get my
teeth fixed for cheap. As in most places, there are good and
not so good dentists. One higher-dollar dentist in Tijuana
attracts clients from all over the world.
    Hot springs on both sides of the Salton Sea are fun but
overcrowded. I put a little iodine in them to make sure I do
not pick up any bad bugs. East of Camp Verde AZ is an old
wintering spot the Mob used back in the 1930s. It is on the
E. Verde River, next to a hydroelectric station, and has a
small hot springs in a cement tub. While you soak, you can
look at the big carp floating around in the river. The Mob had
another spot in the mountains south of Elsinore CA, but this
hot springs has been commercialized, and that area has few
squat spots. The San Francisco hot springs are at the eastern
edge of NM below Megollon. The big pool is only luke warm, but
there are smaller pools near by that are hotter. While you
soak, you can sometimes see mountain sheep cavorting on the
ridge. I met a nomad hanging out there who financed his travel
by filling his big trailer with drink cans found along the way.
    Magollon was a mining district. I always carry a metal
detector and gold pan in such areas. Rock shops have good
books on sniping, and metal detectors. I once washed up an old
safe. A friend comes up with nuggets quite often in certain
areas. Another seems to find stashed hoards and rich gold
deposits by dowsing. Of course, much more money has been spent
on speculation than has been produced by mining. And each
issue of Calif Mining Journal tells of Forest Service assaults
on small-time miners.
    One character I knew, made good money in a rocky canyon
area collecting pretty fireplace rock he sold to builders.
(Most cities now have landscaping-rock outfits that are doing
great.) A few weeks ago, a girl friend and I were snooping
around an abandoned mine and came up with iron pyrite and gold
ore that would be gorgeous fireplace rock. Later we found
many pounds of ore that was almost solid silver crystals.
Silver City ID had rich ore like this, and when I was a kid,
some pure silver chunks were still lying around old cabins.
    If traveling north from San Diego, I stop over at Harmony
Grove, 5 miles west of Escondido. This is a high-energy
vortex spot that makes the hair on my arms stand up. It is a
mecca for psychics. There were ancient writings here from some
advanced culture of the past, but the huge rocks got stolen in
the 1990s. Half way up Rawson Road in Morongo Valley, there's
a different kind of vortex. It is an interdimensional portal
and at certain times some bizarre things happen in the area.
The whole badlands area north of Indio has little valleys with
smaller other-dimensionals running around.
    Further north, the military bases have "whackenhut" guards
that are nasty to curious people. One guy told me he got in an
old tunnel and ran across a newer tunnel that carried high-
speed underground trains hauling goods between bases.
    Each year I see more locked gates and "keep out" signs all
over the West. If worse comes to worse, I sometimes just

explain to a property owner that I would like to squat a while
(cleanly). I am seldom refused. Parking in front of a house
is safer than on the outskirts of towns that are patrolled by
police. Al Fry, Idaho 836, January 2004

How to squat in an empty house.
     Who owns empty houses ? Many government departments do;
mis-management and bureaucratic delays can cause houses to
remain unoccupied many years. Private developers leave houses
empty so they can make a fast buck, or to keep rents high by
limiting available housing. Wealthy individuals own houses
they may use only occasionally. Deceased estates without
living relatives, are administered by the Public Trustees
office, which may take many years to settle their fate.
     Finding empty houses is generally quite easy: an unkempt
look; mail oozing out of mailbox; overgrown garden; power
off (check the electric meter); broken windows and doors.
     You should always knock on the door before entering or
prowling around the house. Sometimes old people are living in
their home without maintaining it well. Then take a closer
look. Is there thick dust inside ? No obvious signs of
occupation ? Are any floorboards missing ? Are the electric
and gas meters still there ? How many rooms ? How is the
overall structure ? You need to know what to bring to fix it.
     Try to find out who owns the property, so you will know
who to negotiate with if necessary. In Netherlands at least,
only the owner or agent of owner (who can be but is not
necessarily the police) can legally evict you or ask you to
leave; not the neighbors, nor the police without direction
from the owner. The neighbors may know who owns the house.
Quite often your first contact will be with the neighbors,
who you will eventually have to contend with anyway; best
present yourself as honestly and openly as possible. The land-
titles office is another way. Their system may seem mind-
boggling, but it provides info on recent transactions and
proposed developments. The staff are quite helpful and you
can't be denied info though you may have to pay for some.
     The best time to check out houses is during daylight on
a weekday; less conspicuous, and you can see more. Best to
first just look; don't bring tools such as crowbars that
police could use as an excuse to arrest you for breaking and
entering. Getting in is generally quite easy: often through
broken doors or windows previously forced by other visitors.
Vandalism often indicates vacant houses; the local kids may
use the place. As well as making it quite easy to just walk
right in, that can be a good argument to use with the owner
for letting you live in the house rather than leaving it empty.
As long as you don't damage the property, you are not illegal.
If you do break something accidentally , then leave immediately and return after a lapse of several days.
     A few hours to a few weeks may pass before the owners
realize that someone is occupying the house. Use this time to
make the house livable. Try to keep the house occupied
constantly at first, or until you can come to some agreement
with the owner. If after a few weeks you have heard nothing
from the owner, you can start to get more comfortable; it is
harder to evict well-established households than people who
appear to be just using the place to crash in.
     First thing to do is change the locks and secure the
house. Most barrel locks are easily replaced by using a few
tools (screwdriver, hacksaw, pliers). Deadlocks may have to
sawn off and replaced totally; these cost more but are more

secure. Door and windows that can't be immediately repaired, can have wood or chipboard nailed on them for security.

If the water is off at the taps, find the main and turn it back on, after checking the pipes. If the water was turned off because water rates were not payed, go to the water authority and pay off some. If plumbing isn't intact, hoses and clamps can be used for at least temporary plumbing.

Get electricity and gas on as quickly as possible. If the wiring is okay, you have a legal right to have electricity connected, but may have to pay a security deposit. You may be asked to show proof that you are leasing; just say you are living there and have a right to services. It may not be a good idea to tell them you are squatting. If electric wiring or gas pipes are damaged or broken, get someone who knows what they are doing to fix them !

As a squatter, you have almost no rights. But if you are threatened with eviction, there are things you can do to postpone eviction or even negotiate a settlement that allows you to stay. Try to talk to the evictors; evictions have been stopped at the last moment. Quite often you will be told lies, or at least bent truths, as to the history and future plans for the house (demolition, renovation, etc) in an effort to get you to leave. If you are asked by the owner or owner's agent to leave and you don't, you can be arrested for trespass.

Ways to resist eviction: Get friends and other squatters to come around when eviction is due; people showing support can stall eviction. Leaflet or door-knock surrounding houses; try to get some local community support. Talk to the media, though be careful as the media may not portray you and the issue favorably; alternative media, local papers, noticeboards, etc, best. Visiting and perhaps protesting outside the offices of owners can sometimes cause them to back down.
(From http://squat.net/archiv/squatbookl/index.html , sent by Bruce

(Comment:) When cleaning up dust, be careful to not breathe any. Eg, wear dust mask. Dust that includes rodent or bird feces may carry serious diseases. (See Jan 91 DP, p.12)

Living on a floating island in New York City.

For the past 25 years, Mario has lived in Mill Basin, a backwater of Jamaica Bay. At first he stayed on a friend's house barge, then on an old house boat by himself, and now on a 2000-sq-ft floating island made of old docks roped together; presently moored 60' behind Macy's in Kings Plaza.

Mario sleeps in a 200-sq-ft wooden hut with a woodstove and copper cookware, and two storm windows. He gathers firewood from the shoreline. "If it's free, it's for me." Elsewhere on his island are tomato and pepper plants growing in pails, a tiki bar, and a tanning area for when women friends visit. Kelly, 30, says Mario's island is a "riot". "I get seasick so I can't go out on deep water. But there, the water's calm."

Mario has many friends in the area, some of whom live on boats in the marina. Many never leave the basin. Ray, 45, a retired fireman, says, "It's so relaxing being on the water." About Mario's island: "You should see this place in summer. It booms. Guys bring their boats, blast their radios." Another friend says, "There's something about him. People just go to him. You go down, you bullshit about your life. He tells you what's going on. He don't look like much but he's a very smart man." Ray explained why Mario gets to live on his own island. No one else does. "No one else tries. At first, King Plaza tried to throw him out. They couldn't do it.

Everybody came: police, harbor patrol, coast guard. Everybody
likes Mario. We are trying to get him a mooring permit."
Of Cuban ancestry, Mario was born and raised in Florida.
He left home at 14 and landed in the Bronx. For a while he
had an incense shop in NYC but "lost the place". Then he
cooked "at a restaurant in Flatbush." Then he worked for a
friend lobster fishing, but only for a few years because it is
"too rough and not enough - no way to make a living." Now he
fishes some. Using for bait little black crabs he finds under
rocks on shore, he goes out in his small outboard boat an hour
before high tide, and drops a line in the basin "near the
wooden poles where the black fish feed on the barnacles." He
sells some to a Chinese fish store. He keeps a bicycle on
shore. Toni Schlesinger (Village Voice 12Dec00, sent by Drew)

Lone woman is only resident of forgotten Maine town.
Hibberts Gore is home to Karen Keller, 50, who lives on
640 acres overlooked by surveyors and mapmakers and unclaimed
by any county, deep in the remote reaches of Maine's vast
wilderness. She was not discovered by officials until she
filled out a census form. "I love it here. The first time I
laid eyes on this place, I knew, this is for me." When she
first moved there 15 years ago, Keller was married. But the
couple split and she decided to stay.
She lives in a cedar-shingled A-frame house, hunts deer
with a bolt-action rifle, grows vegetables and fruit, hauls
water from a well, chops firewood, and cooks her meals on a
wood-burning stove. She is coping with her manic and depress-
ive episodes - without the help of drugs or the stress of main
stream life. When she's feeling upbeat, she roams the fields,
climbs bridges, cleans, plays with her cat and dog, and walks,
walks, walks. "It's like tripping naturally on speed." When
she's down, she toughs it out by making herself get out of bed
and do one chore. (from Examiner 17July01, from Roger Knights)

Backyard sheds now popular as offices and bedrooms.
Backyard sheds traditionally house lawn mowers and trash
cans. But in the insane CA real-estate market, where many
families can't afford bigger homes, gussied-up sheds are housing people. At The Shed Shop in Fremont, sales of "room-
addition alternatives" have tripled in the last 5 years.
Instead of spending big bucks for a traditional addition, and
living with sawdust for months, homeowners hire the firm, or
rivals like Tuff Shed, to build customized wooden-shingled
backyard structures. Sizes range from 4-by-8 to 12-by-16 feet;
average price $3100. Construction takes only a day or two.
Customers then add insulation, dry wall, carpeting, electricity
- or hire contractors to. Most building codes ban plumbing.
Most customers use the sheds for home offices, art studios
or hobby areas. But some space-starved families use them as
spare bedrooms or guest rooms - even though most building codes
prohibit sleeping in them. Daniel McGinn (Newsweek, 29Sept03)

Philosopher has camp site that is both sylvan and urban.
For the past 17 years, Donald Kearney, 61, has lived
rustically in the middle of Boston. He lives in a self-made
tent in the woods near Jamaica Pond, less than a mile from the
middle-class Brookline home where he grew up. Though he has
enough money, he has little desire for more than a plastic tarp
for a room, several heavy blankets, and the 11 newspapers he
reads every day and then uses to insulate his tent.
Like Henry David Thoreau whom he has long admired, Kearney

loathes government and social conventions such as paying rent and concealing opinions. "Living outside with nature means living in the most intimate way." Raised by a Jewish mother, and an Irish father who played horn in the Boston Symphony, Kearney calls himself a Lepre-Cohen. "It is peaceful, no one bothers me, and there's no better place to read than under natural light." One of the hard-core homeless who refuse to sleep in city shelters, Kearney and about 300 men and a few women live outdoors year around, surviving the coldest nights.

Though Kearney's home is concealed by a thicket of oaks and pines and hemlocks, the property owner knows he is there. But "as long as he takes care of the environment and himself, we let him live his way." Kearney does not reveal his exact location in the large stretch of woods; he doesn't want more visitors. A few times, thieves have stolen his blankets.

Though Kearney spends much time alone in the woods, he goes downtown nearly every day, dining in soup kitchens, speaking out at rallies and lectures on college campuses, attending classical concerts, and collecting newspapers. He also visits friends: other homeless people he buys food for and talks politics with. Occasionally he ventures to Watertown to see his sister, who hosts him for holidays such as Passover and receives his subscriptions to several Conservative magazines including National Review and Weekly Standard. Social workers who know Kearney say, that unlike most soup-kitchen patrons, he helps wash dishes and mop the floor after meals.

His sister, an Ivy-League-educated accountant with her own business, isn't sure how her brother ended up so differently. He doesn't do drugs or drink, she says, and with a trust fund left by a wealthy aunt, "he can certainly afford an apartment. I just think he genuinely likes living in the woods."

Kearney began sleeping outdoors when he was young and went to camp in Maine where, as a gifted clarinetist, he won awards for his chamber music. Over the years he sought more isolation, living for months at a time in NH's White Mtns and ME woods. David Abel (from Boston Globe, 3Dec02, sent by L.Smith)

(Comments:) Note the author's derogatory labeling of Kearney as "homeless", though, inconsistently, elsewhere refers to "his home". Ie, if you have a home that officials and the lap-dog media don't approve of, you are "homeless". (Next, will people who live in unapproved ways, be called "lifeless" ?)

Make sure any lamp wick is ALL natural fiber.
Burn a bit at one end. If only fine ash remains, it is probably natural. If a hard lump remains, it is partly or entirely synthetic. Much string that looks like cotton, is actually part polyester for strength.
Recently I prepared a replacement wick for a wax lamp (see Sept 04 DP p.2) from string (that had sewen shut a grain bag) that LOOKED like cotton (fuzzy). But, in the lamp, it burned and melted away in less than a minute. Holly, Febr 04

A tiny fan will greatly increase a wood-stove's efficiency.
Or, if electricity is not available, sheet-metal baffles around a longer chimney. Air-tight stoves are the only kind to buy. If you make a stove, allow a foot of space above the door for smoke collection. Al Fry, Idaho, 2001 ?

Wet boots can be dried by filling them with warm sand.
Usually they will dry overnight. Al Fry

Dwelling Portably   April 2004

Tick-borne diseases: a pound of prevention - or a TON of cure.
Compared to other arthropods (including insects), ticks
are more often infected and more likely to transmit an infection. And some tick-borne diseases, especially Lyme, can be
very difficult to diagnose and cure. I read several books
from a library. By far the best was "Everything You Need To
Know About Lyme Disease and Other Tick-borne Disorders" by
Karen Vanderhoof-Forschner (Wiley, 1997, 249p.6x9, $15 cover
price). But the title exaggerates: much is NOT known.
Karen learned about Lyme the hard way. Infected by a tick
while pregnant, the disease spread to her fetus (though MDs
assured her that did not happen with Lyme). After various
mis-diagnoses and inadequate treatments, Karen finally got
effective treatment and slowly recovered - but her son died.
Consequently she founded the Lyme Disease Foundation to pool
the considerable but scattered knowledge.
"Ticks transmit more kinds of micro-organisms than any
other arthropod, including mosquitos", perhaps because of their
mode of feeding and relatively long lives. Almost everyone in
the U.S. is at risk, including a city dweller who uses parks.
Lyme has been vastly under-reported for various reasons,
and some other tick-borne diseases even more so. Karen
estimates that over a million U.S. residents are infected. In
CT, one person out of 29; in RI, one in 42; NY 59; NJ 93; DE
107; WI 124; PA 159; MD 267; MN 309; MA 330. However, infection rate varies from area to area within a state: in the worst
areas, a third of the population may be infected; and some
states not listed may have places with much Lyme. Though south
eastern and south central states do not have much Lyme, other
serious tick-borne diseases are common. Ticks are much more
common in eastern than in western North America; the reason
may be that ticks need a moist environment year around.
"Owning a pet, especially a cat, puts you at increased
risk." Though dogs seem to get more ticks, a cat may be more
likely to bring a tick to a human, because cats groom themselves more/better than do dogs. Eg, a cat picks up a tick
outside, comes in, grooms itself, and removes the tick before
it gets firmly attached - which then gets onto a human. Whereas, a tick that gets onto a dog is likely to remain on the dog
until fully fed. However, for that reason, a dog may be worse
than a cat for increasing the tick population. (My conjectures)
Not mentioned by books: if you have an animal, either keep it
in or leave it out. Don't let it in and out.
Ticks "tend to live in close proximity to potential hosts.
This frequently places them in the dense overgrown area between
a manicured lawn and a forest." A tick doesn't move more than
ten feet under its own power, but may be transported long
distances by animals, especially birds. A tick rarely climbs
higher than 3 feet above ground, and cannot jump or fly.
Ticks typically seek prey by climbing upwards on vegetation, waiting until a prey brushes past, and then grasping it
with one set of legs. However, larvae may actively seek prey
instead of waiting. Most ticks prefer non-human animals: esp
deer, mice, chipmonks, rabbits, dogs, birds; but will feed on
whatever animals are available.
For protection, all advice I've read seems inadequate.
Most authors say: wear shoes (not sandals), socks, long-sleeve

pants and shirt; light colored. Tuck pants into socks and shirt into pants. That way, a tick that gets on your foot must crawl up the outside of clothing to reach bare skin. But how likely are you to spot a tick on clothing which probably also has on it stickers and bits of debris ? If you don't spot the tick until it reaches your neck, it will likely get into your hair where it will be more difficult to see and to remove. Also, long clothes not comfortable/healthy on hot days.

In CT, the state with the most Lyme, almost no nudists get tick-borne diseases. From that, a researcher concluded that ticks don't bite fully-exposed skin. Unfortunately, not true. "Most likely, the nudists simply had more opportunities to examine their own bodies and the bodies of companions, making them more likely to spot and remove crawling ticks."

In our (H&B's) experience, ticks bite bare skin much less often than covered skin. During tick season we usually have bare legs. If ticks seldom climb higher than 3 feet, they most often grasp legs. But we've had few bites on legs. Most were on bodies; some on arms. In many instances we were bitten after coming inside, often at night. I suspect the ticks rode in on our clothes, then crawled around until they found skin covered by clothes or bedding. So perhaps the most important precaution (which none of the authors suggested): Remove outside clothes before coming inside. Leave outside clothes outside. Carefully inspect before coming inside. While inside, wear only clothes that never go outside.

"One of the most effective pesticides is permethrin, which is a synthetic imitation of natural substances called pyrethrum found in chrysanthemums and other flowers." Sold in most garden shops. Soldiers apply it to their uniforms and find that it lasts through several launderings. Permethrin kills, within minutes, ticks and most other arthropods that contact treated fabric. It has little toxicity to mammals, because it is little absorbed and rapidly inactivated. Occasionally people report local irritation. Although registered as a possible carcinogen, it is believed not toxic after it dries. Do not apply to clothes while wearing them, and do not touch the clothes until dry. "A good idea is to treat one special outfit and then wear that whenever you go outside." However, permethrin is not a repellant, which means that a tick that grasps bare skin and doesn't then wander onto fabric, could bite.

(Is permethrin really better than the natural substance ? Or is this another case of a corporation slightly altering a substance so they can patent it and charge more ?)

To remove a tick, Karen says, "it is almost always better to wait until you can secure the right (fine-pointed) tweezers, especially if it is only a matter of a few hours." But elsewhere: ticks who "are systemically infected" in salvary glands as well as mid-gut, "may be able to transmit the pathogen in only a few hours." (Ticks with only a mid-gut infection, may need 24 to 48 hours.) So, I might wait a few MINUTES, but NOT HOURS ! If lacking fine-pointed tweezers, I can usually improvise an adequate substitute in a few minutes. Most tweezers have points that are too broad, and would squeeze the tick's body, spreading its fluids. Do not use; or sharpen.

Grasp tick as close to skin as possible. Gently pull straight back, away from skin. Do not twist tick.

If mouth parts remain in the bite, should they be left ? Or removed, which may require digging with a needle ? Authorities disagree. After removing tick, apply antiseptic to bite and tweezers, and wash hands thoroughly. "Alcohol or Betadine" suggested by one book. [Other possibilities (I don't

know relative effectiveness): soap and water; iodine water
solution or tincture (which you might have for sterilizing
water); eucalyptus or tea-tree or other very-pungent oil;
hydrogen peroxide; chlorine bleach, maybe diluted (not good
for you, but tick diseases much worse); conifer resin; tart
(acidic) berry juice; urine; booze (ethyl alcohol is much
less toxic to humans than is isopropyl "rubbing" alcohol).]
     Place tick in closable container. If you will send it
to a lab for analysis (cost $25 to $60) "you must keep the
tick alive." A few grass blades or moistened tissue in the
container will suffice for a few days. Make sure the lab will
test tick for all pathogens known to be in area where bitten.
     If a tick remained attached more than two hours, or if
attachment time not known, some of the MDs who are knowledgable about Lyme (most MDs aren't), recommend taking oral antibiotics immediately, without waiting for symptoms. "On the
one hand, you may be taking $20 worth of medication unnecess-
arily (and possibly getting bad side effects). On the other
hand, you may be avoiding a nightmarish scenario that involves
$30,000 worth of intravenous medicine... Given the early
dissemination of the Lyme bacterium throughout the body and
into the brain, I think that waiting for a telltale rash is"
foolish. 67% of Lyme patients with an early rash, already had
the infectious spirochete in their spinal fluid.
     Four weeks of doxycycline or minocycline, long-acting
members of the tetracycline family, are commonly recommended.
They are well absorbed on an empty stomach and thus can be
used at a low dosage, and some of those drugs reach the
central nervous system. Also effective against some other
tick-borne diseases including relapsing fever, tularemia,
ehrlichiosis, Rocky Mountain spotted fever. "Not recommended
for pregnant or breast-feeding women, or for children under 8."
Possible side effects: yeast infection, nausea, blurring of
eyes, dizzyness, liver and kidney disorders, intracranial
pressure (simulates brain tumor). Avoid dairy products, iron
supplements, antacids; they interfere with absorption.
     If we (H&B) lived in an area with much Lyme or other
bacterial diseases, I would want antibiotics ON HAND, so I did
not have to wait until I could get to a doctor and drug store.
Also, an ignorant or timid MD might insist on time-consuming,
expensive tests before prescribing. A friend who knows an MD
could probably procure antibiotics easier than I could. Or,
in Mexico, antibiotics can be purchased without a prescription.
Animal-feed-store antibiotics, such as fish-cycline, are a
possibility, but might not be absorbed as well or reach as
many organs. Anti-biotics are perishable; store in the coldest place available. They don't help viral diseases; eg, flu.
     As with other spirochetal infections such as syphilis and
relapsing fever, the first symptom is often a local skin rash,
but it is not always present, or can be overlooked, esp on
dark-complexioned people. Don't confuse a rash with the
inflammation at the bite that usually develops within a few
hours but starts to disappear within 24 hours. The rash does
not develop so soon, and it lasts longer. "Early dissemination is characterized by flu-like symptoms such as headache,
stiff neck, mild fever or chills, swollen glands, muscle ache,
and fatigue. Often the symptoms are not unduly alarming, and
many people do not seek medical attention." The early symptoms may go away on their own. "But if the underlying infection has not been treated appropriately, the disease can
progress, sometimes within a month, sometimes not for a year
or longer, to late-stage dissemination, when damage to multiple

body systems can occur (and) the disease is securely lodged in the body, difficult to diagnose and much harder to treat."

How sick and what symptoms, depends partly on what strains or microbes. On Shelter Island NY, "60% of black-legged ticks studied were infected with more than one strain of Borrelia burgdorferi (Bb)", the Lyme microbe. In CT, 20% of patients with Lyme also had at least one other tick-borne disease.

"There are many strains of Bb, and a drug effective with one may not work on another" (esp if not treated early).

Though ticks are the main carriers of Bb, it can also pass via placenta (pregnancy), raw milk, sex (at least among mice), blood transfusion, and getting urine of an infected animal on cuts, eyes, mucus membranes. Biting flies and fleas suspect. Mosquitos can become infected but because Bb can live only a few hours in a mosquito, transmission is unlikely.

As of 1997 there was no reliable test for Lyme. In its absence, most U.S. MDs won't prescribe the powerful drugs needed to cure Lyme after it disseminates. In 1992, the average cost of treating Lyme disease was $62,000 per person, and half the costs were incurred BEFORE diagnosis !

Ticks spread at least 8 other serious diseases in U.S.:

Rocky Mountain spotted fever (RMSF), a rickettsia. Despite name, 60% of cases in east. Tick can transmit within a few hrs. Onset sudden: high fever, rash resembles measles, 3-8% fatal. Tetracycline or doxycycline or chloramphenicol.

Ehrlichiosis, a rickettsia. Mostly in se and s central. Symptoms, none to severe; resemble RMSF; 5% fatal. Quite a few kinds of ticks transmit. Tetracycline or doxycycline.

Babesia microti, a protozoa. Mostly coastal and n midw. Like malaria; some strains deadly. Clindamycin & oral quinine.

Tularemia, a bacterium. Mostly s central and sw to CA. Many kinds of ticks cause half the cases. Also biting flies, drinking contaminated water, touching infected animals or eating their under-cooked meat. In over 100 mammals; some birds, amphibians, fishes. Painfully swollen lymph glands. Streptomycin or gentamycin or tetracycline or chloramphenicol.

Relapsing fever, a spirochet related to Bb. Mainly w and sw. Spread by soft ticks often in old cabins, mines, caves. Can transmit within 15 minutes. Tetracycline or doxycycline.

Powassan encephalitis, a flavivirus. Mostly e N. Amer. Also spread by raw milk of infected goat. No antibiotic for it.

Some of these diseases are carried by the same ticks that carry Lyme; therefore a single bite can transmit more than one. Except soft ticks, all adult females in U.S. have a circular black or dark shield on the front portion of their back, with the rest of back red-brown or brown. Ticks other than Ixodes also have various white markings on their backs. Ixodes don't. Adult males have all-dark backs. Unlike mosquitos, males bite. But the adult female is most apt to spread disease because it must feed before it can lay eggs, and it feeds longer.

The black-legged tick, Ixodes scapularis, in e and midw N.Am can transmit Lyme, babesioses, granulocytic ehrlichiosis, Powassan encephalitis. The western black-legged tick, Ixodes pacificus, looks identical and transmits same diseases, but only 1% of them carry Lyme, vs 30% of their eastern relatives.

The lone-star tick, Amblyomma americanum, in se as far n and w as RI, IA, TX, is a major carrier of tularemia and monocytic ehrlichiosis and maybe other diseases. White spot on back of adults. "Aggressive and seeks out humans to bite."

Several Dermacentor species (dog ticks), the most common ticks in N.Am., spread RMSF, monocytic ehrlichiosis, tularemia and probably others. Chalk-like markings on adults' backs.

Portable dwelling myths and realities.

Many people believe that living without a house (or a big RV) must be arduous and uncomfortable. That attitude is fostered by some wilderness-experience providers who dare you to take their training to prove how tough you can become.

Camping doesn't require exceptional fortitude or strength. Before Europeans came, millions of Amerinds camped full time. (Only a few tribes built permanent lodges.) They included small children, pregnant women, elders, injured. (Tips for learning how to camp comfortably are on page 3.) Holly & Bert, Jan 04

I want a tent that is warm in winter and easy to set up.

In a few hours at most. Thanks for your reply (in May 03 DP p.16), but I don't have time to try to build something.

What is the best 4-season tent I can buy? Or what features should I look for ? I'd like enough daylight inside to read and write. (I go to classes 3 days a week, and work freelance many nights and weekends, so I prefer to stay in camp on free days.) High enough to hang clothes, and sit comfortably in a chair.

I can't afford to rent solo, and I don't like sharing a space. (My work provides more than enough relating to people.)

Also, I need a good rechargable flashlight for following trails and at camp. (My present flashlight is bright enough, and I can set it down and then point beam where I want it, but its battery is costly and doesn't last long. Eve, CA 950, Aug

(Reply:) I don't know of any tent for sale that meets your requirements. (If any reader does, please write.) "4-season" means: you can stay ALIVE winters, but during extremely cold weather you may be COMFORTABLE only when in bed.

IF you have or can easily buy replacement poles for your present dome tent (in case poles don't survive the following), you might try: Remove its fly (top tarp) if it simply clips on (if not, leave it on). Spread over the tent a big thick (insulative) quilt, or maybe two rectangular sleeping bags opened and zipped together. Above, erect two (for less dew) tarps, big enough to reach to the ground on 3 sides and provide some rain-sheltered space in front. Space them one above the other, not touching each other or the quilt. If the quilt blocks ventilation, DO NOT USE ANY FLAME INSIDE.

Or, if buying a "4-season" dome tent, look for one with strong poles (probably more than 2); ie, a tent rated for high wind or accumulated snow, so the poles will support insulation layed on top. But I doubt that such a tent will admit much light. (For features I'd like but haven't found, see p. 7.)

For hanging clothes and keeping most equipment, I'd get a second tent. Some car-camping tents are tall enough and somewhat portable. Then rig big tarps, overlapping, above both tents for extra rain shelter and for dry passage between tents.

I've seen ads for rechargable flashlights: some plug into the grid; some set in sunshine to solar charge; some you shake for a few seconds every few minutes. I don't know how good. Also see Dec 03 DP, p.4,5,6. Bert, OR 973, Sept 03

Low/no-cost lamp is easy to make.

Materials: empty tuna or catfood can; cotton cord or other NATURAL fiber (synthetic burns stinky); thin stiff wire with insulation removed; candle-remains; extra empty can.

 Braid wire around wick.

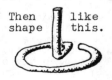 Then shape like this.

Assembly. To stiffen the cord, braid two thin wires around it. (Ordinary string will soon put itself out by slumping into the liquid wax puddle that develops.) Then shape wick as shown, so one end sits straight-up, self-supporting inside the tuna can. Top of wick should not stick above top edge of can. Melt wax in other can and pour into tuna can over centered wick. Fill nearly to the brim. Let cool and harden. Your new lamp is now ready for use.

When wax level gets low, causing too much flame, add pieces of wax. When I use at camp, I set lamp on a flat rock, to reduce risk of knocking it over. Brijji, UT, May02 bridgepeter@yahoo.com

(What Bert did.) Had no tuna can. I used a tiny aluminum pan 1½"D ¾" high. (It had been one of a dozen mini-lamps - also called "votive" or "tee" candles. As the wax burned away, I'd added more. But its wick, too, had gradually burned away in a few hours got too short.)

For a new wick, I used loosely-twisted cotton cord, 1/12 inch diameter.

The first wire I tried, a paper clip, was too thick. After a bit of wick that protruded above the wire burned away, the flame went out. I suppose that wire conducted away too much heat.

The next wire, copper, fine hair size, was too thin. Cord not stiffened enough.

Somewhat thicker copper wire, coarse hair size, did fine. Stiff enough, yet not so thick it snuffed the flame. Steel wire might be better: stiffer per thickness. But none here thin enough.

To wind wire onto an 8-inch length of cord, I tied thin string to ends of cord and suspended it quite taut. I twirled cord between fingers while moving wire along; then reversed to spiral other way.

The cord was long enough to make 3 wicks. I dripped melted wax from a candle onto the cord near where I would cut, to make sure wire did not unravel when cut. Also, waxed wicks light easier.

I shaped the stiffened wick as shown, except circled twice to provide spare length. I set it in the tiny pan, put chunks of wax around it, and lit. As the chunks melted, I added more until the pan was nearly full of melted wax. The wick got tilted but still burned okay.

The wick burns away much more slowly than on original mini-lamps - and most candles. Because the wire's conduction cools it some ? When, after a week, it got too short, I raised more, grasping it low (scorched part fragile), using improvised wooden tweezers. (Metal tweezers stuck to wick, because their conduction solidified wax near wick.)

Total work appreciable, but overall easier/better than what we'd done previously: lay wick on sloping side of a clam shell. It needed more frequent adjustments, and often went out or flamed too high. Thanks Brijji !

Julie Summers described a lamp somewhat like Brijji's in Sept84DP p.4. She threaded hollow woven cord such as some shoelaces onto stiffish wire coiled like Brijji's. She burned tallow and various oils as well as wax. (I don't recall trying. Maybe we had no hollow cord.) More on candles in May97p.6 & Oct93p.1.)

This kind of lamp needs more careful attention than does a candle set in a secure non-flammable holder. It is more dangerous if knocked over because more of the wax is liquid; and, if wax burns low, the entire wick may catch fire.

Mounting solar panel on travel trailer.
To not have the fumes and fire hazard of candles, I built a 12-volt lighting system. A 35-watt PV panel recharges a used auto battery. (More in May 97 DP.)

Instead of drilling potentially-leaky holes in roof, I glued on the mountings with Barge cement and regular clear silicone caulking. Has held for over 4 yrs thru high winds and severe winters.

I first cleaned the roof. After gluing down the mounting, I also put a thick layer of silicone ON TOP OF the mounting foot. I applied silicone to an area 3 times as wide as the mounting foot, so the silicone has more surface to stick to. David French, SD, May 98 (Was only in Net Suplmt then, hoping for more info about the mounting feet.)

(Thought:) Why not just bolt panel onto a wood frame (eg, two 2-by-2s glued to plywood cross pieces) slightly longer than the trailer is wide, drilling bolt holes in the 2-by-2s as needed ? Then, hold the frame on roof with ropes from 2-by-2s down the sides of trailer and tied to frame. Put something soft and not slippery (closed-cell shipping foam) between plywood and roof to cushion.

That seems more reliable. (How long & well will cement adhere to the roofing tar ?) Also, frame with panel is easily removed when traveling, if hurricane, if hail, etc. Also, frame can be tilted so PV intercepts more rays. (Panel flat on roof not good in winter when sun low.) B

Living in vans and travel trailer.
I lived in an outfitted mini-van for over a year. Then the two of us lived in a larger van for 6 months. We had a king-size bed, propane heat, cook stove, and solar electric system.

Though we were comfy, we wanted more space and facilities. So we saved until we had enough money to buy a 1982 Shasta 16-foot travel trailer we tow with our van. It more than meets our needs.

Some folks buy big expensive RVs they must finance - but lose them to the repo man if they are layed off work. That is why we waited and saved, and chose a low cost used trailer we could buy outright.

For money, we prefer to wait until our funds run low; then get a job and save like mad until reserves build up; then camp until our funds get low again.

Places to park. If you are self-contained, construction sites are good; often you can live free with electric and water and sewer hookups provided, in exchange for your presence providing security. Similarly, industrial sites and equipment enclosures. We recently site-sat a truck rental place. No pay, but parked free. Sometimes you find an employer who will not only pay for day work, but let you stay as night watch.

I presently work for a transit system part-time. We sometimes over-night in their lot; also at Walmart and other shopping centers. On weekends we're at campgrnds: drain tanks; charge battery.

Usually we winter as caretakers at a private campground after they close. They pay only $15 per week, but not many chores to do: in autumn we winterize the plumbing; in spring we get everything running again before leaving.

Some summers we camp-host at state parks; usually for 2 or 3 weeks, but a park may want you to commit longer. Some remote parks give small stipends, but usually no pay. However, we get a site, electric hookup, pool use, and other amenities free. All we did was check the rest rooms twice a day, and alert the park staff to any problems. Parks also hire seasonal workers and pay quite well. Check with park offices.

We've seen more and more van dwellers here. John & Rose Ward, PA 174, Aug 2003

How we go to and from cities.

Most of our camps, though remote from settlements, are within 60 miles of DP's po box. If friends are camped nearby and happen to be going through there, they may be able to bring our mail to a stash shared. If so, we might stay in the woods many months. Otherwise we go once a month or so, and shop then too.

For travel on highways, we bike, bus, hitch, ride-share; depending on season, weather, road, distance, and what is available. To find ride-sharers, I may hitch back in late afternoon when many commuters go home, and ask ride-givers if they go regularly. If hitching, I always offer a $ or 2 to help pay costs. For ride share I offer more, because driver must commit to time and place.

We bicycle to a ride meet or bus stop, or all the way if city near. We leave bikes stashed near a paved road, and may also have a temp campsite and gear there so we can hike there the day before and rest a night before traveling on.

Bike trips longer than a few miles we do only on early Sunday mornings when traffic is light, during late spring and early summer when dawn comes early.

We bicycle mostly on paved roads. Gravel is riskier, wears tires faster, and not much faster than walking. B & H

Learning to dwell portably with comfort.

Some people try to do too much too quick. Perhaps inspired by a movie or book, they hike many miles into a wilderness with a single backpack load of gear and grub, and then try to live off the land. Most soon hike back out - IF able to. A few, better prepared or unusually talented, survive uncomfortably for a few months or years, but grow dissatisfied and eventually leave, saying: "Been there, done that."

Bert and I learned gradually: first day hikes, then summer weekend backpacks into nearby woods, then summer camping for longer periods. Any time the going got unpleasant, we'd head for other shelter where, after drying off and warming up, we'd ponder what went wrong and how to do better next time.

The biggest problem with our bit-by-bit approach, was finding energy and time while still employed (sporadically; fortunately neither of us worked steady full time) and renting (various cheap rooms and out-buildings with improvised furnishings - probably "substandard",but codes seldom enforced unless complaints).

We had read quite a few books and they helped, but most were broad (to sell widely); not focused on one area.

Neither of us had "outdoor survival" training. Most such courses teach how to stay alive until rescued or until you find your way home - which IS IMPORTANT, but not much help learning to camp as a way of life. If you seek, try to find some that deals with the climate and terrain where you expect to live. Check nearby colleges. Some offer rec courses (no credit) open to outsiders.

Some readers assume that portable (backpacking) dwellers live much as do vacation trekkers: each morn, pack up all gear, carry it in one trip to the next site, and set up camp - day after day. NO - that's not what we do.

Though we sometimes go on long treks, or visit cities where we stay a few days, we live mostly at base camps where we may remain (except for short trips away) a few weeks to a few months.

General advice. At first for backup, remain close to familiar shelter. Go slow, stay observant, be thoughtful. As you see things, ask self: how could that be dangerous - or useful. H & B

Experiences camping in northern BC.

I've been in one place since late Oct. When I moved here, I didn't have enough time to build a proper shelter, so I made a lean-to (resembles a bimini on a boat) out of ten-foot-long pieces of black pond-liner. (Last year, I saw a road-construction forestry crew using it around a culvert. I went back after hours with my freighter pack-frame and EMT shears and some rope, and cut pieces out of scrap left behind.) It feels and looks very tough - hail proof, much stronger than my toughest tarp, which I have to double up to keep me completely dry during the heavy downpours here.

Under the plastic I stretched a piece of barbless fencing I found, from which I hang clothes to dry. The fencing is also handy for keeping bedding and other gnaw-able materials suspended where pesky ground critters can't easily reach them. The plastic and fencing are tied out to live deciduous trees.

Under the lean-to, I made a bough bed 8" thick, beside a big dead-fall log which provides a windbreak. 1000 yards away is a brook running year around.

The terrain here consists of a series of terraces. In the valley's bottom is a river; above that a cliff; then a terrace on which is a public road; then another cliff, and then a 50-yard-wide terrace on which I'm camped. Above me is another cliff and terrace. My camp is near the back of the terrace for less wind and more seclusion from the road.

I've seen deer and rodent tracks in this area, but animals don't bother me. No humans have come near. But I do fear people finding my camp and stealing or vandalizing. I'm too close to the road to have fires or make noise. After the snow melts, I'll move to a higher level for spring and summer. Bruce, Feb 2002

I moved my camp 50 yards to a higher elevation. Took a full day. I'm now even closer to year-around water. May 02

One day around noon, a domestic dog ambled through my camp. In less than 3 minutes it disappeared into nearby woods not to be seen again. No sign of owner. That prompted me to move yet another 100

Sept 2004

yards, going higher, still in same area. Also, during hot weather, the creek I'm near still has small pools whereas the lower part of the same creek goes dry.

I am camped beside a small cliff off which sound bounces, so I don't hammer or make other loud noises on still days.

So far, at my higher site, the only visitors have been chattering squirrels and local birds. Black bears have long been out of hibernation: I've seen their scat and tracks. But they've not bothered what little dry and tinned food I've had at ground level. I NEVER cook or eat meat or fish at my camp. Those odors are quite strong and more attractive to bears than are rice/beans/lentils. Jy 02

I had thought my latest camp was high enough and far enough from the road to be secure from human intruders. Wrong ! In early August, on separate occasions, two mushroom pickers discovered my camp. They had spotted some of my white and colored buckets. I got face-to-face contact with both who were apparently alone. One was Native-American, about 30, quiet but friendly. I felt he wasn't likely to steal my belongings. The other was Caucasian, 30ish, wearing bright white T shirt, blue jeans; short hair. He didn't look like a mushroomer; more like a nosy undercover cop. However, I will stay here the rest of winter.

This summer was nice: humid but with lots of sun. Many berries. Chinook fishing great. But August was tough for me financially so I didn't go moose hunting with my brother. He lost his 20 year job at a local sawmill because of the lousy economy and mismanagement. He is still bitter. No other job skills.

I pick wild mushrooms in the fall. But I haven't made big dollars: prices low past 8 years because of world-wide economic slump; weather too damp or dry and areas over-picked. Now, local native bands want to charge picking fees !

This area has many logging roads. Most go uphill, winding, for miles, but don't connect with other logging roads. Many are blocked to keep out unwanted motorists. I hike along some to check them out, but fear meeting bears. Sept

So far, all my camps have been within 2 or 3 miles of civilization. I use adult-size bicycles with carrying racks for transport. I don't stash bikes at my camps. If I did, I'd probably hang them from tree branches to keep ground critters from nibbling tires or valve stems or seats. Lately, some have been discovered and had tires slashed. So I have many bikes and keep them in various places as backup in event that one gets stolen or vandalized, or breaks down.

I go to town every 2nd day. I salvage from dumpsters, pick up mail, search internet on library's computers, visit thrift/2nd-hand stores and job banks. On weekends I often stay at camp: cook; wash clothes; tidy up; sew broken gear; saw firewood, etc. Keeps me busy.

Mushroom pickers are here again. Many have annoying habits: defecate without burying; litter; vandalize; steal; raid my provisions. I stay away from one of my camps on weekends because the pickers come in groups of 2 or 3 then. I'll be glad when the season ends, and when kids
Sept 2004

go back to school in early Sept. The woods will be quieter then. Bruce, Aug03

(Comments:) In woods here, we've had no unwanted human encounters, and less vandalism and stealing than you report. Because we are usually further from settlements ? Because these woods are more difficult to hike through ? Luck ?

The drawback of living remotely or in difficult terrain: going to a city is quite an expedition. Consequently, we go much less often than you, and don't have time there to access internet, etc.

How we choose and prepare camp sites.
Holly and I have dwelled portably for nearly 25 years. Though sometimes we camp on river floodlands during dry season, undeveloped city parks, railroad right-of-ways, and overgrown vacant lot, 90% of our living has been at long-term sites in forested mountain areas.

We may live at a good base-camp site seasonally for several years; using different sites different seasons. At each site, we may stash some equipment, stored in pails/totes/barrels, rather than move it all. (Duplicates are often cheap at yard sales and thrift stores.)

Except maybe in summer, we prefer sites that are high enough to be above the cold air that collects in valley bottoms during clear still nights, but far enough below ridges to avoid high winds and lightning. (When scouting, we may climb mountains to view surroundings but we don't live on mountain tops.)

For winter, we like a south-facing slope with no trees tall enough to block the low winter sun. During spring, we prefer a spot within easy hike of nettle patches and other edible greens. During summer, we prefer an east-facing slope for morning sun and mid-day shade, that is near many berries, and perhaps within hiking range of a creek with swimming hole and fish, or the ocean. For autumn we might camp on private land posted "no hunting" if working for owner; otherwise dense conifer forest with little browse attractive to deer and elk. (We prefer autumns for temp jobs. Less competition because pro harvesters are busy with commercial crops, and most kids are back in school; and cooler but mostly dry.)

Our typical base camp is 10 to 60 miles from the nearest city; at least a mile from any settlement; at least 1/4 mile from any paved or graveled road; at least 100 yards from any much-used game trail (or we may reroute a trail).

For winter and spring use, for max sun (when it shines), we may choose an area that was clear-cut a few years ago, and now has bushes and small trees big enough to discourage hunters (can't see deer before deer smell or hear them), and brambly enough to keep other hikers on trails; but without growth tall enough to shade our site.

I may scout and start preparing such a site soon after logging, but not move there for several years. For least digging, I look for a natural hole (formed centuries ago when a big tree fell, uprooting, then rotted. I remove remaining slash (else it will entangle as vines grow and be more difficult.) I might lay long branches across the hole interweaved, for vines to grow upon and form a natural over-roof. But I leave clear exposure for a sun-facing window.

I decide where I want trails, clear slash (left from logging) off them, and distribute slash on unwanted paths.

Other possible winter sites: places where poor or shallow soils stunt trees; steep slopes recently thinned that might have spots still sunny because, by luck, no tall trees close down slope. CAUTION: very steep slopes are prone to landslide ± ten years after logging, when old roots rotted and new roots not yet deep.

Most winter/spring sites need shaping. I prefer to do that in the early spring prior to the winter we will move in; the soil is softer (damp), and spring growth of vines will help cover dirt piles.

We stop using a winter site when the trees grow tall enough to block the sun.

Time scouting and preparing a good winter/spring base camp might total 100 hours or more, but is spread over many weeks and is thus quite congenial.

Moving a base camp requires much more than one back load. Assume we move in summer to an area we've not lived before and do not have supplies stashed. In the first load we might carry: tarps, insect net, sleeping bags, pad, canteen, knife, small saw, trowel, and ready-to-eat food for a few days, packed in wide-mouth plastic jars which, when empty, can hold water. We prepare a temp site, choosing a levelish spot we can clear and smooth quickly. (Seclusion not very important if we won't be there long.) From there we scout for water and a better site.

In the next load, we typically bring cooking utensils and more food, and bow saw and shovel to prep the better site.

If we move during winter, we go to a site previously prepared at which we have supplies stashed. B & H, Jan 04

More about hidden underground home.

Doug Underwood (one of his chosen names) says he has been a nature lover since he was a boy in Binghamton NY. Born about 1960, one of 7 children of a judge, Doug often sought solitude on the banks of the Susquehanna River. "I had imaginary friends - Indian spirit guides who would show me secret places where I could escape adults' peering eyes."

When Doug was 20, his father died. Doug dropped out of college and became a carpenter. In the 1980s he moved to Nantucket, a 57 sq mile island about 20 miles off the southeast coast of Cape Cod MA, where his family had often visited during Doug's childhood. Many wealthy people vacation on Nantucket, causing it to have some of the most expensive real estate in the northeast. During summers, landlords "charge $300 a week for a room in a basement." Working as freelance carpenter and painter off and on, Doug became a familiar sight to permanent residents as he bicycled around the island wearing a small knapsack, to jobs and shops, and sometimes pausing at the tavern for a beer.

Doug made a small underground abode, then, after hard thinking, decided to build a larger home. After much scouting he chose a spot with sandy soil on land owned by the Boy Scouts, near an estate owned by TV newscasters.

"I planned everything - the logistics were huge. I figured out exactly how many studs I'd need, how many sheets of insulation." Some items he found at old camp sites around the island; some he bought. He carried the materials on his back hundreds of yards into the woods.

He worked stealthily, often at night. While digging the 8-foot-deep hole, he covered it during daylight so it would not be seen from the air. Installing walls and roof took a weekend. Total cost: 6 weeks labor and less than $150.

The finished structure "is easy to heat, easy to cool. It is basically stormproof, bombproof, and the wind blows right over you." It includes a main room 8 by 8 feet; two anti-ways; a skylight; and a small cellar where food and drink can be kept cool.

Furnishings include: a queen-size loft bed, hinged so it folds out of the way when not in use; pine paneling; floors of Belgium stones he found; a wood-burning stove made of stone; a kitchen sink; a plastic tube attached to a jug of warm water for showering, with a plastic curtain drawn to confine splatters; and a home-made portable toilet. Shelves of books and music tapes line the walls. A cinder-block-size battery provides electricity.

Few people venture into that area. Trails through thick underbrush seem to lead nowhere. In winter, temperatures sometimes drop to 12°; and in summer, ticks bearing Lyme disease are active. Doug routed paths so they led away from his home. And he made 4" blocks with bottoms carved like deer hooves, which strap to his feet. "Like walking on stilts." If snow less than 4" deep, they leave tracks that look like deers'.

Even on a moonless night, Doug found his way without flashlight, moving past bayberry bushes, blueberry patches, scrub pine, and fallen dead trees, thru matted twigs and branches. Arriving at a jumble of dead branches concealing a small rise in the earth, Doug set aside some branches and lifted a hatch to enter his home. "Each path is a separate dance, which I memorized."

Doug lived there 8 years. Only a few close friends visited, including his mom who was pleased to find it clean and neat. But many islanders heard rumors.

In Nov 1998, Jack Hallett, a local man, while supposedly crawling on hands and knees looking for deer sign, saw a stove pipe protruding a few inches above ground. He told a police officer. Early the next morning, they went there and encountered the startled occupant. Doug invited them down for coffee.

After they left, Doug alerted the island's NTV channel 13 and told why he lived as he did. For a while, Doug was a celebrity, interviewed by major media. Doug used the exposure to criticize some islanders for turning an environmental gem into an overdeveloped resort. That did not endear Doug to those islanders.

The police thought Doug was on the newscasters' estate, and ordered him to vacate in 4 days. Then it was learned he was on Boy Scout land, and the local leaders decided to let him stay. But (perhaps threatened with fines if they didn't evict), they changed their minds, and got a ruling ordering Doug out within 30 days. His home was then destroyed.

Sept 2004

Richard Ray, a health inspector who visited the home, said, "Many people would be envious of his living conditions." But in court, Ray claimed the home had 23 health code violations including with toilet, heating, ventilation.

Doug's achievement polarized island residents. "I'm either a folk hero or a vagrant. They either like me or hate me. I've lost friends over this, but I've made a lot of friends, too." Some call Doug a tax-dodger who wants the benefits of year-around Nantucket living without helping to pay for "good" government. But Dr.Tim Lepore, med director of the hospital, says that's nonsense. "He's not driving (a car) crazy; he's not contributing to congestion. He works and he goes home. He fits in very easily." Lepore offered Doug space in his back yard for a new underground home.

Doug, who said he had homes hidden elsewhere, including in Catskills near NYC, and CO and HI, left Nantucket for a while and lived, he said, in a home he'd built behind a waterfall on the Delaware River in PA. But Doug returned a year later, drawn back by "an intense spiritual attraction." Also, many houses being built, so Doug's skills much in demand.

Doug says, most islanders now accept him, but that an unswayed minority still regard him as an outlaw. (From Boston Globe 3Dc98 and 6Je01, and Long Island Newsday 2May99; MUCH THANKS to L.Smith for getting these via internet.)

(Comments:) The newspapers differed as to how Hallett discovered Doug's home. Neither tale seems likely. Doug was very careful with construction and trails, so I doubt he would leave a stove pipe easy to see or bump into, or light a fire in daytime when smoke might be visible, esp in Nov when days short and nights long.

Hallett's tale may be a cover story. My guess: "concerned citizens" heard the rumors and complained to police. Police learned who Doug's friends were, picked one they could intimidate to show them.

What Doug did after discovery: alert the media quickly, seems wise. Officials then had more difficulty misrepresenting Doug. Even so, they tried to malign him by claiming that 6'4" Doug had assaulted or threatened people. That may have been exaggerations of minor spats in taverns.

The news reports, like most media, were to entertain; not how-to. I put in the little they gave, and tried to fix obvious goofs and fill in a few blanks.

The reports gave Doug's official name. I've not used it in case Doug has moved and prefers that notoriety not echo.

I suspect that Lepore's offer was merely a gesture. If Lepore did let Doug build on his land, Lepore might be fined or sued for code violations.

Hide-outs behind waterfalls provide dramatic scenes in movies, but do not seem desirable for living in. I wonder if Doug hoped to send any hostile pursuers on a wild waterfall chase.

Doug's ability to memorize a trail so well he can follow it in total darkness, is a talent neither of us have. Even with a flashlight, I have difficulty because surroundings look different in light beamed from me than in light from sky overhead. My feet may feel a main trail, esp if wearing mocs, because soil is packed firmer. But, if dark, I often stray, bump into things, and then wonder which way I strayed. Bert & Holly, OR

Suggestions for hiding a camp.

Make use of what occurs naturally in your area. Here there are many steep, bramble-covered slopes where hiking is difficult except on roads and trails: where humans don't go unless they have strong motives. If you live where slopes are slight and woods open with little undergrowth, concealment may be more difficult but perhaps you can be more remote. (Eg, maybe you could ride mtn bikes through the woods - not practical here.) Or, if you have deep snows that remain for months, that may hinder - but also an advantage for hauling in a year's supply on a sled. Likewise, deserts and swamps and rocky outcrops all pose problems - and offer advantages.

Generally avoid unique places: the only grove of trees on an otherwise treeless plain; the only dry mound in a swamp; the only island in a lake; the only known spring in a desert (better to collect and store occasional rains); a hot spring (except where many hot sprs); a choice fishing or hunting spot.

Route any trails around your camp; not to it. Don't end a trail abruptly; continue it to a plausible destination (eg, spring, fruit tree, view spot); one you go to occasionally so that portion of trail continues to get wear.

To get from a trail to your camp without causing visible wear, look for any natural objects. Any boulders you could step on ? Any branches you could go arm over arm along. If bringing many back loads to (re)supply a camp, may be best to prepare a temp trail. Tie vulnerable vegetation out of the way; bring everything in; then re-naturalize. Put back vegetation; remove any that got damaged.

We often use staffs to assist trail access. Its print is much smaller than a footprint and, if carefully placed in among ground debris, not conspicuous. An expert stilt walker might be able to leave no footprints at all. We are not that adept, but a staff enables us to step further and more irregularly without losing balance. A staff (provides a third leg) is also helpful for hiking on steep slopes that lack hand holds, for crossing rivers, and for fighting off any cougars, bears, wolves, or whatever, (though not had to - so far). Make staff strong enough to take all your weight and long enough to reach the ground on your downhill side when on a slope.

Mocassins are better than hard-soled shoes in most woods here. They not only disturb the ground less, but are safer on side slopes (less apt to sprain ankle) and give better footing on most logs and boulders. Rubber mocs made from truck innertubes (see Packet or Set R) are less slippery than leather mocs.

The lower your shelter, the less visible; also less prone to wind damage, and warmer. For a long-term camp, we usually dig out enough to put roof flush with the ground. One time, mushroomers got within ten yds without noticing it.

For camo, at least in these woods, black or brown or dark grey are better colors than green. Human eyes are very sensitive to shades of green; no wonder, our ancestors had to distinguish edibles.
Sept 2004

Our variously green pails and totes and barrels, though much better than white or red, do not blend well here. On other hand, green outer clothing is less apt to be mistaken for a deer.

Clear plastic tarps may be visible a long distance, esp in winter when many bushes and trees are leafless. Black plastic is quite visible if sloped; it reflects sky. But it's not as visible if hung perpendicular to ground. Note: if on slope, on downhill side hang the plastic like $\diagdown$; not like $\diagup$.

Best for concealment from the air: many evergreen trees/branches above; next best, an over-roof of dead branches with vines growing on it; next best, cloth with a varied pattern of moss and fallen leaves on it, which may be less visible than camo cloth. (Spotting from air not likely unless there's an open fire or something else conspicuous. I've read of plane crashes, with survivors trying to be seen and many planes searching - without success.)

Do noisy activities elsewhere; maybe in the bottom of a steep, crooked canyon or at a temp camp. (Twice we've heard noisy parties on neighboring mountains, playing loud music audible for miles. The party lasted a few hours; then, promptly, everyone went away.)

Don't cook when you think people or big predators are nearby. Odors can drift far, esp downhill on calm eves.

If, despite your precautions, someone comes near your camp, don't assume (s)he saw it. Very few hikers are looking for campers. Most are looking for mushrooms, saleable greens, deer, trees, survey marks, whatever. They see only what they are looking for unless something unusual attracts their attention. Your imperfectly concealed camp will be more visible to you than to most others because you know what to look for.

If you are quite sure someone HAS spotted your camp, may be best to greet them, be friendly - and try to ascertain their motives and likely behavior. Exception: if you think they're hostile, get away promptly if you can without being seen. Better to let your camp be ransacked than to confront them. Keep valuables in safe cache; not setting out.

Don't camp close to a concentration of careless campers who might provoke a mass round-up. (We read of one along a NV-CA river a few years ago.) If dozens comb area, they will find most camps.

Learn about all the backwoods activities in the area. Even though you have more enjoyable and profitable ways to spend your time than (eg) gathering greenery that will become wreaths at some rich guy's funeral and then into trash; may be wise to do some, to learn what gatherers seek and where they go. Buyers will show you what they want, and suggest places to look. During autumns we like to be within hiking range of our winter site, to pick any edible 'shrooms as soon as they arise. (Some years we gather and eat $300+ worth at retail. Usually can't get them to a buyer easily enough for selling to be worthwhile.) Be sure to identify mushrooms VERY WELL before eating. Some good tasting ones are deadly for humans, though some other animals eat them without problems.

Sept 2004

My dream tent for winter camping.

Arc-shaped (like a quonset hut), it's supported by (maybe) 5 flex poles that intersect each other for bracing. (Arc tents that have only 2 poles, need tie-outs of ends.) Possible pole placement: (Know a better way ?) Fabric not shown.

Side-walls/ceiling have tough outer fabric to withstand hail and falling branches. Maybe not waterproof. (Coatings seem not durable, esp on cloth exposed to weather.) When rain or sun protection needed, black polyethylene film (common plastic), cut to proper width, is layed over tent and clipped to rings along tent's bottom. Non-bunching fasteners (like clothespin ties, see 1995-96 Summary or Ap92DP) connect clips to the plastic - which may not survive long but is cheap and widely available. The plastic extends a few feet beyond tent's entry end and can be tied out to provide somewhat-sheltered space there. The tie on one corner is easily reclipped high for entry and exit.

The ceiling/side-walls have (maybe) 6 liners, spaced approx 3/4" apart for insulation. The next-to-inner liner is a vapor barrier to keep moisture (from breathing and sweat) out of the outer layers. (NEXT to inner, so human contact does not soil or damage it.) The INNER liner is removable for laundering.

The floor has 4 layers, all but one removable. On the ground is a plastic tarp, separate from tent, to keep tent's bottom clean. Next is a tough rot-proof fabric, sewen to tent. Next a foam pad; either closed cell, or open cell sealed within plastic. (It's in addition to any pad with bedding.) The floor's top layer is cloth; tough but easily washed. The foam insulates the inner layer from the ground enough to prevent condensation.

One end of tent is all window; at least two layers of transparent plastic, UV resistant; flexible but stiff enough to remain unwrinkled and thus easily wiped off; maybe polyester. The window usually faces the brightest, most open sky. The panes zip to the tent, and are removed: for backpacking (better rolled than folded); for cross-venting during hot weather (net window substituted); and to replace. (Likely the first parts ruined by UV.) The ceiling overhangs window a few inches and window slants inward, to minimize rain splatter. The slanted window also reflects sky into the ground instead of across the valley.

The tent's other end is for entry and ventilation. It has 6 lightweight porous curtains spaced apart; one is netting. The curtains can be zipped completely closed to block wind or crawling bugs; or, if few breezes and bugs, hung closed without zipping bottoms, with enough slack to crawl through or reach items outside; which eases access and reduces zipper wear. Curtains removable for max venting or to wash. (People brushing under them will gradually soil them.)

Inside is maybe 6½' long, 4' wide, 3' high: roomy for one; comfy for two to sleep but not do much else. Outside, 7¼ by 5 by 3½. Maybe 25 pounds total; 15 pounds without poles, window, floor-pad.

side view, cross-section

```
       liners ⌐
  ← window    curtains →
     Poles not shown.              in/
     All layers not shown          out
← 
south
```

Problem: The window usually faces down slope for max light. But, if it does, the tent needs a terrace at least 9' broad (7½-long tent plus 1½' stand-up space at entry end). Unfortunately, most terraces are narrow. May need to dig a trench into the bank. Putting window on side of tent would ease siteing, but greatly complicate this tent.

I'd like, attached to tent, a big 6+' tall fully-enclosed anti-way for doffing outside clothes and as rain-sheltered storage. Best shape and size depends on site and weather, and therefore is best designed and rigged by the user.

Cost ? The many layers need careful sewing. Even if made abroad in quite big quantities, my guess: $1000+ at retail. But only a month's rent in many places.

Not worth trying to hand-make one or a few for ourselves. So, until such a tent is for sale, we will continue to winter in wikiups we rig out of plastic plus whatever is available near site.

Most of our wikiups are roomier than this tent and thus better at a base camp we occupy continuously for many months. But our wikiups require much time to set up and take down (and if left up unattended, mice soon move in); whereas in an hour this tent could be set up, or taken down and stored in a barrel. Bert

Totes are not insect-proof.

The lids do not fit tightly enough. Small red ants nested in a 20-gal tote holding solar reflectors. Not damaged only because ants didn't use them. Trash barrel lids, too, seem not tight enough.

Most pail lids do. We've stored food, clothes, papers in many rain-sheltered pails for many years without damage.

The only rodent penetration was of a plastic trash barrel full of jars and bags, left over winter at a summer camp site. Oddly, the hole (big enough for a small rat) was near top. Did rodent get locked in, and gnawed to get out ? Holly

I use many 20-litre buckets for storage.

Ones with good-fitting lids. Also, medium-size totes. Dried foods I keep in 3-foot-long steel ammo cans. Bruce

Water storage during freezing weather.

Some 5-gallon water jugs froze solid. I now use gallon milk jugs, filled only half full. Half full so if they do freeze they are less apt to burst. Milk jugs so if they do burst they are easily replaced. However, I try to prevent freezing by keeping them out of the wind behind natural barriers such as big trees and boulders. Bruce of BC, 2003

I prefer pots with solid steel handles.

Riveted on. Bakelite plastic handles eventually crack or are melted by too hot a campfire. Or worse, the screws come loose repeatedly. I prefer folding handles but they are harder to find.

Cast iron is too heavy.

I buy my cookware and most of my equipment at thrift stores. Shopping tip: many items that don't sell at weekend garage sales, get donated to stores on Mondays. They are usually put out for sale by noon. Bruce of BC, 2002

(Comment:) Pots that have lost their handles have advantages. Though more difficult to move while hot (need heavy gloves or rags), they fit better under a transparent shroud when solar cooking, or insulate more compactly in bed after a brief simmer. And more compact to transport or store. Sometimes cheap or free at yard sales, thrift-store trash, unofficial dumps along logging roads.

If pot has a handle, I prefer welded. If it breaks off, it will probably leave the pot entire, whereas a riveted or bolted handle may leave holes that leak.

The pots we use for solar cooking.

The ideal pot is dull black, inside and out. None of our pots are. Some got darkened while cooking over fires, but more grey than black, and wears off.

I found two pots in a fussy 2nd-hand-store's trash. One small (3 cups), shiny black outside and in (teflon); no lid.

Other pot is mid-size aluminum, black teflon inside, Bert painted outside. (No free/cheap black paint. Bert mixed soot scraped off stove, with oil poured off of white paint.) Needs 2nd coat. Paint survived solar cooking but wouldn't fire.

Solar cooking equipment.

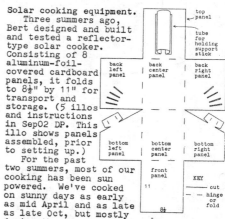

Three summers ago, Bert designed and built and tested a reflector-type solar cooker. Consisting of 8 aluminum-foil-covered cardboard panels, it folds to 8½" by 11" for transport and storage. (5 illos and instructions in Sep02 DP. This illo shows panels assembled, prior to setting up.)

For the past two summers, most of our cooking has been sun powered. We've cooked on sunny days as early as mid April and as late Oct, but mostly during the sunniest months which here have been July, Aug, Sept. Thus, year around, about one-third of our cooking has been solar - well worth it given problems and costs of other heat sources.

We soon learned: one reflector cooker isn't enough. Bert made a larger 8-panel, identical except scaled up: 13½" x 17" panels covered with foil 18" wide.

Bert also made a 3-panel "corner" reflector (see May93 DP or Summary) with panels 14x14" (size of some cardboard on hand). Though not as potent as 8 panels, it sufficed to cook on hot clear days. But mostly it provided hot water that reduced cooking time on the 8-panels; both a second batch that same day and, by insulating over night, the first batch the next day - helpful because
Sept 2004

many mornings are cloudy until noon.

Though the 3-panel concentrates sun less than does a properly-set 8-panel, it does not need adjusting as often.

To heat and store water for cooking, we used a gallon narrow-mouth brown glass jug I'd scavenged (had aloe vera extract). We didn't want to heat cooking water in plastic because, not only does near-boiling water weaken most plastics, but heat may greatly accelerate leaching of any toxins out of plastic.

For insulating water overnight, Bert lined a 6-gal plastic pail with plastic foam: rigid foam top and bottom; flexible packing foam rolled up around the sides; into which the jug fit snugly easily. (A wide-mouth gallon jug might fit, with foam, into a 5-gallon pail.)

Concentrated sun had changed the (vinyl?) bowl, used as shroud when first testing, from transparent to whitish. Luckily I'd found many big scraps of transparent plastic (polyester?) in Kinkos' dumpster (used to laminate). Somewhat flexible but stiff enough to hold a shape, and thus easier to put on and off a pot than is an oven bag (which we would have used otherwise). From it, Bert made various-size shrouds that fit our pots. It has endured sun well. After a while it delaminates, becoming slightly less clear but more insulative.

Bert stapled together ends of side-piece to form cylinder, then fastened on top piece. Some fastenings did not hold well. Our final way: bend ends of tab to insert into slot. Number and exact size of slots/tabs depends on diameter.

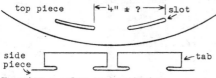

top piece ←—4" ± ? —→ slot

side piece ↙ ←tab

Choosing a solar-cooker design.

The main reason Bert designed our 8-panel reflectors rather than using SCR's CooKit design: an 8-panel folds smaller and thus stores easier. Also, it may be more effective in autumn when the sun is not high here. (CooKit is mainly for tropics where mid-day sun always high.)

SCR (p.B) sells two CooKit versions: one, foil and cardboard, won't take rain; one, foil and plastic foam, endures rain but crushes easily. With either, foil gradually loses shine. If/when a more durable CooKit is made, we may buy one to test along side our 8-panels.

Last summer, Bert added a 9th panel to our small 8-panel (a "fore panel" is attached to the front panel). It boosts power during high sun (near noon from mid May thru July) but helps little when sun low. Conversely, the top panel helps much when sun low, but not when sun is high. If in tropics, we might not want a top panel, because its hold-up stick takes time. (CooKit has no top panel.)

The big-8 accomodates a larger pot than does the small-9, which is why Bert made it. If pot small, big-8 is more tolerant of azimuth. But big-8 needs more materials and stiffer panels, gets more wind force, and won't fit in 5-gal pail (will in 10-gal tote). If adjusted

Sept 2004

frequently, small-9 should heat a small pot as fast as does big-8. Holly, OR

Tests compare solar reflectors.

I used 3 identical one-gallon jugs full of water; plastic, deep blue (not best color but I wanted identical jugs). NO SHROUDS. Jugs' bottoms insulated from reflectors by $\frac{1}{4}$"-thick styrofoam. Started 1:30 on 22July02, water 85°. Left caps slightly loose to vent steam. Ended 3:30. Water 150° on big-8; 135° on small-9; 130° on 3-panel. Big-8's jug evaporated cup of water; others little.

Because big-8's jug got hotter, it lost more heat, so big-8 did better than temperatures indicate. Small-9 had more panels. Why was big-8 best? Big-8 was newer (in use a month, vs 5 months), so its foil was shinier. Jug was too big for small-9: parts of jug were beyond area getting most sun. 3-panel did almost as well as small-9, despite less area and less concentration of sun, probably for both reasons above.

Reflective areas: big-8, 1785 sq in; small-9, 841; 3-panel, 588. Approx ratios: 2.8 to 1.4 to 1.0.

To learn effects of shine loss, on 10Sept03 I tested side by side, heating blue jugs, the original big-8 and a new big-8 same size. In 3 hours, 60° water heated to 152° by new, 142° by old. Bert

How solar and flame cooking differ.

With flame (wood or propane), heat comes from below, so the food cooks from bottom up. Even in an oven where all air nearly the same temperature, a bread heats more on bottom where covered by pan than on top where evaporation cools.

With our solar reflectors, heating is usually greatest on top where both direct and reflected rays shine, whereas the bottom gets only reflected rays. The lower the sun, the less the difference, because fewer rays shine on top and more reflect in onto bottom. Also, the higher the pan, the less the difference, because more space between bottom-center reflector and pan lets in more rays. By setting pan on clear glass jars 3 inches high, we were able to cook breads quite evenly without turning them over.

When cooking in water, we completely cover the food; else food above water may scorch before food in water cooks.

With nettles and other greens, we heated water nearly to boiling (at least 170°) before putting in greens. The hot water instantly wilts the greens which are then easily stirred down into water.

Bert and I cook bread differently. Regardless of heat source, he sprinkles flour on pan, and then around edges of bread, to prevent sticking; and uses low heat because he fears burning.

Whereas, when cooking with propane or wood in an aluminum pan with patina (a tough thin coating that develops), if I get pan hot enough or cook long enough, a bread usually comes free as the crust forms. (If dough very moist or getting sour, sticking to pan is more likely.)

When we switched to our solar rigs which provide only low heat, at first I cooked bread like Bert does. Then I tried spreading a thin coating of oil on pan (with finger). The bread tasted better to me, so I kept using oil, even though for health I prefer to cook without oil (which heat may degrade). But even with oil, I sometimes had to shake pan vigorously, or invert and knock it on something, to jar the bread free.

With solar, I form dough approx one inch thick - slightly thicker than with flame so I need not tend as often. Bert forms loaves thicker. Sun-cooked bread tastes different than flame-cooked. Does the top, cooking before middle, seal in volatiles that otherwise evaporate?

I tried frying pans and teflon-lined pot; covered and uncovered; loaf's top sprinkled with dark poppy-seeds, or not. None affected cooking-time much. What did: sun height. In mid summer near noon, a loaf cooked in approx 1½ hours. Later in season, 2 or more hours needed.

I made a few cakes (moistish bread dough with molasses and cinnamon added), cookies, and blackberry pies (thin layer bread dough; then berries 3 deep; then another thin dough). All cooked fine. Peanuts, soybeans, sunflrs toasted fine; never burned (unlike with flame)! Holly

Report on one day of solar cooking.
(No two days quite the same.) 1 Aug 02, 45° latitude, solar noon 1:30.

9:15. Set gallon 60° water heating in brown glass jug with shroud on 3-panel reflector. Sky partly cloudy until noon.

12:40. Water in jug 150°. Used two cups to start one cup lentils cooking in small stainless pot with lid and shroud on small 9-panel. Also used some water, diluted with cool water until "warm to wrist" (100°?) to mix with flour and yeast to start dough rising we will bake tomorrow. Refilled jug with cool water. Jug water now 110°. Again on 3-panel.

1:12. Started cooking coolish dough (made from flour ground in early morn and yeast-risen today), approx 1½" thick in aluminum frying pan sprinkled with flour, with cover and shroud, on big 8-panel. Pan set on jars 3" tall.

3:35. Air between bread and cover 190°. Tasted small bit from center interior. Not as done as we like.

4:24. Air 220°. Bread done. Removed.

4:29. Water in brown jug now 160°. Moved to (now vacant) big 8-panel.

4:32. Lentils 195°. VERY done - soft, as Holly likes. (I like firmer) Removed.

5:58pm. Water in brown jug now 183°. Put jug with water into insulated pail.

8:30am next morn. Water in insulated jug 119°. (Air about 55°.) Bert

Solar reflectors' problems and fixes.
To better hold top panel's support stick, I lashed its bottom to a bowl (cut-off plastic jug) into which I put rocks. The lashing goes through holes I bored in bowl's side. The stick needs a small fork or lump at its bottom; else it may slide up out of the lashing.

Play of the support stick and Tyvek hinges let wind gusts flap the top panel back and forth, esp on big 8-panel.

The only structural failure so far: on my first big-8, a Tyvek hinge holding center back panel to center bottom panel tore; weakened by repeated foldings when putting rig away. (I'm surprised it tore instead of ripping off the cardboard.) For big-8s, I'd like stronger hinges.

For my first big-8, I lacked enough stiff cardbd. Some pieces I stiffened more by gluing on other pieces, cross-laminating. (Cardbd stiffer one way than the other.) Even so, the panels often warped as heat and humidity changed; but were easily bent back approx flat.

I made the new big-8 out of old 1/8" plywood I found. Portions had rotted, but much was sturdy enough for panels. Much stiffer than cardbd. Design change of tabs: instead of flaps that fold out to hold tab in slot, I put a hole in each tab through which a peg goes. Because paneling is thicker than cardbd, it needs bigger gaps between panels to allow folding, and panels must be folded in order; else hinges get over-stressed.

Because the bigger reflectors have bigger problems, I probably won't build more unless cooking for many people. For our largest pot now, the small-9 is big enough though not as fast as a big-8.

The small-9's fore panel needs frequent adjustments; else its reflection misses the pot. I probably won't fasten a fore panel to future reflectors. If I want one temporarily, I'll set an extra reflector in front of the front panel.

Breezes sometimes flipped the front panel over onto pot, partially shading it. I tied on a little tray on which I set rocks, to limit panel's motion.

When I made the first reflector, I didn't glue foil to cardboard, because I thought white glue wouldn't adhere to foil. Instead, I folded foil over the edge of cardbd. But the foil sometimes came loose, esp near the hinges where only tabs of foil folded over. So, when repairing, I tried gluing edges. Held better than expected.

So, when I made the new big-8 I glued all foil edges (glue seams ½" wide). On the edges not joining other panels, I folded foil over the edge and glued foil to the shady side. But on edges joining other panels, I glued foil to sunny side. That enabled me to use one long Tyvek hinge (glued to shady side) on each joined edge. Simpler and stronger. So far, the glue has held as well to sunny as shady side. (I thought heat might weaken it.) If I build more big-8s, I will make panels 13.9" by 18" to utilize full width of foil, and glue all edges of foil to sunny sides of panels.

3-panel reflector. If each panel is joined to the other two, they can't fold for storage. But if not all joined, the back panels will blow over unless held by something. So I added a second bottom panel. Each bottom panel is hinged to a back panel, but the back panels to each other, but the bottom panels not joined. To set up, I place one bottom panel under the other. The pot then anchors the whole rig. I partially covered the under panel with left-over foil scraps, which adds reflective power if back panels set wider than a right angle. The best angle depends on width of the pot.

All aluminum foil is not manufactured equal. Our first reflectors were made with Reynolds. But I didn't have enough for the second 3-panel, so I bought another brand, 18" wide, 37½' long for $1 at a dollar store. The box says "heavy duty". But it is thinner than Reynolds, and got wrinkled more when rolled by factory. Worse: a moist jug, set directly on the foil, corroded it enough in two hours to lose shine. Bert
Sept 2004

If panels not 8½x11".

To build the big-8, instead of recalculating all measurements (in Sep 02 DP), I made a special ruler with each "macro-inch" (mac) equal to 17/11" (39.3mm) and each 1/8 mac equal to 4.9mm. (Check: 11 macs = 17 inches.) I then simply made all measurements in macs. This works ONLY if a panel's ratio of width to length is 8½ to 11. Above are some other sizes that use 12" and 18" wide foil efficiently. B

panel	mac	1/8
in	in	mac
inches	mm	mm
9¼x12	27.7	3.5
12x15½	35.9	4.5
13⅞x18	41.6	5.2
18x23½	53.8	6.7

The Encyclopedia of Edible Plants
of North America. Francois Couplan's prodigious work includes approx 4000 species of 850 genera. However, many are tropical plants found only in s FL. Not for identification; no descriptions.

Genera rated "A1": tasty, healthful, easily gathered and prepared; and abundant throughout N.Amer: Urtica (nettle), Quercus (oak), Stellaria (chickweed), Chenopodium (lambs qter), Amaranthus (pigweed), Malva (mallow), Brassica (mustard), Raphanus (radish), Rubus (blackberry), Sonchus (sow thistle), Taraxacum (dandelion).

Couplan says the young leaves of Hypochoeris, a relative of lettuce and dandelion, "can be eaten raw. They are crisp and have a pleasant flavor, exempt of bitterness, and make very good salads." But, inconsistently, he rates it only D1 (not very edible). Where we are, H. radicata (gosmore) is much less bitter than dandelion. But species may vary. Perhaps Couplan wrote his praise before he encountered one less tasty - and revised his rating but not his praise.

"The very young tops of Salsola kali (russian thistle) are tender, salty and edible raw. The plant soon becomes woody and spiny and turns into well-known tumbleweeds blown by the wind for miles. Rich in many minerals." The seeds, too, are said to be edible.

The leaves of most Dodecatheon (shooting star) species "are one of the best tasting salad ingredients to be found in the mountains" near the West Coast. The flowers, too, are edible raw.

Papaver (poppy). The young basil leaves of several species, formed before the plant blooms, are excellent raw.

"Many of the Chenopodiaceae have the ability to grow on saline soils from which they derive a salty taste."

"The young shoots of Pinaceae (pine family, including also firs, spruces, hemlocks, doug-fir), rich in vitamin C, are excellent raw, added to salads and other dishes." But some other conifers, including arborvitae (red cedar), some junipers, and especially yew (easily mistaken for hemlock) are toxic.

Oxalis (wood sorrel). "The leaves, flowers and young fruits of various species are edible raw." However, "all species contain oxalic acid and potassium oxalate... People subject to arthritis, rheumatism, gout, asthma and kidney stones should abstain." Also, regular ingestion for several months can inhibit the body's absorption of calcium.

The leaves of Oxyria digyna (mountain sorrel, arctic and high mtns) are edible raw or cooked. They contain oxalic acid, but "it can be eliminated by boiling in a change of water." (Also true for more-common Oxalis (above) ?)

"The very young fronds of Pteridium aquilinum (bracken fern), picked while still tender before they have started to unroll, taste very good" but should be either thoroughly cooked, preferably with change of water; or else soaked for 24 hours in water with wood ashes. When raw, they contain a carcinogen and a vitamin-B1 destroyer. Members of the first scientific expedition to cross Australia from north to south (1860-61) died from beriberi (vit-B1 lack) after feeding on a thiaminase-rich fern, nardoo (Marsilea drummondii). This fern was commonly eaten by aborigines, but only after soaking in water which rids it of the heat-resistant thiaminase.

"The tender young leaves of maple are good raw or cooked. They are rich in sugar. The seeds are edible but often bitter" which can be eliminated by boiling in a change of water. Maple sap, for making sugar, is most sweet and plentiful when, in early spring, "warm sunny days are followed by very cold nights" (common in northeast). Climate is more important than species of maple.

The sweet aromatic juniper "berries" (fleshy cones) are a well-known condiment. But too big a dose, or continuous long use, can irritate the kidneys.

"The sweet taste of licorice is due to ... a saponin 50 times as sweet as white sugar.... If used regularly over a long period of time, it can be a cause of hypertension (high blood pressure)."

"In moderate amounts, the essential (odorous) oils of crucifers (mustards, cresses, cabbage, etc) stimulate the appetite and activate digestion. But big doses strongly irritate mucous membranes and cause digestive or urinary problems.

Pods and seeds of various lupines (legume family) have been eaten, but "contain toxic alkaloids which must be removed by boiling in water."

"After peeling off the bitter outer layer, the inner part of the stem of Arctium (burdock) is one of the best vegetables; tender, crunchy, sweet, with a delicate artichoke flavor. It can be eaten raw or cooked in various ways. The new unfolding leaves are edible raw" but soon become very bitter. "The roots are good raw or cooked, have a pleasant artichoke taste and a sweet flavor due to inulin" (up to 45%), a sugar easily assimilated even by diabetics. Best when fresh. Sold in NYC markets as "gobo" (Japanese name) "for quite a high price" but can be picked free in nearby empty lots. Harvest after their first growing season, in fall or winter - before the flower stalk develops.

"The cambium layer of Alnus rubra (red alder) was eaten by Indians."

California Indians often preferred bitter acorns, as they keep better (due to their tannin) and are more abundant than sweet acorns. Tannin is soluable in water. To eliminate, chop up acorns and boil "in several changes of water until bitterness" gone and water clear.

Pine nuts "are very nutritious. But they turn rancid rapidly and must be stored in an airtight container."

"Bitter almonds (Prunus amygdalus) and their essential oil have been used

Sept 2004

to flavor desserts. However, this can be dangerous as 30 to 50 kernels can kill an adult if ingested at one time." Humans can detoxify hydrocyanic acid, which is also in plum and peach pits, apple seeds, and many other fruit seeds, but only in small amounts, gradually.

P. emarginata, bitter cherry. "The pulp is thin and sweetish. Local Indians removed the kernel from the stone, crushed it, leached out the cyanide with running water, and ate the result as a mush, or dried it for later use."

Beans contain much iron (more than lentils, known to be a good source).

The seeds of lima (Phascolus limensis) and some other beans "contain cyanogenetic glucosides which yield by hydrolysis toxic hydrocyanic acid." It "can be eliminated by boiling the seeds in water for a long time. But it's not destroyed; merely transferred to the water which should be discarded." Poisoning due to improper cooking, is quite frequent.

"Raw beans (and beans newly sprouted) contain a toxin, phasine, which causes serious digestive disorders (sometimes fatal) by inhibiting enzymes and destroying red blood cells. Prolonged cooking (but not simple drying) eliminates this toxin. Bean sprouts must not be eaten raw until leaves are green...."

More toxic warnings about cultivated than wild species, but probably only because more is known about them.

Kudzu, Pueraria lobata. "Young leaves, flowers, unripe pods are edible raw or cooked." In Japan, roots are gathered in fall and starch extracted by grating, soaking in water, filtering, letting starch settle, pouring off water, drying, and crushing into powder. Much valued for nutrients and easy digestibility. In southeast U.S., commercial harvesting could benefit "the producer, the local rural people, and the native plants oppressed by this aggressive invader."

A common error: "The proteins (in grass-family cereals) are incomplete: that is, they don't have all essential amino acids." No. They have all, but (eg) corn has only 2/3 the ideal amount of lysine. So, unless eaten with something rich in lysine such as legumes, portions of other amino acids are not well used.

Couplan, French, uses some British English. Eg, "saccharose" vs "sucrose".

1998, 512p., Keaten, 27 Pine St, Box 876, NewCanaan CT 06840; $20. Revu, H&B

Plants and Animals of Pacific Northwest.

In this book, Eugene N. Kozloff describes approx 300 plant species and 100 animals. The 123 line drawings and 321 color photos are helpful to all who wish to learn the area's flora without delving into technical works with keys. Few mentions of edible and other uses. Some tidbits I found most interesting:

"Any delicate trailer (stems tend to sprawl) with square stems (and usually also downward-directed hooks on the corners) and with leaves arranged in whorls, will almost certainly be a Galium. If you pull the plant across your hand, you will notice that the hooks make it cling...." Common names 'bedstraw' and 'cleavers'. (Cleavers grows, sometimes abundantly, in many places around here. We (H&B) often eat the young growing tips (stem with leafs)

raw in spring. (More in June 89 DP.))

Yerba buena, Satureja douglasii, is in "the same genus as the kitchen herb called savory or basil-thyme" and is "a low creeper of the mint family... rarely missing from an oak woods." Also in dry conifer forests. Kozloff doesn't mention, it makes a mintish-flavored herbal tea.

Kozloff says salal berries, Gautheria shallon, "taste something like huckleberries marinated in a dilute extract of fir needles"; and serviceberries, Amalanchier alnifolia, are "neither sweet nor juicy." I've found both very varied. Some of both were sweet and delicious.

Pacific dogwood, Cornus nuttalli, "ordinarily has a single trunk." To help identify in winter, branches bud as whorls of four though all may not develop, whereas maples branch in pairs. Also, "as branches grow outward, they curve upward." (In spring, big showy white flowers open before or with leaves. Wood is fine-grained, dense, hard when dry; used for salmon-harpoon foreshafts, shuttles for weaving, bobbins, tools and "dogs" (skewers), hence name. Root-bark tea widely used as quinine sub to treat malaria. Berries eaten raw or cooked.)

1976, 270 pages, $15 in 1986 (ppd?), U of WA Press, POB 85569, Seattle WA 98145. Review by Julie Summers

Many wild herbs yield tasty seasonings.

I have learned to enjoy the natural flavors of most wild plants I eat; salt or other seasonings seldom desired. But some other foods I like to spice up. To them I add a herbal mix I blend myself.

Seaweeds provide mostly potassium chloride instead of sodium chloride (table salt). Almost any fresh, non-rotting seaweeds can be collected, dried, powdered, and used as salt. They taste like table salt but milder. WARNINGS: Never eat any that are not fresh or that have foreign growth on them; or gathered near where sewage is dumped into ocean.

The leaves of all Atriplex species can be dried, powdered, and used like salt. Commonly called "saltbush" due to high mineral content and salty flavor. I've also tried burning dried Atriplex leaves and using the ash, but prefer the flavor of the unburnt leaves.

Related to Atriplex is Chenopodium, a genus of the Goosefoot family. Best known is lambs quarters, a nutrient-rich spinach relative found world-wide. All species edible; flavors vary slightly.

Many other herbs, though not salty, are tasty. Choose strong-flavored herbs so that you need only small amounts.

Most members of the mustard family are excellent cooking spices: shepherds purse, wild radish, sweet alyssum, water cress, and the rockets, as well as those called "mustards". No members are toxic. (Watercress may have liver-fluke eggs. We cook. Cooked flavor quite bland.)

The leaves of many wild sages, dried and powdered, can be added sparingly.

Though not salty, licorice-flavored fennel seeds may be a good addition.

Wild and cultivated onions, garlic, leeks, chives, ramps are best fresh.

Never use any wild plants for food or spices you've not positively identified. Christopher Nyerges (shortened from Gentle Survivalist of a few years ago)
Sept 2004

Easy-to-make tool cleans the insides of jugs.

A dirty film gradually develops in water jugs.
It grows algae and (?). Ordinary brushes don't reach
well inside narrow-mouth jugs. To make scrubbers that
do, I bend a piece of wire in the middle to form a
handle, and lash a wadded rag or piece of soft foam to
its ends with rubber bands or cord.

I like to have three scrubbers. For two, I use
coat-hanger wire. It is fairly stiff yet can be bent.
One scrubber is quite straight for cleaning a jug's
bottom. The second is curved to reach portions below
the handle. The third scrubber, made from more-
flexible wire and with a smaller wad, is for reaching
into the handle. With some difficulty, I have been
able to clean all jug handles encountered except for
newer bleach jugs which have tiny openings at top. H&B

Jug showers versus spray showers.

Three writers have recently said they prefer spray showers,
including at least one who has also used jugs. But none said
why. Back in May 82 DP p.1, Julie Summers said she sometimes
showered with squeeze bottles - to use less water.

Carefully-applied squirts from a squeeze bottle may rinse
more efficiently than do less-easily-controlled gushes from a
jug. A fine spray from (eg) a window-washing bottle might be
most efficient of all. However, I think an orchard sprayer,
such as the rig shown in Feb 04 Supplement, would be LESS
efficient, because the flow is less controllable.

If rinsing is more efficient (by whatever means), it will
probably be SLOWER, and you will be wet longer. That is
tolerable or even desirable in hot weather. But when cold, I
like to get rinsed as quickly as possible, even if I use a
little more water. Usually we have enough water. If not, I
wash a few high-priority parts and postpone the rest. Next to
hands and crotch, the parts I wash most often are feet and
lower legs because any hike gets them muddy. For them I often
use a squeeze bottle, because it is easier to handle than a
gallon jug and I don't need much water. (Also see LLL "Simple
Shower", and DP May93 p.1, Oct95 p.1, May96 p.1, May97 p.7,
May98 p.8, Aug00 p.1.) Holly & Bert, Oregon 973, Dec 2004

Some potato-chip bags have shiny reflective insides.

They are more durable and remain more reflective than
aluminum foil. Useable for solar cooking. I sometimes find
such bags in dumpsters. Lauran, Arizona 857, May 2004

RV-type propane equipment better than lighter-weight gear.

If buying propane equipment, get refillable tanks. One-
gallon tanks are made (in case 5 gal is too much to backpack
to a remote temp camp). With the tank, you will need a
regulator (a disk-shaped thing that screws into the tank), a
LOW-pressure stove (like used in most RVs), and a hose or tube
to connect. Shun the little cans and the stoves that fit them.
They are not only more expensive (per propane) but also more
hazardous and wasteful because high pressure feeds the stove.
Also, I've heard the stoves' tiny holes are prone to clog up
and impossible to clean. If at a camp too briefly to want RV-
type equipment, solar or fire cook, or bring ready-to-eats.

Don't drive with engine running too slow.

I purchased "How To Keep Your VW Alive, for the Complete Idiot". Good book. It answered many questions. And I learned I did things that sent my engine to an early grave.

At gatherings, I was referred to as "lug head". I thought it meant I was often working on my van. But, no, it referred to my lugging the engine. Near the campground, I drove at low RPM to make less noise and not disturb the other campers. But quietness not worth ruination. 3000 rpm best for my VW. (I'd been driving at 2000-2500.) Eugene Gonzalez, NC 287, December

I prefer tents that are tall enough to stand up in.

For me, squat tents are not worth the lesser price and weight. I'd thought I'd seldom stand (true), and lower would heat easier (true), and the occasional crouch to dress or exit would be no big deal (false). Could be my age - 55. Ken, WA 982, June

(Comments:) Other advantages of low shelters (of any kind): less likely to be crushed or toppled by wind, and less unwanted ventilation during winter storms; easier to conceal; a hunter's stray missile may go over, not thru.

Ways to obtain stand-up height in a squat shelter: dig a hole in the middle; build a small dome (might be pop-up) on the roof. Most of our shelters have not had stand-up room.

Bear damages and scatters items in an unattended stash.

When moving base camp, I left a pile of remainders near the former site, awaiting further sorting and salvaging. Mostly old plastic tarps and various plastic containers. Nothing valuable. No food. I returned a year later - and found the stuff scattered. Pails had been tossed ten yards. They had claw marks on them. My guess: Some rodent had nested in the pile. Then a bear came along, smelled the rodent, and swatted things helter-skelter in a frenzy to catch rodent. Bert

Methods of processing acorns.

Oak trees grow throughout the world. Over 200 species include deciduous and evergreen trees and shrubs. All oaks are easily identified by their acorns which are nuts set in scaly caps. The tons of acorns that fall to the ground every fall are mostly discarded by gardeners. How sad. In a world with frequent food shortages, it seems wise to learn about an abundant food that was eaten by many of our ancestors.

The tannic acid in most species of acorns makes them too bitter to eat raw. Humans are rarely if ever poisoned by them because no one with normal taste would eat an acorn raw. S/he would just spit it out. But tannic acid is easily leached out.

A quick method. Put two pots of water on the fire. While they are heating, begin removing the shells from the acorns. This can be quite a task if the acorns are still somewhat fresh and not dried out. I have set freshly-collected acorns into the hollow of a rock, hit them with another rock, then easily removed the shells. I put the acorn meats into the first pot, and continue removing shells until I have enough.

Let the water and acorns in the first pot boil for about 15 minutes, or until the water looks dark. Pour off that water but not the acorns, pour in hot water from your second pot, add cold water to the second pot, and put both pots back on the fire. Again let the first pot boil for 15 minutes or until the water gets brown, then change water, etc. Repeatedly boiling and changing water will remove the tannic acid in 45 to 60 min. Occasionally take out an acorn and taste it. After the acorns are no longer bitter, I change water and boil once more just to

make sure. You can then add wild vegetables and other items.
    Though quick, boiling removes much of the flavor and oil
of the acorns. Slower methods are better for nutrition and
taste - and don't require metal pots and fire.
    Neat but not quick. Shell the acorns and leave them
whole. Put them into a mesh bag. (An onion bag
is suitable if it doesn't have any holes big enough for the
acorns to slip through.) Place the bag of acorns in a flowing
stream, secured so it does not drift away. The running water
will leach out the tannic acid in 2 to 7 days, depending on
species. (Various quicker methods that use cold or warm water,
require grinding the acorns. Described in original article.)
    Acorns are 65% carbohydrates, 18% fat, 6% protein. Their
flavor is somewhat like graham crackers but highly variable.
    Though the leaching removes most of the tannic acid, a
little remains. If you start eating many acorns frequently,
add a pinch of charcoal to your acorn products. That will
neutralize the tannic acid. Christopher Nyerges (much shortened from Wilderness Way v6n4, sent by Bruce of BC)

(Comment:) Many edible plants contain some tannic acid. They
include thea (ordinary tea, esp if boiled long), coffee, some
grapes and wines, and (I suspect from the taste) artichokes.
According to the authors of "Why We Get Sick" (reviewed in Sep
02 DP), humans can detoxify small amounts of tannic acid.
Also, many people seem to like the taste (an indication that,
as with many substances, small amounts may be beneficial even
though large amounts are toxic ?).

Be careful if gathering mushrooms to eat.
    Many species of wild mushrooms grow naturally in our area.
Some are delicious, but many may not be edible, and a few have
potent toxins that can permanently damage organs - or kill.
    ACCURATELY IDENTIFY each and every mushroom as an edible
species before eating. Despite folklore to the contrary,
there are no simple tests that will distinguish edible from
poisonous species. Many edible species have toxic look-alikes:
learn what these are and don't rely only on photographs or
drawings. When in doubt, throw it out !
    Never eat any mushrooms raw. Cooking improves flavor,
digestibility, available nutrients; and eliminates some toxins.
However, cooking will not eliminate all kinds of toxins and
will not make poisonous mushrooms edible.
    When trying a mushroom species for the first time, eat
only a teaspoon full and wait at least 24 hours before eating
any more - even if other people have eaten the species without
problems. You may have an allergy to that particular species,
just as some people are allergic to shrimp or strawberries.
Keep a whole uncooked sample in a cool place in case you later
need to confirm identification. Do not consume alcohol when
first trying a mushroom. That may intensify allergic reactions. Also, some Coprinus with alcohol cause discomfort.
    Do not eat spoiled/moldy/rotten mushrooms.
    Do not eat fungi growing on ornamental trees. The fungi
may absorb toxins in the wood. (A recent illness in Eugene
was caused by eating Laetiporus growing on black locust.)
    Be careful where you collect edibles. Mushrooms can
readily pick up chemicals from the environment. Avoid lawns
where fertilizers or pesticides might have been applied; the
sides of busy roads; near old dump sites. Cascade Mycological
(Comments:) Mushrooms were esp bountiful here this   Society
autumn. We ate many, mostly chantrelles. From Sept thru Nov,

we probably averaged at least a pound a day, each. We heard
that chantrelles were selling for $6 to $9 a pound in stores,
and gatherers were getting $4-$5. But we were too remote for
selling to be practical. A few times we had slight nausea or
louder-then-usual ear whistling (indication of toxin ?) which
soon went away. We were not eating any other suspect food.
But the symptoms did not correlate much with amount eaten. On
a few days when we ate several pounds and nothing else, we had
no adverse symptoms (other than not feeling peppy - mushrooms
are not high in calories). Was the cause a little rot or mold
we failed to trim off ? Or had one of the mushrooms grown near
a poisonous specie and absorbed a little of its toxin ?
     We usually cooked them alone, so that remaining silt
(impossible to clean perfectly) dropped to the bottom of the
broth and did not contaminate other food. We put in little or
no water, because the mushrooms quickly exuded ample broth.
     Mushrooms are richer in B vitamins than most vegetables.
But we wonder how well they digest. Though we tried to chew
them thoroughly before swallowing (not easy, because they are
slippery), our feces became voluminous. Holly & Bert, Dec 04

More about Mexican border opportunities and problems.

Algodones (west of Yuma) exists to take care of gringo
dental and medical problems. Small town, many English-speaking
dentists and MDs, laid-back border crossing. I don't know much
about hotels and camping opportunities there, but Yuma is not
far away. Michael Trend, AZ 853, 2 June 2004

     Since May, Nogales police have arrested 12 Arizonans
during an enforcement effort targeting people suspected of
buying tranquilizers or painkillers without Mexican prescriptions. In Sonora state, an American prescription must be shown
to a Mexican physician who will rewrite it, for it to be legal.
"We won't go back to Nogales, said Karen Tafoya, 54, of
Apache Junction AZ. "We've gone to Algodones and always felt
very safe." Several other Phoenix-area residents said they
have not encountered problems in Algodones. They say pharmacies there cater more to their needs and rarely require
prescriptions, so they are shifting their business to there.
     Noe Ramirez, an employee of Farmacia Algodones, said no
arrests are happening in Algodones because it is in Baja,
whereas Nogales is in Sonora, and the prescriptions laws differ.
(from yumasun.com 25June04, sent by Michael Trend)

     I drove from Mexicali to San Luis Rio Colorado today. When
I crossed to AZ, I got asked for ID for the first time in ages.
Evidently, border officials are now supposed to ask for ID from
everyone who crosses. I don't know how thorough the checks
will be, or for how long. Michael Trend, 20 July 04

     Algodones caters more to gringos than does Mexicali, so
prices tend to be higher. Michael, 12 Oct 04. (Recent prices
of Michael's dentist in Mexicali: crown $125, cleaning $25,
fillings $30-$50, extractions $30. "She can get along in
English, and is connected with a great endodontist who is
virtually bi-lingual." Also see DP Dec03 p.7, May 03 p.4,
Sep 02 p.12, June 02 p.6; Sep 01 p.14, Apr 01 p.7, May 99 p.3.)

Suggestions if driving in Mexico.
    Don't drive at night. Dusk and dark are the worst times
for hitting black cows and brown burros.
    Mexico has fewer accidents than U.S. or Canada, and most
are fender-benders. During 4 months in Mexico, Liz and I saw
only one accident; whereas during 6 days in Texas we saw two,
including a high-speed collision that destroyed two cars and
several people (two ambulances in attendance). I would rather
drive in Mexico than the U.S. Most Mexican drivers are very
good defensively. They survive by remaining aware of what goes
around them; always on the lookout for the unexpected.
    Mexican drivers seem to do as they please. Laws are used
only in law courts. Because, under Mexico's Napoleonic Code,
you are assumed guilty, it seems laws are made to be broken.
    Newer buses often display a 95 km/hr sign. Any good bus
driver knows that is the minimum speed expected. No one stops
at railway crossings. They merely reduce speed, look, and keep
going. Some crossings are topes (speed bumps) in disguise.
    Every village has at least one pair of the dreaded topes,
10 to 15 cm high, approx a metre wide, and usually all the way
across a road. They can be of concrete, blacktop, bricks, or
shiny steel hemispheres. If you don't slow to a crawl, they
will tear your suspension apart. As warnings, there MIGHT be
official highway signs showing 2 or 3 bumps, or handpainted
boards (probably put there by local victims) saying TOPES.
Other indications that topes are near: "40 km/hr maximo"
(almost certain); "65 km/hr maximo" (probable); sounds of
trucks accelerating; sign with village name; rocks piled on
sides of road (to prevent going around topes); people selling
items on side of highway (they stand where vehicles go slow).
    On highways, when a truck in front of you turns on his
left signal light, it means it is safe to pass if you are not
being passed and you are quick. Whereas, in cities when the
same driver signals left, it means he is going to turn left.
Sometimes drivers forget where they are or forget to signal.
    Highways are well marked, with numerous directional signs
at intersections. And there are lots of km-to-go signs -
except when you are low on gas. Getting lost in cities is easy;
just follow your map or rusted detour signs. Mexicans don't
take down detour signs - maybe they will be needed again. If
you get a map, get a good one that shows all of the streets.
Don't worry about being able to read the street names; you
won't find the faded street signs because they've been painted
over, fell off, or are hidden behind trees.
    Canadian and U.S. auto insurance is of no value south of
the Mex border. You don't need insurance in Mexico but it is a
gamble: save money and drive carefully, vs have an accident
and go to jail. The first time we went to Mexico, we got Mex
insurance; the second time we didn't bother. John & Liz Plax-
ton (from "RVing in Mexico & C.Am", Faraway, 1996; sent by Bruce)

(Comments by Bruce:) Starting from Kelowna BC, John & Liz
visited Mexico in 1994/95, in a Class C Motorhome, and on a 305
cc motorcycle. Before going, they'd had only 20 hrs of Spanish
lessons and no understanding of Spanish phonetics.
    After reading Michael Trend's short letter (good tips) in
Ab #3, I looked at guide books available. One of the best was
Lonely Planet's "Mexico", 8th edition. It had articles on
cycling, train travel, hostels, lesser-known cities/towns, and
other info not in Frommers and other big-name guide books.
Also recommended: "The People's Guide to RV Camping in Mexico"
Carl Franz; Travelers Guide to Mexican Camping" Mike and Terri
                Dwelling Portably   April 2005

Church;   "Nothing to Declare" (woman travels alone)Mary Morris.
     Mexican beaches are considered public property. You can
camp for nothing at most of them, but security non-existant.
     Cabanas are basically huts with palm-thatch roofs. Some
have dirt floors and nothing inside but a bed. Others have
electric lights, bug nets, frig, fan.   Rentals, $10-$35 U.S.

Hitchiking and busing in Mexico.

     I had reached San Francisco before realizing that I had
forgotten to bring my passport. I called my roomates in
Portland, but their search was unsuccessful, so I entered
Mexico without it. Just across the border, I tried to get a
tourist visa. The immigration officer would not accept my
drivers license. He wanted a passport or birth certificate.
Finally he accepted a photocopy of an expired passport (which
I had along because it showed me with long hair). 90-day visa.
     I met up with Andy a week later in Xalapa, Veracruz. We
planned to hitchike through Veracruz, then to Chiapas (Andy's
plan) or to Yucatan (my plan). Andy nixed my plan by inform-
ing me that the Yucatan Penisula was, not the endless jungle
I had imagined, but a hot dry plateau. Though this was my
third year in Mexico, I had never read far enough in any
travel guide to rid me of my misconceptions.
     Andy and I bussed to the edge of Xalapa. For hitching,
we picked a bad fake-out spot where we thought people were
pulling over for us only to realize they were turning onto a
gravel road 50 feet past us. I was strumming my jarana,
hoping people would be more likely to pick up a musician.
     Four hours passed before a semi-truck heading for the
port of Veracruz picked us up. The truck had poor suspension,
bouncing us up and down on the bed behind the driver and
co-pilot. He asked me to play a song, but I was jerked around
so much that my hand kept missing the strings. Three hours
later, we got off at intersection with south-bound highway.
     It was early afternoon. We had chosen to avoid the four-
lane behemoth, and were on a two-lane highway that rolled down
the coast. No rides ! At sunset I decided that all the
stories I'd heard about ease of hitching in Mexico were bull.
It's not any easier than in the U.S. It's just wait, wait,
wait, ride, wait. Fortunately there is a difference between
the U.S. and less-affluent countries. In the U.S., if you find
yourself on I-5 at sunset halfway between nowhere and somewhere,
you are stranded. You can sit in an all-night gas station
drinking coffee and asking customers for rides. Or you can
sleep in a field next to the highway. Whereas in Mexico, where
busses are most peoples' transportation, you can flag down the
next one and keep traveling - until your money runs out.
     I'd been on that highway before and knew that it came to
the beach about 30 km ahead. So I suggested we bus it, spend
the night on the beach, and resume hitching in the morning.
     At sunrise, we swam in the brownish-blue water of the Gulf
of Mexico before returning to the highway. The day was hot and
there were no trees for shade. We waited 5 hours for our first
ride, with a quiet friendly grain salesman in a VW bug.
Unfortunately, he was only going 60 km. The area we passed
through, Los Tuxtlas, became an incredibly green patchwork of
plantations: coffee, tobacco, banana. Our next ride was with
an old man who just pointed at the back of his truck and said
get in. It was a tall wood-slat-sided truck; the kind used
to haul pigs or a heap of used tires. After we were in back,
he seemed to forget about us. He stopped along the way to chat

with people in small towns. He even stopped for dinner at a
restaurant without bothering to let us out. Sometime after
dark, I had to jump from my sleeping bag and move out of the
way as he hoisted a refrigerator into the truck with us.
     We landed inside the city of Coatzacoalcos late at night.
By then, I was tired of hitching and frustrated with our snails
pace, so I told Andy I wasn't about to spend 3 more days on the
side of the highway just to save $12 bus fare. He wanted to
keep at it, but that also meant finding a place to sleep for
the night, so he gave in and we hopped on a bus toward Palenque.
(From a zine by Skot, ±2002. The author may be Michael Cabello
who had a long report in Apr 01 DP. From Chile, bi-lingual.)

A short freight hop as a learning experience.
     I chose the evening of Thursday, 4 July 03, to embark on
an adventure in the spirit of those who, for me, are some of
North America's greatest heros: the truly tough men and women
who sleep under bridges, work for minimum wages - and think for
themselves. My home town, Peterborough, is on a hundred-mile-
long branch line of the Canadian Pacific that goes from Toronto
in the west to the end of the line at Havelock in the east.
Enough volume is shipped to warrant an out-and-back train from
Toronto almost every day. There is no set schedule, but for a
few weeks prior to my trip I had payed close attention to when
trains were moving and in what direction. I had Friday off
work, and thus had time to ride a train and return home in time
for work Sat morning. Late Thursday night seemed a good time
to catch an eastbound, and I knew from experience that trains
travel very slowly through Peterborough, especially at night
when they don't whistle for crossings. If nothing came during
the night, I would wait until noon, sleeping near the tracks.
     At 11 pm I bicycled downtown, locked my bike at a grocery
store near the old station, and wandered around for a while,
finally settling down on a bench by the river to read (always
bring a book). When I became sleepy, I checked the most obvious
spot first: in the bushes near a bridge. TOO obvious. The
cardboard that I could barely see in the dark was already
occupied by some other tramp, who was invisible until I was
almost sitting on him. A quick apology and I was on my way, to
what turned out to be a better spot, near the station, which
would allow me to climb the train from the old platform. So
it was that I fell asleep in the bushes beside Jackson Creek,
across from the station, my bag tucked under my arm.
     I had slept about an hour when my rumbling ride came
along. As I stood up I saw the three bright lights of a freight
engine. It was moving very slowly and I was close, so I stayed
where I was until the engine units passed. Then I ran across
the small bridge to the station platform as the train was
passing it, grabbed a ladder, and climbed. Did I use one hand
or two ? Which foot went first ? Did I get on the grainer
platform from the side or the back ? I don't remember. I did
it all instinctively, making me think I was born to do this.
     An auto was at the first road crossing (about 25 metres
from my catch point), and the driver likely saw me settling in,
but that did not worry me. As we rolled across the Otonabee
River bridge, I became aware that I was on the 'wrong' end of
the grainer - where all the air brake equipment is; the result
of my 'just get on the damn thing' haste. And it was the FIRST
car behind the two engine units, causing me to worry that the
car might be set off at a siding. But I had not known what cars
might be behind. Fortunately, the train went unbroken.

Freight hoppers say that most rail workers are friendly, and Peterborough and Havelock seemed unlikely to have bulls. Even so, I hid inside the cubby hole with some old rags as we crossed the swing bridge over the Trent-Severn Canal.
The railway usually sends someone by road to turn the bridge just before and after the train passes, which allows boats to pass through most of the time. I did not want to be visible to the bridge swinger. Turned out, this was not a problem.

As we rolled past the siding at the east end of town, the train's slow speed made me think it might drop off cars. So I wore my pack and leaned out the side of the car, watching for anyone to climb down from the engine. I repeated this a few times during the trip; I was prepared to bail out if it seemed like anyone might see me. Finally, the train picked up speed.

I settled in for the ride and relaxed. The floor of the grainer was a safe spot to leave my bag, with no worry of it bouncing out onto the tracks. The compressor made a pretty good seat, although I wasn't sure how safe it was to leave my feet down among all the steel bars and lines.

I had wondered how loud the train would be. My only previous experience was riding a flat car for three days in Mexico (with the bull's permission). Noise had not been a problem there. But down by the wheels between two empty grainers, earplugs are a great asset. Every once in a while I took them off to hear the roar and clatter of steel.

The urban fog of light was left behind, revealing a cloudless night full of stars. Farms went by at 30 miles per hour, seeming fantastic. Grade crossings flash by, some lit, others dark. The whistle wails regardless. We cross rivers. The old grain elevator at Indian River siding stands somberly in the dark, a reminder of days before trucks. And out from behind it, like a fire on the horizon, the moon is climbing orange and crescent through the trees. As the train slows once again, I climb to the top of the car to take in this festival of light: to the left, the Big Dipper and Belt of Orion. Out in front, the trees illuminated by the headlights. They light up a power line suspended across the track; reminding me that being up that high is not a good idea, although that line had ample clearance. As the train swayed from side to side, I climbed back down to the safety of the platform.

The only town on the way to Havelock is Norwood. We barely slow: apparently the residents don't mind the sounds as we whistle and roar past, crossing the main street on an overpass. Soon after, highway 7 curves in parallel to the rails. Little traffic: a few late-night trucks. One passes, slightly faster.

We slow as Havelock approaches. As the train comes to a stop for the brakeman to throw a switch, I disembark. No sense riding into the yard; though little chance of being caught.

I settle down in some long grass. I hope a train will leave for Toronto early in the morning. That would provide a good opportunity for photos; I didn't take any at night. But the crew slept until ten, then bumped cars around for an hour, then headed north to the mines at Nephton. Fortunately I got a ride home with an acquaintance working in Havelock. Sloth (www.northbankfred.com/sloth2.html , sent by Bruce of BC)

Personal rail-vehicles are much used in Columbia.
Some railroads have stopped running trains but, like in U.S., the tracks are often left in place. Two sizes of rail-vehicles were shown on Mexican TV.
A small one holds two people. A long pole is used to push

it along. It is light enough for two people to remove it from
the tracks if it meets another rail vehicle.
     A big one can carry 8 people or considerable cargo. It
rides on 4 metal wheels. To propel it, a motorcycle is mounted
so its rear wheel rests on the track. A 125cc engine suffices
because it travels slow, 15 or 20 mph max. It has the right-
of-way if it meets a smaller rail-vehicle. If used as bus,
fare for a 20-mile ride is about $1 U.S. Herbert Diaz, CA 939,
                                                          Sep04

Rides unicycle in places where bicycles can't go.

     Tom Acevedo starts at the foot of Mary's Peak southwest of
Philomath and wheels all the way to the top; then all the way
back down. "It's called the 'evil trail' because there are
lots of rocks and tree roots, and most of it is steep." Even
some mountain bicyclists fear it. Tom unicycles every day,
rain or shine. "I go out in McDonald Forest mostly and also on
the Bald Hill path and the trails in Peavy Arboretum" When he
is at the coast, he unicycles on the sand at the edge of the
water. He has also unicycled with groups in the woods behind
Fall City, in Sierras, in Utah, at Lake Tahoe. "We get on the
internet to find one another and then agree where to meet."
     Tom, age 50, has a desk job at Hewlett-Packard. He says
he was out of shape physically when he began. "At first I'd
practice for 15 minutes and then have to take a nap. I'd go
along the 3-foot-high fence in our driveway, ready to reach out
and grip it to steady myself. You do fall off when you're
learning - and afterwards too" although far less often, Knowing
how to fall is important. Protective gear helps prevent
injuries or at least lessen impacts. High-top boots provide
ankle support. Velcro keeps leg "armor" in place from ankle to
above knee. Elbow guards slip over the arm and fit snugly.
Gloves have padded leather palms. On top is a helmet.
     Tom has 5 unicycles plus parts for more. Why so many ?
The tire size determines the speed. Each tire size is for a
specific use and terrain. The bigger the tire, the shorter the
cranks. If too short, you can't stop yourself easily.
     The 36-inch-diameter 2¼-inch-wide Coker pneumatic tire is
for level trails. It can go faster than a person can run. But
Tom tries to keep it under 15 mph (it has brakes) so that he can
dismount by slipping forward off the seat and running.
     "This next one is my favorite. It's got hydraulic brakes,
a Yuni frame, and an inner tube in the seat for more comfort.
It has a 26" tire that is 3" wide. It is for mountain trails,
and can go through gravel and on grass and in places where
bicycles can't go. I can hop around on it like you do on a pogo
stick." And he does. Gloria Clark (Northwest Senior News, Aug
(Comment:) This article was much more informative than was 04)
the one from Atlantic Monthly in April 04 DP. Apparently the
wheel is direct drive, like on old-time high-wheel bicycles.
No gears. To change speed range, you change unicycles ! B & H

I lived on the water for 18 months - free.

     Free boats. (I even turned down a 35-foot motor boat.)
Free mooring - friends let me tie up to them. I like being on
the water. I met the Floating Neutrinos (who crossed Atlantic
Ocean in a boat built entirely of salvaged materials). They
make rafts, boats, docks out of free recycled materials. I've
done it too, and so have others. Basically: Get materials
that float (foam, plastic bottles, etc). Encase them (in fish-
nets, scrap wood, etc). Build on top of it. Zalia, OR 972

Choosing a boat for transportation or living on.
     Select your boat for the type of activity you intend, the
kind of water in which it will operate, the speed you will
require, and the sleeping/cooking accomodations you will need.
Keep your needs in mind when you look at or discuss boats.
     Three general types of boats: open boats with no accomo-
dations which may be used for fishing or water skiing; semi-
enclosed boats with minimal accomodations for two people;
fully-enclosed hulls you can live in. Visualize your trips.
How long will you be on the water ? How many people aboard ?
Thorough planning increases your chances of filling your needs.
     Long-distance sailboats are designed differently than
powerboats. They have slow displacement-speed hulls. For
ocean crossings, a sailboat with auxillary engine and adequate
accomodations is generally best. Endurance races across
oceans have involved both monohulls and multihulls. Much can
be learned from these demonstrations of strong hulls and
stronger crews, but don't choose a boat designed for racing
unless racing will be your primary activity.
     Most sailboats are sloop rigged, because one mast is less
expensive than two. However, for long-distance cruising, some
owners prefer a ketch rig (two masts) because, when wind speed
increases, they can furl (roll in) the mainsail and proceed at
optimum speed without excessive heel (tilt).
     The longer the boat, the more comforts it can accomodate,
but the more expensive it will be to buy and operate. Where
will you keep your boat ? What are the fees ? If the dock is
in a shallow waterway, the boat must be shallow draft. Deep-
keel ballasted sailboats are often restricted to deep water-
ways that have no bridges that would slow access to the ocean.
     A fishing boat for protected waters is usually a small
open boat with helm (controls) in the center or at bow so that
most of the deck is open to walk around on while boarding a
fish. But if going well offshore to fish, you will want a
different hull. Suitable boats usually have part of the
forward half fully enclosed and watertight so that water blown
aboard will be deflected and not swamp the boat. A deep V
(high deadrise) power boat is probably best for ocean fishing.
     If you plan scuba diving, the aft deck should have a
transom (swim) platform or a sloped ramp for easy access to
the water. Secure storage must be installed for air bottles,
regulators, wet suits. The forward half usually contains helm,
seating, galley, head. Arthur Edmonds (from summary/ad for
book "Buying a Great Boat", Bristol, off internet, from Bruce)

(Comment:) Used boats, usually in need of repairs, are sometimes offered cheap or free because the owners have no place
to put them. However, regardless of price, a boat (or any
item) is no bargain if it is not what you need. Holly & Bert

Some rivers are suitable for secluded houseboats.
     The floodlands and bayous of the Mississippi River and
its larger tributaries comprise thousands of acres, mostly
uninhabited and perhaps unowned. Many other rivers in at
least 20 states include such areas. Rarely traversed by
humans; the only visitors are hunters, fishers, trappers,
surveyors and engineers working on the river, biologists
studying the plants and animals, an occasional posse, some
adventurous explorers, and refugees from the rat-race.
     Rivers frequently change course, devouring old land and
creating new land that is unregistered and perhaps unknown.
Boundaries are usually vague. A close study of county records

and maps may reveal bits of land that nobody owns or that have been forgotten. Or, you might find a sizable mud bar left by a flood or channel-change, transplant willows and bushes onto it, seed it with edible weeds, riprap the up-current end with rocks so it won't wash away in the next flood, A new island !

Many sloughs are perfect for living: deep enough for big fish to lurk, and for mosquitos not to breed; and with enough level fairly-clear land for a garden, plus gathering grounds for wild fruits, berries, nuts, greens, etc.

Lost and wild animals live in those lands: horses, mules, cows, goats, fowls that have wandered or been abandoned, or lost from shipments or swept down the river and never found. If the creatures give birth, the young grow up feral and not owned. Some big predators live there and are seldom hunted because travel is difficult. Snapping turtles grow as big as wash tubs and can grab an adult bird swimming on the surface. In some places are alligators and alligator gar big enough to kill a cow or human. Ocean sharks sometimes swim up fresh-water rivers for hundreds of miles, and may remain in fresh-water lakes. Reportedly seen in remote places are 3-foot-tall red-furred primates that live in small families. They are primarily vegetarian and very secretive.

The riverbanks and floodplains are littered with debris from many floods: logs, planks, boards, boxes, small buildings, entire walls of houses with doors and windows, boats, chicken coops, pianos, light machinery attached to work tables, and anything else that will float. A shanty boat or small cottage can be built and furnished entirely from free findings.

A raft can be built by lashing together logs or timbers. For more floatation, lash empty sealed 50-gallon drums under it. To replace lost caps, drive wooden plugs into holes. Tar or paint the timbers and drums heavily and often to prevent rot and rust. Also tar the drums inside after thoroughly drying them, by pouring in thinned hot tar and rolling the drums around. Build a deck out of boards, and on that build a shack or rig a tent. Leave part of the deck vacant for sunning and fishing, and for maneuvering the raft.

At first, furnish your floating home with anything close at hand. Then, as you have time, search for better furniture. Walk along the high-water marks, indicated by small stuff deposited in bushes and tree branches which catch an amazing variety of items including many clothes. Look in the trees where high water may leave chairs and tables. Look in back-water driftwood piles for heavier objects which may be half-buried in mud. Metal objects heavier than water will be on the bottom, often in bedrock cracks or whirlpool holes where they were left when the swift currents that were rolling them, slow. If you can spot the natural eddies and backwaters of the various water levels, you will discover frequently replenished treasure troves. But test mud and sand before stepping on it. Some that looks solid will suddenly drop you in over your head. When exploring a new bar, esp one under water, carry a long long pole to arrest your plunge and help you scramble out.

A shantyboat, carefully situated and tied among the bushes, may never be seen even by boaters. Keep your home small and unobtrusive, either naturally weathered or painted a drab color. Don't attract attention. Most people won't bother you even if they find you. Don't leave obviously illegal items in sight. Check laws before hanging fish, crayfish, turtle (etc) traps.

Many river people use a big rock as an anchor. Do not anchor in the current: waterlogged tree trunks may roll down the bottom and roll over your anchor line, pulling your craft under water if your anchor line doesn't break first. The water level will rise and fall, and could deposit your boat on land. Listen to weather and water-release reports on radio.

There are several ways to move if you want to. Use sweeps (very long oars) which can be just wide boards bolted to 2-by-4s which are mounted on 4-by-4s attached to the sides of boat.

Or, in shallow water, you can pole. If the bottom is rock or gravel, shod one end of pole with sharp-pointed metal. Or, if the bottom is mud, attach a flat board: hinged on the end and braced so it opens to give broader traction when pushing, but folds when the pole is pulled from the muck.

Or, walk along the bank pulling the boat by ropes attached to bow and stern. If moving upstream, a pull on the stern rope steers the boat away from the bank; a pull on the bow rope steers the boat toward the bank. Even pulls on both ropes keep the boat moving. A few minutes practice will teach you.

For low speeds and short distances, a motor is probably too much trouble. Fuel, repairs, noise, licensing, rules.

Controlled drifting is usually safe IF you know what is ahead. Drifting when unaware, as from a broken or cut anchor line at night, can be very dangerous. You can be tipped over by an obstruction, stranded in mud, set on a bar, tangled in down trees, wrecked in rapids, or swept over a dam. Useful to have a government-survey river map.

The water will probably be contaminated. Boiling will not remove toxic chemicals. Nor will iodine or chlorine. A reverse-osmosis filter will clean anything, including ocean water, and is even better than distillation. Read carefully the spec sheet that comes with the filter. Paul Doerr (much condensed from Doe #49, 2002)

(Comments:) Many years ago, Paul traveled on his boat all the way from the East to the West Coast. Paul did not say how much and how recently he has lived on floodlands or bayous.

What does a river dweller do when a flood comes ? Perhaps if the flood isn't sudden, as the river rises and nearby land is submerged, s/he can keep moving the boat away from the increasingly swift currents in main channels; then, as the flood recedes, do the reverse - though might get stranded. B&H

Trouble in Seattle's "Jungle".

For a while, Franz Dyduch considered the homeless camped near his house, in the densely-wooded strip known as The Jungle, to be his neighbors. He fed their dogs and drank beer around their campfires. But in January the relationship began to sour. His home was burglarized weekly. When his daughter admonished the campers, she was pelted with rocks, and one morning she found human feces outside her dad's door. She attributes her 84-year-old father's fatal heart attack in April to the stress. "We've had homeless people who've been delightful neighbors for years, but they were different from the trash that harassed them and chased them out ... and took over." Others reported seeing open drug dealing, needles on school playgrounds.

The anger peaked in August with a series of burglaries. One resident came home to find a strange woman in her living room, filling bags with loot. The two fought before the burglar fled into the Jungle. Outraged neighbors armed with baseball bats descended on the Jungle but left without fighting.

Shannon Mills lost birth certificates, passports, check-books in a burglary. Worried about being the victim of identity theft, she joined a neighborhood group that organized

citizen patrols. She makes a distinction: the homeless people
are "not the ones breaking into our houses and stealing our
stuff. It's the criminal element that are ruining The Jungle."
     The Jungle has inspired controversy and brief hassles for
a decade. But a rising volume of complaints prompted the city
to launch a sustained assault. The estimated 80 Jungle
residents were given 24 hours notice to leave. Then state
crews mowed acres of underbrush to expose encampments. New
roads are being cut and graveled through The Jungle, allowing
police cruisers to patrol the area.
     A similar assault in 1998 provoked noisy protests. But
last month's eviction came as a surprise. Rev. Rick Reynolds,
director of Operation Nightwatch, sees it as evidence of a
"meaner mood" in tolerant Seattle. "I'd like to know where
they're supposed to go. They're not going to be able to (find
space) in the shelter system, and most don't have resources to
rent apartments. The pattern in big cities is: who can be
the meanest and shove them onto someplace else."
     A city liaison person claimed, "This is not a campaign on
the homeless. We wouldn't even be here if they treated the
environment and the neighbors with respect."
     Joe Doney lived in The Jungle in the mid 1990s during
another city assault. He found a cohesive community of people
who took turns guarding each other's belongings. The city is
"swatting the beehive. They are scattering the people."
     Last week, a handful had returned to the section north of
Beacon Avenue South. Complaints from neighborhoods abutting
I-5 green space to the north are on the rise, including the
foot of Capitol Hill and University District.
     A police sargent said, the police are stretched too thin
to issue reams of trespass violations. There have been "home-
invasion burglaries. That's the type of crime we go after.
Trespass is way way down the list." Jonathan Martin (from
Seattle Times 19 October 2003, sent by Roger Knights)

(Comments:) The problems mentioned are mostly CAUSED BY
GOVERNMENTS that criminalize drugs (as well as low-cost housing).
Most burglaries are to pay for drugs. If drugs were legal,
addicts could get enough money by (eg) collecting drink cans.
     I read: a century ago, before the War On (some) Drugs,
heroin was sold by drug stores; price about the same as
aspirin. But there were FEWER addicts than now, because there
were not huge profits and strong incentives to hook more people.
     Solutions ? Don't expect governments (which are, first
and foremost, giant terrorist gangs) to do much if anything
that is truly helpful. Instead, avoid or minimize time in big
cities and other places exposed to bullies (whether in uniforms
or not). Spread out, and have as neighbors only compatables.

Some Wal-Marts no longer allow over-nighting in parking lots.
     Many Wal-Marts long had an unofficial policy of letting
RVs and others   over-night, assuming that stay-overs will
buy stuff. We suspect the privilege is rescinded because of
abuse. We saw a rig pull in, drop its levelers, open the
awning, unhook a towed car - and leave to shop at another
store ! Others park by the front door and hog several spaces.
Others stay out of the way but seem to live there permanently.
     Some Wal-Marts are in shopping centers not owned by Wal-
Mart. They never allowed over-nighting. RVers who tried, were
chased off by security thugs or, worse, had their rigs towed.
     When we want to stay over at a shopping plaza, if there
isn't a mall manager, we try to ask the manager of the lead
                    Dwelling Portably   April 2005

store. If they say "no", we simply go to another place. But they almost always say "yes", as they're not often asked.
John & Rose Ward (from Living Mobile 3-04)

We have lived in various RVs and buses.

Now Millie and I are busy converting our third bus. Soon it will be our full-time rolling home. We have loved and used alternative energy systems for many years.

Our previous bus-home didn't have much: just two medium-size solar panels, a charge controller, and three big truck batteries. It worked fine in our situation then. But, if you are going to spend much time in the boondocks and want to be really comfortable and self sufficient, you need more.

For our new bus, we have a hefty array of four Uni-Solar panels (two 64 watt, two 22 watt), an Air-X Southwest wind-power generator, a solar hot-water pre-heating system, a composting toilet, a grey-water purification system, two solar air heaters, dual inverter system, solar oven, and other things.

We chose this system, instead of a typical mass-produced RV, because we like to travel but also like to be able to squat and live comfortably in one spot for a couple of months at a time. Our ideal situation is renting or land-sitting a place out in the country, which is usually quite a ways from the nearest RV dump station and electrical plug-in.

Millie and I don't like to stay long in campgrounds. That gets pretty expensive. More important, campgrounds are often noisy. We prefer being out in the country somewhere pretty.

A more important reason for our many alternative energy systems: we expect RISING COSTS for camping. Not just campground fees, but also dump station fees and propane costs. Dumping your holding tanks will get more expensive: many septic systems are overloaded; many cities and rural areas are having a problem handling all the sewage.

Electricity costs are rising too. WHEN (not if) California or other state has major black-outs/brown-outs again, the state will care more about its voters and their TVs and air-conditioners than about transient RVers. We can expect new legislation penalizing so-called recreational use of electricity in campgrounds during an emergency. We might be charged outrageous fees - or might not even be allowed to plug in.

Rather than bitch and moan after the fact, we can do something about it now. By adding a composting toilet to your rig, you avoid the hassle and growing cost of dumping a black-water tank. By having a realistic hybrid solar/wind system, you only plug in when you want to, not out of need. For water conservation, add a rain water collection system.

Upgrading our system is easy in our bus - in comparison to a "normal" house where they sometimes have to knock down walls and split open concrete floors. Forward thinking helps.

With our new systems, we only have to replenish propane, water, food. Our bus carries at least a month's supply of food at a time, and we never camp far from a water source. We are able to purify water from a stream or creek.

We will pre-heat our water using a solar system, which cuts propane consumption amazingly. We can use this water directly or, if we want it hotter, send it through our ten-gallon Atwood RV Hot Water Heater. When the sun is out, even in winter we can bake and cook using our Global Sun Oven. We have a Danby Consul Propane frig/freezer; efficient.

To warm our bus, we have a wall-mounted catalytic propane heater and a little stainless-steel wall-mounted Dickenson wood stove. It doesn't take up much room but is big enough to heat our bus. It gets out the condensation that builds up in a well-sealed RV that uses propane as its main heat source.

We will add a solar air heating system. They are easy to build, or you can buy pre-made. They are basically a rectangular box that is layered and covered with a suitable clear plastic or solar glass. They can either be mounted permanently on a vehicle's exterior, or designed to be taken off and stored for the summer. They work by thermal convection: taking air from inside the vehicle and passing it through the box where it is warmed by solar radiation. They quickly pay for themselves.

A system like ours isn't cheap. So far we have $8500 invested. But this kind of system allows you to camp comfortably in the middle of nowhere and be as self-sufficient as possible. You can put such a system together a piece at a time. But, if you can afford it, do it all at once. A big retrofit job can get messy. Michael and Millie (Sent by Bruce, off internet but no web addr. The Mobile Homestead, POB 6584, Sitka AK 99835)

(Comments:) Amazing - all the stuff they think they need to be comfortable. Some seems sensible: the solar items if they usually park where there is sun. A composting system may be worthwhile if someone is stationary enough to garden (see Ab #4). But carry it around on a bus ? Sanitary disposal of human waste is usually quite simple - especially in the middle of no-where (see May 96 DP).

Michael and Millie expect grid electricity to become very costly or hard to get. But propane, along with diesel fuel and gasoline, will likely become even more scarce and costly. There are more and easier ways to generate grid electricity than to extract or synthesize liquid and gas fuels. B & H

The "heat-resistant silicone rubber cement" is a special type.
(It was mentioned in April 04 DP, p.10.) It's called "RTV Silicone". Sold by auto parts stores and auto section of Walmart, etc. Comes in black, red, blue, clear. Zalia, Apr04

Hubbards Shoe Grease waterproofs leather well.
I've used it on hunting boots and other leather gear. Made in U.S. from pine tar and other ingredients. A small can lasts me a long time. Bruce of BC, 2004

Some shipping bags useful for temporary storage of big items.
Or even as giant sleeping bags. They have a thin paper-like material covering a p.u.c. plastic bladder type bag. Sizes 3 ft wide by 6 ft tall, and larger. I have occasionally seen them left in empty box cars with air trapped in them. They have small air valves somewhere on the outside. Just don't get caught by a bull (cop) trying to salvage them. Bruce

Aluminized-plastic "emergency" blankets at a dollar store.
$1.25 Cdn, made in China. I've also found tools, hardware, magnifiers, reading glasses, even eyeglass repair kit.
Bruce
(Question:) Were they the kind with aluminum that easily rubs off the plastic ? Or more durable ? I'd like to try such material on solar cookers in place of aluminum foil.

I find many uses for disposable plastic gloves outdoors.
Such as picking up greasy or sooty things around camp. Although not as tough as latex or nylon disposables, they are adequate for many jobs. I go through many pairs a month. At a dollar store I bought 60 pairs for $1.25. Bruce of BC

Clothes pins have many uses besides hanging clothes.

Eg: clamping glued pieces together while the glue hardens; holding fabric while sewing; temporarily holding a cord in place (may be quicker than tieing and untieing a knot); hanging messages on lines where there is no bulletin board; holding open a curtain or drape; closing plastic bags containing things I want to access often, or quicker than a rubber band allows; serving as extra hands while doing complex tasks.

I keep several clothes pins within sight in my living/ working area, so they are accessible, and so they may remind me that I have what I need. Julie Summers, 1999

(Addendum:) If a stronger grip is needed than the clothes pin's spring provides, after I put on the clothes pin, I wind a thin rubber strap (cut from innertube) or long rubber band several times around clothes pin between its pivot and jaws.

I sometimes do this when tieing out a plastic tarp, to grip its edge without bunching it (as does a ball tie, and to a lesser extent the grip-clips sold). I roll the tarp several times around a twig, grip that with a spring clothes pin, strengthen grip with a rubber strap, then put the tie-out cord through the spring. (Illo in Apr92 DP or 95-6 Summary). Bert

Vise easily improvised using a stump.

This can firmly hold an object being worked on, such as wood being carved or metal being filed.

Select a stump a few inches in diameter that is still firmly anchored in the ground (roots not yet rotten). Split its top downward a few inches by sawing, or by tapping with a small log on the back of a strong knife. Spread the split with some kind of wedge (thick knife, chisel, sharply rock, carved stick). Insert into the split, the object to be gripped. Remove the wedge. Tighten the grip by winding a rubber strap many times around the stump. (If no elastic strap, strong cord can be substituted. To tighten, insert a stick between one loop of the cord and the stump, and twist the loop of cord.)

If the object is narrow, the strap can be below it (as shown). If the object is wide, to keep it in the split while working on it, may be necessary to put the strap above it; in which case, before winding on the strap, wrap a cord tightly around the stump below the bottom of the split to prevent the split from extending downward and weakening the grip. Bert

Northern Bush Craft, by Mors Kochanski.

"This book is not simply a manual on wilderness camping or survival, but rather discusses the basic existence skills that allow you to live in the bush on an indefinite basis with minimal dependence on technological materials and tools." Unlike primitive-skills books devoted to stone-age methods, this book emphasizes early iron-age methods, especially use of a steel knife and axe. This 2nd edition is profusely illustrated with over 300 line drawings and 34 color photos (the latter sensibly grouped in back, minimizing printing costs).

I highly recommend this manual to anyone who, after long careful preparation, plans to move far back into the northern

Alberta wilderness or similar forests and seldom if ever come out. (A broad belt of Northern Forests with similar climate and plants and animals, extend across Canada and curve south into U.S.)

Much of the contents are not too relevant to people like us who are usually within a few-days hike/bike of a sizable city. However, almost anyone will find info that is useful at times. One risk: some readers could get so fascinated by bush crafts as art, that they neglect methods that are less impressive but more practical in their situations.

Of most interest to us, was the chapter on saws, the book's shortest (10 pages). "The saw and axe are complementary." The axe is more hazardous, "requiring experience and constant attentiveness to use safely" - esp dangerous after dark. Whereas a saw may be used by a blind person for many jobs. "The axe takes weeks of constant use to master, whereas the saw requires a few hours...." Most of the work is done with the saw; the axe is back-up. Limbing is easier with the axe. "Wedges are easily made and pounded in with an axe. The axe is more versatile" and is chosen if limited to one tool.

A saw "can fall and section a tree with a fraction of the exertion" an axe requires, "and with greater convenience in confined or awkward situations, such as cutting in dense growth or above the head. With the assistance of wedges, a saw can fall a tree in directions impossible with an axe alone.... The saw can make squared ends ... or boards with a minimum of waste." A hand-powered saw is quieter than an axe. "The axe is more durable.... The cutting edge can be maintained with locally-found natural stones." A saw blade is comparitively fragile.

"A saw frame (of a bow saw) should be heavy enough to keep its blade under considerable tension." Function and durability should not be sacrificed for compactness and portability. "All saw blades should have guards to prevent cuts.... Using a saw above the head puts sawdust in the eyes.... Keep the eyes closed enough to help the eyelashes exclude the dust."

"A gently used saw will stay in working order for a long time.... Use (only) the weight of the saw at first.... As you become more skillful, you may apply downward force with the wrist of the hand holding the saw. When you can use the saw smoothly and unconsciously after having developed a sensitivity to its cutting action, you will know how much force to use to make it cut even faster.... If too much force is used, you will tire quickly. Any technique that adversely affects tooth arrangement should be avoided, such as twisting, kinking, bending, heavy pushing or pulling or downward force." Cutting close to the ground so that dirt gets into the cut, or sawing sandy driftwood, will quickly dull a blade. Sharpening gets 4 pages.

Axes get 34 pages. "The full-size axe with a handle length of about a metre is the safest as it normally deflects into the ground before reaching any part of the body." The hatchet, or short-handled axe, though the most portable, is the most dangerous. However, Mors tells how to use hatchet least riskily.

Tree falling gets 12 pages. Falling is dangerous, esp if tree is bigger than a foot diameter or crowded or dead or leaning. Many cautions given, including some I don't recall in "Professional Timber Falling" (review in June 1989 DP).

Knives and knife-sharpening get 26 pages. Knives are versatile. Eg, by bending a wrist-thick limber tree, a sharp knife can cut it in one stroke. Many tips are given for efficient use and safety. Some of the techniques shown seem risky to me unless one is very skilled and careful. Not mentioned: jury-rigging a vise to hold the wood (see p. 1).

Dwelling Portably   September 2005

Fire craft gets 60 pages. "When all else fails, fire is the simplest means of providing comfort and warmth against cold and wet in the Northern Forests. If you were dressed in the old European tradition, with numerous layers of fluffy wool adequate to deal with bitter cold, you would likely be wearing about 9 kg (20 lbs) of clothing. If you were unable to dry your clothing out, within 5 days you would be carrying 6 kg more weight of accumulated frost. The efficiency of your clothing would be so impaired by this frost build-up you could die of hypothermia within a week." Not mentioned: wearing a vapor barrier to keep body moisture out of the clothing. A big plastic bag, with holes cut for neck and arms, may suffice. For comfort I wear it over the inner layer; not next to skin.

"When you stop moving in cold weather, the first thought should be to light a fire. Your hands should not be allowed to become so numb that fire-lighting becomes difficult...." Bow drills get 14 pages, flint and steel 4 pages, matches one page. (Not mentioned: propane lighters; big flexible plastic lens, which can ignite even damp tinder quite quickly - but you do need some sun.) Kindlings get 10 pages; fire arrangements 7 pages. For most uses, esp for warmth with an open-fronted shelter, Mors prefers a fire with logs laid parallel. However, if the only fuel is long poles and you lack a saw or axe to cut them, or if a fire is wanted only for cooking, cross the poles in a star array and light them where they cross. Pot support gets 8 pages; cooking 12 pages.

Fire safety gets 5 pages. "A common, though unnecessary practice, is to ring open fires with stones", believing that "the stones confine the fire and make it safer; yet many forest fires are in fact traced to such fireplaces." When the fire is extinguished, "stones that are not moved aside can harbour hot spots... There are, however, justifiable uses of stones in a fire: to store warmth in a closed shelter; to support pots when no other means are available." Not mentioned: rocks provide a low wind break, so that gusts are less likely to scatter glowing embers. With any fire, unless roots are removed from soil or the soil is very damp, combustion may spread through underground roots that act like fuses.

Making cord from natural materials gets 12 pages. "The time and effort in making a cord should be matched to its intended use. A quickly and crudely made grass rope will do as a lashing in shelter building. A carefully and precisely twisted bow string may take hours to make."

Shelters get 34 pages. Most are open-fronted, used with a fire in front. To be effective, "the occupant must sleep parallel to a fire that is as long as he is tall. The back of the shelter must be near enough to the fire to be warmed by it" and very close to occupant to prevent cold air infiltrating between occupant and shelter. "The bed, the fire, and the wind must be parallel to each other" so that the smoke blows away instead of blowing or eddying into the shelter.

"The proper management of a fire in front of an open shelter demands constant attention resulting in relatively short periods of rest.... Whatever needs to be warmed must be positioned close to the fire and exposed directly to the radiation. Any warmed air rises, providing little warmth...."

"The conical shelter is very efficient. It provides a large floor space in relation to the amount of cover required. The shape allows for standing room in the middle, and an easily heated low overhead volume. The design is stable in wind and useful in heavier forms of construction." Also, unlike a dome, a cone has no flat area on which rain could puddle and then drip through any leak; and, if big sheets are available, a cone can easily be efficiently and snugly covered by wrapping.

"Birch bark makes an excellent cover that is reasonably portable. It can be peeled almost all year around." Processing birch bark gets 12 pages. Formerly, most Northern Forest nomads used tanned hides. Felt mats were popular in some places. "Hair or wool covers have a good reputation for being rot resistant, insulative, rain deflective, light and durable." Also common: "mats woven from various weeds". "In Lapland, natural cover materials were replaced with canvas in summer and horse blankets in winter. Now, such covers are made of durable woven polyethylene." That was the only mention of plastics. Plastics may have disadvantages in Northern Forests: easily melted or ignited; not very durable; not easily repaired; some kinds brittle when very cold. But why didn't Mors discuss them ? Perhaps, as a Wilderness Living Skills Instructor, Mors often leads expeditions of people who don't like the look of plastics, especially in a wilderness setting.

Enclosed shelters get only 7 pages. Most are snow caves. Any enclosed shelter is warmest if the entrance is well below the sleeping level so that warmed air does not escape when the entrance is opened. The final "ideal shelter, difficult to achieve with wilderness materials", has a cover that is "portable with a reflective inner lining, opaque to vision but translucent to day light." What material ? Not said.

Useful plants of the Northern Forests get 60 pages: paper birch, alders, white and black spruces, lodgepole and jack pines, balsam and subalpine firs, poplars, quaking aspen, willows, saskatoon, red osier dogwood. Ribbed baskets get 4 p.

Moose get 18 pages; varying hares 12. Anatomy, habitats, habits; how to call, hunt, butcher, tan, and use all parts.

2nd edition 1988, 303 p. 5x8, $13 cover price; Lone Pine Publ, 414-10357-109 St, Edmonton AB T5J 1N3. (Thanks to Bruce of BC for sending. He says there is now a 3rd ed. Revu, H&B)

I broke a Mora camp-knife blade during sub-zero cold.
I was prying on a big dry log. The knife had cost me nothing; I'd found it two years before. But, to replace it, I paid $14 Cdn for a new Frost knife. Both Mora and Frost (brand) knives, made in Sweden, are often recommended on survival web sites for value and reliability. Bruce of BC

My Swiss Army knife broke three times.
The first two times I sent it back to Switzerland (lifetime guarantee). But the third time I said "NO" ! Now I use a stainless steel 'US' military pocket knife. Cost one-third as much and has not broken. Zalia, OR 972, April 04

The $6 Walmart Multi Tool is not as good as a Leatherman.
But it will do 80% of what a Leatherman will; plus I can afford to replace it if it gets lost or stolen. I have used it to do repairs on my bicycle. Zalia, OR 972, April 04

Repairing sails without sewing.
I use heavy dacron or spectra fabric patches, plus 3M 5200 fast cure and 3M 950 seam stitch. Put a plastic sheet under the ripped area, to work on. Wear rubber gloves. For big repairs, enlist extra hands. Leave frayed yarns and pin in place. Then place seam-stick "sutures" across the rip. Apply thin beads of 5200 close to both sides of the rip

and also about a half inch inside the outside edge of the patch, all the way around. Carefully lay the patch in place, then apply firm pressure with a plastic squeegee. D.Smith, FL 322,

(Comment:) Sails must withstand much force. So that method might also do tents and heavy garments. I've read, most sails are polyester, some are cotton. So, before trying to repair other fabrics, I'd test scraps or consult 3M's spec. H & B

Are ice sailboats useful for transportation ?

For a while during childhood, I lived near a sizable northern lake that froze over most winters. I recall seeing ice boats. They went much faster than water sailboats, I suppose because friction of a skate on ice is much less than friction of a hull in water. They may have been used for transportation as well as play. (When not frozen, travel to/ from that lake's only city was quicker by passenger boat than by bus, even though the boat was slower, because the road went round about, while the boat went direct.) Bert, Dec 04

Precautions if traveling on ice.

Winter 1997 was a bad time to go onto ice in northeastern U.S. In January, a pair of cousins who drove onto a Maine lake, lost their 4x4 and almost their lives. A week later, a night-time father-and-son snowmobile ride across a frozen pond ended with only the son coming home. Of the approx 4000 Americans who drown each year, half of them do so in the off season. Though falls through ice accounted for only 2% of snowmobile accidents, they caused 18% of snowmobile deaths.

The surest way to reduce your risk is to know the ice. Never rely on appearance alone. Snow can camoflage thin ice, ridges can obscure cracks, open water can resemble ice in the sun's glare. Visual danger signs include slush, cracks meeting at right angles, branches frozen in the crust.

Before stepping onto ice, look for posted warnings. If none, test the ice every 15 feet with an ice chisel. If it doesn't break through, it's probably safe to walk on. Then, to determine if it is vehicle-ready, go out on foot with an ice auger, drilling small holes at 150-feet intervals where you intend to drive. One formula: vehicle weight in tons, find its square root, multiply by 4; equals minimum thickness in inches. 4" for 200 pounds, 6" for 2000, 8" for 4000.

As for when to start checking, forget the calender. In Maine, "I've seen ice in November able to hold a man and a machine, whereas last winter we never got enough ice." Temperatures should be in the low teens or lower for a solid week before you should think about walking on ice.

If you go on the ice, go with a friend, wear a whistle, avoid hip waders or boots that can fill with water, and bring 50 feet of rope. If your friend falls in, "there is nothing worse than standing there and not being able to do anything." If you fall through, remain calm - don't waste energy. You have a few minutes to get yourself out before hypothermia sets in. Tell your partner to back off. If he has a rope, rest your arms over the edge of the ice and have him throw an end to you. If not, have him find a long stick. And carry an accessible knife, screwdriver, or something else pointed to stab into the ice to help haul yourself out. Otherwise, face the direction from which you came (where the ice will probably be strongest), place your arms flat over the edge, rock yourself up and down a few times, and hoist yourself over. Then stay low and slither away fast. Paul Scott (from Men's J, Feb 2000, sent by Lance)

A line across raging river allowed safer crossing.

A few winters ago, to help set up and stock a base camp, I had to repeatedly cross a small but fast-flowing river with heavy backpack loads. The thigh-deep stream had an uneven rocky bottom not visible through the silt-laden water.

During low water of autumn, I had scouted a shallow place and rigged twine across. I had only hay-twine, used. I chose unfrayed pieces, not yet cut, or else cut with the knot (from hay bailing) at one end. I tied them together using the hitch (in Oct94 DP and Summary) that doesn't weaken twine much. I tied two lengths of the twine (for redundancy), separately but adjacent, to trees on opposite sides approx ten yards back from the banks. I put the twine quite high so that any snags being swept down stream would hopefully not catch on it.

Just before crossing, I slacked the twine, so I could cross a few yards downstream of the anchor trees, to put less stress on the twine. I removed pants, but left on tennies and let them get wet. I held the twine on my downstream side so, if I lost hold, the twine would remain within reach. I kept my feet spread apart upstream-downstream, and braced myself fore-aft by keeping tension on the fore twine - facing toward the anchor tree I was approaching.

If I had not prepared twine, I might have tied a longer line to one tree and crossed farther downstream. Bert, OR 973

I use a fishing pole as a bicycle flag pole.

If it hits (eg) an overhead branch, it gives and bends instead of breaking - and it is also usable for fishing. I attach the pole to the bike with hose clamps, or insert it into an aluminum tube (doesn't rust) attached to bike rack. I tie on more than one flag, streamer, windsock for extra visibility and safety. I've used fishing poles this way since 1985. Zalia

I have caught long rides on tractor-trailer flatbeds.

I sneak on and hide under tarps that were loose or not snugged down. I mostly do this at night. I have never been caught, but I don't do it often. Bruce of BC, 2004

I built a big horse-drawn caravan for $1500.

My old gypsy caravan, in which I had lived for 14 years, was only 8 feet long. Over half of that was occupied by a full size bed. With my daily cheese-making and cooking, it was very crowded. So I was ready for something larger.

I already had wagon running gear ($350) to build on. So, when in March 03 I sold some goats (3 milkers, a buck, 9 kids) for $500, I invested the money in lumber, plywood, and iron supports. Later I spent about $600 for paint, trim, insulation, etc. So I now have a light-weight easy-pulling (rubber tires) wagon that will house me for many years to come. The horses and harness are worth about twice that. Thus, for the cost of a used car, a person could build a caravan and never again pay rent, license, registration, insurance.

My new caravan is 12 feet long. With the same size bed, it has over twice the kitchen area. This spring I am adding a solar panel and fluorescent lights. Bear, ID 832, May 04

A year caretaking; then back on the back roads.

In June 2003, I drove my new caravan about 200 miles along the same route as my 02 trip (see Dec 03 DP). While on the Salmon River I met a man who needed a caretaker for his remote ranch. Good caretaking jobs are sometimes hard to find. This job found me because of my caravan. People just have to stop and talk to the weird guy driving horses in the wrong century.

This ranch is the place I've been looking for. It has a good road to haul hay in on, but is snowed in for six months every year. It is 50 miles to the nearest store so I plan on going to town only once every 6 months. My mail box is 12 miles away - an 8-hour ride out and back, so I don't get my mail very often. In winter the only easy way in or out of here is by snowmobile, or one could cross-country ski. The nearest plowed road is 20 miles away over a mountain. A friend who was fur trapping in the area last winter, brought me my mail and a few groceries. I have the place to myself most of the time. The owner was here only four times last summer.

My new home is 80 acres of creek bottom meadows bordering the River of No Return Wilderness. It is 15 miles by trail from the wild and scenic Middle Fork of the Salmon river (which has 12 hot springs along its shores). My horses and goats have abundant grazing here, which they share with deer, elk, moose. I've also seen black bear, fox, coyotes, eagles, wolves. Caretaking a place this remote is not for everyone, but if you enjoy nature and don't need to go to town often, it is ideal. Time to fire up my wood-heated hot tub and sit back to watch the animals grazing in the meadow. Last evening there were 12 deer, 9 elk, 8 horses, 5 goats. Bear, May 04

(Later.) In July I quit the caretaking position. The owner went back on his word. Rather than deal with a dishonest jerk, I hit the road. I had been pretty isolated for a year and needed to see old friends and meet new people, so I headed up river to the Stanley area where I had lived for four years in the mid 1990s. Life on the road sure is different than life on a remote ranch, but fun in its own way.

7-21. After a week of repacking wagons and shoeing horses, I got on the road at noon and drove 12 miles down Morgan creek to the Salmon river. I pastured the horses on an island away from the roads. Hippies from New York stopped by camp asking about the local hot springs. They had been to the Rainbow gathering in California.

7-22. Drove through Challis and up highway 21 to the Bayhorse campground. It was about 15 miles of heavy traffic. The horses did real good except for Ritta, the 2-year-old, who still does not want to lead on the pack string. She broke loose and followed along at her own pace, in and out of traffic.

7-23. Drove 23 miles to Holman creek. This is the worst stretch of road on the trip. No good place to camp. Even this spot is not great: too close to the road and not much feed. Had two flat tires today. First, a tire on the goat cart was leaking. A very helpful man in Clayton changed it for me, put on a new tire and tube, and refused payment. Two miles further a tire on the wagon went flat. I hitched a ride back to Challis with the rim and bought a new used tire.

7-24. Moved just a mile to the end of Slate creek road and camped in an old pasture where the horses have plenty of feed. After yesterday's travails, we needed a day off.

7-25 19 miles to Casino creek and camped in the cattle trap where, 11 years ago, I first saw Mitasunke (My Horse - Lakotah). She belonged to a fence contractor who was camped there. I traded one hundred hours of work for her. She is still paying me for that labor, raising foals and carrying a pack load in the back country.

7-26. Day off. I visited with several friends who stopped by camp. I lived right across the river for 3 years.

Dwelling Portably   September 2005

There is a big summer house being built in "my" old horse pasture. On the 75 acre ranch that had one house in 1993, there are now eight big summer houses - and no horses.

7-27. Moved just 1½ miles to a spot near Boat Box hot springs. Someone has put a big redwood tub where the 2 ft by 4 ft boat box was when I lived here. The new tub is nice but it takes a lot of river water to cool the 130 degree water to get a soak. More up-river friends stopped by camp.

7-28. Drove 8 miles through Lower Stanley and Stanley (tourists everywhere) to the end of Cow Camp road by Stanley Lake creek. Had my first run in with a federal employee who felt he had to try and bully me. He claimed that I needed a permit to graze my horses on public land. I told him he was a liar and a criminal, and if he continued to harass me I'd see him in court. He left in a hurry.

7-29. Eight miles to Vadar creek rest area. I watched a hundred elk grazing in the meadow across the road.

7-30. Eight miles to Capehorn creek at the end of Bear Valley road. Off the pavement for a while.

7-31. Eight miles over Capehorn summit to Bruce meadows in Bear Valley. This is one of the largest alpine meadows I've ever seen. Elk everywhere you look, and Sandhill cranes filling the air with their weird calls.

8-1. Hiked 3 miles down the creek to Bear Valley hot springs. Large hot pools filled with naked women. Paradise for an old hippie.

8-2. Moved 2 miles up stream to a quieter spot a bit further from the road. This is the road into the head of the Middle Fork of the Salmon river, one of Idaho's most popular white water rivers, so it is very busy and dusty.

8-6. Stayed four days in the last camp and then found a spot just a half mile up stream that is off the road and has lots of feed. Real quiet here. The only noise is the cranes. A pair walked into the meadow by camp. Beautiful birds.

8-9. The horses saw a wolf last evening. I saw them looking at the road into this meadow, but I could not see what they were looking at. But when I went for a walk this morning, I saw a pile of wolf shit in the wheel track I made coming in.

8-10. Drove 5 miles up Bear Valley creek. The feed here is coarse swamp grass.

8-11. Moved one mile to a big meadow with good feed. Camped 100 yards from the road on the creek. This is a side road so the traffic is light. I watched a coyote stalking Little Big Man out in the meadow this afternoon. I think the coyote was over-ambitious. 1100# of horse might be too much !

8-12. My rooster was a big hero today. A hawk tried to grab a hen. The rooster flew up at the diving hawk and drove

8-15. Drove 9 miles to Fir creek and camped   it off. ¼ mile from the developed campground. Hiked down to BearValley hot springs for a soak. Right at dark a fool with a trailer full of mules pulled in right next to my camp. I've got four loose horses. I expect to hear fights all night long. Millions of acres of forest and this ass has to camp on my picket line !

8-16. Eight miles back over Capehorn summit. Steep hard pull but the horses did real good. I tried tying Ritta to the pack string. She broke loose twice, broke two halters, two ropes, the rigging ring, and pulled Trisha's saddle off. After that trying day, when I let the chickens out, they went down to the creek for a drink. The white hen drank at the beach where I was watering the horses, but the rooster tried to drink where the bank was two feet high and the water was two feet deep. He jumped off the bank into the water; I guess the creek was so

clear that he couldn't tell how deep it was. Sure was funny
watching a rooster play at being a duck.

8-17. Two miles down Capehorn creek to where it crosses
the highway. The old timer camped next to me packed into this
valley and into Bear Valley 50 years ago. He had lots of
stories of pack-string wrecks and cattle drives back when the
Stanley basin had only dirt roads and no tourists.

8-18. Three miles to Knapp creek at Marsh creek. There
is a sheep camp a half mile from me. When the flock arrived at
dusk, the colts all freaked out. They had never seen 1000
sheep before. They ran out to the road, then back to mama,
several times before I got Trisha and Bob caught.

8-19. Same camp. I went over and had coffee with the
Peruvian herder this morning. His boss showed up and I spent
the day helping sort old ewes and lambs out of the flock.
I enjoy working with sheep. They smell better than cows.

8-20. Same camp. The herder came looking for a lost horse.

8-21. Moved 3 miles to Blind summit at the head of Marsh
creek. The sheep owner stopped by to check out my wagon. A
Forest Service officer stopped by to visit; not hassle me.

8-23. Four miles to Archer creek at the sheep sorting
corrals. Lots of Sandhill cranes along the creek. Cold rain
all day. I'm glad I have a wood stove in the wagon.

8-29. Four miles to Marsh creek by the highway. Ritta
kicked a truck in the headlight. He was trying to pass us on a
narrow part of the road. I'll have to tie her up tomorrow.

8-30. Back on the pavement again. 14 miles to Stanley
Lake creek at the end of Cow Camp road. Tied Ritta to the
wagon and she threw herself on the road and got road rash on
both knees and a hock. I hope she has learned to lead.

8-31. Eight miles to Boat Box hot springs. I took a two-
hour soak as soon as I got the horses put away.

9-1. Same camp. I spent all day at the hot springs.

9-2. 17 miles to a friend's mining claim up the Yankee
Fork. I need to get off the highway for the weekend. An old
crane is at the mine. Osprey have built their nest at the top
of the boom. The birds provide many hours of entertainment.
As they are alert to threats, they make good watch ~~dogs~~ birds.

9-5. Three miles to the fish ponds below Ramey creek.
These ponds are left over from the HUGE gold dredge that worked
the Yankee Fork in the 1950s. The dredge, still here, is now a
museum. This river bed was turned upside down and now is
nothing but rock piles and holes that are stocked fish ponds.
Anyone who wants gold jewelry should see this place. An entire
river valley destroyed for greed and vanity.

9-6. Same camp. Lots of fishermen but few fish caught.
These stocked rainbows have seen every kind of lure and don't
rise. They think food comes in a pail at the hatchery.

9-7. 15 miles to the pasture at the end of Slate creek
road. The trip back down river is no fun. The same campsites,
the same road. The horses are tired and foot-sore. Paved
roads are hard on horse shoes. I'll be glad when back on dirt.

9-8. 23 miles to Bayhorse campground.

9-9. 15 miles to riverside camp by the cottonwood island.
Tomorrow I'll be back on Morgan/Panther creeks for the winter.

The wagon trip was about 270 miles. Most days I just
moved enough to find grazing for the horses. I met many
interesting people and soaked in a few fine hot springs. The
wagon worked fine. It is heavy and I need to harness 4 horses
on the passes but it pulls easily on level roads. I had no
problems with traffic or the law, although one sheriff's deputy

said he'd had many complaints about me slowing traffic. He
agreed that I was legal and no one had cause to complain. Many
people stopped to take pictures and praise my free lifestyle.

I'm settled in for the winter on a remote ranch on Panther
creek, busy building fence to pay my rent. I'd like to take a
long trip next year, perhaps to the southwest, but I'd like to
find someone to drive my old wagon. Leaving a pile of stuff
stored here is a pain. Many people talk about how they'd like
to live free like me, but so far it's just talk. I guess, when
there is no more oil, then people will have to use horses again.
I'll be ready to teach what I know. Bear, ID 832, May & Oct 04

Are you ready for a mobile chicken farm ?

Suppose you live in a van, bus, old RV, or horse-drawn
wagon. With a little thought and work, you could have fresh
eggs wherever you travel. For two years I lived in a homemade
camper on a pickup. For most of that time, six hens lived in a
coop on the roof of the cab. Now hens travel with my caravan.

The thing that makes it possible, is the desire of hens to
roost in the same place every night. They see their coop as
home - no matter that it has moved 500 miles since yesterday.
The only major drawback is that you can't move camp while the
chickens are out grazing. You must wait until dusk when they
go to roost. What do you do on long trips with few stops ?
Feed and water the chickens in the coop.

If the only place to put a coop is up on the roof, get
banties, as they can fly. My big old hens can only hop a
couple of feet, so their coop is under the wagon.

A small utility trailer that can be towed by a car or van
could house a goat or two plus a coop of chickens. Turn road-
side bushes and bugs into milk and eggs !

A coop under a rig should have a wire mesh floor so the
poop falls to the ground and fertilizes a new spot every time
you move. A coop on the roof should have a solid floor with
sawdust or old newspaper as bedding and be cleaned weekly.
I think I could make a pack-horse coop and take chickens trail-
riding into the back country. With a calm horse, it would work.

I can hear you doubters now: "This crazy idea is way too
much hassle." Well, food is never too much hassle when you are
hungry. Once you eat an egg from a free-range hen, you will
never go back to factory-made store-bought eggs. If you can
feed yourself, "they" can't control you by rationing your food.
                                                          Bear

In October, a black bear bit holes in many of my pails.

Replacing them is laborious. Previously for two years,
I had stored most buckets and totes on the ground. No problem.

I am now sprinkling full-strength ammonia around tree
trunks in hope the smell will repel bears. I also clothes-pin
garbage bags to clothes lines. Even a slight breeze causes
the bags to rustle, which may scare animals away. Too soon to
know if those repellants are effective.

I now keep most of my food buckets at one main camp, and
hang them 12 feet up or higher on tree branches with a rope.
I plan to replace the rope system with some sort of metal-cable
crank system for winching buckets up and down.

I may build a primitive tree house if I find a suitable
tree that is secluded enough. Bruce of BC, February 2004

(Comment:) Physical barriers, such as the cable system you
plan, seem better than odorous chemicals, because the latter
are temporary at best. We haven't had much bear damage, maybe
because most wild areas here are small enough for pesty bears
to roam to folks' gardens - and get shot.   Sept 2005

Choosing a tree and means of support for a tree-house.

The higher I go in a tree, the greater my sense of freedom and the farther I may be able to see. However, I also think about ease of climbing up and down, chances of falling, likelihood of injury if I do fall, maximum wind speed the tree may experience, and quality of support for it. Kid's tree-houses are seldom over 10 ft high, to minimize injury if child falls.

Trees are stressed by wind, esp during storms. Trees cope by losing parts of their structure: first leaves, then small branches, then big branches. As each is lost, the tree's wind catchment area decreases, which reduces the force and the risk of the tree blowing over. Adding a tree-house, increases the wind catchment area. In high-wind areas, tree-houses should be in the lower third of the tree, where wind speeds are lower and the wind-force's leverage on the tree's base is less. If wind poses a serious threat, build only a small tree-house and round its sides to reduce its sail effect.

The branches to which the tree-house is attached, must be strong enough to take the weight and wind-force of what they are supporting. Simpler to build on a few strong supports than many small ones. Branch strength varies among species. Generally strong: oak, beech, maple, fir, hemlock. For a one-storey tree-house with four attachment points (one at each corner) and no overhanging parts, minimum thickness is about 8 inches. If more than one storey, or the extra leverage and weight of overhanging sections, 12 inches or more. If your branches aren't this thick, use more attachment points so that the weight is spread among more branches.

If you use two or more branches or trunks or trees to support a tree-house, attachments require extra care. In a strong wind, a tree and its branches will twist and sway a lot. If your house hinders this movement, it could be destroyed. This can happen esp if building across two very long branches, because the wind moves them a lot. Different trees and branches will move differently; supports must be able to cope with that; either have a strong rigid framework or a flexible framework.

Rigid framework. If the branches are not very large, or heavy, you may be able to fasten rigidly to them. The small wind forces can be withstood by the supports and the floor beams. This method is not suitable for large spans or for use between thick trunks. Recommended only on branches 6"D or less.

Flexible (or floating) framework. This is the best choice because very low stresses are created; so smaller, lighter, cheaper wood can be used. However, it may be more complicated. The idea: fix one end of a beam to one trunk or branch, and support the other end on a sliding joint. When the trunks move differently, the support slides across the joint and no big stress is put upon the support or the beam. One such joint is a J-shape metal bracket. The top of the J is bolted to the tree; the hook of the J supports the beam, enabling the beam to slide in one direction. This isn't suitable if the beam may get twisted sideways in the bracket and prevented from sliding. Another way: attach one end of a steel cable to the tree-house's frame and the other end to a higher branch. This is cheap and effective, but be careful how you attach the cable. Suspend it from an eye-bolt fitted to the tree at right angle to the cable and attach it to the support with another eye-bolt. This is important so that, when wind moves the support, the cable doesn't rub away living bark and damage the tree. (From http://www.corbinstreehouse.com , sent by Bruce of BC)

(Comment:) In a windy place if using a bracket, I'd prefer a d shape. The house might tip out of a J shape.

Father and daughter lived four years in Portland forest.
An Australian cross-country runner, scouting routes thru
dense woods, spotted a girl and an older man with bushy white
hair and beard at a "well-established transient camp" in a
remote part of the northeast section of Forest Park. Carved
into the ground nearby were two swasticas. The runner and his
wife called police at 9:06 am on April 28 and gave the location
citing Thomas Guide map, page 565, block G6.
That afternoon, four cops on ATVs searched the slopes for
more than an hour with no luck. "We had little to go on."
The next morning, the runner escorted police back, using
a compass to lead them on foot through waist-high foliage far
beyond marked trails. A police plane flew overhead, but the
pilot said the dense fir trees concealed the ground.
After 1½ hours search, they found an elaborate camp dug
into a steep hillside about 500 yards above and sw of St Helens
road 1¼ miles se of St Johns bridge. Inside a 20x20-ft tarp-
covered wood-framed shelter, they found sleeping bags laid out
on plastic ground-covering, a makeshift table carved from tree
bark, a stove, a large metal pot, a partially burnt log, tools
including a hand-saw and rakes, girl's shoes, a doll, a stack
of old World Book encyclopedias and other books. Nearby was a
rope swing, a tilled vegetable garden, and a creek with a pool
shallowly dammed by rocks. But no one was in sight.
Police, armed with rifles and shotguns, stayed around for
an hour, keeping silent. "We didn't know who we'd encounter."
As police prepared to leave, a police dog disappeared over
a hill. The handler found the dog 50 yards down a ridge,
sniffing at a man and girl huddled behind a tree. Immediately
police separated them; one cop questioned the girl while the
other interrogated the man. The man, Frank, said he was a 53-
year-old college graduate and Marine Corps veteran who had
served in Vietnam. He said the girl's mother was institutionalized in NH where his 12-year-old daughter, Ruth, was born,
and the two now lived on a $400-a-month disability check.
He said, rather than live on the streets and expose Ruth
to alcohol and drugs, they had hiked deep into Forest Park and
set up their camp. He taught Ruth using the encyclopedias.
They went into the city twice a week to shop and to attend
church. He said he was a devout Christian and explained that
the swastica was an ancient Chinese symbol for prosperity and
purity and good fortune before the Nazis had adopted it.
Frank and Ruth told police that the runner was the first
person to find their camp during the four years they had lived
there - and were stunned that police found them. Their biggest
worry was being split up. "Please don't take me from my daddy",
the girl pleaded with the cop as they sat on a log talking for
half an hour. Police were impressed that the two were clean,
well-fed, healthy. Police "persuaded" Frank and Ruth to leave
their camp, promised to help find them food and shelter, and
said they would try not to separate them. The father and Ruth,
leery at first, led police down their zigzagging trail to St
Helens Road, carrying some of their belongings in two backpacks.
A cop said, "All of us had difficulty negotiating the steep
path, except for Frank and Ruth."
Police fingerprinted both and did a thorough national
criminal background check which came up empty. A pediatrician
examined the girl and found her free of illnesses and tooth
cavities and signs of physical or sexual abuse, and as smart
as a 16-year-old. After some prodding from supervisors, the
sargent alerted caseworkers of the state Dept of Human Resources. Informed that there were no signs of abuse, they allowed

the pair to remain together. A homeless outreach worker found
them a spot in a family shelter for two nights. But they could
not stay there indefinitely. Instead of turning them over to
state authorities, the sargent found them a place to live and
Frank a job on a horse farm in Yamhill County.

For the past two weeks they have lived in a mobile home.
Frank is now mowing lawns and learning to drive a tractor. The
two ride bicycles to a nearby church on Sundays. Maxine
Bernstein (from Oregonian, 15? May 04; sent by Pam in Oregon)

(Comments:) The police, sensing that the episode would get
much media attention, claimed they were trying to help Ruth and
Frank, and perhaps actually were more considerate than usual.

Ruth and Frank were lucky that Ruth was not forced into a
foster home. The sargent seemed reluctant to notify DHR, maybe
because such agencies are prone to seize children on the
slightest pretext (I've heard they get paid per kid), and
foster homes are prone to abuse (they, too, get paid per kid,
so they have an incentive to crowd in all the kids they can
get - and some kids will be bullies !).

The Oregonian headlined their front-page article: "Police
rescue a father and girl." RESCUE ? !!!!! Ruth and Frank had
lived healthily in those woods for 4 years. They did not need
or request "rescue". (Big media are seldom more than propaganda. One reason: if they don't "cooperate" with police and
other officials, they won't be given "news". Also, their
staffs might get traffic fines instead of warnings - etc !)

After a few weeks at the horse farm, Ruth and Frank left
and disappeared. They wrote a note to the owner saying they
did not like all the media attention they were getting. Now
more experienced, hopefully they won't get "rescued" again.

Note that Ruth and Frank were eventually found, not by the
police or an airplane, but by a dog. If, upon spotting the
police at their camp, instead of hiding nearby and waiting, if
they had immediately left, would they have gotten away ? Seems
better to chance theft of camping equipment, than to confront
police or other dangerous people. Even though someone believes
they are "innocent" of any "wrong doing", no knowing how police
may construe what they see or what fingerprinting
and a "thorough national background check" might show up.
(Recently, a Portland man (a lawyer, no less), who had not been
out of the U.S. for ten years, was imprisoned because his
fingerprints supposedly matched prints left near the train
bombing in Spain. Fortunately, Spanish police found the man
who had actually left the prints. Did the FBI's fingerprint
system goof ? Or were the police 'framing' him ?)

(Based on what little advice we've seen on an ACLU info-
card, and in lit from other sources:) If you are with other
people and get confronted by police, try to STAY TOGETHER. If
questioned separately, any differences in what you say can be
construed as evidence of guilt. If the police insist on
separating you, or if they question you for longer than a
minute and then refuse to let you go on your way, assume you
will be arrested, and SHUT UP. Thereafter say only, "I have
nothing further to say until I obtain adequate legal information", or words to that effect. Police will usually not tell
you that you are under arrest until they put hand-cuffs on you
and haul you away, because they want to get as much info out of
you as they can before you shut up. Any info you provide, no
matter how innocuous it seems to you, may be twisted by police
and prosecutors and used against you. When they arrest you,
police are supposed to tell you that anything you say may be
used against you. Whether or not they do, SHUT UP.

Can orbiting spy satellites spot your camp ? Probably not.
        Supposedly they are capable of (eg) reading a newspaper
headline from orbit. But they'd have difficulty finding a
newspaper because, the higher the magnification, the smaller
the area viewed. Testable with a variable power scope.
        According to 25May03 "Ask Marilyn" (Vos Savant) column,
"satellites view the entire Earth almost daily at a resolution
of one kilometer and biweekly at a resolution of 30 meters."
That means, something smaller than 30 meters (100 ft) won't be
seen unless it is intense, such as a bright light at night. H&B

Using a shake-light at base camp and on trails.
        In Dec 03 DP, I said I'd buy one when the price got under
$10. Well, at a mobile sales (a dealer who travels to small
towns with tools and farm things), John and Rose Ward of Living
Mobile saw new HDC shake-lights (stock #CLFL/38978) on sale at
$5. They bought a few and sent me one (MUCH THANKS !). Made
in China, marketed by Homier Distributing Co, www.homier.com
(no mail address). $6\frac{1}{2}$" long, 1" D except $1\frac{1}{2}$" near light end,
$\frac{1}{4}$ pound (half the weight of our Russian squeeze-light).
        Instructions say: If completely drained, 3 shakes per
second for 30 seconds will fully charge the capacitor "which
will give up to 5 minutes of continuous bright light." "During
prolonged use" shake 10 to 15 seconds every 2 to 3 minutes.
Shake with "moderate force" while holding horizontal. "Shaking
too hard may cause damage" as may bumping or dropping .
        HDC claims the light is "visible for over a mile" which
may be true. But the beam is too narrow (eg, 3" at one ft) for
most tasks. Immediately after shaking, its beam is brighter
than the incandescent-bulb squeeze-light. But the squeeze-
light's beam is broader (3 times,if set broad; $1\frac{1}{2}$ times,narrow)
and therefore better for following a trail through brush at
night. On trails, the best way I've found to use the HDC:
leave on and shake a few times every few seconds. The shaking
bounces the beam around - which helps illuminate more terrain.
        Though most of HDC's light is focused into the beam, the
clear plastic case passes enough light to reduce night vision.
I shaded it by holding that portion of case in my hand.
        Unlike present squeeze-lights, a shake-light
can be used solo for tasks requiring two hands.
But for most tasks, the HDC must be set into
something to hold it and spread the beam. I used
a ceramic mug. A chunk of soft foam keeps the
shake-light upright. White cardstock, half way
around behind, holds a cardstock top on which is
glued slightly-wrinkled aluminum foil to reflect
and diffuse the beam. So rigged, the HDC is
approx as bright as an ordinary candle for only
a few seconds after shaking. The light fades
fast at first, then increasingly slower. After
15 minutes, the HDC-as-lantern still gave enough
light for me to (eg) eat without spooning food
onto my lap. It continues to glow dimly for
many hours; helpful for finding it at night.
        Experimenting, I shook the HDC rapidly but
gently for 30 seconds - so gently that the
magnet barely bumped its stops. I switched it
on briefly to notice brightness, then shook it
VIGOROUSLY for 10 seconds. Much brighter.
        This autumn, for 3 months we've used the
HDC most every night or morn for an hour or more.
No failures so far.   Sept 2005

card-
stock
Al
foil
foam

Instructions warn: "DO NOT attempt to remove the LED or any internal part", but also claim "water and weather proof", so I assumed its innards were sealed. I noticed the end piece screwed on. Thinking it held only the glass lens, I unscrewed it, intending to remove the lens to broaden the beam. WRONG ! All the innards slid out ! I reassembled with difficulty. The only sealant is a rubber gasket between the lens and an internal tube. So I'd say it is water RESISTANT, maybe as much so as is a plastic pail with a gasketed lid.

A good feature: the switch does not penetrate the case. Instead it is magnetic and actuates something inside. A feature to look for in ALL kinds of flashlights.

The sliding magnet that generates electricity is strong and easily attracts steel objects even through the case. HDC warns, keep shake-light away from tapes, pacemakers, etc.

In Living Mobile 4-04, John and Rose reported on their HDC. "3 minutes of vigorous shaking results in about 6 minutes of usable light, with the light becoming noticably dimmer at the 4 minute mark... The more we use it, the longer it seems to shine. We didn't get even 6 minutes ... when it was new."

We seldom shake our HDC longer than 10 seconds because we are concerned about life of the LED (see next item). Our HDC fades gradually; no abrupt change. Nor have we noticed any change with use. White LEDs are a new product (not yet made the same ?) and individual LEDs may vary. Bert & Holly, Dc 04

Preliminary report on an Eveready "Energizer LED Lantern".

It "folds to put the light where you need it". $3\frac{1}{2}$x$2\frac{1}{2}$x$1\frac{1}{4}$" when folded, 6 oz when 4 AA cells installed. It appears to contain two LEDs (white unfortunately, yellow would be more efficient) which beam most of their light through two small translucent tubes which diffuse it. So, it emits a broad glow like a candle, rather than a narrow beam like most flashlights.

It does not say what kind of AAs, but the package mentions "battery changes" (not recharges) so I assume alkalines. However, because flashlight makers tend to run LEDs at higher power than they are rated for, I installed NiCds. NiCds give only 1.2 volts per cell, vs alkaline 1.5 v). With NiCds, the lantern is about as bright as a candle - adequate for reading or hand-writing if the material is placed close.

When I installed the NiCds, I also stuck in wires at the connections. The wires go to a small socket, so I can recharge it simply by plugging it into our photovoltaic panel.

The little info with the lantern did not say how long the cells should last. I measured 25 milliamps on dim and 50 ma on bright (two settings). That means: new 500 ma-hour NiCd AAs, if fully charged and used until 80% discharged, might last 8 hrs on bright and 16 hrs dim. NiCds lose capacity as they age.

It has been very useful this autumn, because we are able to recharge it some on bright cloudy days when our pv does not generate enough voltage to recharge our main 12-volt system.

Sent by Al Fry (MUCH THANKS) who did not say where he bought it or how much it cost. He noted, "Direct viewing of bulbs is irritating to eyes." Bert & Holly, December 2004

My Brinkman two-AA-cell white LED flashlight is bright.

It cost $12 or $15 at Walmart. It is the only TWO cell LED flashlight I know of. Others require 3 cells, usually AAA. Most white LEDs need 3.6 to 4.5 volts - higher than the 2.5-to-3 volts that two cells put out. Zalia, Oregon 972, April 2004

Charging multiple batteries off of one photovoltaic panel.

In full sun, our big (1x4') pv panel puts out 17 volts -
ample for charging a 12-volt battery. But when cloudy or
partial shade, it puts out less than 12 volts. The big pv's
cloudy performance is poorer than the small pv on our Casio
calculator which operates in quite dim light. Dim-light
performance of pvs depends on how they were fabricated (and
age ?) - something to check for if buying a pv that you would
like some power from during long cloudy periods.

Previously, to get something when cloudy, I clipped the
the pv to just one or a few cells of our main 12-volt battery.
This autumn I devised an easier way: I hooked it to other
lower-voltage batteries through separate resistors and one-way
diodes. See below. The "12 volt batt" consists of ten NiCd
cells (originally 20 amp-hours capacity but now, over 30 years
old, MUCH less). The "5-volt batt" are 4 NiCd AAs in the
Eveready lantern. The "3-volt batt" are two alkaline AAs
being recharged, which power our Sony "Walkman" radio/tape-
player ($3 at a thrift store). We play it while sitting doing
inside tasks (NOT while hiking). Voltages are slightly higher
while the batteries are charging or when fully charged.

We tried the Walkman on two NiCd AAs (2.4 v), but it did
not play. Three NiCds (3.6 v) might blow it. So it needs
alkaline AAs. They warn: do NOT recharge. But none have
blown up - yet. Two "Duracell" swelled and leaked a little.
(We recycled.) No problems with others so far. We have 8 or
so that we recharge in rotation. Some we salvaged from toys we
found at an informal dump along a logging road. Others came
from a pail of discarded batteries for recycle, at a university.
We also tried recharging alkaline D cells (used by a different
radio at a summer camp) with a small pv that puts out 60 ma in
full sun. All leaked - but still worked. To recharge, esp
"non-rechargables", best do it VERY SLOWLY with LOW currant.

The resistors are to limit current when the pv gets full
sun; else the AAs would be charged too fast and damaged.
Also, the resistors allow the 12-volt batt to get charged. If
the pv puts out 1 amp (1000 ma) at 14 v (voltage limited by 12-
volt batt), the 5-volt batt takes 26 ma and the 3-volt batt 24
ma. The other 950 ma goes into the 12-volt batt. The NiCd AAs
say they hold 500 ma-hrs and to charge 14 hrs at 50 ma max.

At our present winter camp, even on sunny days the big pv
gets full sun for only an hour or two. More typically, with
cloudy sun or partial shade, the pv puts out 8 volts, in which
case the 5-volt batt gets 8 ma, the 3-volt batt 10 ma, and the
12-volt batt nothing. The 3-volt batt gets some charge when
the pv puts out as little as 4 volts. (Diode loses a little.)

Recently I found various-size NiCds and a 9 v lithium in
recycle. (Why were rechargable NiCds discarded ?) More later.
                                                          Bert

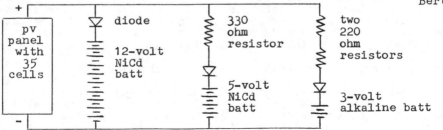

Dwelling Portably

May 2006 $1 per issue

or Shared, Mobile, Improvised
Underground, Hidden, Floating
POB 190-d, Philomath OR 97370

What is wrong with this bridge ?

This drawing is from
"Pioneering" pamphlet #33588,
which came in a boy-scout
magazine. It suggests
activities to "enhance
outdoor skills, especially
knot-tying and lashing"
and "an understanding of
some of the principles of
engineering as they build
temporary structures and
camp equipment" and to
"increase self-
confidence."
The pamphlet
includes some
good info and
ideas. But

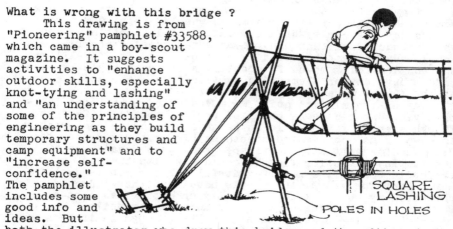

SQUARE
LASHING
POLES IN HOLES

both the illustrator who drew this bridge and the editor who
approved it, deserve to lose their merit-badges. Why? Page 124.

How can nomadic or primitive-living people find one another ?

I know about Rainbow Gatherings, but unfortunately they
are only held once a year, and the only way to find out where
and when is by using a computer (which I don't use).

Most primitive-skills festivals I know of cost money as
well as the time and effort of getting to them.

A common angst with many people who live this way, myself
included, is loneliness. If you've found your soul-mate, you
are one of the rare, lucky ones. Many more of us are the
"freaks" and "weirdos" of our neighborhoods; rarely if ever
meeting people who want to drop out of main-stream society.

Solitude is beautiful, but so is good company. We can be
stronger together. Thoughts ? Resources ? Gumby, NC 275,Jy05

(Comments:) Loneliness is not just a problem for nomads (etc)
but for most people. Though they might live in (eg) similar
tract houses, they differ in important ways and have difficulty
finding compatables. "Mainstream society" is mostly a
statistical fiction. Everyone is a "freak".

Most nomads (etc) have an easier time than most other
people, because we aren't spending most of our lives working to
pay rent. We have more time to find a long-term companion.

For how, seek opportunities fairly near by, so that you
can spend more time in places good for meeting people. Your
area (NC, etc) is culturally diverse, so a long move may not be
necessary. For nearby gatherings, check bulletin boards and
local event sheets. And keep in mind that every popular park
and beach and library is a gathering of sorts.

Don't expect to meet anyone who shares your exact
interests. Be flexible. When Holly and I met, perhaps our
most important commonality was dissatisfaction with the
heavily-promoted options (such as expensive housing, and steady
full-time jobs to pay for it). Bert, OR 973, March 2006

How Rose and John developed their mobile dwellingway.

I (John) don't think that I ever made a singular decision
to live in a mobile dwelling. I built on an extensive camping

experience of over 20 years. After my last house was sold, it was no suprise to my friends that I moved into my 84 Dodge mini-van. Some people thought I was nuts, and others wished that they could do as I was doing.

I was dating then, and one of my litmus tests was, how the woman reacted to my little home on wheels. Many women look at a house as a security blanket, and since I didn't have one, I was not surprised that many of my dates reacted poorly. One young lady was not bothered by my lack of a fixed dwelling; she and her folks moved frequently, a la gypsy style, so she didn't have any problems with my lifestyle. She still doesn't, as she (Rose) became my wife !

After the minivan quit, we moved into an 86 Dodge full-size van that had been converted for our nomadic lifestyle. Though someone living solo in a van can be quite comfortable, the two of us soon wanted something bigger. But rather than get rid of a perfectly servicable van, we purchased an 82 Shasta travel trailer that we could tow with the van. Now we are quite content, and very grateful for our mobile dwelling-way. Over the years many people have said that I should chronicle my mobile life; thus Living Mobile was born as a way to share knowledge within the nomadic community.

Many in the nomadic life use RV's, though their RV's are often old. Others use cars, trucks, vans they have modified, or simply occupied as mobile shelters. I distinguish those who are mobile by choice, from people who are homeless but would like to return to "normal" life. John & Rose, PA 174, March05

How did you come to live your choice of dwellingway ?

Did you consciously decide to leave so-called modern life, or did your dwellingway evolve over a period of time ? Did you both learn your lifestyle by trial and error, or did you build on the works of others and maybe have help ? John & Rose

(Reply.) Holly and I learned gradually. We'd both been some-what outdoorsy tho not into uncomfortable or dangerous feats.

A big "bottom line" for both of us, was the high cost of conventional housing, esp housing that was comfortable. Before meeting Holly, I had rented various rooms and structures - always the cheapest I could find because I considered the rent money ill spent. Consequently, most were not very comfortable. Some had no heat; others only an UNvented gas cook-stove. And some landlords soon kicked me out. I usually payed the rent on time and I did not smoke or have animals, but I ate and sometimes cooked (on electric hotplate) in my room. For food, as for shelter, I believed in spending little money so that I needed to spend little time working at jobs I mostly disliked.

(I went to restaurants only with dates. Likewise to entertainment that charged admission. I was generous with women, at least by my frugal standards, because I didn't find many who were interested in me - despite my spending much of my free time looking for them (for which I traveled to beach resorts or sizable cities, because seldom were there many women near where I worked). The "litmus tests" were mostly the women's. I simply tried to get acquainted with every woman I saw who looked good to me and who did not seem busy or in a rush or with a man. I am not quick-witted verbally. Though I tried to be polite, my conversation openers were usually trite/banal/awkward/contrived - as well as "out of the blue". I got rebuffed maybe nine tries out of ten. Of the women who at least talked with me a while, not more than one in ten dated me. Of those, most did not date me more than once or twice.)

Dwelling Portably   May 2006

Though I enjoyed travel to/through new places, I hated commuting. So, if I couldn't rent something cheap close to work, I slept in my car (an ordinary sedan), usually parked at my work place with boss's permission - sometimes in climates with winters colder than Oregon's.

The shelters that Holly and I have had while "camping out" have been MORE comfortable and no more crowded than almost all the housing I'd had previously. Exception: one winter camped in the Rocky Mtns while still quite inexperienced. That prompted a move to the West Coast, 25 years ago.

The housing Holly had had before we met, was generally more comfortable than what I'd had - but cost her much of her earnings. And she, too, had had problems with landlords.

As we recall, after getting together, over a period of several weeks we consciously decided that we wanted to live differently than most people lived, though we weren't sure how. We talked about RVs and boats, and looked at a few, but decided they were too expensive if big enough to be comfortable, and too insecure. We also thought about trying to build something permanent in some very remote area, but decided it would be difficult to sustain, and too much to lose if it was discovered or for other reasons became untenable. Holly was even less enthusiastic than I for anything requiring big investments of money or time. So, somewhat by elimination, we arrived at what we have. Comfort is a big thing for us: comfort not only within our dwellings, but minimum DIScomfort while operating our support channels. (I DIS-fondly remember going out on cold mornings and removing snow from my car so I could drive to work, and then having to work out in the cold.)

During a cold spell a month ago, in early morning, 23° outside, 52° inside. By mid-day, 45° outside and sunny (cold days here are often sunny), 65° inside thanks to solar heating. (A more-typical winter morn, 35° outside, 60° inside.) And our heat is free and effortless: our bodies; our plastic-covered earth floor (which stores heat); the sun (sometimes); and cooking in the evening (which consumes 5 gal of propane in 4 or 5 months). Meanwhile, house dwellers who heat with electricity or gas are paying BIG BUCKS. Or, if with wood, spending much time tending the fire and cutting and transporting wood. So - WHO is "roughing it" ? ! Bert & Holly, Oregon 973, March 06

My son and I are now living in an old school bus.
It is about 30 feet long inside. It has a wood-stove, sink, two beds, table - all built in. I parked it on a friend's land. I pay him rent, which includes water and electric hook-ups (plenty of water, but electricity is limited by an extension cord - only enough for lights, radio, TV-VCR).

Long term, I am interested in solar electric in case I unplug from the grid. My bus is wired for 12-volt lights and radio, etc. No phone line; I have a pager.

I bought the bus in Oct 2003 for $2000. I'm working 40 hours a week to pay down the loan I got to buy it. The bus is drivable, but not insured or licensed so it stays put.

Living in vehicles is illegal here, but this is a tolerant place and, if nobody complains, officials ignore it. (They feel: better in a bus than "homeless".) Many other people live in buses and trailers on this island (population 12,000; doubles in summer with visitors and tourists). Rents and house-prices are high. I get plenty of free firewood from a lumber yard, so no fuel bills. (They even cut the wood into short lengths and put it in a free box by the road.)

I heat water on the woodstove in big pots. I like to soak

in a hot bath, and I enjoy long showers. This week I put some coils of black rubber hose on the roof of the bus and got some very hot water - enough for a short shower. I am adding a small water tank to increase volume. I am also working on a bigger solar system, using recycled solar water-heating panels (formerly heated swimming-pool water). I found some leaks in the panels; also, the water pressure here (municipal system) is too high, causing more leaks.

My 14-year-old son and I dug/built an outhouse, and are working on a second one. Most people here use septic fields or a municipal system (which dumps the "treated" sewage into the ocean). A public health nurse said an outhouse is better than those two options. Aarran, Saltspring Island BC, June/July 05

(Comments.) Out-HOUSES (difficult-to-move structures over big pits) may be better than septic fields or municipal systems (which need many miles of pipes that can leak - or be ruptured by an earthquake or flood !). But a big concentration of feces buried deep is likely to pollute ground water. (Unnatural. What animal digs a big hole and shits in it repeatedly ?) Better to make small shallow deposits - which are soon broken down by soil microbes, enriching the soil. To build a portable rain/snow shelter, lash together poles to form an A-frame and tie a tarp onto it.

I wonder if your bus also has insulation built in. A bus dweller in Toronto said his "tin shack" was difficult to heat. "Metal is a good conductor of heat. Accumulated snow would melt off the roof." (Long report in May 97 DP.) But Toronto has colder winters than where you are. Bert

Having a motor vehicle can help in some situations.
A young lady walked into our favorite pipe and tobacco store and asked to use the phone. The manager pointed to the pay phone outside. She responded that she didn't have any money. He allowed her to use his phone. She called several homeless shelters - and finally found one that had an opening.

The manager later told me that she had lost her job, and that everything she owned had been repoed. I responded that, had she at least owned a suitable car or van, even a cheap one, she would have a place to stay and store her stuff; and would be better able to find work, even temp work, and to get there.

Personally, I think that to rely upon the kindness of others, or on homeless shelters, for something that a person should provide for themselves, is pathetic. Perhaps it has something to do with the victim mentality, fostered by big daddy government: you can't care for yourself, but big daddy will take care of you. This is why I like the DIY of the punk and nomadic communities. Rose & John, Living Mobile, PA,Mar05

(Comments.) There are good reasons for her to feel victimized. Big Bully and his accomplices victimize everyone (though some more than others). Eg, at her former job, how much of her earnings were taken, directly by taxes on her, or indirectly by taxes on the business (which partly comes out of what she could otherwise get payed - her employer won't willingly lose money or cut profits - at least not for long). At her former apartment (or house), how much was her rent (or payments) inflated by all the restrictions on building ? However, I agree that some kind of backup would have been desirable.

But would a vehicle be the best kind ? Costly, not only in money (purchase, maintenance, fuel, insurance, licensing, maybe parking) but in time and stress and risk. And, if she had had one, would it too have been repoed ? Also, living

comfortably in a vehicle takes learning, which takes time.
(I was not very comfortable sleeping in a car, because I didn't
have the time, or at least take the time, to learn how and to
equip it adequately. I regarded it as temporary. Likewise the
rooms I rented - and my jobs.)

Nor, would the kind of shelters we enjoy now, necessarily
be a good backup for her. They, too, require learning.

The most practical short-term backup for her, might be for
her to pre-arrange reciprocal house-sharing with other employed
women. Ie, if I can come sleep on your floor, you can come
sleep on mine. If the latter doesn't happen, she can give the
other woman some money when she gets some. (Most people are
unemployed at times, but also earn quite high pay at times.)

Long term, she would probably be better off with a
dwellingway that doesn't require much money. Holly & Bert

San Diego police harass occupants of big vehicles.

Every night, Harry Wells slips behind the wheel of his
1976 Itaska motorhome and steers it out of a Mission Bay
parking lot, across I-5, and into the hills of Clairemont.
Wells looks for a parking space where his motor home won't be
a nuisance. Then he sets the alarm for 6 am and he and his
wife, Barbara, settle in for a night's sleep.

The next morning, he drives the motorhome back to the bay
parking lot before his presence can be detected by residents
of the neighborhood. Both the Wells work for temp agencies:
Barbara as a nurse; Harry as a telemarketeer.

When the Wells moved into their motorhome last year after
a string of bad luck, they joined more than 31,000 California-
ians living in vehicles. More than 2700 live in San Diego
county, angering some house-dwellers. Officials responded to
complaints by amping up enforcement of parking regulations in
bay and beach lots, which prohibit parking from 2 to 4 am, and
by eliminating parking spaces in the bay lots and along Morena
Blvd where Wells formerly parked without annoying homeowners.

The changes have sent Wells and other motorhome dwellers
into residential neighborhoods to park overnight. Wells said
he has been glared at, has had ice thrown at his motorhome,
and has been awakened at 5 am and asked to leave. "We're
trying to keep a low profile", said Well, 54. "We don't want
to bother people." But Chris Rink, chairman of Clairemont
Mesa Planning Committee, said motor homes take up parking
spaces and that residents worry about who is inside them.
"They don't contribute to the neighborhood."

Bay Park resident Mike Vinti said he has called police
ten times in the past 18 months about motorhomes parked across
the street from his home. While some of the occupants could
be homeless, he said many of them are living in expensive new
motorhomes. "I feel those people are cutting corners. There
are places for them..." But many motorhome dwellers say they
can't afford to pay for a permit or to park in RV parks, such
as Campland on the Bay - which charges $37-up per night.

Wells, whose only criminal record is a traffic violation,
says he doesn't like avoiding police, but he is doing what he
has to. When he and Barbara, 56, decided to buy a motorhome
and live in it, he never expected it would lead to being
harassed. Wells was laid off from his job as a loan processor
last June, and the couple were evicted from their rental home
in North Park when the owner decided to sell the house. Using
what was left of their savings from a disability settlement,
the couple plunked down $2300 for the motorhome and moved in,
after putting some of their possessions in storage. They also

have a Nissan Sentra, which Wells uses to commute to work.

A proposed San Diego ordinance would prohibit parking recreational vehicles on city streets from 2 to 6 am, and for more than 4 hours at any time. Police said, existing rules, which ban parking any vehicle on city streets for more than 72 hours, are difficult to enforce. Santa Barbara limits RV and trailer parking to two hours; Encinitas bans overnight parking of RVs on its streets without a permit. Kristen Green (from 23Je05 San Diego Union-Tribune; sent by Phyllis (thanks)

Thoughts about dwelling in vehicles.

If we were to choose between a house and a motor vehicle, we'd get a vehicle. As long as it keeps running, it can take us places that otherwise may be difficult to get to; and, if we get hassled, we can more easily move. Whereas, in a house you "own" (actually you are just leasing from the government), you are a "sitting duck" for anyone who wants to "get you".

Unless I had a very profitable business that needed a van, I think I'd choose a fairly big hatch-back car. I'd remove the rear seats and install a secure deck under which I would sleep; and (if I lacked a better place) eat, read, write, listen to music on earphones, and sponge-bathe a few body parts. (But I'd shower, and do any cooking and any noisy activities elsewhere.) I'd insulate my sleeping compartment well (easy, because small) so I wouldn't need artificial heat.

The deck would be low enough to not obstruct the windows, and would have stuff on top of it so that its purpose would not be obvious to someone peeking in. With such a vehicle, I think I could park even in neighborhoods lousy with housing-bigots without getting hassled. (These are off-hand thoughts. Experienced vehicle dwellers will probably have better ideas.)

When selecting a vehicle, unless I planned to drive it many miles (which I'd do only if essential for a business), I'd choose something cheap. It would likely not only burn more fuel, but not be capable of going many miles without costly repairs. But those are not big financial concerns if not going many miles. As for environmental concerns: LOW-mileage use of an old "gas hog" consumes less resources and generates less pollution than does manufacturing a new vehicle. Bert

Lew carried all his tools in a van.

So he could do just about any job on site. Small table saw, planer, chop saw, Skill-saw, Sawzall, jig saw, router, and several portable drills - along with other carpentry and plumbing and electrical tools. He did foundation work to cabinet work - and took everything to the job. It's a great idea for a young builder - keep it portable so you can go anywhere in the country. There's a great demand for solo building like this. Lloyd Kahn (final thoughts in his book Home Work, listed in "Off the Beaten Path")

I purchased a small 2-stroke, 25cc, 9-pound bicycle engine.

From www.bikeengines.com. I rode 1100 miles from Tucson to Seattle last fall with no problems hauling 65 pounds of gear on a BOB trailer. Speed depends on load, terrain, wind; but I averaged about 25 mph. I get between 180-240 mpg depending on terrain, load, speed.

The engine installs above the rear tire on the gear side. I installed it in about an hour. It uses a drive ring that snaps onto the spokes, and a belt that goes from that to a gear on the engine. Three gears are available: trail, standard, highway. I ride a lot with loads behind me so I usually use trail gear. But on open flat roads, even with a load, the standard or highway gears result in faster speeds and better gas mileage. Changing gears take about 5 min. The engine kit is designed for mountain bikes with 24-26" tires.

I have really enjoyed this engine. It seemed pricey at $600, but I have since let my truck insurance expire (because I hadn't driven it in a year) which saved me $400 - plus much gas and oil. The engine has saved me money, at least compared to my past habits, and it gives me the mobility I need without the hassle of licensing, insurance, special permits (none are needed in the U.S. unless an engine is over 50 cc). Another web site to check if interested in serious hauling with a bike: www.bikesatwork.com. They have a 8-foot model that can haul several hundred pounds as well as long items. I intend to get their 5' model to haul my tools to the small home-repair jobs I do for money from time to time. Lauran, AZ, July 05

(Question:) How noisy is the engine ? Quiet seems important for safety - hearing approaching vehicles. Even with a good stable rear-view mirror, may not see vehicles soon enough to get safely off the road if no shoulder or if gravel-and-sloping shoulder; especially if winding road.

I wonder, in how many states is riding on the shoulders of freeways legal ? (Was in Oregon.) That seems safer than riding on almost all 2-lane highways. Bert, Sept 05

(Response.) I arrived in Tucson after riding, with bike engine, 2317 miles over 38 days, hauling 55-75 lbs of gear (depending on food/water levels). For the most part I enjoyed myself. The noise isn't bad: it is behind me and on the right, so it "trails" while riding. I do have rear-view mirrors, one on each end of the handlebars. I would never ride without them, engine or no. I focus the left mirror for cars and the right mirror on the load to make sure it is covered and secure.

I do wear ear-plugs while riding, not because of the engine but rather the traffic noise which frays my nerves after a few hours. The ear-plugs don't eliminate sound, but buffer it enough to make it tolerable yet allow me to hear.

I frequently check the mirrors and so am rarely caught off guard by upcoming vehicles. But it does happen (eg, fast vehicle, sharp curve) and is jarring. On this trip it happened less than ten times, as I recall.

I put a bright green neon "wide load" sign on the back of the trailer, partly for visual safety and partly hoping that a little humor might help keep a potentially annoyed driver respectful. I also have on the trailer a 5-foot pole with a red neon flag. Both increase visibility.

I now have just over 4000 miles on the bike engine. Counting the $600 price plus two belts totalling $80, but not gas and oil, the engine has so far cost 17¢ a mile. As for durability, the company said: their longest-running engine to date has 20,000 miles on it, and they have not had any engine failures during the 6 years they have been selling them.

Regarding freeway riding, my understanding: legal only if no other route is available. That is too bad, as I've twice had to take an Interstate and I've felt much safer having so much room between me and vehicles. Lauran, AZ, Jan 06

(Comment.) No matter how visible the rider's flags and clothes, riding thousands of miles on highways seems dangerous. Many motorists, esp drivers of big trucks (who hate to brake because they need much time and fuel to regain speed), feel that roads belong to them. (They pay to use them; bicyclists don't.) Often they try to squeeze by where   isn't room, hitting

the bike or forcing it off the road. Though an engine-assist
bike has the advantage of being on the road less time to go the
same distance, its higher speed increases the time needed to
slow and get safely off the road onto a bad shoulder.
      For long-distance seasonal traveling, I'd try hard to
arrange rides. Many "snow-bird" RVers go south in autumn and
north in spring, and may welcome fuel contributions. If we
spent much time around big cities, I think we could make
connections. Even from the smaller cities we infrequently
visit, we were able to get rides SOUTH the few winters we went.
Coming back north was a problem, partly because we usually
returned in February (because of DP mail obligations), and most
"snow-birds" don't go north before April. So we usually had to
hitch. (Hitching has become very risky now that cops have
hassle quotas and may try to pin unsolved crimes on non-natives
- TX is notorious for that. Hitchers are stationary targets
and thus easier to hassle than motorists.) Holly & Bert

Bicycle trailers, one wheel or two ? My experience:
      The 2-wheel Burley Nomad feels stable while riding and can
often carry more weight comfortably. The BOB's single wheel
tracks beautifully behind the bike's rear wheel and so is the
best choice for trail riding and backwoods going, but is
awkward to back up and park.
      The Burley, even with 100 lbs in the back, doesn't put
more than 11 lbs on the tongue. Whereas the BOB has more
tongue weight per load, and so can be harder on the bike and
you feel it more.
      The Burley, which has a rectangular bed, is easier to load
and manage, whereas the BOB is teardrop shape.
      The Burley tracks a bit to the left, to keep the right
tire out of ditches when on narrow shoulders. On my bike, its
wheels are inside the width of my handlebars, so I can easily
judge where I can and can't go safely. The BOB's width is
about from one pedal to the other. Lauran, AZ, July 05

Venom extractor proved effective on tick bite, but fragile.
      I bought a Sawyer "Extractor" kit at BiMart ($14). When I
attached the smallest cup to the syringe, the cup cracked. The
store exchanged my kit for a new one.   I'd put the cup on tight.
Now I leave it looser. But it seems delicate. Also, it says: do
not get the syringe wet. Durability ? Made in China.
      I used it on a tick bite, after removing the tick with fine-
pointed tweezers. The Extractor drew out fluid and blood. The
bite healed quicker than usual with less redness and soreness.
      Later Bert and I tested, on unbitten skin, the Extractor's
cup with mouth suction as well as with the Extractor. It applied
stronger suction than our mouths could, raising a bigger hickey
in 30 seconds. Also, Extractor suction can be more easily
applied for several minutes than can mouth suction. Recently I
found that, by attaching the cup to the Extractor with surgical
tubing, I can use Extractor in tight places. Holly, Jan 2006

What is wrong with the boy-scout bridge on the first page ?
      The brace ropes at the end are steep, putting stresses
that are unnecessarily high on the support poles and ropes.
The anchor stakes will probably pull out of the ground,
collapsing the bridge and dumping the boy.
      The anchor ropes should be longer and anchored farther
away, so they are not as steep. Also, those little anchor
stakes don't look strong. I'd tie to the base of a big tree.
Or, if none is available, to the base of a BIG stake, deeply
buried, with its TOP braced to the BASE of a smaller stake.
Av Dave, Oregon 978   May 2006

Surviving in the hills and towns of western North Carolina.

During Eric Rudolph's 5 years as a fugitive, despite a nationwide manhunt and a million-dollar bounty, a hobo came closer to catching him than did any federal agent.

The search for Eric, accused of abortion-clinic bombings that killed two people and injured 100, had focused on the densely-wooded mountainous western tip of NC. Eric had spent his teenage years there and had returned as an adult in the early 1990s, supporting himself doing carpentry.

In letters to his mother, written from jail, Eric described how he repeatedly sneaked into Andrews (population 1600) at night to scavenge food - even after scores of federal agents who were hunting him had set up their headquarters there !

Eric describes one mid-Oct foray. "On this particular night the air was cool, fall having started a month before. I was hesitant to get out from under my improvised bed, which was made of leaves and plastic." But he was hungry. He needed food. Forget hunting. That summer he had found an easier if riskier way of getting it. Shortly before midnight he started toward Andrews. "The mountain trail down to the road was steep and full of obstacles. Traversing it in the dark without a flashlight was done primarily from memory. Each step must be calculated and correlated with the surrounding shadows produced by the trees and the general landscape. Once you get used to the step count and how the trail looks at night, it becomes fairly easy."

At the road, he paused in a clump of bushes and shrubs and waited for traffic to subside. Then he headed to "a real godsend - two big, well-tended gardens right on the way to town. I had to be extremely gentle with the frozen plastic (which protected the plants from frost) for across the street, on the porch of the gardener's house, was my nemesis: a 20-pound pile of canine crap waiting patiently on guard for the slightest noise. A sound from the garden would send him into a rage, forcing my hasty retreat. I tried to make friends by feeding him (scavenged McDonald's hamburgers), but he would have none of my bribery. He hated me, and I hated him.

The gardener reminisces: "Someone could get a dozen ears of corn and you wouldn't know it. Now my brother, he got to missing a lot of tomatoes."

On that night, "everything went smoothly and I proceeded to bag my take and put it under bushes on the side of the road where I would retrieve it on my way back."

At Andrews, the road crossed a highway and then a river. Instead of using the well-lit bridge, Eric waded the river wearing waders he'd "improvised out of plastic garbage bags and string." In Andrews, "my first stop was the green garbage can behind Gibson Furniture" where he often found magazines and cigarettes. "A little work back at camp, cut the filters down and wipe the remainder with a clean towel, and you have nicotine-induced bliss." Then, behind McDonald's, he picked through the burgers tossed out at closing; and behind the grocery store he looked through its trash bin. Sometimes he even went through the cinema's trash for unsold popcorn.

Other nights, Eric obtained hundreds of pounds of corn, wheat, soybeans from silos. A mix of them, boiled, then pounded into pancakes and fried, proved to be "a staple that sustained me for many years." He would climb to the top of a silo, open the hatch, and scoop the feed into doubled trash bags (which he'd salvaged, washed, dried). He temporarily stored the bags of grain in garbage cans he'd previously stolen and set behind a lone (abandoned ?) building across the road. "One night I had to wait atop the silo for a few hours as a state trooper set up across the road to lay in wait for hapless speeders. He would race off to catch one, and after writing his ticket he'd return." Another time, Eric thought he had been spotted by a hunter along the creek behind the building. He scurried up a ridge and watched - but the feds didn't come. "For whatever reason, the hunter didn't divulge what happened." To haul the cans of grain to his camp, on Halloween he stole a pickup from a used-car lot. The pickup was found a few weeks later. The owner says, the police "didn't even dust for fingerprints or anything."

A scary encounter happened one night when Eric was searching through trash for materials to improve his leaf sleeping bag. "Right on top was a large piece of plastic perfectly draped over the top of a long rectangular box. I proceeded to fold it up. (Then) the box began to slowly open, like a coffin lid in a vampire movie, and there in the box was the barely visible figure of a human being. My thoughts started racing. Was this an ambush ? Did someone see me going through the garbage on a previous night and set this up?" The figure spoke to Eric, in a voice that "came hard - probably damaged by years of alcohol and cigarettes. Suddenly it came to me. 'This is a bum'." Eric replied, then slowly moved away. But Eric worried: "Did he recognize me ? Would he run and tell ?" (Many "wanted" notices with Eric's picture had probably been posted.) I made my way quickly back across the river, splashing through the cold water." After climbing the far bank, Eric looked back. The person hadn't moved. "But was he just waiting to catch his breath before leaving ? Then, after several tense moments, the person lit a cigarette, and every few drags he would let out a few gut-wrenching coughs. After finishing his cigarette, he lifted the lid on his box, climbed back in, and lay back down to sleep." But Eric waited a week before going into that town again.

On a Saturday night in May 2003, Eric went to a grocery store in the neighboring town of Murphy. "A Saturday night is a good night for garbage. I had a pile of bananas already, but thought I could get more and end my fruit drying early this year. Pushing aside my fears, I left my camp."

To cross a bridge, if a car approached he'd have to "hang over the side of the bridge on the other side of the rail", the shallow river 50 feet below. "Finally I get over the bridge and make my way through the field toward the dumpsters. At this point, (to see) what is coming around the sides of the building, I have to rely solely on the sight of (glare from) headlights. So I sit in the field looking from side to side, waiting for the patrol." The cop drives by "usually once an hour, but on weekends, with drunks and teenagers to deal with, his schedule is uncertain. For 3 years I have dodged him; on many a cold night he has come within inches of finding me. One night, while I was hiding in the dumpster at Taco Bell, he got out of his car, went into the dumpster area, and urinated on the dumpster I was hiding in. But on this particular night the cop was the least of my worries. Having to haul 200 lbs of fruit up to camp was on my mind. I run toward the dumpster." But when Eric was halfway there, the cop's car came whipping around the corner of the building with lights off. "This is unusual, for he never (before) turned them off, and this is how I've spotted him coming around the building."

The Murphy police officer had been a cop for less than a year when he spotted Eric and arrested him. Blake Morrison (condensed from 6July05 USA Today)   May 2006

Another method for cleaning a narrow-mouth container.

I fill it about 1/3 full of coarse sand, add a few drops of soap and enough water to make a slurry, and shake well. With persistence, cleans even stubborn deposits. Lauran, AZ, 2005

Attaching jug lid with duct tape, makes berry picking easier.

After making sure that the jug and lid are clean and dry where the tape will adhere, I firmly press the tape on. (If the tape does not adhere as well as I'd like, I reinforce by putting a second piece cross-wise over the first piece and around the jug.)

Then I twist and scrunch together the linking part of the tape to create a cord. The cord must be long enough so that movement of the lid does not put much force on the tape where it attaches. Twisting/scrunching shortens the tape, so allow extra length.

After losing one snap-lid, I did this. It proved a great convenience when picking, because I put the lid on and off frequently: on, when I move over rough ground where I might fall, or through (eg) rye grass which can splatter barbed sharp-pointed seeds in among the berries; off, when I reach the next berry bush. Also, when I remove the lid, I can just let it dangle; I don't have to put it somewhere.

If I tumble, a snap lid-and-jug is not as secure as a screw lid-and-jug, but the lid is easier to put on and off.

I rig a harness (not shown - an old pant leg, or a strong bag with straps ball-tied to it, might serve) around the jug so that I can wear it, leaving both hands free for picking.

Holly

Eating Nopali cactus - and removing stickers !

De-thorned Nopali leaves are found in every Mexican market's produce section. Nopali (prickly pear - Opuntia polyacantha), a succulent, is endemic to all of the American West, from Sonora north into BC. Boil in soup; or stir fry strips; or add diced to salads; or cook with sweetener and then dry, making candy.

Smaller northern variants may lack the sweet purple fruit found on the Sonoran kind, but are good eating. Free for the harvesting at roadsides, or from public lands (except in Arizona which has no-picking laws).

You need to work carefully to avoid the stickers. I use a long-bladed knife to chop free the leaves, and then two tong-like sticks to carry the leaves to a campfire for scorching off the fuzzy thorn tufts. If, despite precautions, you get the hundreds of tiny hair-like thorns stuck in your hands, smear a thin coat of white (Elmer's) glue over the affected area, let dry for 15 minutes, then peel off the glue film with the thorns all at once. Otherwise, make sure before-hand that those tiny tweezers are still inside that Swiss knife - and allow 30 min for picking the thorns out one by one. Brijji, Utah, Dec 04

(Addendum.) Prickly-pear grow in desert areas of BC, like the Okanogan near Osoyoos and Keremeos. Aarran, BC V8K

Ways we use damaged plastic containers.

Some pails had slits when acquired (caused by too-deep cutting when originally opened) or developed cracks. Others got punctured by a bear's teeth or claws (report in May 06 DP). Some lids had pour spouts which soon broke off. While awaiting better containers, we repaired with duct tape. Our patches endured a few months, even when rained on.

Punctured pails are still useful under cover for grouping small items. Or, a pail or jug with a hole in one side, can be cut in two and its good half used as a basin. Holly & Bert

Huge hasty hazel harvest hardly hearty.

In years past, we sometimes encountered hazel nuts while foraging berries. We picked a few but didn't get enough to excite us. However, the summer before last, we were in the right place at the right time - or so it seemed. Many bushes, some bearing dozens of good-size shells.

The nuts were not yet fully ripe but if we waited, the critters would get them. We picked and picked - many hours. Picking is slow because the husks are almost the same color as the leaves and difficult to spot. Got 15 gal - BEFORE husking.

To dry, each day we set them out in shade, some in net bags, some on old window screens we'd fortuitously found. Each evening we put them away in pails. That went on for a few wks.

To husk, Bert half filled a 10-gal tote and, wearing rubber mocs, tramped on them for ten minutes, picked out the shells and husks that had separated, and tramped on those that remained - again. That wore away the inside layer of the Rubbermaid tote ! After husking, we had maybe 5 gallons.

To shell, we used nutcrackers and pliers - and discovered that the nuts which had seemed plump when unripe, had shrunk: the largest to pea size, most to lentil size. A third of the shells contained no nuts. Hardly worth shelling by hand. (We thought about passing them through the grain grinder set loose, but didn't try.) We still have about 2 gallons unshelled.

Except for blackberries and possibly nettles, none of the foods we commonly forage provide as many calories as we expend harvesting them. But they provide variety: trace nutrients. Calories are cheap to buy and quite light to transport IF in dry seeds such as grains and beans. (We seldom buy canned or fresh foods: not only are they mostly water; they are more perishable and generally more polluted.) Holly & Bert, Feb 06

Participating in Nature: Thomas J. Elpel's Field Guide.

"In order to survive on a particular food source, you have to be able to harvest more calories than you expend. Many 'edible' wild plants require so much effort to harvest that you could starve to death even if you ate all day long every day."

Bitterroot (Lewisia sp.) "The foothills behind our home have small colonies - not enough to justify harvesting. However, I discovered a patch of 1000s of plants 35 miles away. I collected over a gallon of the whole plants during a one-hour harvest in May. Trimming away the vegetation left approx 1½ qts of roots. Pealing off the bitter bark took another 8 hrs ! The peeled roots cook up nicely in a stew. They are starchy, gelatinous, and filling. However, it is important to remove all the red bark. Even a little bit will make the whole stew bitter beyond edibility.... I've since learned that the Flathead Indians test the roots in mid April to see when the bark slips easily.... As with many wild plants, precise timing is the critical factor.... You have to get the roots at exactly the right time to be able to process them efficiently.

When he started camping, Elpel tried to subsist on foraged foods - and was usually hungry. Now he also takes food along.

"Much of the wilderness goes unused. People stay on a handful of well-defined trails leading to a few spectacular lakes and peaks. The smaller streams, trickles, springs and ponds are usually unused and unknown.... People rarely wander off the beaten path except in hunting season, so for the most part you can have the woods to yourself...."

"In all my reading I found very few shelters that could be built relatively quickly and still keep a person alive and comfortable. And those, unfortunately required materials that were not present in my area...."

"Instead of merely giving you some various shelters for you to replicate, I want to teach you how to THINK shelter. You see, every time and place is different, and at every time and place your own personal goals or objectives will also be different.... The type of shelter you build, and the location you choose for it, will vary tremendously depending on the TIME, the **PLACE**, and your **GOALS**. Therefore, every primitive shelter you ever build will be completely unique, and suited to the particular conditions at hand...."

Though some other primitive-skills books give more details, Elpel's advice seems sounder because he tells what has actually worked for him, including problems encountered. His specific suggestions are esp applicable to where he lives: in sw Montana about halfway between Butte and Bozeman.

"I rarely build freestanding shelters like the wickiup. I use the same principles but I prefer to begin by selecting a campsite that takes advantage of some natural features of the environment. For example, in an area with sizable trees, I look for a big tree that has fallen over, leaving just enough space for me to crawl underneath, that can be improved upon by leaning slabs of bark against one or both sides of the tree to widen the dry space underneath. Slabs of bark are natural shingles and really easy to use.... Simply start at the bottom of your shelter and layer the bark up to the top, so that the water will always fall from one bark shingle to another...."

"A tarp or poncho is an easy one piece shingle...."

"On winter camping trips I wear sweat pants over my jeans so" I can easily "stuff grass or other insulation inside...."

"The leaf hut is an excellent shelter in areas where there is a lot of dead organic matter on the ground, such as deep layers of tree leaves. The inside is shaped like a sleeping bag, defined by sticks leaning against a horizontal ridge pole. This is typically covered over with two feet of leaves, serving the dual purpose of insulation and shingling.... It stays warm with only your body heat." But, where Elpel lives, there isn't enough accessible organic matter for leaf huts to be practical. "It makes more sense for me to adapt my shelter to the local resources such as dirt, logs, stone, than to hike 5 or 10 miles to bring back a huge quantity of cattails." For a temp camp during cold weather, Elpel often first builds a fire to warm the ground before improvising a shelter on it.

"Most primitive skills literature and archeological records are oriented toward bulky material culture like baskets, pottery, weaponry. By the time you make these, plus your bow drill set, your shelter, and your tanned hides - you need a pickup truck to move to your next campsite." Elpel favors traveling light, carrying minimal tools and supplies.

1998, 198p.8½x11, HOPS Press, www.hollowtop.com; in 2006, Granny's Country Store, POB 684, Silver Star MT 59751, $25.

(Partial review by Bert, who had time only to read the
shelter chapter (18p.) and skim plants (30p.) before returning
it to a library for a friend. Others: mind (attitudes) 27p.,
fire 20p, cooking 20p, animals 26p, clothing 20p, ecology 16p.)

Different ways for different people in different places.

(Thoughts stimulated by the foregoing book.) Elpel makes
much more use of fire for warmth than we do, probably because
he lives in a colder climate. Also perhaps, most of his camps
are brief, without time for much insulating; whereas most of
our winter camps are used for weeks or months. (At our camp
this winter, with body heat only: during a cold spell, early in
morn, 23° outside, 52° inside; typical morn, 35° out, 60° in.)
Our camps might seem luxurious to Elpel, who often
improvises shelters in small holes. Our shelter, this winter
and most winters, is in a hole, but a big hole (natural, but I
also spent many days digging to shape it). However, our camp
is our home. (We type our zines on a 70?-year-old manual
typewriter.) Whereas Elpel also has a house in town, built by
he and his wife mostly out of natural materials at the site.
(He composes his books on a computer.)
Like Elpel's, each of our camps is different, even though
it may consist mostly of the same materials. (I've used
"wikiup" as a generic term for various kinds of insulated
shelters, most of which were not free standing.) B&H, Feb 06

I spent several snowy winter months in a 5x7x5-foot wall tent.

Made from blue poly tarps. I kept a fire going in a home-
made 5-gallon-can wood stove with a 4" galvanized pipe. The
tent was cozy - and toasty (in the small space the stove had
to be a little too close to my sleeping bag).
Now, years later, I'd think twice before breathing so much
air containing substances that out-gas from heated plastic and
galvanized metal. I'd use less plastic, esp where it is exposed
to heat. Also, I recently read that galvanized coatings contain
much cadmium and other toxic metals; so I'd pay a bit more for
the better stove-blacked pipe and burn it out thoroughly before
closing myself in with it. I think that most toxic building
materials out-gas less as they age. Doug, WA 988, March 2006

(Addendum.) Re out-gassing. That is what we found with a
small Stansport dome-tent we bought 15 years ago. At first it
stunk, probably from a fire retardant (notoriously toxic) that
government regs require. (Aren't you glad that gov protects
you ?!) At first we did not occupy it. Instead, for a few
summers, we hung it (so mice could not easily move in), erected
and opened, in the shade (so that sun would not deteriorate the
nylon). The smell SLOWLY went away. Now we often live in/out-
of the Stansport during summers, and don't notice any odor -
all the more reason to buy/scavenge USED tents/clothes/materials
(we'd bought the tent new), but wise to launder before using.
B&H

Giant blanket, draped over dome tent, added warmth.

Last autumn, our move to a winter base-camp got delayed
(by projects that took longer than expected). During November
we were still at a summer site, living in and out of our 6x7x4'
Stansport tent. Most days were still sunny and pleasant. But
the long nights got cold, often frosty. The tent was within an
open-fronted plastic rain/wind shelter. With both of us in the
tent, typical dawn temperatures: 30° outside, 40° inside -
tolerable for sleeping but not for tasks requiring bare hands.
Years before, we had acquired (from a dumpster ?) a BIG

blanket.   (Too big for any bed I can imagine. Original use ?)
It had languished, STUFFED (with difficulty) into a 5-gal pail.
(For our bed, we prefer sleeping bags opened out, or quilts -
more warmth per weight.) I draped the blanket over the tent.
It reached most of the way to the ground on all sides. It
warmed the inside at dawn to 50° - tolerable for hand work.
     Would several blankets, sewed into a dome shape, have
provided more warmth yet allowed enough ventilation ? Another
winter, I had covered a dome-tent with a 3-inch-thick layer of
moss (report in Apr 2000 DP), which had kept the inside 30°
warmer than outside. (Last autumn, not time to gather moss.)
     The Stansport tent (made in Taiwan) has held up well -
better than expected. No broken poles or balky zippers - yet.
But its biggest load was that blanket when damp with condensation; no snow load or gale wind. (Longer report in Sept 02 DP.)
                                                           B&H
Cave dweller discovered on militarily-restricted land.
     During his 4 years there, Roy Moore carved out a comfort-
able home. The 56-year-old veteran had solar panels wired to
car batteries for electricity, a wood-burning stove, a bed, a
glass door, a satellite radio, and ten 18-inch-high marijuana
plants growing in soil outside the   cave.
     The cave is in Los Alamos Canyon, a quarter mile from
Trinity St in Los Alamos and a half mile from Omega Bridge. It
is well-hidden at the bottom of a steep cliff in a restricted
area belonging to Los Alamos National Laboratory (LANL).
     On Oct 13, a **LANL** employee spotted smoke and called the
fire department. The deputy chief said, the fire in Roy's
stove, the first of the season, had released a plume of soot
and black smoke. (Presumably, Roy had had fires for previous
winters without producing smoke that had been seen.)
     LANL said, the cave is not near any critical or high
security areas. However, the marijuana prompted someone to
call the Los Alamos police who arrested Roy, charging him
with possession - a felony. Roy pleaded innocent and was
released on $5000 bond. (Jason Auslander, Albuquerque J,290c04)
     Roy then moved to the eastern rim of Pajarito Mtn, an
extinct volcano. His camp, below a ski resort, overlooked LANL
and the Rio Grande valley. Three months later, a Forest Service
law-enforcer asked Roy to move. He then moved in with his
daughter and her boy friend who have a studio apartment in Los
Alamos. There, he baby-sits his grandkids.
     A former computer programmer, Roy quit his job in 1996 and
sold all his possessions, to simplify his life so he could
focus on developing his unifying theory of the universe. He
moved from Amarillo to Los Alamos because of its proximity to
LANL and its dense population of PhDs and deep thinkers. He
has given talks at the Los Alamos library.
     Roy said, during his 3-month stay on Pajarito Mtn, he
enjoyed watching the ravens and deciphering their different
calls, noting how the calls changed as the birds became familiar
with him and learned to associate him with food scraps. Adam
Rankin (25De04 Alb.Jnl.; off internet by L.Smith - THANKS)
(Comments.) No mention of how Roy's second camp was found,
nor of what happened with the marijuana charge.
     Encouraging ravens to come around by providing food scraps,
seems risky. Ravens, and other birds of the crow family, are
especially likely to carry West Nile Virus.
     Media give a biased impression of the risks of dwelling in
ways not approved by Big Bully, because, with rare exceptions,
only people who are discovered, are publicized. My accessment:
          Dwelling Portably   September 2006

Suppose I camp 30 miles from a city and bicycle there once a
month. The biggest dangers: (1) getting hit by a vehicle
while biking; (2) catching flu (or ?) while in the city. B&H

Fires thrive on attention.
Move together pieces of wood that are too far apart, or
spread those that are too close together. A fire tolerates a
void under it but not within it. Fuel should be put on in time
to be adequately dried and preheated.

The cure for a smoky fire is often a matter of proper
adjustment of the wood. If that does not help, the fuel may be
too green or wet. Putting on dry, finer fuel will help burn up
more products of inadequate combustion and the improved thermal
column will carry the troublesome smoke up and over your head
more effectively. Mors Kochanski, Northern Bushcraft (reviewed
in SeO5 DP

A "Dakota Hole" cooking fire did not work well for me.
Its configuration was mid-way between Tim Leather's (May94
DP) and Eugene Gonzalez's (Apr01 DP). Bert dug it but then got
busy doing other things, so it was I who tried to cook with it.
The fire was smokier than an open fire. The connecting tunnel
kept getting clogged with fallen dirt and/or ash, but even when
open seemed to not supply enough air. So I soon changed to one
hole with a metal grate over it and the pot on the grate.

Bert now wonders if the pot was too big for the hole, thus
acting like the damper on a stove's chimney. We will try again
when we have more time to experiment. Holly & Bert, Feb 2006

Durability and reliability of various fire starters.
Most storable: a magnesium bar that has an artificial
flint on one side. With a knife, scrape off a small pile of
magnesium shavings as tinder, then strike the flint to put
sparks into the shavings. I had to strike quite a few sparks
before one ignited the magnesium. It works as well now as it
did 23 years ago when I bought it. However, I haven't used it
much so I don't know how many fires I could start before either
the magnesium or flint was used up. (Reports in May82 & Se82 DP)

Propane lighters have worked okay after several years of
storage, but I noticed some corrosion of the flints. Also, the
lighters have quite a few parts that can go wrong.

I bought some Coghlan "waterproof" matches 23 years ago.
I also coated various Diamond matches by dipping both ends in
melted paraffin. After soaking in water as long as 20 hours,
the $2\frac{1}{4}$" Diamond kitchen (strike-anywhere) matches lit best.
Whereas, after soaking only 3 hours, the Coghlan did not light
until both matches and strikers (not strike-anywhere) had dried
many hours. However, now, after 23 years storage, Coghlan's
still light fairly well; Diamond's not at all. Julia Summers,
(Comments.) More about Julia's match tests in Fe82 DP.   OcO5

The most durable and reliable lighters we have: big (8x10)
flexible plastic ridged-lenses. They can ignite even damp
tinder, and have nothing to get used up and little that can go
wrong. However, you need sunshine - which is not usually when
you want a fire. So, you also need a way to keep an ember. H&B

Further report on solar cooking: our problems and fixes.
(This is an update to reports in SeO2, SeO4, ApO5 DPs.)
During 2005, like in O4 and O3, we began solar cooking on
sunny days in May, and solar-cooked almost exclusively from
July through Sept. Though Oct included many days with sunny
afternoons, and we had no problem heating water for showers and

clothes washing, the sun was no longer bright enough long enough for reliable cooking. (During Oct and Nov, still at our summer camp, we fire cooked on a stove made from tin cans (somewhat like Fred's in May03 DP). In late Nov, we moved to a winter camp where we still have propane.)

The biggest change: completing the third big 8-panel reflector (panels 13x17"). Instead of aluminum foil, I covered the panels with aluminized plastic from a "space blanket". We were given the blanket many years ago, but had not used it, and with our mode of camping, seemed not likely to.) Upon opening it, I found that a big irregular area in the middle was not aluminized (which might not have much affected its usefulness as a blanket because the person would be laying on that portion). However, I was able to trim enough aluminized pieces.

I also found that the blanket consisted of one layer of plastic with an aluminum coating (unlike some snack bags which seem to sandwich the aluminum between two layers of plastic). So - indecision ! Should I glue the plastic with aluminum-side out, or plastic-side out ? The aluminum side was shiniest and the aluminum seemed to adhere well. (I had to rub vigorously with paper to get any off.) But how well would it withstand repeated wipings/washings to remove dust or grime - or when food accidentally dropped on it ? On the other hand, if the aluminum faced inward, would glue adhere to it ?

I put plastic-side out. Later I put aluminum-side out on a foam disk that sets under a glass jug for heating water - and the aluminum came off on the jug !

At first, the aluminized plastic was shinier and tougher than aluminum foil. But NOT more durable: after two months use, the plastic began disintegrating, mostly on the bottom center panel which receives the most concentrated sunlight and heat. Would the plastic have endured longer if put on aluminum side out, so the aluminum shaded the plastic ? When I replace it, I'll try shiny snack bags if I've found enough to cover one panel; otherwise aluminum foil.

We'd also like a better material for insulative shrouds over the pots. The salvaged transparent plastic we've been using, disintegrates after two summers of sun and heat. (We tried patching with transparent packaging tape, but sun/heat soon unstuck it.) We are hoping to find, at yard sales or in dumpsters, small sheet-acrylic aquariums. (Acrylic supposedly endures sunlight well.) Until we do, we will try oven bags draped over racks made of wire coat-hangers.

We have not had a really good solar cooking site. For the past few years, most of our summer camps have been on north-facing slopes (because foraging is usually better there - south-facing slopes get too hot and dry) and not far above valley bottoms. Consequently, any low haze/fog/smoke weakens the sun-shine; and distant trees and hills block the sun early morns and late afternoons, so we may get only 6 hours of sun.

Overall, solar cooking takes less labor than does wood-fire cooking (counting collecting and cutting wood) and no more labor than propane cooking (counting buying and transporting propane), but requires that one person stay nearby while cooking (for several hours) to reposition the reflectors. What would help: rotating platforms that automatically track the sun. They are made (sometimes used with pv panels) but aren't cheap.

B&H

How to increase storage life of dry foods.

Keep them dry, and as cool as possible. Rough rule: each 10° drop in temperature halves the rate of deterioration. Eg, if sunflower seeds can be stored one month at 70° before more than a few become rancid, their life might be 2 months at 60°, 4 months at 50°, 8 months at 40° (typical frig), 16 months at 30° (freezing), 32 months at 20°, 64 months (over 5 yrs) at 10° (typical freezer). In our area, average temperature of a buried barrel with an inch of styrofoam or a few inches of dry debris over it, is 50° to 60°. Coolest on a steep north-facing slope.

For extremely long storage, removal of oxygen from the air in the storage container is recommended. (See article in Ab#2.) Not quite as good: replacing most of the contained air with carbon dioxide from dry ice. (Wait for the dry ice to evaporate before sealing the lid tight; else it may explode!)

Find a hot spring and build your own soaking pool.

Guide books give the locations of popular pools, but they may be crowded or require permits. However, throughout much of the West, many unknown or unpublicized hot springs are free to anyone who finds them. By snooping around the right geo areas (eg, near known hot springs) you may spot the tell-tale (bright green) mossy rocks or, in winter, steam. A few hours work will create a delightful spot for relaxing.

A friend and I discovered hot water bubbling up through sand along a river. We made a pool by laying boulders around a 15-foot circle and scooping away the sand. We added sand bags (made from old Levi pant legs) and a drain pipe. We brought in clay from up the river which, after settling, reduced seepage out through the sand. That gave us a perfect cold-weather pool next to some scenic rapids. While trying it out, a couple of river otters came to see what we were doing.

In earlier experiments I tried metal tubs. But they either got destroyed or were taken out by the Forest Service. Some years ago, a local bath house was torn down after some nit wit slipped on the moss and sued the Forest Service.

Though most pools with substantial flows are safe, much-used pools in (eg) S CA can carry pathogens. I put a dash of vet-supply iodine in them. A few pools have tiny worms growing in the moss. I screen out the moss and put a little soap in the water to deactivate the worms. A long soak in hot water can dehydrate; keep a jug of drinking water handy. A brief dip in cool water will usually restore energy. Al Fry, ID 836, Jan 06

How we dispose of feces, in winter and summer.

During winter when at a base camp with a well-insulated shelter, we usually defecate inside. We shit on several sheets of paper, which also serve to wrap it. (Details in May 96 DP.) We temporarily store it in a pail with lid on, kept outside. When the pail is full, Bert takes it along while foraging or fetching spring water. He empties the pail into some natural depression, well away from our camp and any water, and not within sight of trails, and covers with a little dirt/debris/leaves. We don't dig latrines at a camp where we may remain long, because doing so would disturb much vegetation.

When at a short-term summer camp, we usually dig a narrow-hole latrine (described in a Light Living Library paper). We seldom shit directly into the latrine because it is usually not close and has bushes around it. Shitting on paper is easier.

The only problems we've encountered: During winter, hungry critters often dig up feces, creating a visible mess. (The paper is more visible than the feces, and more durable.) During spring, stinky mushrooms sometimes grow on the feces. Neither problem is serious if the deposits are not near our camps. At some places during summer, the soil, dry then, is very hard.

Report on Yukon in northwestern Canada.

If I had to travel much through the Yukon, I would bicycle, even though that is time consuming. Hitching is tough there, though legal and you do get rides eventually. May be, my attitude and dislike of hitching shows on my face. Companies like Greyhound bus lines have a monopoly on adult bus fares.

In 2005 (a rough year for me financially), I traveled out of town less than in 2004, but I covered many more miles. In Oct, I and my brother (who drove his pickup-camper) went on a 5-day weekend holiday roadtrip to Whitehorse and back. My brother is a redneck hunter and drove there to visit a friend living in Haines Junction. Campground fees are about $13 a night. We usually parked the pickup-camper on some back road in wooded surroundings, out of sight of traffic and residences.

In some ways I find Yukon more appealing than my home area (in central BC). Much wilder: fantastic fishing, hunting, camping. And, in summer, 24 hours of daylight. But Yukon is an EXPENSIVE place to live. Groceries and other supplies cost much more. I pity some of the people there, such as lodge owners, who rely on tourist dollars to keep their businesses open. If you were poor, you would have to be very resourceful or inventive to survive year around. Most people in Yukon shop at Whitehorse, a city of 30,000 people, for all the amenities and services it has to offer. Bruce of BC, January 2006

How to learn more wilderness-survival skills.

Nothing beats experience. I've attended survival classes in NJ, NC, VT, ID; most affiliated with Tom Brown's Tracker School. These classes lasted a weekend to a week, and cost $800 of more ! They do show you many things but, after the class, without intensive practice, you're really not much better than before. For these classes to really be useful, you need to practice a lot; but, ironically, if you are that motivated, you don't really need the classes. The best thing about the classes is having the chance to meet like-minded people, form friendships, and make connections.

I think it is better to save your money and buy or borrow good informative books. Tom Brown Jr's field guides are good (tracking, wilderness and suburban survival, etc), but intent-ionally incomplete. Tom believes you learn more by figuring part of it out for yourself, but this can be frustrating. Euell Gibbon's books are great for plant info if you can already identify the plants. For identification, I think Peterson Field Guides are best, esp the one on edible plants. Peterson uses drawings, which better emphasize indicator marks. Audubon is good for identifying trees (bark is hard to draw). The Foxfire series is interesting/informative, but not always practical (mountain-man-style living). Newcombs Guide to Wild-flowers may be the easiest to use. No field guide is complete.

Learn about the things around you (ecology is fascinating) and as for survival skills - practice, practice, practice. Do not get discouraged; your mistakes are your best teachers. Go easy, be patient with yourself. If possible, seek people with similar interests for moral support. How strongly do you want independence and freedom ? Gumby, NC 275, July 2005

(Addendum.) A good book for this area is Plants of the Pacific Northwest Coast, MacKinnon & Pojar editors, Lone Pine. It covers from the Umpqua/Siuslaw divide south of Eugene to the Kenai Peninsula sw of Anchorage, and east to Cascade summits. (Despite the wide range of latitude, many of the same plants occur throughout that area.) Reviewed in Apr01 DP by Julia Summers who calls it "THE BEST field guide i've seen - and at a reasonable price" ($23 ppd for 539 pgs 8x5 - subsidized by Canadian taxpayers ?). Though a beautiful book, with both color photos and line drawings good for identification, it does not list many uses. Eg, it includes Hypochoeris radicata (gosmore, which, second to nettles, is the green we eat most of) and several of its difficult-to-distinguish relatives, but said nothing about edibility. For that, good books include Plant Uses of BC Indians, Nancy Turner; Wild Edible Plants of West, Kirk. An excellent book for all of N.America is Encyclopedia of Edible Plants, Couplon (reviewed in Sept 04 DP). H & B

When seeking edibles, evaluate plants plentiful in your locales.

Plant books tell about many wild edibles in a region. But if you go looking for all of them, you will probably spend much time looking without finding many edible plants, because most grow only in certain habitats. A more productive approach: first notice plants that are plentiful in places you go and identify them (easiest when flowering, using a book ordered by type of flower), THEN check for edibility. Bert & Holly

For nutrition, consider what remains after preparation.

I was surprised to see an article of mine that was in Sept 1986 Coltsfoot, quoted in Apr 04 DP. I'd written: "Boiling destroys vitamin C", which is true. The DP author then claimed: "A more accurate statement would be: vitamin C is destroyed IN PROPORTION TO light and heat, NOT instantaneously when a food reaches boiling" (and goes on to cite test data).

That gives the impression that one is still getting a significant amount. Linda Clark wrote, in Know Your Nutrition, 1981: "But those who insist we get enough vitamin C in our foods should realize that, according to a study made in Ireland, 80 percent of the vitamin C in our food is lost in cooking.... Even exposure to the air can cause a loss." George Sherwood, NY 147, Mar05

Sour about substitute sweets.

Claim: Unlike refined cane/beet sugar and corn syrup, maple sugar and honey are safe because they are absorbed slowly.

Dis: Except for flavors and impurities, maple sugar consists of the same sucrose that is in cane/beet sugar, and honey consists of sucrose plus the same glucose and fructose that are in corn syrup. All are soon absorbed if eaten/drunk on an empty stomach. Honey contains natural toxins that flowers put in nectar to deter bugs that dine without pollenating. (Raw honey may contain microbes that babies' immune systems can't cope with.) Refined sugar may contain small residues of toxic chemicals. Neither contain the vitamins (etc) needed to utilize them. Both are unnatural: 99.999% of our ancestors (stone-age and before) rarely got concentrated sweets. Thus humans did not evolve to cope with them. H&B

Our experience with various storage totes and barrels.

We are now using about 25 totes of various brands. (They had vent holes under the handles. Purpose ? I covered the holes with duct tape, inside and out.) None have leaked, including some setting out with nothing over them. Rubbermaid lids seem to fit more reliably than do the lids of some other brands, both because the Rubbermaid lids have taller lips and because (with the 20-gal size) the sides do not bulge out as much if the contents press on them.

Dwelling Portably   September 2006

Dwelling Portably

or Shared, Mobile, Improvised
Underground, Hidden, Floating

Dec 2007 $1 per issue   POB 190-d, Philomath OR 97370

Earthen floors may or may NOT be warming during winter.

Bert wrote that plastic-covered dirt floors have a big
advantage (over raised wooden floors): heat capacity. "They
help warm your home during winter and cool it during summer."

I don't doubt the summer cooling. But winter warming ?
Only if you live where winters are short and not very cold.
Even there, a dirt floor will be warming only when the air
drops below floor temperature which might be 50o. Not balmy !

But where winters are long and cold, uninsulated dirt
floors will be chilling. Packed dirt is a fair conductor.
Your floor will get almost as cold as the soil outside. Here,
soil freezes several feet deep - and this isn't the Arctic.
(We don't have permafrost. Permafrost poses a more serious
problem; not in winter but in summer when the top melts.)

We tried a dirt floor. COLD ! Something that helped:
bank snow around your shelter, deep and wide. It insulates the
ground from sub-freezing air and slows the frost.

What is better: insulate your floor well along with the
rest of your home, and store MANY gallons of water inside.
During the day while the stove is going, the water warms up.
Then at night you can let the fire go out because the water
will give off enough warmth to keep the air above freezing or
at least from going much below freezing - depending on amount
of water and insulation and outside temperature. (Regardless
of how well you insulate, unless your home is tiny you WILL
need a stove. Solar heating ? Not here. Winter days are
short and the low sun (if any) doesn't give much warmth.)

Recycled milk jugs work fine. They are better than one
big tank because they have more surface and therefore take up
and give off heat faster. Also, if not too full, ONE freeze
won't burst them. (I don't fill them above bottom of handle.)
Repeated freezing/thawing may. Mark, Alaska 995, May 2007

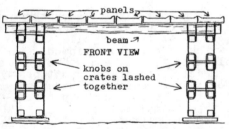
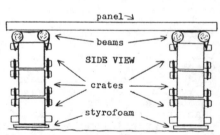

Crates and panels form a versatile portable structure.

A decade ago, we bought the leavings of a family that had
moved away. Some were immediately useful; some we couldn't
use; some were puzzles. We had to take all - but price right.

Among the puzzles were knobby crates and panels of wood,
stiff foam, fiberglass. Parts of a structure ?

Two years ago I got time to play with them. Most needed
repairs; the wood had rotten spots. (I don't know their
history, but I assume they were built for a dry climate - NOT
western Oregon.) I patched those which had rotted least (which
took longer than expected). I'm not sure how the parts were
used, or if I have all the parts, but here is what I did:

Dwelling Portably   December 2007

I lashed together 12 of the crates to form 4 columns, each 3 crates high. I arranged the columns in a quad, setting them on pieces of salvaged styrofoam to insulate their wooden bases from the ground so hopefully they wouldn't get condensation and rot more. Then I set beams between pairs of columns and lashed them to the crates. I used poles as beams. (I didn't find anything beam-like among the parts.) Then I layed panels across the beams, lashing them to the beams and (not shown) each other. Also not shown: pieces of cushiony foam between beams and crates, and beams and panels, to distribute loads.

Result: a gazebo, about 13 by 8 ft, open on 4 sides, but easily covered with netting or several layers of cloth or plastic, depending on weather. The panels, mostly foam, form an insulative roof. But, if rain, a plastic covering is needed to prevent leaks. Inside height, about 4½ ft; adequate for sitting; not standing. (Can be heightened by lashing another crate onto each column, or by digging out the floor.) It is somewhat stabilized by the beams lashed between columns, but would need additional bracing to withstand strong winds.

Advantages, compared to pole/branch-framed structures: Panels are insulative. Crates provide shelves (and totes when moving). May assemble faster. Size can be changed more easily. Saves finding, cutting, trimming poles (if prefab beams are added). Dis: Bulky parts to carry (though quite light), and to store when not in use. Needs level rectangular sites (whereas wikiups can be tailored to space available). With either, winter warmth will depend on the coverings.

I don't know of anything similar manufactured. Feb 1980 MP/DP (in the original first issue no longer stocked; not in the reprint) mentioned a Carry Cabin made in MI that was formed of panels small enough to carry. I've seen/heard nothing about it since. Various lawn sheds are made of sheet metal or wood. But they don't have insulative roofs; and (my impression is) they don't disassemble as easily as this gazebo. (The metal sheds I've seen are held together by many screws.) A few years ago, Rubbermaid made (still makes ?) a small lawn shed formed of plastic panels that fit together easily. Big enough for two people to sleep in, or for storing a few bikes.

I don't recommend hand-fabricating this kind of structure (unless you are a hobbiest who enjoys such work). I suggest molding the parts out of plastic, as are totes and pails - a task for a mid-size manufacturer with appropriate equipment. Choose shapes that are easy to mold, and to ship and store. (I don't suggest this gazebo as a model. Its crates don't nest.) If you or anyone you know works for such a company, please pass on the idea. There is a substantial market for such a product. (Many people can no-longer afford traditional housing.)

What existing things could form structures ? Could milk crates be lashed together into columns and a ceiling ? To insulate ceiling, into its crates put plastic bags of anything fluffy and light (extra clothes; dry leaves; styrofoam chips; crumpled newspapers). For rain protection, suspend plastic tarps above the ceiling, sloping. The space between tarps and ceiling provides an attic for storing LIGHT-weight things.

How available are milk crates ? Do dairies give away damaged crates they would otherwise have to recycle ? **Bert**

Slope tarps quite steep for rain; even steeper for snow.
And place any rafters up-down the slope. (If cross-ways, they may dam puddles - which will deepen as the plastic stretches - which will further stretch the plastic ...!)

Mongolian Cloud Houses: How to Make a Yurt and Live Comfortably.
About half of this book consists of detailed instructions
with many drawings, for   building a 13-foot diameter yurt like
what the author, Dan Frank Kuehn, built and dwelled in for five
years in northern New Mexico during 1970s. Dan used mostly
native or salvaged materials. Many of his helpful tips are
also applicable to other kinds of dwellings.
"One way to initially straighten solid wooden poles is to
tie them tightly into a bundle while they are still green,
carefully aligning each pole. When the bundle is dry, the
poles will keep their new shape."
"If you intend to cut your own poles from the forest,
spend some time looking around in your own neck of the woods
for trees and shrubs that naturally have a straight, vertical
nature. Collect some samples and let them dry."
"I built (the frameworks of) my first yurts entirely out
of willow poles which were readily available but impossibly
crooked. I've since learned that in Mongolia and Europe,
willow, poplar, ash, hazel, and other woods are specially
chosen varieties, cultivated to grow extremely straight."
"Johnson grass (which Dan used in NM; it resembles
bamboo) is considered a pest and you should have no trouble
getting permission to cut it; just be sure you are not
transporting its invasive grass seeds with your poles."
"Cut (poles) as close to the ground as possible and clean
them of branches, carefully working UP the plants so as not to
weaken them at the limb connections."
For covering, "I used 12-ounce untreated canvas. It's
strong and natural but only practical in the driest climates.
There are other, un-natural but more durable cover options...."
"Two trenches on the uphill side of the site are necessary:
one (above the back bank) to allow water coming downhill to pass
around the site; and one (between bank and yurt) for water
coming off the yurt itself." (Illo in book.)
While leveling the site, "if you want raised or sunken
places, this is the time to make them."
Other topics: dimensions of parts for other sizes; how
Dan would build a yurt differently now; traditional Mongolian
methods; many photos, both of Dan's yurts and of Mongolians
and their yurts; reprint of 1930's kids book about Genghis
Khan;   sources for yurts, other nomad homes, supplies, tools.
Though yurts are more complex to build than are some other
kinds of portable or improvised shelters, they seem well suited
to open areas where a few people may be able to move a small
yurt without disassembling it, and where there are strong winds
but not much snow or rain, and where the native woods available
are mostly slender (eg, 1"D) poles. Comparing with tipis:
"Because of the slope of the roof, a tipi can shed rain and
handle a snow load better than a yurt." "A low ceiling makes
(a yurt) easier to heat, and the short poles fit on or in most
vehicles." If they have the same surface area (and amount of
covering), tipi is 15' high, 18' D base; yurt 10' high, 13'D,
and has a little more stand-up height area. (Illo in book.)
160 pages 7x10, 2006, Shelter Publications, POB 279,
Bolinas CA 94924; www.shelterpub.com; $17. They also have:
Wonderful Houses Around the World , Yoshio Komatsu and Akira
Nishiyama, 48p.7½x10, $9. Color photos plus cut-away drawings
with captions show/tell how dwellers live. Homes in Mongolia,
China, Indonesia, India, Romania, Tunisia, Spain, Senegal, Togo,
Bolivia. Some are underground. Book especially for kids.
               Dwelling Portably   December 2007

Latex polymer waterproofs tents effectively.
In my 4-meter cotton tent, during a heavy downpour some
visitors remarked that it was like being aboard the Titanic.
As soon as the tent's skin got soaked through, it no longer
kept out the weather.
I later found and applied an effective product: Kamp-Kote.
Now rainwater can even puddle on top of the tent without drip-
ping in. A several-year-long test convinced me: Kamp-Kote
works. It is a water-soluable latex-type polymer liquid.
Kamp-Kote is ten times better than Scotch 3M, Waterguard,
Thompsons Waterseal; also better than similar more-expensive
polymer products. About $13 a gallon at outdoor-sports/camping
stores. If they don't stock it, they can order it.
You can thin its milky consistency with water for easier
application to cloth. It works equally well with natural
fibers like cotton canvas, and on many synthetics including
nylon taffeta. It dries clear, and, once dry, it does not
stiffen cloth nor add noticably to weight. briggi2u@yahoo.com
July 06

Recently-purchased "duct tape" has weak adhesive.
It sticks momentarily but soon peals off. The slight
springyness of the tape itself is enough to gradually lift it
off of a curved surface or around a bend. The tape peals off
even if continually cool. Brands tried: 3M; Tartan (BiMart).
Tape we bought several years ago, holds better. Eg, Tape-
It duct tape and SpecTape masking tape. I wonder if the adhesive was found to be toxic and replaced with something weaker.
We use the newer tape only for repairing items we also sew
such as clothes. The tape holds the cloth in position for the
few minutes needed to sew through cloth AND TAPE. The stitches
anchor the tape so that it reinforces the cloth. Holly & Bert

Free water barrels have many uses.
Last month at my mobile home in the woods, my ex-food-
industry-sourced polyethylene water drums were showing symptoms
of age. After 27 years in the sun, they were cracking and
splitting and leaking. Time to find replacements.
Prices have gone up. Eg, commercial sources were selling
30-gallon poly drums for $37 each. But a friendly tip led me
to a bottling plant. Coca-Cola plants receive soft-drink syrups
in 2-bung poly drums: 15, 30, 55 gallon. Bottlers try to have
local recyclers pick up the one-time-use barrels. But when the
scrap-plastic-market price is low, the empties tend to
accumulate, uncollected, at the loading dock.
Call on your local bottler's manager, offering to help
recycle those barrels. They may still have a trace of syrup in
them, so rinse well. (Some folks may moan about toxic
substances leaching out of fresh plastic - but, hey, it's a
plastic world we live in - and those barrels are free.)
There are many uses for them apart from water storage.
Make an underground storage cache by cutting open and nesting
together different sizes. Or build a huge floating raft by
lashing together a hundred barrels with bamboo poles.
Or .... ? briggi2u@yahoo.com July 06

(Addendum:) Though harder to find, there are also barrels with
removable tops in which some foods are shipped. Useful for
storing things other than liquids. They are much stronger than
plastic trash barrels, and they seal better. Bert & Holly

Experiences living in a travel trailer in Pennsylvania.

Last year I learned that our trailer's front framing had gotten wet and dry rotted, causing the trailer's front to bow outward. The RV dealer said that, even if they could fix it, the bill would be about $4000 ! We had bought it for only $1200. So, gingerly, we towed the trailer to where we winter.

This spring, as we were readying the camp-grounds for its May-first opening, a carpenter working there told me he could repair the damage for $100 ! But he had other jobs scheduled until years end. I told him to schedule us then.

Normally we have to leave the camp-ground by May first, and wondered how the trailer would fare on roads in its present condition. Then, the camp-ground owners asked us to stay through the summer months, remaining at our premium site (it is the levelest and closest to the hookups), continuing to pay $15 a week. That change was welcome - but didn't last.

The camp isn't a typical RV park where people come and go. Instead, the camp is rented as a whole by various churches and other groups. Normally, each stays a week or so. But for the last few years, one group has rented the place for 6 weeks each summer. Unfortunately for us, that group's leaders wanted the premo site for their RV. Whereupon, the camp owners, instead of telling them that the site had been promised to us, told us to leave. $$$ were more important to them than integrity !

The trailer towed fine, and we are now set up on a family member's property. Though on top of a hill, we are mostly hidden. But we have no electric, water, sewer connections. We have dry-camped before and found that, by being frugal, we can go 3 weeks, using our trailer's self-contained systems.

We might be here for a while, so we are living in the winter mode: hauling in water; using small kitchen bags and kitty litter in the toilet bowl; and running our generator for electricity. Our gen has a low-amp outlet and a high-amp outlet. After we figured that out, we could sleep in relative comfort as the air-conditioning compressor would work properly. The generator runs all night on 2 gallons of gasoline.

(Later.) The 6-week group has now left. We pondered whether to stay on the hill, or move the trailer back down to the campground. Convenience won out, so we moved.

The guy who offered to fix the trailer, now says he can't do it before next year. So we decided that, next spring, we will look for a better used rig. We'd like another trailer, or an older class C, though we'll consider a well-done school-bus conversion. John & Rose Ward, Living Mobile, PA 174, July
& Aug 06

We live full time aboard our boat.

Very comfortably; very economically. We have had no hassles from the marine patrol this winter, even in the warm clime of southwest Florida. Land dwellers have not been so lucky. Lots of meanness. The police harrass. Also, in northeast FL, an older gent was attacked by two 10-year-old kids, which put him in a hospital. Becky, FL 339, Apr 07

I live aboard merchant marine ships. On ship, I pay nothing.

Off ship, I live in southeast Asia, out in the backwoods boondocks. Even there, I can pick up pocket money by exporting coffee and cocoa beans. Alan, 2006

I am rebuilding a '71 Westfalia Transporter.

I will live in it while searching for land, as a communal venture or on my own. Garner, CA 935, 2007 Dec 07

Exploring railroad tracks can be rewarding in several ways.
Most cities have a vast intricate network extending outward. There used to be many vacant structures along the right-
of-ways, but not with today's economy. However, I find many
places to do gorilla gardening, which is no longer possible
anywhere else in Chicago. Do NOT plant on railroad or power-
line right-of-ways. They are heavily sprayed with herbicides.
Also avoid former wastefields.
While near the tracks, you are close to the fastest and
most discrete method of getting out of town: hitch a freight.
What you want is one empty car in the middle of a bunch of full
cars, so it doesn't bounce around too much. I tend to use only
freight and spur lines, not passenger lines. The workers don't
usually bother me, and less danger of getting run down.
If threatened by a flood or by a hurricane which can bring
a flood, to evacuate my first thought is: get on a rail line
(preferably one on top of a large embankment) and start walking.
A problem, esp if there is a social breakdown: other kinds of
people who do this might be potential marauders. Kurt, IL 606,
2006

Wild ginseng is valuable, but harvest is regulated.
Wild ginseng diggers will trudge deep into the hills of
Appalachia today for the beginning of harvest season. Last
year, 4800 pounds of the perennial herb were harvested (in WV?),
selling for about $300/pound. Some people believe the herb
boosts their energy. (newspaper clipping sent by Herbert Diaz)

Antiseptic/healing oils effectiveness increased by covering.
Tea-tree or eucalyptus oil seems to hasten healing of
insect bites, infected thorn-punctures, pimples. But if not
covered, most of the oil evaporates before it can diffuse thru
our skin. To block evaporation, I cover the oil with a piece
of aluminized plastic cut from a junk-food wrapper. (We rarely
eat junk foods, but we collect a few empty wrappers.) Food-wrap
plastic is not only relatively non-toxic, but it is formulated
to prevent escape of food flavors including aromatic oils.
I hold the plastic on by putting sticky tape around all
edges. (I've mostly used masking tape, without noticable ill
effects. Medical tapes safer ?) One application is usually
enough. If not, once a day or so I remove plastic, apply more
oil (maybe alternating euc and ttree), replace plastic, tape.
H & B

Vitamin D is very important for health.
Over 100 scientific studies show that deficiencies not
only cause rickets (deformed bones), but render people of all
ages more prone to cancer, flu, osteoporosis, tuberculosis, MS,
chrohns, diabetes-1, skin infections, and other diseases.
Some of D's health effects have long been evidenced. Eg,
sunshine prevented/cured tuberculosis; cod-liver oil reduced
infections; people near equator suffered much less MS and
diabetes-1. But until recently there was little formal
research, perhaps because unpatentable natural substances such
as vitamins were not profitable for the medical/pharmaceutical
establishment. And in pop nutrition media, D was long over-
shadowed by vit C, probably because D has a narrower safe range:
megadoses of C are generally safe whether or not helpful,
whereas megadoses of D can harm, esp if eaten, but even if
obtained from sun (sun burn, and more risk of skin cancers).
Physiological effects are numerous and complex. For some,
see long articles in 11Nov06 Science News and Nov07 Sci Amer.
Dwelling Portably   December 2007

Most Americans and Europeans are vitamin-D deficient.

400 first-time moms (half Afro, half Euro) and their babies were tested by U Pittsburgh. 90% had taken, during pregnancy, multivits that included D. Half had before. Yet, at birth, blood of 96% of Afro and 63% of Euro moms, and umbilical blood of 83% of Afro and 50% of Euro infants, lacked adequate vit D. A cause of rickets increase in Afro kids. (Sci News, 10Feb07)

In Feb-Mar 2005, blood tests of 420 otherwise-healthy human females in various north European cities (latitudes 52o to 60o; N Am equiv, Calgary-Anchorage) found: adolescents, 92% deficient, 37% severely so; older, 37% def, 17% severly. NvO7
Sci Am

Best obtain vitamin D from sunshine, not from pills.

Because the vit D in pills and foods is fat soluable, it is carried in the blood by lipoproteins (fat-protein combos) and may accumulate in artery walls along with cholesterol, and increase calcium deposits. People who have other coronary risk factors and who ingest much vit D, may harm themselves more than help themselves, especially post-menopausal women.

Vit D that is produced in the skin by sun exposure is carried by proteins (rather than fat) and is unlikely to contribute to arterial calcification. Michael Mogadon, MD, from Every Heart Attack is Preventable ,2001, New Am Libr.

(Though major media have recently publicized D's health benefits, I've NOT seen sunshine's superiority publicized, perhaps because universities/corporations are patenting artificial analogs of D they hope you will buy.)

However, if you live where sunshine is absent or very weak for long periods, and you lack electricity for a special uvb-emitting lamp, fish-oil or D-pills recommended. One vit D researcher in Montreal takes 4000 units/day during winter (which is ten times the official RDA; one-tenth the toxic amount). There is NOT enough D in "fortified" foods nor in most multi-vit pills. As for artery clogging, reduce other risks.

Sunshine during childhood prevents multiple sclerosis later.

Health workers who travel widely, have long observed that MS is rare near the equator but common at high latitudes. "There's a genetic component to MS but also an environmental component." (Probably also various dietary components.) Recent studies "hint that uv rays set a child's immune system on a normal course for life." Though mostly older folks get MS, after adolescence sun doesn't seem to help prevent MS, though it does some other ills. (Science News 28july07)

Too much sunshine is not good for you.

In spite of what sun-worshipers say, ultra-violet rays can dry your skin terribly, esp as you grow older. The sun acts as an oxidant. Look what happens to plastics left in the sun: you can poke a finger through some older tents; a plastic bottle cracks and crumbles. This same force is at work on your skin cells. briggi2u@yahoo.com July 2006

How much sun exposure is healthful ?

With sunshine as with selenium, iron, protein, exercise, and quite a few other things, the optimum range may be narrow. Recent recommendations I've seen: find out how long an exposure turns your untanned skin slightly pink; then expose yourself one-third as long three days a week.
Dwelling Portably   December 2007

Mild exposure directly benefits the skin exposed. So, though a bikini covers only small areas, nudity is better. Except: minimize exposure of face and neck and any other parts that receive much sun during activities when they can't be easily covered or shaded. Change positions frequently.

Complications. Sunshine intensity depends on atmosphere conditions and on sun height (when low, its light goes through more air which absorbs more of the uvb) and on angle of skin to sun. Eg, an hour's exposure that may not pinken skin at mid-day in Dec-Jan nor near sunset any month, may burn it at mid-day in June-July. Dark people (who may need 6 times more exposure than pale people) may not notice pinkening.

Though humans evolved the ability to store vit D for a while, most of our ancestors lived in the tropics and did not need to store enough D to last for several months. Consequently, winter exposure is very desirable when possible. H & B

How to increase sun exposure during winter.

Expose as much skin as is comfortable, except probably not face or neck. If too cold to be nude below the neck, alternate areas: eg, waist-up for ten minutes; waist-down for ten min.

Some ways to increase warmth: Wear insulative head-neck coverings. Stand or lay so that the rays come at nearly a right angle to as much skin as possible. Exercise. Drape a blanket or coat over your shady side. Stand between the sun and something that reflects sun onto you, or that absorbs sun and radiates heat onto you (eg, a broad tree trunk with dark bark). It will also block or slow any breezes.

Build a small portable sun tent, just big enough to lie in (which can also serve as a mini greenhouse). It can be as simple as a lean-to of a plastic that passes uvb. On the back side, put aluminum foil so that you get both direct and reflected sun. Orient ridge east-west.

Ordinary clear polyethylene passes some uv - which is why it soon deteriorates in summer sun. (If used only in the weaker sun of winter, it may last a few years) But I don't yet know how much uvb (needed for vit D synthesis).

Later this winter, we may be in an area where we can build a sun tent - and report. (At our present site, the trees are now tall enough to confine sunshine to spots which move as the earth turns. So, to get much sun, we have to move too.) B & H

Recent wild hazel harvests: fewer nuts but bigger kernels.

A few years ago, we harvested MANY nuts. But, to get them before other animals did, we picked while most were still immature. Drying/curing shrunk the kernels. They tasted fine but most were only lentil size. Last summer and this summer we waited longer - and consequently got fewer nuts. But, after drying, the kernels were bigger: about pea size.

Wild hazels seem to have thicker shells than do domestic hazels. Some can't be easily cracked with ordinary pliers or nut-crackers. Vise-grips crack them ! Bert & Holly

Harvesting tip: the sequence in which plants ripen, varies.

I read that hazels ripen about the same time as black-cap raspberries. Maybe some places some years. Not here recently. Last summer, black-caps were past and we'd been picking blackberries for two weeks before hazels were mature enough. H & B

Prolific "weed" proves to be a nutritious delight.

Following several rain storms, our normally dry, brown, southern New Mexico desert erupted into acres of green weeds. As I diligently removed them from our yard, a neighbor happened by - and suggested we eat them instead. Although I have a copy of Euell Gibbons' Stalking the Wild Asparagus , I had overlooked purslane. This beautiful "weed" is loaded with vitamins, omega-3s, and other beneficial nutrients.

Raw, I found it rather uninspiring. We now eat it lightly steamed. When dressed with garlic, oil, soy sauce, butter, etc, my husband says it is as good as any of the other greens we love. I am also pickling it in ACV. I also chop it up and feed it to our birds, dogs, cats. For recipes, etc, type Purslane on a search engine and you will find multiple sites.

Gibbons wrote: "Originating in India or Persia, purslane has established itself around the world. In America it has found a congenial home, from Atlantic to Pacific, and from Canada to Tierra del Fuego.

"The wild plant is a ground-hugging annual seldom reaching up to two inches high, although it may be more than a foot across. It reaches its best development in rich, sandy soils and so is sometimes a weed in gardens and cultivated ground. Each plant has several tender stems, which radiate from the center of the plant, forking freely as they creep along the ground. The stems are about a quarter inch in diameter near their origin, and reduce in size at each forking. The tiny yellow flowers, opening only on sunny mornings, are found in the forkings of the stems." Lynn, NM 880, Aug 06

What we eat, and how our diets are evolving.

In Ab #6, we will review China Study. Though we question bits of its advice, we rate that book very important. How much has it influenced what we eat ? Not much yet: partly because our diets have long been much like what it recommends; partly because changes we would like to make, are difficult.

One easy change: no more milk ! Bert was buying ± two pounds/year of powdered milk. He liked it, along with sugar, on blackberries, making a sort of iceless ice-cream.

One difficult change: fats. Our biggest source: refined rape-seed ("canola") oil. (Next biggest: sunflower seeds, some raw, some lightly toasted, mostly ground; flax seeds, raw, ground; (we grind them ourselves and eat within a few days); wild hazels; oats.) Bert calculated: during a month this summer, 20% of his calories came from rape-seed oil. (He guesses that 8% came from oils in other foods. Total, 28% - near the high end of the commonly recommended range of 15-30%. My consumption might average 20%.) We'd like to replace the oil with various nuts. But we've not found enough hazels; and stores seldom sell nuts in shells (because most people no longer have enough time to remove shells ?). Consequently, the nuts are not only pricy but often stale, esp walnuts. Nuts keep better in their shells than after the shells removed.

We eat much fruit; mostly berries during their seasons: ± June-Sept. We forage 7 different berries in quantity, but 6 are of the same genus (Rubus: blackberries and relatives). Some autumns we are near abandoned orchards that still bear apples. Other seasons, our fruit is mostly limited to: canned tomato paste (we eat a spoonful along with vit C); raisins (but less as their price rises along with our doubts about their healthfulness); occasionally scavenged citrus, discarded because of cosmetic defects or small rot spots (easily cut out). A few winters we have found rose hips still on bushes.

We eat much fresh greens, esp during spring and early summer. But most are of only two species. By weight, maybe 70% nettles (Urtica), eaten cooked; 20% gosmore (Hypochoeris, a lettuce relative), mostly eaten raw; 10%, all other greens. In some places we have harvested gosmore year around, but it is most abundant and tastiest in spring. (Picture in May 94 DP.)

During the past few winters, we have been near areas where toothwart (Dentaria) is quite abundant. Toothwart grows for only a month or two, but during times when other greens are scarce. Toothwart came up about New Years in 2006; not until early Febr in 2007. The leaves are small: time consuming to forage many - but we do. Toothwart is of the mustard family and "hot", at least when raw. We eat it mostly mixed with other foods. (Pic in Feb/Apr 87 DP) A relative, bittercress (Cardamine), is sometimes abundant on disturbed soil. Raw, it tastes much like toothwart or watercress; appearance resembles watercress. We haven't noticed bitterness in the plants here.

Greens/flowers that Bert or I eat in small amounts: Cleavers (Galium), raw (pic in June89 DP). Dock (Rumex) cooked. Wild carrot (Daucus) leaves raw, a few year around. (I've read, somewhat toxic. Bert thinks, no more so that celery or parsley (same family); likes taste, hasn't noticed ill effects.) Miners lettuce relative (Montia), raw, very little, else it irritates mouth. Oxalis (Oxalis), raw, little. (Green leaves here year-around, but contains oxalic acid which may prevent absorption of calcium. Oxalic acid also in spinach, chard, beets, chen, amaranth.) Violet (Viola), raw, green leaves year around; pleasant wintergreen taste but tough; not abundant. Ox-eye daisy (Chrysanthemum), flowers, raw; abundant, but more than a few causes an unpleasant taste. Mint (Metha) or yerba buena (Satureja): during summer we pick and dry leaves; during winter we occasionally brew tea. Plants featured in most wild-edible-plant books, such as chen (Chenopodium), purslane (Portulaca), amaranth (Amaranthus) don't grow wild around here. They grow as weeds in some gardens. (A few times we've been hired to weed gardens, and got some. A fringe benefit.)

Occasionally we've scavenged "organic" cabbage outer leaves or other greens discarded by a pricy gourmet food "co-op". But we seldom go to cities. When we do, we are usually too limited for weight to bring home fresh vegies/fruit (mostly water), or too short of time to scavenge much. Also, (eg) just a few gosmore leaves may have more vits than a head of lettuce.

We don't eat much meat; average maybe 3 pounds/year each. Chickens on sale. Eggs (often on sale during spring, but delicate). Seafoods when near the coast. Canned tuna on sale. Wood-rats (which we trap if they invade our shelters). One time part of a cougar-killed deer (report in Nov99 DP). We catch many mice but throw them away: too small to be worth skinning and gutting. We get meat-hungry during blackberry season when the berries supply much of our calories without providing much protein; seldom other times. We eat mostly plants for health and convenience: to not get too much protein; to minimize risk of infection from animal or raw meat, and of cooking odors attracting big predators; and for easier food storage.

Most of our calories come from purchased grains: wheat, oats, millet, popcorn. Most protein comes from those grains plus lentils, beans, peas, sunnies; also much in nettles.

Except during blackberry season when we get much vit C naturally, we take a dab of pure C powder (a heap ± the size of a lentil) 2 or 3 times a day, with some fruit or greens if available. (C pills gradually darken as the C reacts with the binders and (we've read) become harmful.) Other supplements taken if/when our food may be deficient: B12, E, A (beta carotene), zinc, calcium (ground limestone), selenium, multi-vits (mostly for B's). We use maybe 30 pounds/year molasses, mostly on oatmeal. Bert uses maybe 3 pounds/year refined sugar, mostly on redberries (Vaccinium). Other than oil and sugar, we eat almost no "empty calorie" foods. (Minerals in molasses.)

As it is, what we eat is probably more healthful than what 99% of Americans eat; not because our diets are superb, but because most people's diets are horrid - including most people who try to eat only "organic" foods; also most gardeners who eat what they grow but also buy/make much junk foods.

A diet that is good for adults is not necessarily good for children. If we had kids, I think I'd try to provide as much meat as they wanted (but NOT hype it). If not enough meat, the youngest children past weaning would get priority. H & B

For solar cooking I use a huge stainless steel bowl.

It is 15 inches across. In it I put a pyrex casserole with lid on. To raise the casserole a little above the bowl, I set the casserole on a trivit or jar lids. I tuck a blanket around the bowl and cover the bowl with a discarded storm window. For more reflector area, I add car-windshield reflectors. They are more durable than cardboard and foil.

Unless you are among trees you need not move everything. I have to turn the bowl once or twice. It gets hot enough that I use pot holders. Wind won't damage it, and spills I just wipe off. I use the bowl also for laundry and salads.

I also tried a styrofoam chest. I put fire bricks in its bottom. I had spray painted the chest's inside and the bricks black. I covered the chest with the storm window. But the chest did not cook whereas the stainless bowl did. Suzanne, OH 451, May & July 06

Update on our solar cooking.

(Also see reports in Sept 02, May 03, Sept 04, Apr 05, Sept 06 DPs. Sept 02 includes plans/instructions for making reflectors that fold up compactly.)

For hinges between panels, the most durable we've found: strong denim (cotton) cloth, held on the plywood by carpenters glue. Tyvek fatigued and tore after a few months use.

New Reynolds aluminum foil is not as shiny as was the old. Apparantly produced by a different process, it has tiny ridges that scatter some of the light. But after the old foil has accumulated several years of grunge, or abrasion caused by wiping off the grunge, the new foil is better. Awesome brand foil, bought at Winco, seems identical to Reynolds. Both are much more durable than another brand bought at a dollar store.

The ideal reflector is without irregularities that scatter
Dwelling Portably   Dec 2007

light. Aluminum foil, despite its ridges and ripples, seems
better than the windshield reflectors I've seen, which were
textured (perhaps so that a reflection won't dazzle a passerby,
cause an accident - and bring a lawsuit !)
    As reported in Sept 06 DP, "space blanket" plastic was
initially shinier and stayed smoother on a panel than doea any
foil we've used - but soon deteriorated. We haven't found
enough aluminized plastic bags (eg, potato chips) to try them.
We doubt that any plastic will long endure the ultraviolet and
heat unless specially chosen for that.
    We salvaged 3 pieces of mirror at a glass shop that also
mounts custom mirrors. Each ± 1x1½ ft, not all the same size.
Ideal reflectors, but heavy and thus difficult to move or
adjust, as well as breakable and with sharp edges.* I want to
compare them with a 3-panel foil reflector, testing side by
side, heating identical jugs of water. * Metal file smoothed.
    Oven bags have endured quite well as shrouds on gallon
jugs heating water. They become less clear, from scuffing and/
or plastic turning cloudy, but not fragile or brittle - yet.
Other shortcomings: Their wrinkles increase surface area and
thus lose more heat than does a firmer shroud. They tend to
touch the jug or pot in spots, reducing insulation.
    We have yet to live near a really good solar-cooking site;
partly because our sites, scouted and prepared before we began
solar cooking, were not chosen for that. Most of our summer
sites have been on north slopes or had trees nearby that block
early and late sun. But despite site and equipment flaws,
solar cooking has reduced propane use by a third. With better
sites, which we are now scouting/preparing, we expect to reduce
propane use another third. We also save time, overall.
    Even on days too cloudy to completely cook solar (most
days here in winter), we save by pre-heating the cooking water,
or by getting the pot of food as hot as possible before turning
on the stove. Even if the water can only be solar warmed, much
fuel will be saved. (With most foods, more fuel is consumed
heating water and food, than maintaining cooking temperature;
esp if, after a brief simmer, the pot is insulated in bed
(which we do). Also helps: while on the flame, shroud sides
and top of pot with several wrinkled layers of foil (we do).)
    Everything we've tried to solar cook, cooked fine - except
popcorn. Though the air between pot and clear shroud heated to
250°F, and probably hotter inside the pot, no pops. How high
a temperature is needed ?! Makes us wonder about popcorn. B&H

Keep your old Coleman stove and lamp burning bright.
    (Responding to Lisa's question in DP's Apr06 Supplement.)
With these stoves, effective fuel flow depends on pumping
enough air pressure into the fuel reservoir. If you can't pump
enough pressure, check the leather cup-like air gasket, set
inside the pump shaft, secured to the thumb-push pump rod. To
access gasket, lever off the pump-rod cap's retaining wire with
a screw driver - on older models. On yet older models, caps
will screw off. Pull out the rod and gasket assembly. Leather
deforms out-of-round as it dried over the years, allowing a
disabling amount of air leakage. Get a leather treatment
product like you'd use on boots to prevent them cracking. Or
else some animal fat; bacon grease will do. Antique leather
does not like mineral oil or motor oil as well as a plant or
animal product. Using fingertips, thoroughly massage the
grease into the gasket, in a way that tends to reshape the cup

form round and outward, so as to restore a snug fit. Reassemble. If this fix doesn't restore pressure, contact me and we can discuss making replacement cups out of scrap leather.

Coleman no longer stocks replacement fuel reservoirs for stoves. These have to be changed out from a scrap stove. (When faced with a missing stove reservoir, I fabricated a propane-feed adaptor out of metal scrap and a bit of welding. This would not be practical for most folks to try at home.)

Fuel choices. Fumes are an inevitable consequence of combustion. That's why many lamps and stoves come with the disclaimer: "Use only in a well-ventilated area." (Makes you want to go solar.) Any kind of fossil fuel will form carbon monoxide. In addition, virtually all petro-fuels, propane included, have unwholesome additives. Even wood fires, esp if pine fueled, put out unhealthy smoke. I've found 91 to 95 octane auto gas to burn clean enough to be an acceptable substitute for "white gas" camping fuels that fetch 3 times the price. Your choice. Happy cooking, briggi2u@yahoo.com

How I transfered propane from one tank to another.

A few years ago, a law was passed forbidding propane dealers to fill tanks that lacked a new automatic-shut-off valve (asov). The asovs are not only costly, but have had problems, some of which LESSEN safety ! So, something differ- ent and probably costlier may soon be required. Furthermore, BC (all of Cda ? some U.S. states ?) forbid refilling ANY tank that is more than a few years old, regardless of condition.

We payed $20 to exchange one old 5-gal tank for a retro- fitted tank. But we have other tanks we want full, as reserve, and sure aren't going to replace them with asov tanks ! Though we have greatly reduced propane use, and plan to quit using it entirely (or any fossil fuels), at present we like propane as a back-up when other cooking methods are not convenient.

I asked John of Living Mobile if the asov would prevent transfer. He asked a dealer he knew (THANKS) who thought not.

None of the hardware stores I tried, had proper fittings. (BiMart formerly did, but now has only a small rack with few kinds of parts.) So I went to a propane distributor whose main business is trucking propane to dealers and big users. The only person there was a very young woman (looked mid teens) working on accounts. She didn't know about the fittings but tried to be helpful. Together we searched through MANY drawers of hard- ware. No single device was suitable. But, on a bench, left from another job, was a 3-ft length of high-pressure hose; and I found POL (put on left) fittings that could plug into the hose and then screw onto the tanks. Cost: about $12 plus a half-hour search. (No one else came in or even phoned while I was there. Probably lucky. If the proprietor had returned, he might have refused to sell to me, fearing liability if I had an accident.) Only friction held the hose on the POLs. I hadn't seen suitable clamps, nor did the woman know of any. So, back at our camp, I wrapped rubber straps around the hose joints.

I put black plastic snugly around the sending tank to warm it faster, and set it in the sun, upright which seemed safest. I set the receiving tank in a tote and shaded it, and poured creek water in around its bottom to cool it. (If too much water, the tank floated and tipped over.) I screwed on the transfer hose. I opened both tanks' valves. I heard a loud hiss that quickly diminished, then silence. But by almost closing the sending tank's valve and putting an ear close, I could hear a soft hiss: gas still flowing - slowly. (I did NOT open the receiving tank's 10% valve to reduce pressure and speed transfer. If I had, gas would have flowed out and been lost as fast as it transfered.) Hours passed. Along with the gas came much heat (boiling requires heat; condensing supplies heat), so I had to keep replacing the cooling water.

After two days the receiving tank was only half full. Thereupon I set the sending tank upside down so that liquid would flow. That transferred the propane much faster, but not real quick: the rate was limited by how fast the sending tank absorbed heat from the sun, to keep its pressure higher than in the receiving tank. After a few hours the receiving tank was nearly full and no more propane was flowing. But the sending tank still held some liquid. At first I thought the residue was hydrocarbons that had higher boiling temperatures than propane. But later I wondered if the asov, which is to prevent overfilling; when upside down, acted in reverse and prevented complete emptying. So I again put the sending tank upright. Transfer resumed - but slow. The sun was setting, a cloudy week was forecast, and twas mid Sept. So I quit for the year. The gas still in the sending tank, we used cooking.

Learning from that experience, this summer I did much better and refilled several tanks. We were near a spring that had water much colder than the not-very-cool creek. Also, I painted the sending tank's bottom black (up to where the sides are vertical) to absorb solar heat faster when upside down. (If any dealer asks why the black bottom, I will say it helps keep the tank cool - which it does if setting on cool ground.) Also, I solar-heated water quite hot. Then, when the asov stopped the flow, I set the sending tank upright in a tote and poured hot water in around its bottom to keep its remaining propane warm. Those improvements enabled me to transfer a tank-full in one day and to completely empty the sending tank. The last transfer I did, the sending tank emptied while upside down. Maybe the asov did not close. (Tending tanks did not take much time. While tending, I also washed clothes.)

CAUTION. I am now careful to always OPEN the valve on the RECEIVING tank FIRST. One time I opened the sending tank first. Before I could open the receiving tank, the hose blew off the POL ! During the few seconds it took me to close the sending tank's valve (difficult to reach because the tank was upside down) I lost some propane. When I put the hose back on the POL, I wrapped the rubber straps even tighter and used more layers.

Someone who has snow or ice available for cooling the receiving tank, can transfer propane faster. Or safer, because the sending tank doesn't have to be as warm. The best time: late winter when the sun is fairly high yet snow is still on the ground. Even if the air is cold, the sending tank can be warmed by loosely shrouding it with clear plastic, and by putting reflectors around it so as to shine onto it. Bert

A propane automatic-shut-off valve (asov) can be dangerous.

Until a few years ago, most propane tanks had a main valve plus a manual "10%" valve. To fill a tank, the dealer opened both valves. While liquid propane flowed in through the main valve, propane vapor came out through the 10% valve. Though wasteful of propane, that reduced pressure in the receiving tank, which enabled it to fill from a supply tank that lacked a pump. More important: when the receiving tank got nearly full, liquid propane squirted out the 10% valve, signalling the dealer to quickly stop the filling. (Because, if a tank gets completely full of liquid and then warms, pressure rises much more than if the tank has some vapor space. That is why drink bottles are not filled completely.)

That system was simple and fairly reliable, but hazardous. While a tank was filling, the cloud of propane could be ignited by a smoker passing near by, or by a spark from static electricity or from a loose or corroded electric connection.

To end that hazard, asovs were required. An asov works like the valves on some toilets that stop the refill. But the asovs proved unreliable. Often they jammed close. That happened once with our tank. The dealer managed to free the asov by lifting the tank and dropping it a half-foot onto concrete ! Worse: sometimes an asov failed to close when it was supposed to. Consequently most dealers, no longer trusting asovs, again open 10% valves - re-creating the hazard that asovs were supposed to eliminate. Worse yet: this summer, the last time our one asov tank got refilled, after filling and AFTER the main valve and the manual 10% valve had been closed, when the dealer tried to remove his filler nozzle, propane spewed out of the main opening - and continued spewing. (There is normally only a brief gush as the filler nozzle empties.) The dealer swung the tank various ways, banging it hard against a metal post. That finally stopped the flow. The dealer said, though many asovs stick shut, that was the first time he'd had one stick open. During many years of refilling asov-less tanks we've never had a MAIN valve fail to close. So I blame the asov. I don't know its details, but either it bypasses the main valve or else its failure kept the main valve from closing.

Holly wonders if my refillings might have damaged the asov. Possible. But a valve so easily damaged is dangerous. (I did nothing as drastic as dropping a tank onto concrete or putting it on a mobilhome parked in hot sun (which I've seen).)

An asov is hazardous not only during refilling, but any time the tank is not connected to an appliance with valve.

We hope to find a propane dealer willing to refill the older asov-less tanks. Though illegal, I doubt there is now much enforcement; else dealers would not be opening manual 10% valves which is probably also illegal. Bert

LED lantern is useful though connections are troublesome.

(Also see report in Sept 05 Dp, p.15.) We've used Eveready's "Energizer" lantern during 3 winters, maybe 2 hours a night, average. It requires 4 AA cells. We have mostly used NiCds, 4 of which provide 5 volts. We've also used recharged "non-rechargable" alkalines, which provide 6 volts.

Though our 12-volt light (which contains scarlet and green LEDs) is much brighter, the lantern has the advantage that its AAs get recharged on cloudy days when our PV panels put out too little voltage to recharge the 12-volt battery.

I used the lantern at 6 am one morn to write a first draft of this. I set the lantern on a squat jar and adjusted the LED portion to shine downward. With the lantern 6 inches above the paper, the bright area is about 6 inches diameter. Bright enough for writing; marginal for much reading. Though no brighter than a candle, the lamp emits no fumes, can't start a fire, and is more easily adjusted to shine where I want it to.

Its main problem, like with all UNsealed low-voltage electric devices: the connections corrode, esp the springy negative contacts. They need attention frequently. Usually,

twisting the cells in place, back and forth several times, rubs
off enough corrosion to restore contact. Bert

A Garrity-Duracell crank-light soon failed.

In May 2006, I bought a "k023 Powerlight", $10 on sale at
Winco. I hesitated: its 3 LEDs are blue-white (we much prefer
yellow); its beam is too narrow (3" a foot away) for most
tasks; I doubt that it is sealed (I don't see how the crank
could be) and thus is prone to corrosion. However, it was
brighter than our little Homier shake-light (report in Sept 05
DP), and we haven't encountered bigger brighter shake-lights
(which ARE sealed) at attractive prices.

Approx 6x2¼x1¼ inches, ½ pound. Our average use: 3 hours
a night during autumn. It needed cranking frequently: though
bright at first, it soon faded. (Likewise, our shake-light.)
The instructions claim: a minute of cranking yields 30 minutes
of light. Well - 30 minutes of DIM light.

Bert experimented, using our solar calculator as a light
meter. He hung the light one foot above the calculator and
cranked approx 2 turns per second. Number of turns, seconds
until the display faded (by then, light quite dim), seconds of
light per turn: 5 72 14;   10 121 12;   20 138 7;   40 198 5;
(second trial to check: 40 188 4.7)   80 338 4.2;   160 448 2.8.
Ie, cranking a few turns frequently, yielded longer light per
turn than did cranking many times less often.

Though brighter than our shake-light or squeeze-light, it
is less satisfactory on rough trails where I want one hand free
to fend off branches and to arrest stumbles, because cranking
requires two hands (one to hold light; one to crank). So I
must stop often. Whereas, a shake-light or squeeze-light can
be activated by the hand that is holding it.

As months passed, the crank-light dimmed more quickly and
I noticed less resistance cranking it. Then, in Dec, it failed
completely: the light became very dim; cranking did not
brighten it, and the crank spun with no resistance, indicating
no generation. Bert opened it (which required unscrewing three
tiny deeply-recessed phillips-head bolts) and measured some
voltages. He thinks the LEDs, generator, battery (tiny 3-cell
NiMh) are okay. The fault: a chip that mates gen to battery.

He thinks he might be able to fix it by substituting
diodes. But first I'll try returning it to Winco, though I
doubt Winco will replace it because they don't regularly stock
those lights. (Winco didn't.) The maker offer a "lifetime
guarantee exclusive of the LEDs". But mailing it back is not
attractive, considering postage and work to package - and
prospects the replacement will fail.

A friend who bought one, hasn't had it fail, but I don't
think she has used it as much. I heard of another one that
broke mechanically but was fixed with a nail.

A friend with internet access checked: www.garitylites.
com. It recommends a minute of cranking at least once a month
to keep a charge on the battery. That surprised Bert who had
assumed that a NiMh like a NiCd (and UNlike lead-acid) could
be left discharged indefinitely without damage. Holly & Bert

Shake-lights are the least trouble-prone of existing types.

Better than crank, squeeze, and battery-replacement type
lights. Reasons: simple mechanically; can be well sealed, so
no corrosion; recharged by the hand that holds it. (Of course
I don't claim ALL shake-lights good.) Yellow LEDs best for
most tasks. Bert   Dwelling Portably   Dec 2007

Dwelling Portably

or Shared, Mobile, Improvised
Underground, Hidden, Floating

May 2008 $1 per issue   POB-190-d, Philomath OR 97370

A Chinese-style wheel-barrow can be used on narrow trails.

A housing of poles and sticks, or scrap boards, is built around a large-diameter wheel. (A big wheel rolls with less resistance than do the small wheels used on most American wheel barrows.) Cargo is carried in front of the wheel and beside it, as well as behind it, which reduces weight on the handles. A strap runs from handle to handle, looped over the user's shoulders (or head ?) which takes the weight off hands and arms. Some wheel-barrows are 3 feet wide and big enough for two people to haul. (From note by Andrew, ME 046, 2006)

handle ↑

straps
not
shown

wheel   angle
iron

lashings
not
shown

handle ↓

(Comment)
I like this idea. Simpler and lighter than a two-wheel cart. (But on a bike trailer I'd want 2 wheels for balance (as does Zalia, next item).) The sketch Andrew sent showed a ⊂⊏ shape. For our use, I think I'd prefer a ◁⊏ shape. Lighter, less wobbly, and the narrow front will hopefully fend bushes aside instead of hanging up on them. Dis: not much space in front for cargo. But enough for a small heavy item, to help balance.

Any kind of cart can be more easily pulled than pushed, esp on a rough trail, because pulling reduces weight on the wheel(s) whereas pushing adds to it. This wheel-barrow might be difficult for ONE person to take through brush where it must be pushed. But if there are two people, the front person pulls with a harness and can provide most of the forward force. The rear person balances and helps lift it over obstacles.

The wheel needs side strength. (I'd NOT use a 26-inch bicycle wheel. See discussion in May 06 DP.) If using a motorcycle or BMX-bicycle wheel: to hold its axle, angle-iron is easy to lash to the frame, but a front fork may be more available. The fork would be horizontal and lashed to stout sticks which lash to the frame. Bert, Oregon 973, Jan 2008

Two-wheel bicycle trailers are best.

A single-wheel BOB trailer does track behind the bike's wheels, but has load and balance problems. I use two-wheel trailers. Much better for balance and load capacity. I have hauled up to 600 pounds, and sometimes have a wide or tall load. You can't do that with a single-wheel trailer. Zalia

Some solutions to problems with small tires.

The tires on small trailers, lawn-mowers, wheel-barrows, etc, frequently develop flats. I have an old 3-wheeler that local kids run around on. The tires are cracked and no longer hold air. Into them I inserted steel-belted thread strips I cut from old auto tires. I positioned the inserts so that the narrow bead strips were against the wider supportive thread.

The tires have more drag and less spring than if inflated.
But I'm not going to pay $150 for new tires.

To make the strips, I snip the steel bead with a grinding
blade, then cut out the strip with a sharp knife. Small narrow
tires may need only one strip. Wide tires need several.

Large diameter bike tires do require tubes. To prevent
frequent punctures by thorny vines, I either buy super-thick
inner-tubes or else use the tire sealing goop. I occasionally
find thick heavy water hose that I can insert into the bike
tires that I use on garden carts.

Though I have the usual tire-patch kits with all my rigs,
I find that shoe goo temporarily fixes low-pressure 4-wheeler
tires that get punctured in the outback. Al Fry, ID 836, 06?

More thoughts about springs on carts and other vehicles.

The fat low-pressure tires on ATVs, not only minimize
sinking on soft ground, but provide some springing on gravel
roads where ATVs often go quite fast.

I think springs of some kind are desirable on a hand cart
if loping (an easy run, 12-15 mph ?). But springs may not help
much if going slow (1 mph ?). The speed at which springs
reduce forces on wheels and load (including any rider) depends
on how bumpy the road is. A one-wheel barrow can more easily
dodge rocks and holes than can a 2-wheel cart. Bert, OR 973

Elastic cords between pack-frame and load may reduce forces.

Compared with a conventional unsprung frame, peak vertical
forces exerted by a 27 kg (60#) load were 1/6th as great and
energy consumed was 3/4ths as great. Science News 13jan07

(Comment) The brief report (based on info from frame's design-
er ?) did not describe test conditions. With a backpack as
with a vehicle, vertical forces partly depend on velocity. I
dislike running with even a light (20#) knapsack. If I must
run, I grab the bottom with my hands to take most of the weight
and to minimize bouncing: ie, my arms act as springs. Whereas
if hiking slow, which I must do on a steep or rough trail: with
a heavy load (80#) the steady pressure on shoulders or head-
and-neck becomes uncomfortable (and prompts frequent brief rest
stops) but I don't notice peak forces. If a trail is smooth
and level enough for fast walking, I notice peak forces somewhat more but they seem less annoying than the steady pressure.
I have backpacked heavy loads for many years, so perhaps I
subconsciously move so as to minimize bouncing. An inexperienced backpacker may bounce more, causing greater peak forces.
                                                          Bert

Backpacking food and other supplies to our base camp.

Our present winter base is about 2½ miles from a road-
head: ½ mile mostly rough trail somewhat uphill; ½ mile on a
smooth but seldom driven logging road, up and down and level;
1 mile uphill, mostly steep, partly rough; ¼ mile partly rough
some up and down; ¼ mile downhill, mostly steep, to our camp.

Downhill is the most difficult: slipping is likely.
Though I may wear tennies the rest of the way, downhill I wear
rubber mocs (made from truck innertubes) - less slippery here.
If my load is heavy, eg, two 4-gallon pails of wheat, near the
summit I split the load and bring it down in two trips.

To carry a heavy load from road-head to camp, takes me ±
5 hours. Ie, I average ½ mph. To go from camp to the road-
head, usually light-weight, mostly downhill, takes ± 1 hr. Bert

The in-route camps we use for city trips have had problems.

We often live at a "winter" base camp from October through May (8 months a year). Consequently we choose a site and build a shelter that provides: enough warm space for indoor activities; security for us while there and for our equipment; sunshine for warmth and light - rainy days often have sun breaks.

The site that is best in those ways is usually many miles from cities and quite a few miles from highways. Consequently, each trip to a city is a minor expedition requiring planning and preparation - and at least one intermediate camp site.

A typical city trip. In advance, ready things to go; and listen to the weather radio, waiting for a mild dry period. Day 0: pack things to go; bathe. Day 1: hike to an in-route camp-site near a highway where we have stashed a tent, bedding, city clothes, ready-to-eat food. Day 2: rest and get ready. Day 3: hike to the highway and travel to the city by the most expedient means (options discussed in May 96 DP); do city things; return to in-route camp. Day 4: rest; select things to go to base camp (and, if time, read bulky magazines and books that are NOT going). Day 5: return to base camp.

Often we don't get 5 good-weather days in a row. If not, we may forgo rest days. Or, after return from city, we may remain at in-route camp until the storm passes. Or we may hike in the rain (but not snow - steep slopes too slippery). Not surprisingly, we seldom go to cities during winters.

We have been quite pleased with our winter base camps, but NOT with most in-route camps. Because the site must be near a highway yet reachable from base camp, and fairly secure, we do not have a wide choice of sites. The least-bad site is usually among mid-size trees (most 2nd-growth forests here) and doesn't get sunshine during mid winter. Even if no recent rain, bushes remain wet with dew, or with frost that melts when we rather it didn't. Also, highways are mostly in valleys into which cold air collects: when hiking from base to in-route camp, as we descend we often notice an abrupt chilling of ± 10 degrees.

For the past few winters, we've used our small Stansport dome tent as in-route shelter. If we leave it set up, that saves time and avoids discomfort (bare hands needed to set it up). Also, we can cover it with blankets or moss for insulation which enables our bodies to warm the inside ± 20°. And we can suspend plastic tarps over it, which reduces dampness and provides a rain-sheltered antiway. But if left set up, it is more visible, and animals might damage it.

At our present in-route site, we have left the tent set up with black-fabric over the tarps, and with mouse traps set in the antiway. A mouse has never gnawed its way into the tent. Perhaps the fire retardant, whose smell was scary when the tent was new (report in May 96 DP) tastes bad.

We usually both go to in-route camp, even if only one of us will go to city, so that we can haul back more food staples. Also for warmth: if we split up, neither shelter is as warm.

At in-route camps, bed covers were a problem. They got damp from invisible sweat, and could not be dried before leaving. We reduced that problem by enclosing our thickest sleepa (sleeping bag opened as quilt) into a big plastic bag (from a furniture store). We fastened the corners to minimize shift of the sleepa within the plastic. Plastic is also over the foam padding under us. In bed we wear clothes for additional warmth and to avoid touching the plastic (which clings to skin and hinders changing position). The plastic over us is not as

flexible as cloth and does not conform to our bodies as well,
but covers us adequately and adds to the sleepa's insulation.

B & H

At in-route camps, we plan to use a bigger tent, heated.

We have never used a stove for warmth at any camp.
Reasons: avoid having to cut and haul and shelter wood, and
tend fire; avoid fire risk and smoke inhalation; increase
privacy (smoke might be seen or smelled; heat detected).

Now we are reconsidering. A wood stove could quickly warm
a tent that is big enough for assembling trip things and to
hang damp clothes to dry. Security might be adequate
if the tent is used only briefly and NOT left set up: our
camp-sites are usually in brushy-brambly areas difficult to
hike through by anyone who hasn't figured out the trails.

We would use the site ONLY for in-route camping, so that
few things remain there. (Recently, we used a summer base
camp as an in-route camp also. It offered some advantages but
was over a mile from a highway: a city trip required following
long rough steep brushy trails in darkness with dim flashlights.
And the many things stored there increased security needs.)

For a stove set-up, I like the arrangement
used in Korea that David French described in
May93 DP. The fire is in the ground; the hot
fumes pass through a tunnel under the tent
before exiting through a vertical pipe.
Advantages, compared to a stove in tent: tent
can be smaller and simpler (no stove-pipe
exit) and stays cleaner. The ground gets heated and continues
to warm the tent after the fire goes out. Dis: more complex
site; must go outside to tend fire. After our problem with a
dakota-hole cook fire (report in Sept06 DP), I think I'd want a
small auxilliary burner at the bottom of the vertical pipe to
preheat it so that it sucks the smoke when main fire is lit.

The tent I'd want: fairly big (6x8 ft, 6½ ft high center)
yet compactable enough to easily stuff into a 20-gallon tote;
integral rain fly (over-tarp); sets up quickly. Maybe no
frame. Instead, the tent is held erect by chords that snap
onto pre-arranged anchor rings. I've not seen advertised any
tent that seemed suitable (but, until now, I haven't been
looking hard). Suggestions welcome. Bert, OR 973, Jan 2008

We now use thin-mat black-fabric for camo here.

Black-fabric, also called landscape fabric or weed control,
is sold by garden suppliers during spring. Compared to
ordinary black plastic, its advantage for gardeners: it passes
water and air. I've seen two kinds of black-fabric.

The kind we use is a thin mat of plastic fibers welded
together in many small spots. Compared to ordinary black
plastic, its advantages for us: it is not shiny; it passes
some light. Compared to cloth: cheaper; lighter weight;
more sunlight resistant than most synthetics; doesn't rot as
does cotton. Dis: not as strong. However, even when hung
vertically alone, it withstood quite high winds. Two years ago
a roll 3x50 ft was $6 (4¢/ft sq). Ordinary 3-mil plastic, 10x
25 ft, was $4 (1.7¢/ft sq). Since then, prices of all plastics
(made from fossil fuels) have risen. We haven't found any mat-
type black-fabric wider than 3 feet, unfortunately - we often
need wider pieces and sewing takes time. (Tried welding. Weak.)

Another kind of black-fabric is wider but quite shiny. It
seems to be ordinary black plastic with many tiny holes in it.

Dwelling Portably   May 2008

In w Oregon woods where there are many old stumps and logs with dark bark or burned black, black-fabric provides better camo than do the mottled green and brown tarps we've seen which seldom match the local vegetation. Bert & Holly, Jan 08

Dwelling in or roaming wild areas, reduces global warming.
Plants respond to increased carbon dioxide by growing faster. And after plants die, some of that carbon remains in the soil. But growth is limited by other nutrients obtained from soil. Humans who frequent wild areas but eat some food grown elsewhere, add nutrients to wild soils. Sci News 15apr06

Whole grains store better than does flour or meal.
This is important to us because we usually buy most of our staples during the dry season (summer) so that we don't have to deal with rain or muddy roads. And, if we can hire a vehicle to help, we may buy enough to last us several years.

Snow-country dwellers may do the opposite: bring in supplies during winter with a snowmobile.

Grains vary in how well they store. Wheat stores well for years, even decades, if kept dry and cool - PROVIDED the kernels are intact. (95% of 15-year-old wheat sprouted, report in May90 DP.) But in whole-wheat FLOUR, the wheat-germ oils soon get rancid. (Notice that stores refrigerate wheat-germ or else sell vacuum-packed jars.) Though wheat-germ is rich in vit E, E is not an antioxidant until converted by our bodies.

Almost all commercial bakers, including purveyors of "organic" breads, buy their flour. Consequently their bread probably contains rancid oil by the time it is sold. Flavorings may mask the taste but don't remove free radicals.

When Bert and I first got together, our main starch was brown rice, boiled. We liked its taste better than white rice; it is less sticky and so doesn't scorch as easily; and we were vaguely aware that it was better nutritionally. Some people have reported storage problems. We had no problems storing short-grain brown rice a few years, kept cool (under 60°F). I wonder if short-grain keeps better than long grain.

Then we learned that rice is the most pesticided of grains. We switched to millet, which is also cheaper. But, though millet tastes fine to us after an absence, we soon tire of it. Does millet contain something our bodies don't want much of ?

We tried wheat boiled: chewier than we like. Wheat slightly sprouted, then boiled, tasted better; but sprouting often isn't practical for us. So, finally, we got a hand grinder and began baking. Usually the only ingredients: flour, water, yeast. Flavor varies: may depend on how long and warm the dough rises. (A few times we got sour dough, unintentionally.) We prefer and usually eat bread that is still warm, directly off the pan. Holly & Bert, OR 973, January 2008

For identifying wild edibles, mice can be your guinea pigs.
Almost every plant that you observe mice or rats eating, can be good for you to eat. They love to spend hours cracking open pinyon nuts, or else sitting on a stump munching a slab of juicy nopali (a cactus). briggi2u@yahoo.com

(Comment) Rodents eat some mushrooms that are deadly poison for humans. I wouldn't be surprised if the same is true for some plants. Rodents and primates have gone their different evolutionary ways for 150 million years or so.
Dwelling Portably   May 2008

Around here, mice and rats are nocturnal. We see squirrels
harvesting doug-fir cones. Seeds edible for humans but TINY.

Calcium-to-Oxalic ratio in green vegetables varies widely.
My understanding. If the ratio is high, the oxalic acid
is bound and calcium is left for nutritional needs. Whereas if
the ratio is low, the oxalic acid will bind not only calcium in
the vegie but other calcium eaten then, preventing assimilation.
In Dec07 DP, I mentioned some vegies that contain oxalic
acid. Bert found more info in Apr/June86 DP. Of 22 vegies
tested, highest ratios (90:1 - 45:1): collards, mustard greens,
kale, cabbage. Lowest (0.20:1 - 0.45:1): swiss chard, spinach,
purslane (Portulaca), beet leaves, poke, rhubarb, chen (Chenopodium). Ie, according to the 20-year-old article (any newer
contrary info ?), purslane (etc) will NOT provide calcium and
may prevent assimilation of other calcium. This doesn't mean
that you should shun purslane (etc). Just make sure that, if
you eat much low-ratio greens, you get ample calcium elsewhere.
Oxalis is often the only green here in winter. Oxalis was
not tested, but from its name and acid taste, I assume it has
much oxalic acid. So, when I eat it, I take calcium (limestone
flour) with it - enough (I hope) to bind the oxalic and leave
surplus calcium. (The article was mainly about miners lettuce
(Montia perfoliata), ratio 8.34:1.) Holly, OR 973, Jan 2008

Be careful if eating fruit partly eaten by other animals.
At least, cut away previously-eaten portions. In Bangladesh, nipah virus is spread by fruit-eating bats, and then by
kids who collect fruit even if half-eaten and sell to venders
who blend fruit into drinks. Purchasers, mostly Muslim, drink
the beverage before it can ferment, which would kill the virus.
(Pasturizing would, too.) Nipah often causes measles-like
symptoms, brain damage, death. Outbreaks of nipah and related
hendra occur frequently throughout the bats' range, from the
Himalayas to Australia. The Bangladesh strain spreads from
bats to people and kills 75% of those it infects. In Malaysia,
nipah spreads from bats to pigs to people; in 1999 it killed
a third of the 265 people infected. Science News 9june07

Pathogens that infiltrate plants are not removed by washing.
In a lab test, uncut apples were dunked in water containing E coli. The bacteria migrated to the apples' cores.
Likewise into unpeeled oranges. Salmonella got into mangos,
tomatos, various leaf vegies. Both microbes got into alfalfa
sprouts. Bacteria in spinach may have caused the 2006 outbreak
that sickened over 200 people, killing 3.
Researchers believe that microbes get into commercial
produce from water used to irrigate or spray pesticides.
Though bacteria that have evolved to infect animals, don't
infect plants as vigorously, they are able to make use of the
defense mechanisms of plant pathogens not harmful to humans.
The 3-page article suggested: use drinking-quality water for
spraying; don't buy damaged produce; get to frig quick.
SN 20oct07, 10nov07
(Comments) Pasturizing will kill the bacteria but will also
deactivate enzymes that may help digestion.
The article did not mention wild plants. They seem less
risky than commercial produce. But I'd either avoid spots that
are popular with animals or else pasturize my pickings. H & B

Plain water was most effective for washing virus off hands.
In a test using norwalk virus, water removed 96%, water plus an anti-bacterial soap 88%, an alcohol-based hand-gel only 50% - which surprised researchers. Science News 10june06

(Comment) The report did not conjecture why. Though soap and water is a better surfactant (dirt grabber) than plain water, it is also a better lubricant. That may have prevented the hands from rubbing each other as effectively. However, for removing something oily/greasy (poison oak/ivy toxin ?) I'd use water AND SOAP if available. Holly & Bert, OR 973, Jan 08

Sand slurry is good for cleaning some containers, not others.
I've cleaned stainless steel cups and bowls with sand and creek water. Worked very well. Soap not needed. But I don't recommend sand for plastic bottles. Sand roughens the plastic, enabling even more scum to grow on it. Zalia, OR 972, Aug 06

Some simple ways to obtain water from the earth.
In my area, water drillers charge $35 per foot. So I drilled my own shallow well, using an auger and muscle.
Though seldom suggested by back-to-land books, collecting seepage is simple. Find a slope with water-indicating plants such as cottonwood and willow. Dig a trench the full length of the seepage; a foot deep may suffice. Line the trench with clay to trap the water. Lay perforated septic-system pipe in the trench. Cover the pipe with gravel. Cover the gravel with (eg) old carpet or burlap sacks to keep dirt out of the gravel. At the pipe's upper end, add a clean-out plug. At the lower end, add a plug and a pipe to the trough or holding tank.
In some places, water veins come close enough to the surface to be tapped by hand pumps. I once had a girl friend who could walk along with her palms down and detect not only where there were veins but how deep they were.
Water can be sucked to surface by a colder temperature. Some older cultures knew this and built stone spring houses or water caves at spring sites. Al Fry, Idaho 836, 2006 ?

(Addendum) A few years ago, Holly and I wanted a new drinking-water source, closer to our camp. I hadn't found a natural spring so I tapped a seepage. Because of climate and terrain, my method differed somewhat from Al's.
A nearby creek had a steep V profile with banks ± 30 feet high. Near the end of dry season (late summer) I struggled along the creek bed (difficult because of fallen trees) watching for tiny tributaries. I found one. It flowed on the surface for only a few feet beside the creek. I did not tap it there because it would be submerged by creek water during the rainy season. I climbed directly up the bank, far enough to be above the creek's flood water. I dug. A foot down I reached saturated soil. The seepage was slow. I widened the hole, forming a ditch across the slope. I piled the dirt on the downhill side of the ditch, forming a dam. A little pool began to collect. I continued the ditch as far as there was seepage, about 8 feet. The subsoil was clayish (which may be why water seeped above it) so I did not have to line the ditch with clay.
From a salvaged garden hose, I cut a still-good portion. I perforated a half-gallon bleach jug. I lashed the jug to one end of the hose. I covered the perforated jug with synthetic loose-weave cloth, to admit water but keep out anything that might block the hose. I placed the jug in the deepest part of

the pool and (temporarily disrupting dam) routed the hose downhill. Muddy water trickled from it. I covered the jug and
filled the pool with pebbles gathered in the creek. I covered
the pebbles with plastic to keep out dirt and rain water. I
covered plastic with soil and debris. (Illo in June/Sept84 DP)
        A few days later. Clear water trickled from the hose;
only a spoonful per minute but that was enough. I inserted the
hose into a narrow-mouth 5-gallon jug (salvaged).
        A day later. The jug was full of clear water. I loaded
it into a crude carry basket I had rigged on an old pack frame,
and put an empty jug on the hose. And so forth.
        For several years, seasonally, we've used that water for
drinking and cooking. (For washing, we have a closer source.)
The only maintenance so far: I occasionally blow into the
outlet end of hose to dislodge silt collected around its intake.
After a heavy rain, I wait a week or more before collecting
drinking water, to avoid contamination by surface water.
        This area has water-indicating plants. Horsetail is one
of the best. But the plants apparantly have DEEP roots for
obtaining water during dry season. Once, in a likely-looking
horsetail patch, I dug down more than ten feet. No water !
        I sometimes find a natural spring along the base of a high
steep ridge, or by following down a dry gulch that flows during
heavy rains. But such springs are seasonal: dry near the end
of dry season; contaminated with surface water during heavy
rains; drinkable maybe half the time. Bert, OR 973, Jan 2008

Does sterilizing water with iodine create toxic compounds ?
        Iodine, either tincture or water solution of crystals, has
long been recommended to backpackers as more effective and
less toxic than chlorine. However a report about city water
supplies in 5aug06 Science News, causes concern. The tap water
of most cities contains myriad toxins, formed by reactions of
disinfectants (eg, chlorine, chloramines, ozone) with organic
matter in the water. Over 500 chemicals are formed. The EPA
put limits on a few but rates 50 others likely to cause cancer.
        One is tri-iodo-methane. Might that be formed when iodine
sterilizes water ? Some organics can be removed by settling or
filtering, prior to iodizing. But not any substances dissolved
in the water. Best find or develop a spring you can trust. H&B

More about small engines that mount on bicycles.
        The 25cc 2-stroke engine (that Lauran uses on bike, more
in May06 DP) is standard on weed eaters and is on many small
yard appliances and some chain saws. 21cc-to-25cc are not
designed for sustained loads and don't last very long. 31cc,
up to 49cc (on many road scooters) is better.
        Two-strokes are noisy and put out burnt-oil smoke. A
4-stroke 2-or-3-hp cast-iron engine is better but heavier.
        The drive ring and belt (which Lauran uses) is the best
way I've seen to add power to a bicycle. Most bike engines
use friction on tire, which destroys tire. Zalia, OR 972, 06

Traveling/boarding/working via relays of friendly motorists.
        My idea. The travelers are driven, each night or every
few days, to a place where they can sleep. At each place, a
different vehicle from another area comes and picks them up,
and they start another leg of their journey.
        This is a variant of what was often done during 1800s.
At lectures and church-halls/rectories, travelers arranged to

              Dwelling Portably   May 2008

board with families for a favor/fee/work. Patty, NY 131, 2006

A way that an employed couple may safely park their motorhome.
If one works nights and the other works days, they can
move back and forth between their employers' parking lots.
The Wells (story in May06 DP) could do this. The husband
works days. The wife, a nurse, can easily find work at night.
I think vehicle living is safer if two people. Suzanne,OH 451

(Comment) Best if every user of the parking lot knows about
the arrangement and approves. Else ? Suppose the woman works
at a place that employs only women. Some "concerned citizen"
may see the MAN in the parking lot - and call police !

Further report about living in a travel trailer.
Our summer was quiet. Though we got kicked out of the
campground even after the owners said we could stay, we got to
live on a hill top, parked in a clearing within a grove of
trees. The spot was so secluded that the owner called on the
cell phone, asking when we would arrive. He was surprised to
learn that we were already there. Aside from the lack of
electrical and other hook-ups, it was an awesome place.
We're often asked why we still live in our travel trailer.
We could say, because of the freedom we enjoy. But, being
practical, it is a way to live within our means. A local man
who lives in an old school bus, moved into an apartment for the
winter. We considered doing so, but were shocked by the rents
being asked. From prior experience, we know that many people
in conventional housing, are living way beyond their means,
often on increasing lines of credit. We think, if something
happens, they would soon be on the street. We prefer paying
cash for everything and owning what we live in and drive.
We never did repair the trailer's framing. If we get
another travel trailer, we'd like a 19-foot. We'd prefer a
driveable, but one in our price range would be a 1970s.
Some of our readers gave us ideas for insulating. We
filled some windows with styrofoam panels, and have a large
plastic tarp covering the roof. That seems to increase warmth.
But the real proof will be less fuel consumption this winter.
A 20# tank of propane normally last us 2 weeks if used with
care. When we lived in conventional housing, we placed clear
plastic film over the windows on the inside which raised the
temperature 5o or so. But we feel that making the small space
of our trailer too tight would be unhealthy. We do tape the
outside of the windows where the windows open. John & Rose
Ward,PA 174,Nov06

Repair your vehicle south of the border.
In Mexico, every town and city has countless small work-
shops, going from early morning until late night, that keep old
rigs running. You can get major engine work, transmission
overhaul, and maintenance/servicing for much less than in the
U.S. Parts too, for older Ford and GM, are available cheap
because there is much after-market parts manufacturing.
My 1992 Ford F-150 pickup slid off the interstate in a
blizzard, then rolled on its side into a hillside median snow-
bank. (Bias-ply tires are not real stable for winter driving.)
The passenger-side door and pickup bed got terribly stove in.
Last year, near Veracruz, I had all the bodywork done,
including fixing old dents, bends, scrapes, dings collected
through normal use. Then, a nice thick shiny coat of primer

and paint, and detailing and painting the wheels, grille,
bumpers. A beautiful job for $250 total. (The shop accepted
some barter, so I actually paid $200 (in pesos) plus 3 old
wrist-watches.) My road shame turned to road pride. In U.S.,
the same work could cost $2500, because here they don't pull
and hammer sheet-metal so much as replace it with new.
　　　　It helps to talk some Mexican, and to spend time with
different shops to find the best price. Riddle: What is
Mexico's national color ? Answer: Primer ! briggi2u@yahoo.com

(Comment) I would go to Mexico (or other country) only if I
had a very strong reason, or MUCH to do there. If I went, I'd
stay until ALL was done. I'd MINIMIZE border crossing.
　　　　"Jump through the hoops"? The "hoops" are RED HOT.
Border guards are cops. Regardless of how legal someone thinks
they are, any encounter with any cop is DICEY !
　　　　Sneak across ? Regardless of how knowledgable and careful
someone is, accidents happen !
　　　　Mexicans whose businesses require border crossing, are
probably more skilled at crossing than is an occasional gringo
visitor. To fix a vehicle, how about finding a reputable
repair-person who crosses quite often (maybe to buy parts not
available in Mexico) and arranging pickup and delivery ? Of
course, expect to pay more than if driving to the shop. B & H

Outlook can affect odds of surviving the unexpected.
　　　　I became interested in Lawrence Gonzalez's Deep Survival
because the author discovered characteristics that help humans
survive drastic situations. The 2003 book's focus is not on
skills or gear, but on outlook. Many of the stories concern
inexperienced individuals who nevertheless managed to get out
of unbelievable situations. "I remember thinking the jungle
trees looked like cauliflowers", said a 17-year-old girl who
fell out of a lightning-destroyed airplane into jungle, walked
out over 12 days, and lived. A Navy SEAL commander said, "The
rambo types are the first to go." Though the book focuses on
some extreme examples, I think it is, nevertheless, an excellent guide for anyone considering woods life. Especially
interesting: along with calmness, curiosity, non-assumption;
a trait favoring survival is NOT being a rule follower. Also:
know local conditions, and know what you don't know - ie, be
aware that familiar can turn into unfamiliar. Included are
research findings, anecdotes, extensive quotes from eastern and
western Classic Lit. Andrew, Maine 046, 2006

(Comment) I read about the girl somewhere. As I recall she
had no parachute but LUCKILY fell through dense foliage.
　　　　That book may be esp helpful to (eg) someone who has never
been in the woods and has NO interest in any woods, but who is
the sole survivor of an airplane crash in a remote forest. But
to someone CONSIDERING woods life, I suggest: give priority to
info sources that focus on equipment and skills and habitats.
The same holds for anyone considering ANY kind of life, whether
in big city, small town, desert, swamp, ocean, or wherever.
　　　　The difference: preparing for what is expected, versus
responding to the unexpected. Sure, no matter how well you
prepare, you may encounter unexpected threats, and your outlook
could affect the outcome. But, if you have time, best learn
what to reasonably expect, and prepare accordingly. MANY more
people are killed or crippled by fairly LIKELY happenings (eg,
accidents to high-mileage travelers; ill health of junk-food
junkies) than by freak events.　　　　　　　May 2008

"BEWARE THE BATS" warns a Science News headline.

Many deadly emerging and re-emerging diseases, including nipah, hendra, sars, ebola, rabies, originated in bats. Not known why. (Because bats are both numerous and may fly far ? And because some hibernate in clusters ?) Also not known why those diseases don't kill bats but kill humans. SN 9june07

Incense and candles pollutes air in churches.

In a Roman Catholic church in Germany, burning candles during a service doubled amount of particles smaller than one μm (the most harmful); burning incense along with candles increased particles 9 times. Amount quicky dropped after candles extinguished but stayed high 24 hours after burning both.

In a Dutch chapel, after candles had burned 9 hours, air contained ten times as many free radicals as by a busy road.

Incense is often used in places other than churches to repel insects or to mask odors. Science News 19aug06

Keep matches and other fire-starters dry.

A few businesses still offer free matches. To protect them from humidity, keep them wrapped at the bottom of a plastic bag. Body heat, too, keeps things dry. Keep bagged matches under your bedding, along with tinders such as dried grass, sage shreds, birch bark. briggi2u@yahoo.com, July 2006

(Comment) Wrapping things in plastic keeps them dry for a while, but water vapor gradually diffuses through thin plastic.

Things beneath bedding may stay dry if the bedding has air circulation under it, such as might be provided by a thick loose mattress formed of conifer boughs. But not if bedding sets directly on the ground or a ground cover. Esp not if the bedding is porous and lacks a vapor barrier (plastic) between sleeper and most layers of bedding. Un-noticed sweat off the sleeper, diffuses through the bedding and condenses on ground.

My experience with a Coleman camping stove.

I acquired a freebie: green case with a red tank into which you pour liquid fuel and then pressurize with a pump integral to the tank. The case had some rust. The tank seemed much used (chipped paint). It held fuel. The pump didn't work.

I reconditioned the pump's leather gasket/plunger with tallow. Now the pump works fine. Thanks briggi (for how-to in Dec07 DP). I followed instructions printed on the stove-case and lit burner. The flame was yellow and not well controllable.

Next day I tried again. This time I realized the case's carrying handle had been in the way of the tank seating properly. I moved the handle out of the way. The tank now fit into place properly which extended the carburator tip deeper.

I lit the stove. This time it burned blue, and I could easily turn the flame up or down: better than on my propane stove which tends to go out when I turn the flame very low.

I had planned to buy gasoline (two service stations said their premium unleaded was 92 octane) but decided to first call Coleman: 1-800-835-3278. Surprise ! After waiting ten minutes a real person came on the line and was attentive, knowledgable, responsive. I asked if I could use unleaded gasoline. She said I could if I had a dual tank, which is coated inside so that automotive gas won't corrode it. But my tank was not dual. Also, auto gas has more additives and results in "more maintennance"; ie, gunking up the carburator. (A new carb costs $7 to $14 depending on model. Coleman also sells dual tanks.)

Dwelling Portably   May 2008

That convinced me to buy a gallon of Coleman fuel, $6.
Though the Coleman stove's lightness is appealing (I don't like
hauling a **HEAVY** propane tank), lighting a propane stove is
simpler and thus seems **SAFER**. Also, propane is cheaper. Lisa
OR 973

Many people are injured by nail guns.
U.S. emergency rooms treat 37,000 people annually. Two-
thirds of wounds were to hands or fingers. "Many injuries
occur when a nail gun discharges inadvertently - often when a
safety feature has been disabled for rapid nailing. Also, a
properly fired nail can ricochet off one that's already set,
or run through a piece of wood into a body part." SN 26may07

(Comment) DP readers probably don't use nail guns to improvise
wikiups or outfit vans, but may take temp carpentry jobs.
I've never used a nail gun. But I've used chain and other
power saws on jobs for others. If a customer wants me to use
power equipment, I want higher pay - which may mean I don't get
the job, because for that much they can hire a skilled carpenter. But that's okay. Better healthy than wealthy. Bert

White LEDs bother people because eyes are accustomed to yellow.
Sunlight, candles, incandescent bulbs are all yellowish.
After getting used to my white LED lights, I LIKE them. But I
had millions of years of eye evolution to overcome. Zalia, 06

(Response) Though direct sunlight is yellow-white, the sky is
blue. When under open sky but shaded from direct sun, the
light is blue-white. So, eyes have had mega-years exposure to
BOTH colors, though the yellow-white has been brighter.
Maybe our white LED lights irritate mostly, not because of
color, but because they illuminate only a small area. The
shake-light is focused: fine for spotting a coon in a tree or
for sending morse-code signals across a valley, but not for
much else. The lamp is dim, so it, too, illuminates small area.
Any white LED has another problem. It consumes much more
power than does an equally-bright yellow LED because: (1) white
LEDs are actually blue LEDs with a phosphor coating that
converts enough of the blue light to other colors to give an
impression of white. The conversion wastes energy. (2) Human
eyes are only 1/4th as sensitive to blue as to yellow, and half
as sensitive to red or green as to yellow. So, a white light
must be more intense than a yellow light to illuminate as well.
Some dealers claim that white LEDs are "more efficient".
Than **WHAT** ? Certainly more efficient than incandescents. Also
more efficient than white LEDs of ten years ago. LEDs are
being improved. Yellow LEDs are now used in traffic lights and
turn signals, so I doubt that their development is lagging. B

Many couples break up when building a home.
Primarily because the job is more complex than it needs to
be. If it were me and I were building a house and I had to
work for a living, I'd look for the simplest method around. My
perspective is that of an owner/builder, not architect or
professional builder. In fact I don't trust experts. (Don't
trust people with initials behind their names.) Pretty much
all the new homes I see being built these days, especially in
the wealthy Bay Area, are disasters.. Lloyd Kahn (in HomeWork :
Hand Built Shelter" (described in OBP) www.shelterpub.com

I do carpentry for friend in exchange for a room. Andrew, ME046

Index

of them along the garden's downhill edges so that their vines could spread outside onto the sifted rock and gravel border.

Bert planted the seeds individually except for the tiny turnip seeds which he sprinkled - not very evenly as we found after they sprouted. The garden was only 4 ft wide, so we did not need aisles (from the sides we could reach the middle), so all space was planted. Seeds ± 3 inches apart. Bert covered the seeds with a layer of soil as thick as the seeds (commonly recommended); not thick enough in our situation - watering floated up some of the seeds. Bert re-covered them.

Despite being tiny, the turnip seeds sprouted well and quickly, and grew vigorously   all varieties, also sprouted well and big initi   ng second leaves. The lentils sprout   he chard sprouted slowly (as Suzanne   . (She had suggested pre-soaking   Bert was in that area only one day.   sprouted and they grew slowly at fi   the biggest plants. The pumpkins sprouted   ong vines.

For protection from small creatures,   door (after patching a few rips with other screening sewed on) was mounted horizontally on corner posts ± 2 ft high. The sides were covered by loose screening hung vertically, with tops tied to the door frame, and bottoms anchored with rocks. When harvesting, we temp removed the rocks and curled up the side screens.

Some turnips seemed too close together. We soon thinned them by snipping with sizzors (pulling might disturb neighbors' roots). That is also how we did a little weeding.

We also soon harvested some chard leaves, but sparingly so as (we hoped) to not seriously injure the plants (which, Suzanne had said, could survive a few yrs and then reseed themselves).

The broccoli was very slow producing flower buds (the part usually eaten), and the buds were small, so we also ate the leaves (which, cooked, taste about as good as the buds).

The beans were slow flowering and producing pods (perhaps because the screening excluded bees which, Suzanne reported in Ab #10, are needed for pollinating). The pumpkins grew big yellow flowers, but most did not develop into pumpkins.

Though the netting was a barrier to most insects, it would not deter deer (which often ravage the gardens of rural settlers in this area); maybe not even rabbits. To hopefully repel animals, and as future fertilizer, we poured pee around the garden, putting most on the uphill sides.

We set several mouse traps, some within the screening, some in crannies under big rocks outside (to not catch birds). But we did not catch any nor see evidence of mouse damage. Something (sow bugs ?) ate small holes in some leaves. But we noticed very little damage by wild creatures - which pleasantly surprised us. Nor did many weeds grow.

For watering, after trying various ways, we used a squeeze bottle, refilling it from jugs in which we hauled water from a small pond we'd dug ± 50 yards away. We tried to water early mornings every 2 or 3 days (depending on temperature and amount of sun), but sometimes missed because of trips away. We simply squirted the water onto the top screening and let it spray through. About four gallons per watering.

By mid Sept our summer camp got sun too briefly each day for solar cooking to be practical. So we moved to our new winter camp. (There we continued solar cooking until much cloudy/rainy weather began in mid Oct). Before leaving, we harvested most of what remained.

Broccoli: We cut off and cooked all leaves and buds, except for a few old leaves past their prime, and a few small new shoots that might continue growing.

Turnips: On most, the leaves had withered; we harvested the roots. Biggest was orange size; most were plum size (small for turnips ?). By the time we got around to cooking them, some had partly rotted where there had been insect infestation. The remainders of those, and the others, tasted okay.

Chard: We harvested some leaves but left many in hopes the plants would survive the winter.

Beans: Only a few pods had developed. Most pod covers were tan (dead). Damp when picked so, to dry them, we put them in a pail with dry newsprint (from a recycling center).

Lentils: No pods had developed.

Late Sept and early Oct were quite warm and sunny except for a few showery days. Then in mid Oct came a few cold days. Frost warnings on weather radio. I don't know how cold the garden got; we were not there then. Then, through early Nov, mostly cool cloudy rainy/showery days.

On 9 Nov, Bert made a day trip to our summer-camp area to fetch things. He briefly inspected the garden. The frost had killed the pumpkin vines but left two immature pumpkins, the biggest orange size. The bean and lentil plants were dead. The broccoli had grown vigorously, putting out many new leaves and, on one plant, buds which had flowered. The chard was still growing. The few turnips we had left still had green leaves. We hope they survive the winter and next year produce seeds. Bert, lacking time and weight capacity, did not harvest anything.

In early Dec, shortly before an arctic air mass moved in with temperature below 20°F, Bert did a final harvest of leaves and shoots of broccoli, but left a few blossoms in hope they might produce seed. I removed the beans from the pail, hulled them, and was pleased that most were dry and looked good. All four varieties. But not many more harvested than were planted. Enough for only one meal. Tasted fine.

Conclusion: Harvests were not near enough to compensate for our labor. But we learned – and may do better next year.

The garden got several hours of sun on fully sunny days from late May until late July – the period when the sun goes higher in the sky than the tops of nearby bushes and small trees. But overall, the spot apparently does not get enough sun for seed or root crops to produce much. Also, the screening reduced sun intensity. So, next year, we will grow only plants with edible leaves: turnips; broccoli; chard (if it survives winter); kale (another cabbage relative) if we get seed; parsley (thanks again to Suzanne). But not lettuce, because we forage much wild gosmore (Hypochoeris radicata) a lettuce (and dandelion) relative that is probably more nutritious than domestic lettuce. (This year, we harvested gosmore all winter near our base camp, despite the Dec freeze.) Holly & Bert

I survived by foraging wild foods and dumpster diving.

And by working odd jobs where I could. After leaving my parents' home at age 17, I was on the road for ten years, living out of my backpack. I developed a taste for traveling lightly. I seldom stayed more than two nights in one place. I went to various political events and alternative gatherings.

As a single woman, I had no problem getting rides. I've been to every U.S. state and Canadian province, most of Mexico,

4

and all of Central America; but not much farther. When south
of the U.S. border, I stayed far away from tourist destinations
and so was always seen as a novelty and was fed by the locals in
the small towns I hitched into.

   After a while I grew tired of always being on guard among
strangers, and having to trick or coax at least one man a day to
avoid rape. (Believe it or not, I've never been raped or beat
up.) I got enough money to buy an old broken-down van and began
to live in it. I got books from libraries and learned how to
fix it. I even replaced an engine. (It had a cracked head.)

   I learned: if all the world's earnings were divided equally, each person would receive $6 a day. But more than 80% of
earth's people live on less than $2 a day. I tried to. But
that was impossible while having a van. And I never camped near
enough to a town to bike there and back. But living on $6 a day
was fun: requiring creativity and meaningful thoughtful
activities. For 17 years now, I've lived on $5-$6 a day.
I drive very little, not only to spend less, but to contribute
less to fuel-related deaths and destruction.

   As for companionship, having a partner has never fit with
my lifestyle. I have sweethearts here and there. I've gone to
Rainbow gatherings since 1978. I no longer love them as I once
did, but I still get lots from them.

   I have a desert 'home' I return to each winter. I've been
there nine winters so far; no one has found it yet. I have to
hike two miles to reach it, and 2½ miles to backpack water. But
I love it: 360° views with no neighbors. It is perfect for my
needs: so quiet and peaceful; beautiful because my time is my
own to invest in qualities I want.

   To build it, I bent cattle panels between boulders. Inside
is lathed and stuccoed. Outside is covered with plastic, then
rocks and recycled 'windows' or glass, and stuccoed between
rocks. I've invested about $200 into it.

   (In a sharply-focused color photo, her abode resembles a
rock outcrop. Terrain seems to slope gently. Waist-high bushes
with sparse foliage; patches of cactus; no trees visible.)

   During other seasons I live in a small vehicle. I removed
all seats except the driver's. Kitchen in right front. Cupboards along one side in back. I sleep with my feet between the
driver's seat and kitchen. The car is cozy; does not need heat.

   In early spring I carry in all my supplies to my campsite
and don't go back out (except for a trip to a gathering) until I
leave in the fall. I take a shovel and hand-rake for building a
a road to where I'm camping. I cover my vehicle's tracks behind
me by replanting trees and bushes, and spreading grass seed I
gather or buy. For crossing creeks, I have two 7-foot-long
steel ramps (custom made, $50). I try to find camp-sites on the
far sides of creeks. (Few folk will cross creeks and get wet to
go exploring.) After each crossing, I remove ramps and meticul-
ously repair the creek's sides, to leave no trace of my passage.
Rockann (pen name given by H&B, so readers may refer to article)

Silicone caulk plus thinner seam-seals tent; waterproofs pants.
   Before bicycling from Tucson to Seattle last summer, I
needed to seam-seal my tent. I dislike the pricy containers of
seam-sealer that dry up so quickly. So I tried using D.A.P.
100% silicone caulk (±$3.50), thinned with a solvent. (Gasoline
or paint thinner will do. I didn't try alcohol.) After it
dried, I dusted the seam with corn starch to lessen the sticky
feeling. One tube of caulk will waterproof MUCH fabric, and

I've stored caulk for more than a year without problems.

I also tried coating the inside of nylon pants. Applying two thin coats with a brush seemed to work well. I didn't take those pants with me to Seattle, so I don't yet know how long the coating will endure. Lauran, March 2009

Experiences with two different bicycle-assist engines.

The first engine I told about (in May 06 DP) is a 23cc two-stroke. I still have it. 7000 miles to date.

This past summer I purchased a 35cc four-stroke, slightly heavier, same drive system, different sounding, no mixing of gas and oil. I thought it might be better because 4-strokes are cleaner burning than 2-strokes; and there is 'talk' of eventually outlawing 2-strokes because of emissions.

For the 2-stroke I had a pretty good system for mixing oil and gas, so I didn't find non-mixing to be that great a convenience. The 35cc engine definitely could pull the weight all day with an easy cruising speed of 25 mph - though I find 22 mph more congenial for safety.

A disadvantage of the 4-stroke: I had to change the oil. Not a big job, but something I didn't need to do with the 2-stroke. I also needed to check oil level - though it NEVER needed topping off. To change the oil, I removed the engine from the bike (a 5-minute job), tipped it upside down into a suitable container, let it drain, then remounted the engine. Total time: less than ½ hour. I preferred to do this near a gas station to which I could take the oil. Once I simply took the engine into the gas station and asked if I could pour the oil into their waste barrel. They were fine with that.

The 4-stroke engine performed well except at altitudes above 7000 feet (Colorado). Trouble starting, fouled plug, very rough idle, etc, due to engine not getting enough oxygen. The 2-stroke has an adjustment for altitude. I talked with the owner of the 4-stroke business. He told me to send him the engine when convenient and he'd put an adjustment screw on the carburator. When they sell to someone living at high altitude, they put in different jets. I am one of only a handful of people who use these engines for long hauls through different altitudes, so I tend to expose these problems.

I hauled a Burley trailer weighing 60-80 pounds, depending on food and water load. Going up mountain passes, I needed to pedal to assist the engine. But that is well within my strength level. (I'm 52; in good shape compared to most women my age.)

I like both engines, though I slightly prefer the 2-stroke. It doesn't go as fast (which I don't care about) but is peppier responds faster, which is nice. It also can be put in any position without problems. Eg, when I camp at night, I often go into trees/brush, etc. That may require putting the bike under fences, or laying it down so that car headlights don't shine on my reflectors and reveal my location. Two-strokes are designed to be run in any position. Whereas 4-strokes must stay fairly level. Users have reported: if a 4-stroke is tipped past a certain angle, oil gets into part of the carburator, requiring work to clean it out. I was aware of that, so I kept the engine level. But there were times when I was put at risk or inconvenienced more than I like.

I was told the 4-stroke would get as good or better gas mileage than the 2-stroke, but it hasn't. I averaged 180-200 mpg with the 2-stroke and 140-160 mpg with the 4-stroke.

The 4-stroke has a lower throatier sound - a bit more

tolerable. But the 2-stroke sounds better than some 2-strokes.
Their db levels are about the same. A personal preference issue.
    I looked at cargo bikes. But for my needs they seem big,
awkward, extra heavy, cumbersome. I often need to get the bike
off into brush. A cargo bike would be more of a hassle.
    On a trip in Idaho, I found and purchased a Raleigh that
isn't made anymore. It's a cross between a comfort bike and a
recumbent. I REALLY LIKE IT. Pedaling it uses slightly different muscles, more glutes and hamstrings. When I sit on it, my
feet are flat on the ground. Its wheel base is slightly longer.
I am AMAZED at how much nicer it rides on a dirt road. Much
smoother, less bumpy. I don't know how much this is due to the
longer wheel base or to the type of tires. I haven't put the
engine on it as I love riding it as is.
    I also like its seating position. Riding long distances
on conventional bikes with my head facing up and forward, puts
an awful kink in my neck. I suffered a very painful herniated
disk two years ago. I'm not sure that extended bike riding
caused it, but I don't think it helped. This new bike lets me
sit more upright with little or no kink in my neck. The pedals
are slightly more forward than on a conventional bike, but not
as far forward as on a recumbent. The one thing I'll change:
its wide-berth comfort-bike seat. Because of the slight angle
of the pedals, there is nothing behind my butt to push against
when pluggin' up hills. (Not much of a problem here in Tucson,
but Seattle was another matter.) I need a seat with a small
back, maybe 3-4" high. I may design it myself, or see if any
type of modified recumbent seat would work.
    If you go into a bike shop, a current model, "Electra
Townie", is much like it, I think. Lauran, March 2009

(Comment) I wonder what type of handle-bar you use on a conventional bike. Or, how you position the hand grips. I HATE a
bar that droops; requiring me to sit hunched over – and then
strain my neck to look forward. I want to sit upright. When
climbing hills, I often stand on the pedals. (This is with a
2¼-speed bike. Typically, one speed won't stay in gear well.)
Yeah, more wind resistance. Not a big drag at my 10-15 mph
cruising speed, but I suppose it would be at 25 mph. B & H

My wife and I car-camped in Nashville for five years.
    At night we parked free, behind a brake place, in exchange
for night-watch services. (I found that opportunity by distributing hundreds of fliers to businesses, delivering them before
the businesses opened. Very few responded.)
    At the brake place, we had to drive away each morning by
6:30 when they opened. During summers we usually drove to a
park and stayed there until after dark. We then drove back to
the brake place and parked in the alley behind it. We typically
ate supper at K mart, then went to a library until 9:00, then
returned to the brake place, got into our car, and went to bed.
We slept in Geo Metros by removing the front seat, adding a
foam-rubber mat, and sleeping longways.
    Leaving each morning always felt good, because we had beat
the system out of rent; enabling us to afford a decent car,
and to save money – with which we eventually bought an old 30-
foot travel trailer and fixed it up (report in March09 DP).
During our 5 years car-camping we saved thousands on rent, and
had our freedom – but nothing is perfect. Our car costs $500
a month, including car payments, insurance, gas, etc.
    I sang and played guitar in bars. (Report in Ab#9) When

not playing, I usually kept my music equipment in storage units. But when I came home at night, the storage unit was closed, so I had to leave my equipment outside the car.

A few times, people tried to rob us while we slept. A man tried to steal my guitar from my car, but I woke up and ran him off. A female sneak thief tried to steal my wife's purse by reaching inside the window, but my wife woke up and gave her hell. So we got a dog and chained it to the bumper to warn us. Late at night, kids sometimes woke us by throwing rocks at us. Mexicans tried to steal the car. The neighborhood was racially mixed, and some blacks tried to make us pay them protection money, but we never did. In winter nobody bothered us much, but in summer kids and Mexicans roamed at night. We were hassled 4 or 5 times a year. I did not have a fire-arm, but I kept a baseball bat or crowbar or heavy wrench handy.

Once, as I drove off, I heard something dragging under my car. I stopped and looked. It was a man who had passed out. I called an ambulance, but he got up and ran off.

In Nashville, to sleep on business property, you need written permission from the owner - to show the cops when they come and wake you, which they will eventually. After you explain what you are doing, the cops will tend to leave you alone - unless new cops take over that beat; then you can expect to be bothered again. Cops' reactions to us ranged from helpful, to feeling sorry for us, to distainful. If any gunshots sound nearby at night, cops may question you. We were never arrested but always lived in fear of the law and outlaws.

In summer, fleas and mosquitos could be bad. In winter at night, we needed plenty of quilts over us. However, Nashville seldom gets colder than 20°F.

The library helped us get through many days and nights. Library people are nice here. Downtown, they are quite tolerant of the 'homeless'; many come from the mission. The library never gets new books, but the magazines are current. I'd never steal from the library as they are the only free thing here.

Nashville is quite dead at night; not as much happening as you might expect. It is a work-and-go-to-bed town - the buckle of the Bible Belt. It is a rich man's town. It tries to copy LA and NYC. Nashville has poor areas right next to rich areas. East Nashville is poor-to-middle-class; probably the friendliest area. West Nashville, Franklin, Beele Meade, Brentwood, Bellvue are rich and snobby. The rich and some middle-class whites won't hardly speak to the poor. If you drive an old car through a rich area, the police will be called. Nashville is 25% black. Some blacks are prejudiced, but most are friendly if you are. Blacks and whites bond against Mexs.

Broadway, famous for country-music dives, now runs off the poor. Costs $12 to park and $3 for a beer. The middle-class young go there, but poor rednecks are not welcome. How ironic; country music was originally the music of poor whites.

Rooms rent for $400 a month. Apartments, $600 up. Trailers $135-$150 a week. No rent control. Most people here put their money into cars and housing, and don't have much else. No state income tax, but TN has one of the highest sales taxes in U.S.

Nashville now has a "quality-of-life" ordinance, so the cops can harass and fine the poor. They want the poor out of sight. But sleeping in cars on city streets is not illegal here yet. There is a tent city downtown on the river. Some intolerant people wanted to run them off, but the mayor let it stay. 50,000 people were unemployed in 2009. 6000 'homeless'.

8

Nashville ranks third in U.S. for violence against the homeless. Car-camping is stigmatized here. I never let straight people know that I car-camped. So why did we car-camp HERE ? We grew up here and knew people. Would I ever car-camp again ? Not in Nashville. I have been here too long and done all that a poor person can do here. But I might in a much bigger city. It would have to be a place with many music jobs. But during this depression, I doubt that there is such a place.

Advice if car-camping. Keep tools with you and learn to fix your own car. Use window tint; don't use curtains, they would be a give-away. And do not leave bed covers visible in the car during daylight. Or, get a van with no windows and you can park most anywhere, as long as no one sees you get in and out. (But I've heard that such a van may attract attention some places; eg, parked on a street in a residential neighborhood.) If woken by someone at night, do not respond unless you are sure it is the cops. (If you don't respond to a would-be thief, he may break in. Or, if legally parked on a street with a vehicle in which you are not visible, why respond to cops ? If you lay still (don't rock vehicle) they won't know anyone is inside.)

Go to bed early and get up early before locals can see you. Before parking on business property overnight, get written permission from the owner. Keep a big wrench for protection. (Not illegal.) Stash your money away from the car, in case you are robbed. If you need warm places to spend time during cold weather, look for stores with delis, such as K-mart and Krogers.

Keep a low profile and enjoy your freedom from rent. You can move around nightly and enjoy the adventure. Enjoyment depends on attitude. Make a game out of hiding your lifestyle from the public. They think it is a moral crime to be poor. So build up your savings - then you can laugh at them. Car-camp until you can do better. If 'better' is not better, you can go back to car-camping. Or ?

I know people who live in the woods near the interstate. They sell firewood at the exit. They do not bother to own cars. They built a cabin and use a propane heater. They get by on $40 a week. They seem rather happy. Marty Brown, 2009 & 2010.

A do-it-themselves village near Portland of houseless people.

I heard an hour-long discussion about "Dignity Village" (DV) on OPB's "Thinking Outloud", 26nov09. DV has existed 8 years. DV is situated on asphalt pavement near Portland's airport. A prison and golf courses are near by; not much else. DV is 40 minutes by bus from downtown Portland; a big problem for DV residents who have jobs or are seeking them.

DV presently has 60 residents/members. Apparently most are men. A few are couples. No kids mentioned. When DV began, most residents lived in tents. But now most have 8-by-10-ft cabins. Some have wood stoves inside. A few have photo-volt panels on roof for elec lights and devices. None have running water or grid elec. Apparently most cabins were built by their original occupants. There are toilets outside (like those at construction sites ?). DV has a "common room" with wood stove wherein the discussion was conducted. On cold winter nights, a few houseless non-members are allowed to sleep in it.

The site was provided by Portland city. Residents pay $20/month, which goes for insurance the city requires. Legally, DV is a "non-profit corporation". On-site management and maintenance is by DV residents elected to their positions. Several were interviewed. One, the gate-keeper, said that residents

are not allowed to bring alcohol or illegal drugs into DV.
Police have visited DV once a week, average - a high rate for a
village of 60. Mostly in response to calls from DV.

DV wants to construct a shower/toilet building with water
and sewerage hookups, but needs $14,000 merely to pay for the
permits and inspections required - the charge for ANYTHING
legal built in Portland ! The $14,000 does not include the
costs of actual construction or hook-ups.

DV has had various micro-businesses: candle-making; a
hot-dog cart; an e-bay store; firewood sales (more scrap wood
is donated to DV than it uses): total, $1500/month. These may
be businesses conducted by/for DV; not including members'
individual activities. Some gardening is done in pails and
raised beds. (All ground is asphalt covered.)

Interviewees included several-year residents, a recent
arrival, an ex-resident who remembered DV's founding. But the
person who got the most radio time is not a DV resident. Her
main job: administering Portland's ten-year program to "end
homelessness". She is also city liason with DV; she collects
info about the people in DV. Her line: Though DV is commended
for doing as well as it has done (maybe the best such effort
anywhere in U.S.), "we" want to get all "homeless" people into
conventional housing that is affordable. (Ha ha ! With $14,000
required to merely get a permit ? Fat chance. But SHE has a
well-paid position.) She said, "Children belong in a house
with electricity and running water."

Electricity and indoor plumbing are relatively recent
inventions. They are costly luxuries, not necessities. Our
ancestors got along without them, and most people in the world
still do. I am saddened and angered when some people want to
force their preferences onto others.

Also said on the program: There are 1600 houseless people
in Portland. Their rates of addiction and mental illness are
no higher than among low-income people with houses. Poverty is
the main cause of houselessness. Holly

To sleep warm during cold weather, use plenty of covers.
Most sleeping bags are rated optimistically even when new,
and their effectiveness declines with use because stuffing gets
compressed and voids develop. Presently, sleeping INSIDE
our winter base camp, where seldom colder than 50°F, we are
using one old rectangular sleepa (opened out as a quilt) inside
a cover bag to help keep it clean and together, plus a quilt.
When much colder inside than 50° (20° or colder outside, seldom)
we add a third quilt (quite thick sleepa opened out). Under
the covers, we usually sleep nude except for knit caps and (on
Holly) long thick socks. We have a 4th sleepa in a pail near by
in case of extreme cold, but haven't had to use it. (Only a few
times a century does w Oregon get colder than 0°F.)

If occupying a semi-buried shelter long, what is under us
is less important for warmth than what is over us, because the
ground will gradually warm. We presently have barely enough
foam (open-cell on top of closed-cell) for cushioning. (We've
more foam stashed, but other things have had backpack priority.)

Some years ago, Lazlo Borbely, car-camping in WV, wrote in
DP that, when colder than 40°, he slept with his head under the
covers. 40° may be my approx threshold. If 50°, when I get
into bed, to warm up I usually keep my head under for a few
minutes and may blow exhaled air toward my feet. But after
CO2 accumulates to cause hard breathing, my head comes out.

Whereas when colder, the ventilation is greater (depends on the difference in temperature as well as thickness of covers) and my head stays under (though more air leakage around head than around body). I also wear a second knit cap. Bert

Use ground as floor ? Or insulate floor from ground ?
     Which is better for warmth during cold weather ?˙ That depends on the site, soil, depth of floor, occupancy.
     We have used the ground as our floor, covered only with plastic film plus maybe thin foam and linoleum. That is simpler than insulating the floor, and is usually as good or better for warmth IF the shelter is underground or earth-sheltered deep enough that the floor is several feet below the depth to which the ground usually freezes (if it does).
     Insulating floor from ground may be desirable IF the floor is at or close to the surface.
     As insulation, soil is much less effective PER THICKNESS than are fluffy or porous materials that entrap air, such as dry moss, loose leaves, crumpled newspapers, feathers, foam. (The still air is what insulates; the moss (or ?) merely serves to keep the air quite still.) But soil can insulate effectively if SEVERAL FEET of it is between the inside and the cold; ie, if the floor is quite far below frost level. (Exception: where soil is very porous (eg, loose gravel) and cold rain or snow melt percolates through. In that case, the water could be diverted by plastic tarps on the surface around the shelter. But insulating floor from soil might be easier.)
     If ground is floor, what will the floor temperature be during winter ? Unless there is water flow, many feet underground the soil temperature remains close to the average year-around outside temperature, because the soil stores heat (or cold) and many feet of it insulates effectively. Where we are, deep soil is 50° to 60°F, depending on slope and elevation. (South-facing slopes are warmer than north slopes; moderately-high slopes are warmer than valley bottoms and high altitudes.)
     When in winter we return to a well-insulated partly-underground shelter that was vacant for several weeks, the floor will typically be ±50° and the inside air close to that temperature - desirable if outside air colder. After one night occupancy, the floor will not have warmed much and the inside air may warm to only 60°. But if we stay several weeks, our body heat (and cooking, if done inside) will gradually warm the floor to ±60°, with the inside air typically fluctuating between 60° and 80°, depending on outside temperatures (typically lows of 30° and daily highs of 50°) and our activities. Generally coolest at dawn and warmest late afternoon. (Some data in March 09 DP.)
     If insulating floor from ground (I never have), I'd use a floor material that will store much heat and thus help warm the shelter during cold periods. Barefoot Architect book (review in Ab#10) suggests dark-colored stones or ceramic tiles. But damp soil stores more heat per weight (because of its water content) and is generally more available. I'd put plastic film above and below it to confine the moisture. The insulation under it must support the weight of the soil plus the occupants and their equipment. I might try alternate layers of plastic film and scavenged styrofoam chips (used for packaging; they don't have many other re-uses). I'd reserve foam SHEETS for walls/ceiling.
     Raised wooden floors are desirable only in special situations: on flood lands where the floor must be above high water; on very steep slopes where terracing would be difficult; on

permafrost; in earthquake zones for a structure built to
'dance' over the ground (suggested by Barefoot Architect).
        (Raised wooden floors began as status symbols centuries
ago when only the rich could afford them. Peasants had dirt
floors, covered at most with straw. Back then, no plastic
film or linoleum or automatic-machine-made carpets. When they
became available, floors could have been made better without
becoming more costlier. But no - building codes were imposed
which required complex floors along with many other non-
essentials. That made houses much more expensive, forcing
house dwellers to work longer hours and pay more taxes.)

"Earthquakes don't kill people. Buildings kill people."
        Recent earthquakes in Haiti and Chile prompted us to
review our seismic situation. Odds of a big quake off Oregon's
coast within the next 50 years, raised to 80% after researchers
found that the fault slips oftener here than farther north.
        Crustal plates gradually move relative to each other. But
edges may hang up. The force increases until it overcomes the
resistance and the edge breaks loose. That's the quake. The
more time since the previous quake, the greater the force that
may build up, and the more violent the quake.
        During the past ten thousand years, intervals between giant
quakes here ranged from 200 to 800 years; average 300 years.
The last giant quake: 310 years ago - accurately known because
the tsunami swept all the way to Japan and was recorded.
        The fault is only 75 miles from the coast. A tsunami would
smash ashore in a few MINUTES. Coastal residents are being
warned: if you feel the ground shake, IMMEDIATELY head for high
ground. DON'T WAIT for evacuation instructions. Past tsunamis
here were as high as 40 feet, sediment deposits indicate.
        Our base camps are high enough and far enough inland (± 10
miles) that even a 100-foot tsunami would not reach us. Most
years we are ON the coast no more than a few days, and our temp
camp is usually up on some hill, so that is not a big concern.
        A quake's effects inland depends on type of soil. Safest,
solid rock. Riskiest, deep sediments, esp if soaking wet - as
they often are here during winter. The sediments will slosh
about, like liquid in a pan that's jolted, thus amplifying the
movement. Thus valley bottoms are usually riskier than higher
ground. Portland and the Willamette Valley is at high risk.
Also risky, steep slopes which may avalanch, esp road cuts.
        Because Oregon hadn't had big quakes recently, most bridge.
and buildings are not as sturdy here as in Calif. So, minimize
time in schools, stores, offices, libraries, multi-story apts,
etc; esp those built before 1995, which was when past earthquakes were discovered. I've read: the wood-frames of most
houses are resistant, but plaster and sheet-rock may crash down
furnishings be tossed about, conduits ruptured, and escaping
gas be ignited by a pilot light or electric spark. Barefoot
Architect has some advice re quakes we've not seen elsewhere.
        Our new winter shelter SEEMS fairly safe. No big trees
near. A ± ten-foot-bank is on one side. It is stabilized by
old tree roots and by new trees and bushes as they grow. So
I don't expect a MASSIVE land slide. The bank sheds dirt and a
few rocks, esp when the ground thaws after a hard freeze (one
in Dec 09). I left a two-foot space with a ditch between the
bank and our shelter's surface: wide enough to crawl through
to remove fallen dirt. So a quake may only fill the ditch.
        One change: We had many jugs of water inside, setting

quite high. (Ceiling ± 4½ ft) We'd put them there because they stayed warmer, and because not much floor space, and because they might freeze outside. But if a quake upsets our shelter, those jugs could come bombing down. So now, we leave most jugs outside. We bring in a few to warm up, a day or so before needed. If freeze forecast, we bring in all - despite clutter.

During winters we cook mostly with propane, usually once a day. After cooking, we turn off the tank's valve, mainly to reduce leaks, but also for safety in case a quake ruptures the connections. The stove is inside; the tank is in the antiway.

We've read: the N Amer region most at risk is the Ohio Valley and adjacent areas. That area has several major faults and deep sediments. A quake there two centuries ago, was so powerful that in Boston, ± 1000 miles away, churches were shook enough to ring their bells. No seismographs then, but estimated magnitude: 8.0 to 9.0. (An 8.0 quake is 30 times as powerful as Haiti's 7.0. A 9.0 quake, 900 times.) Another quake is overdue. The early 1800s quake killed few people because few people lived there then. But a quake there now could demolish buildings in an area hundreds of miles across and kill or injure many millions. A book, "8.5", dramatizes what may happen. Though fiction, it is well-researched seismically, I've heard.

The few radio reports we heard about Haiti (we don't listen much) described destruction and death, but didn't mention what a geologist said years ago: "Earthquakes don't kill people. Buildings kill people." Haiti, quite far south and surrounded by ocean, has a warm mild climate. So why were so many risky buildings built ? Why not more use of tents and other soft lightweight shelters.? Haiti also gets hurricanes. What would withstand BOTH, yet be economical ? STRONG tents ?

Animals behaving strangely sometimes give advance warning, perhaps because, before a VIOLENT movement, the ground may creep enough to open deep cracks, letting unusual odors to surface. Most mammals can smell much keener than can humans. B & H

Since getting my first vehicle, I've lived with a kitty.
Cats are quiet, bury their shit, and provide for themselves where there are trees they can climb to protect themselves. When in a desert lacking trees, I keep my kitty inside at night and lay a trap-line of 15 little head-snappers around our camp. If I wake early enough to beat other critters to my prey, I typically harvest 4 or 5 mice. Keeps kitty fat. Rockann

Preventing and responding to animal attacks.
Each year, nearly 5 million Americans are bitten by dogs, and a 4th of the bites require medical attention. Of 500,000 emergency-room visits prompted by bites; approx: dogs, 90%; cats, 8%; rodents, 2%. I've never encountered aggressive dogs in the wilds, but have been charged by many dogs when on roads and streets and sidewalks. I fought them off with sticks and rocks, or outran them on a bike. So, the most important preventive: minimize time near the abodes of people who keep unchained dogs. I've never encountered an aggressive cat. I assume most cat bites are inflicted on people who handle them.

Once, years ago, I encountered a rat in a storage tent who, instead of fleeing, stood its ground and bit the stick with which I attacked and killed it. We then discovered: it was a male trying to defend its mate and young who had a nest in the tent. (Brave, but their choice of nest site was a fatal mistake.)
If bitten, the most effective treatment: "Immediate and

vigorous washing and flushing with soap and water, detergent, or even water alone." (If a snake-bite suctioner is at hand, I'd then try that.) Then "apply either ethanol (eg, booze) or tincture or aqueous solution of iodine, or povidone iodine" (if at hand; if not, I'd use isopropyl alcohol or diluted bleach (though more toxic) or hydrogen peroxide (though less effective).

As for rabies: 19 cases in U.S. from 2000 to 2006 of which 18 fatal, caused by: bats, 13; raccoon, 1 in VA; mongoose, 1 in PR; transplanted organs from one donor, 4. Bats are the only rabies reservoir in Oregon. Foxes often acquire rabies from bats, and rabid foxes may attack humans. In OR, 2000-2008, of animals tested who were rabid: bats, 93 of 905; foxes, 6 of 25; dogs, 0 of 337; cats, 0 of 738; other, 0 of 258. In OR, rabies prophylaxis strongly recommended if bitten by fox or bat, unless animal can be caught and tested and is not infected. "However, prophylaxis should not be undertaken lightly", because costly (mean, $3700) and time consuming. In 2000, a survey of 11 u-associated ERs, found that prophylaxis administered "inappropriately in 40% of cases". (from CD Summary, 26may09)

To stop a charging bear, a can of hot-pepper resin with compressed air is more effective (92% of time) than a fire-arm (75% of time) said a BYU biologist (Outdoor Life, Mar09). Why ? Not said. But in May09 Backpacker, "Most canisters produce a visible 30-foot cone of spray", whereas gunshots must be accurate and even then, the bear may reach you and maul you before dying. "Aim for the bear's eyes and face, and pull the trigger when the bear is 40 feet away. As soon as the bear is disoriented, leave the scene as quickly as possible." On average per year, one person is killed and 12 injured by grizzly attacks. "Out here (in WY) we have many times more black bears than grizzlies, but we have fewer encounters with blacks. Blacks are scared of humans because they are hunted; grizzlies are not", said an elk hunter (in OL) who was injured and probably would have been killed if his companion (dad) had not killed the grizzly "with a single well-placed arrow". The federal "bear recovery coordinator" disputed that, saying: "Bears are not taught anything by being killed." No. But the bears who AVOID humans are more likely to pass on their traits to offspring. Either that official is ignorant - or wants more money thrown his way.

General advice for defense against big predators: If with companions, stay close enough to each other that a predator who sees any of you sees all of you. A predator is less apt to attack a PACK of creatures who appear defensive than a loner. For defense, unless you are a fast-draw expert, you can get a spear or staff into action quicker than a gun or pepper spray; important esp against cougars because they often ambush. (Advice not seen elsewhere: When on a road, we usually walk on the downhill side, thinking that a cougar waiting in ambush will likely be on the uphill bank so that it can leap farther.)

If a predator is encountered, stand tall, look big. Maybe open coat or raise knapsack over head to look bigger. Don't stare at it. Slowly back away. Speak in a low voice. Ie, act differently than its usual prey. DON'T turn and run. That will likely prompt a race you will LOSE. If attacked, fight back aggressively with whatever is at hand. Bert & Holly, Oregon 973

Pet animals are the source of many deadly/crippling diseases. Especially in young children. (CD Summary, 5aug08, 19aug08) (Comment) I hope toy makers develop robots that are more appealing to kids than are puppies (etc) - AND are not toxic.

Prions contained in dirt are very infective.

Prions are mis-shapen proteins that cause brain-destroying diseases (eg, mad cow). "Prions linger in soil for at least 3 years by binding tightly to clay and other minerals." Prions get into soil when an infected animal dies; also from urine and saliva. Animals often swallow hundreds of grams of soil per day when eating plants, drinking muddy water, and licking the ground to get minerals. (Sci News 11feb06,21july07) (Comment) Though probably more of a problem with domestic animals, esp animals concentrated in feed lots, some wild animals get prion infections. When foraging plants growing close to the ground, esp where animals frequently graze, I'd wash plants thoroughly. Boiling doesn't deactivate prions. H&B

Mysterious malady cured by discontinuing treatment.

Bert noticed a tiny sore on the edge of the web of skin at the rear of his arm pit. I examined it, saw nothing, but felt a minute swelling. A bite? Or a pimple starting ? I dabbed on a little tea-tree oil but did not cover it.

The next day, the spot, still slightly sore, was redish. I dabbed on more tea-tree, then covered it with a small piece of aluminized-plastic food-wrap, taped on, to slow evaporation of oil. But the tape did not adhere well to the edge of skin.

The next day, a penny-size area was now red and tender. Before Bert sacked out, he had me dab on more tea-tree; then lay with his arm snug against his arm pit to hold in the oil.

The spot got no further attention for a few days, but Bert continued to notice tenderness. When I again inspected it, I saw an irregular maroon-colored area with abrupt boundaries, approx one by two inches, all tender when touched. It seemed to be spreading ! But what was IT ? And why the strange shape and bruize-like color ?

Bert finally guessed that the tea-tree was irritating the tender skin in his arm pit. The irregular shape was where his arm had fit snugly against his arm pit and confined the oil.

Now, approx a month later, the skin looks and feels normal. What caused the original sore ? Maybe mechanical irritation. One night had been unusually cold. Instead of fetching another quilt, Bert had slept with sweaters on. Maybe, during a deep-sleep period, a seam had pressed long and hard against his skin.

We've not noticed bad effects of tea-tree on other skin. But we put it only on a small area and seldom more than 24 hrs.

The moral of the story: You don't have to go to pricy MDs who prescribe pricy drugs and very costly surgery, to suffer bad side effects. You can do it yourself, cheap. Holly

How to distinguish hyper-hydration from dehydration.

Though drinking too little water is much more common than drinking too much, either is harmful. And some of the symptoms are similar: dizzy, tired, vomiting, shakes. Nor is frequency of drinking a reliable criteria. During hot dry weather, one may drink often, but sweat out more water than is ingested without noticing because the sweat quickly evaporates. Dehydration is also common during cold weather, esp at high altitude, because of moisture lost by breathing hard to get enough oxygen while working/hiking vigorously to help stay warm, and because of reluctance to drink cold water. Symptoms that differ:

Too much: Urinating often and much, and the urine stream appears colorless or very pale. You might also notice water

sloshing in your belly. If too much, quit drinking. Maybe eat
a little salty food. Stay warm. Note STREAM: urine that looks
colorless in a narrow stream, will look yellow in a container.
    Too little: Urinating seldom and little, or not for many
hours, and the stream is quite yellow. Urinating might also
be irritating. If too little, drink more WATER (NOT "sport
drinks"; their sugar/salt is dehydrating.) Or, if no water,
maybe eat edible succulant plants you KNOW WELL, that are NOT
sweet, salty, bitter, or other strong taste. Stay cool.
    If hot, whether or not dehydrated, get out of the sun.
Remove clothes. (Except, if no shade, loose clothes, opened,
might reduce heating.) If no shade, rig some from clothes or
whatever is at hand. Eg, ball up a small garment, set it on top
of your head to maintain an air space; then drape a big garment,
preferably white or light colored, loosely over it. Or, if
sticks and twine available, rig a parasol (shade umbrella) or
mini roof. If enough materials, form two layers with an air
space between. (A single layer will get hot and radiate heat,
esp if material dark.) Unless without water and close to source,
postpone travel until evening or (cooler) very early morning.

Potassium is as vital as protein for building/retaining muscle.
    In people over 65, muscle mass correlated with the amount
of potassium in their diets. "The body converts protein and
cereal grains to acid residues. Excess acid triggers breakdown
of muscle into compounds that ultimately make ammonia which
removes the acid. Potassium-heavy diets, being alkaline, can
buffer those acids without scrificing muscle." Fruits and
vegetables are rich in potassium. Science News, 29mar08
    (Comments) I read elsewhere that some grains (eg, millet)
don't have acid residues. (But we tire of millet faster than
other grains we have eaten. I don't know why.) And that some
fruits (eg, plums) have an acid residue.
    Safer to get potassium from food than from mineral supple-
ments. Too much potassium is toxic. A balance of potassium
with sodium and other minerals is needed.
    Getting enough potassium may be a problem for people in
northern climes who live off the land year around, because their
diets may be mostly meat. It has been a problem for us some
winters, because our diet was mostly grains, esp wheat. (This
winter, luckily, gosmore (Hypochoeris radicata) has remained
plentiful near by, though we wonder about the effects of eating
so much of IT. We've also eaten legumes and tomato paste.) H&B

To reduce risk of breast cancer, do NOT wear bras.
    And gently massage breasts daily, starting nearest the arm
pit, suggests a New Connexion article. Reason: Unlike blood,
which is circulated mostly by a heart, lymph flow depends on
body motions. If circulation is hindered by a bra or by not
moving enough, carcinogenic toxins (both natural and human-made)
accumulate in tissues. (But, while massaging, if you feel any
lump, DON'T massage it - and seek further diagnosis.)
    I read previously, in Naturally, that breast cancers are
very rare in cultures where women don't wear bras. But possible
co-factors: more movement; less junk foods; more babies
starting at age ±20, who are breast-fed.(epidemiologists say).
    People tend to blame chronic illnesses on things they CAN'T
control, such as unlucky genes or pervasive environmental
pollution. Though those are likely co-factors, the most
important causes are often things that people CAN control. H&B

Ab

c/o Lisa Ahne, POB 181, Alsea OR 97324. #9 Dec 2009.
$2 for big-print copy until all sold; $1 for tiny
print. Ab discusses how and where to live better
for less. Ab, an ab-apa, encourages readers to send
pages ready to copy (text 16x25 cm or 6.3x10", black on white,
on one side of paper, compact). Usually published UNedited.

WOOD STOVE for MAD HOUSER HUTS in CHICAGO

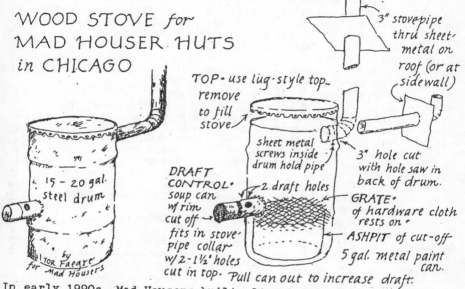

TOP· use lug-style top remove to fill stove

3" stovepipe thru sheet-metal on roof (or at sidewall)

15 - 20 gal. steel drum

sheet metal screws inside drum hold pipe

DRAFT CONTROL· soup can w/ rim cut off → fits in stove-pipe collar w/ 2-1½" holes cut in top·

2 draft holes

3" hole cut with hole saw in back of drum.

GRATE· of hardware cloth rests on ·

ASHPIT of cut-off 5 gal. metal paint can.

Pull can out to increase draft.

by Tor Faegre for Mad Housers

In early 1990s, Mad Housers built ultra-low-cost houses and
gave them to houseless people. 6x8x8 ft, no elec or running
water, not to code. But occupants preferred them to official
shelters that were so regimented that residents could not hold
a job. In Jan 09, Tor wrote. "Mad Housers are no longer in
action, though I think about a revival." For more info:
Tor Faegre, 1600 Ashland, Evanston IL 60201. 847-869-1969

I choose comfort over appearance.

I wanted to sew cuffs onto a long-sleeved sweatshirt whose
arms were too short. Conventionally, seams are sewen with the
raw edges and stitching facing inwards. But when such a seam
is pressed against the skin, as does the cuff seam when I'm
writing and my wrist is pressed against a table, there can be
irritation, even soreness. So I chose to face the seam's raw
edge outward. Feels better. Julie Summers, OR 973, Jan 09

For foot comfort and health, change footwear often.

And don't wear the same ones again for a week. There is
not any best kind or brand. Boots, shoes, tennies, mocs,
sandals, thongs, and various hybrids all have good qualities -
and bad ! Wear any one everywhere or long and it will rub a
spot raw, or collect thorny debris, or not block sharp objects,
or not keep feet warm, or not let sweat evaporate.

We don't buy footwear new. We make mocs from discarded
truck innertubes. We've found many tennies in a thrift-store
dumpster, and got some dress shoes at a church give-away.
Sterilize in a laundry drier, or by sunning in a clear plastic
bag on a hot day. (170°F kills harmful microbes.) H & B

Thank you for the DP and ABs. I notice DP is becoming more focused; and absorbing extraneous but interesting material is for AB to do. good stuff. I agree with you about choosing a place based on climate/terrain and likeminded folks. Personally I would - or might - have ended up in the south but the culture was too psycho. And summer heat was awful. The terrain and winters were more to my liking.

Religion: while we do have our crazies in the NE they are fewer than in most other areas Ive travelled. NE religion is traditionally very personal, not something to bludgeon others with, despite puritan heritage. My own background is that of a seeking Christianity, not dogmatic. The problem is religio fascism in times of unrest, i.e. nativist Father Coughlin types. Desperate people seem to either organize(Argentina in the 90s, midwest farmers during foreclosure sales in 30s, miners since the 1870s) or cling to insane theology.

Anyway I live here cause I like it. 12 years so far. I have hitched extensively, camped illegally, walked and biked much, and only once interacted with cops when my car headlight was out. But I am White, and Black friends tell a different story. Maine is 98% white.

Old time Skills: where do OTS leave off and new skills begin? To start with I think useful to talk about attitudes, then develop particular skills or tool proficiencies, observation techniques, from there.

Patience: OTS, or post oil skills (POS), rely more on human energy and natural process (the flow of a river to move a boat). Walking takes time. The use of some tools can be dangerous in the hands of inexperienced, impatient users.

Familiarity: with ones abilities, limits, with others one is with, with ones environment, with tools/gear one uses, and so forth.

Ability to make do: Not needing to have everything be 'ideal', being able to make and mend with whats at hand. Some connection with familiarity. One friends old truck (1966) was simple, he was familiar with, and we fixed it numerous times with rope, wire, once a plywood washer to facilitate holding axle on, once a rope to hold driveshaft. Ability to improvise, do without, conserve.

Of course these are all vonu skills too.

In terms of actual skills, I would start with knife and axe craft. Many books on the subject incl. _The Axe Book_ which is excellent. With these two tools one can get fuelwood, clean out animals/butcher, cut poles for shelter, make other tools, crafts, etc. A good axe is hard to find, old ones best, 3# with no marks on the poll (opposite to the blade). A poll struck with steel i.e. to drive a wedge, will deform head, ruin axe. A good knife can be found at Woodcraft (woodcraft.com) which carries the line of Frost swedish laminated sttel knives/wood handles, thse are inexpensive ($10) and very good. I like the medium, wide blade. Cant recall if a sheath is included, sometimes in stores they will come with a thermoplastic sheath. The axe rough shapes, the knife refines. Made a bucket yoke with these 2 tools yrs ago, also new tool handles, spoons (yeah, I know, not necessary-but nice) toggles for coat closure, and with a hand saw, a frame for a 24" buck saw blade. Your experience with the h'ware store bowsaw is sadly typical of the state of tools today. One must either buy expensive custom tools or (as I do) haunt the used tool sellers (many here). I will send drawings/instructions for bucksaw if you wish, it is portable and sturdy but not as handy as bowsaw or as compact. Also, induction hardened teeth on a saw of the Swede-style can be sharpened with a diamond file. not easy though.

Thanks to Chris Withemi for his piece. Good to hear how children can/do grow up freer.

Here we have some locally organized buying clubs for bulk foods. Comes from Assoc. Buyers, etc. Decent. Much agglomeration happening w/bulk food buying as United gobbled up the little guys.

NOTE: FEB 09, ANDREW IN ME,

(Thoughts) Andrew advises, be familiar with your own abilities. YES ! For that reason, I do NOT want an axe. An axe is too dangerous unless the user is skilled with it. I would not use an axe enough to develop and maintain skills. An axe is easier than a saw to resharpen, and is faster for some tasks IF one is skilled. But I'll make do with saws and knives.

Holly and I have quite a few knives, here and there, bought cheap at yard sales, etc. Most are not the best but are adequate for our tasks. A few have broken but we have spares.

Apr/Oct 1981 DP has plans for a bucksaw frame. I've never made one. A few times I've used a broken piece of bow-saw blade without frame. Not very efficient, but light and compact: adequate if not much sawing needed. Andrew says: be willing to make do, vs insisting that everything be ideal. YES !

About attitudes. Often more important than how skilled someone is, is what they DO with whatever skills they have. Years ago, DP got a letter from someone who said he knew HOW to build. He said his problem was, finding WHERE to build. He was seeking a county where he could build a conventional cabin with conventional conveniences (eg, a drive-way) without getting hassled about permits and building codes.

We don't know of such a place. Though some counties and states are PRESENTLY not as bad as some others, they may change ANY TIME and become as bad or worse - and require that existing structures be expensively brought up to code - or demolished.

He may have been an itinerant carpenter, in s CA winters, n CA summers. If so, he was probably more skilled with tools than I am. I build things, but not very many. And I've never apprenticed, or taken courses, or diligently studied a manual and practiced techniques. If he watched me build, he could likely show me ways to use a tool more efficiently and thus do a task faster and better. None the less, I had built comfortable shelters for Holly and me, whereas apparantly he hadn't for himself. Why ? Because I am willing to build and utilize shelters of kinds and in ways that don't attract hassles.

But I still wonder why he hadn't. In Oregon (and many states ?) small buildings (8x12 ft max ?) don't require permits. Does CA not allow them ? Or not allow sleeping in one ? Or was he fixated on building something bigger ? I don't know.

Regarding familiarity with abilities of self and others. Seems to me, that is gained mostly by DOING - and quite often making mistakes. Gauging that a repair, though not ideal, is probably adequate, comes from making other repairs, some of which sufficed, some of which didn't.

Holly and I like having our own junk piles. Most items will never be used, but some will - and we can't predict what will and what won't. We scavenge much from impromptu (illegal) dumps beside logging roads; some from recycles and dumpsters.

Regarding tools and materials. What can be accumulated now that may become valuable and tradable during future conditions - which are NOT predictable ! I'd avoid high tech, except for things I want to use SOON. Dmitry Orlov (reprinted in Ab#6) suggested buying and storing photovoltaics. But pv prices have trended downward, and may decline greatly when a cheaper manufacturing process is developed. So, unless demand increases SOON, pv bought now is likely to lose value.

The future can NOT be predicted well. Many wild cards. Any preparations will likely be needlessly early - or TOO LATE ! Thousands of people will make and publicize predictions. A few are right on, partly BY LUCK. Only 6 predicted this depression. B&H

Comments on the tribode: a structure for living on the ocean. The tribode may work in reasonably protected waters but it is wacky. It will be tough to resell. D.S. in FL, Nov 08

A 60-foot-tall structure on the water will draw the attention of both local authorities and the USCG. The USCG has a rep even among 'normal' boaters as being thuggish, and a 'weird' boat, let alone structure, seems to bring it out more. I know of two boats here declared unseaworthy and 'grounded'.
Carbon fiber is extremely pricey and toxic (epoxy bonds it). It's also UV-sensitive; needs paint or other UV blocker.
The structure is quite top heavy, and I'm not sure the splay of the legs makes up for it. A center of gravity 40 ft up, compared with a boat's COG which is below the waterline. The tribode seems more suited to calmer waters, where swells are more common than breakers. Andrew in ME, Feb 09

Your write up was interesting, but, as you said, it's not "a complete, detailed, proven design ready to build." Is that as far as you will go with your idea ? Or will you provide detailed plans ? If so, how soon ?
Have you built anything similar to a tribode ? What ? How much have you lived out on the open ocean (not just in a marina) and where and when and in what ?
Your pen name suggests that you are involved with aircraft. Have you designed, built or flown seaplanes ? Salt water wrecks equipment not built to withstand it. Even a cabin 32 ft up will get some salty particles. Bob, CA 908, Feb 09

I like the idea of homes that are mobile without depending on roads for mobility. I also like the idea of each family being independently mobile (vs leasing living space on a cruise ship.) But I wonder where and how a tribode dweller could buy more supplies at reasonable prices; a problem for a family living in a remote wilderness or even an isolated small town.
It was a problem for boat dwellers (whose reports were in the bulletin of the Seven Seas Sailing Assoc, SSSA, who swapped with DP years ago). Though the Caribbean has many independent island nations, for boats in that area, the best places to buy more supplies and replacement parts were Puerto Rico and Virgin Islands, as well as U.S. mainland. Go there and you will likely have to deal with USCG and other officials. Bert, Mar09

Reply to D.S. in Florida. Ease of resale depends on numbers. If as many people want tribodes as want boats of a certain type, resale will be as easy. I'd build a tribode now only if I wanted to use it for a long time.

Reply to Andrew in Maine. USCG, I agree. Tribodes are not for U.S. waters nor for any coastal waters. For shallow waters I'd favor something like that boat with legs that could raise itself out of the water. (Mentioned in March 09 DP.)
Stability. I assume you had not seen my "limits" (on "Tribode" p.8). They may assuage your doubts. The CG of an empty tribode is $\sim$ 16' above sea level. When inhabited the CG is lower unless the cabin is heavy loaded which I warn against.
Some boats have CG below the water line. Some don't. Mono-hull yachts with deep heavy keels do. But their heavyness reduces yielding when struck by waves. That increases stress, which requires more strength and even more weight and cost. Most multi-hull boats are light-weight shallow-draft with most of their structure and volume above the waterline. Their CG

is lower than a tribode's but their hull spacing is much less.
     The price of ultra strong fibers will come down as patents
expire and as new kinds increase competition. If building now
I might use carbon fiber on the booms where stiffness is very
important, but I'd use fiberglass on floats and cabin.
     Yes, epoxy is toxic but has been used many years and safe-
guards are well developed. (Fiberglass particles are hazardous
too. They can behave like porcupine quills and penetrate flesh.)
     Yes, epoxy is UV sensitive. On a tribode instead of paint-
ing I might wrap most parts with a plastic film that blocks UV.
Films are easier to replace than are paints. Wrapping isn't
practical on most boats because of their complex shapes.

Reply to Bob in Calif. How far I go with the idea depends on
how much interest it arouses. I haven't yet built any vehicle
or structure for salt water use. Before offering plans I would
build a tribode and rigorously test it, and live in it on
stormier waters than I recommend frequenting with it.
     Yes, salt water can wreck equipment. Salt water is not
especially harmful to most plastics. Less so than to metals.
Any wetness can harm wood. Fiber-reinforced wood seems the
easiest materials for building a prototype for testing the
configuration, but probably not for large-scale production.

Reply to Bert in Oregon. I'm not familiar with SSSA. But my
impression is that most boat dwellers use the ocean only for
travel to lands that interest them. There they dock, moor, or
beach. While sailing they cannot easily obtain supplies.
     Tribodes are for ocean living, not mainly for travel. I
agree that a family living isolated on the ocean would have the
same problems as on land. But I doubt that many tribode
dwellers would live isolated. There are easier ways to be
isolated for anyone who wants that. The advantage of tribodes
is that their dwellers can congregate without having to go into
ports, and they can easily change neighbors when they desire
that. For vehicle dwellers on land, somewhat similar is The
Slabs in southeast Calif. But that will continue only as long
as government agencies tolerate it.
     A congregation can attract supply boats or, if big enough,
ships that act as department stores, perhaps making circuits of
several tribode groups along with small islands. On land there
are mobile merchants who go to small towns and offer merchandise
not available locally. Ave Dave, OR 978, May 09

     (The first 6 pages about tribodes were in the original Ab#7.
We now offer all (so far) 10 pages (5x8, quite big print)
separately for $2. I hope to obtain 2 more pages about it or
related topics. (12 pages are easier to bind than are 10 pages.)
What other mobile structures exist or are contemplated for
RESIDING on (or above or under) deep water in mid ocean ? The
Ab#7 reprint contains everything in the original issue except
the tribode: 16 pages originally, now tiny print, $1.)

"20,000 Nations Above the Sea" is an article in July 09 Reason.
     It talks about an organization to promote the idea of
seasteading. It is run by Patri Friedman, son of David and
grandson of Milton Friedman. Patri formerly worked for Google,
has connections with Silicon Valley money people and has gotten
some financing from them. Jim Stumm (in Aug09 The Connection)
     I found Reason in Corvallis city library and briefly read
the article. The group seems to be thinking of building islands,
not mobile structures. Bert   Ab #9   Dec 09   Page 5

Our experiences buying dry foods, including wheat from growers.

Until recently we did not search for growers. Nearby stores sold the foods we wanted at affordable prices.

When Bert and I first came to this area nearly 30 years ago, there was a funky co-op that emphasized nutritious foods and that minimized their expenses. It sold 50-pound bags of organic hard red wheat for ± 20¢/pound. Other stores charged almost that much for non-org hard red wheat. So we chose org. And wheat became our biggest source of calories; replacing rice (the grain most pesticided). We bought non-org lentils, beans, oatmeal, popcorn, millet, sunnies, etc, because we ate much less of them and, for them, org cost much more than non-org.

At that time, what was "organic" was a matter of trust and reputation. So, the extra cost of org was due only to more field labor or less yield; not to hoop jumping.

That all changed. The co-op gradually became fancy, pricy, hypy; and emphasized very-costly highly-processed more-tempting-but-less-nutritious foods, bought by affluant but deluded folks who seemed to believe that anything "organic" was healthful. It no longer had space for extra 50# bags of wheat.

Also, organics became certified: growers had to fill out forms and pay for inspections, etc, which raised costs. Also, rich folks were discovering organics faster than growers could switch, which bid up prices. So, we quit buying organic.

For a while we bought most dry foods from a small local wholesaler. For 50-pound bags, non-org hard red wheat, ± 18¢/ pound; other foods ranged from 25¢ to 45¢. The wholesaler did not get much walk-in trade; the store was small and crowded, difficult to get around in. Then the owner retired. The new owner enlarged and remodeled. But apparently sales increased less than did costs. A few years ago he went out of business. Now, no nearby wholesaler (we know of) sells to walk-ins.

We had food reserves, so no immediate problem. We hoped to find and pool purchases with someone local who was buying at wholesalers in Portland (± 150 miles away). So far we haven't. We don't have a motor vehicle. Nor do most local friends. Nor are they buying 50/25-pound bags when here. Most are in this area only in summers when wild berries and greens are abundant.

Winco is the only nearby store that stocks many dry foods. (Winco has stores through-out Northwest. Headquarters in Boise. Winco buys 25-pound bags to fill their bulk bins. They some-times have extra bags they will sell. But the bags are not setting out; you need to find a stocker. Nor do they sell bags for less than bin price; despite that reducing wastage, and saving plastic bags and stocking/clean-up labor. Some prices reasonable: eg, oatmeal 42¢. Some prices weirdly exorbitant: eg, 70¢ for non-org hard red wheat when growers were getting only 10¢. Whereas unbleached white flour was 30¢ and cracked wheat 35¢, despite needing more processing. Why ? Probably no demand: Winco has only one bin of each (vs 7 bins of oatmeal). Is their buyer corrupt: eg, paying a high price to a relative who grows wheat ? Or lazy ? Or over-worked and lacks time to find a low-priced source ? We don't buy wheat from Winco !

Years passed and our reserves dwindled. Then we learned of a friend of a friend who was buying white wheat from a local grower to feed chickens. We got a sample. Direct from the combine, it included many wild rye-grass seeds which have sharp barbs. But after grinding, the fragments were too small to be a threat. The bread tasted fine. And 95% of whole kernels sprouted, indicating good condition. So we ordered 400 pounds.

Price, 11¢/pound, which was what big buyers in Portland were then paying growers for wheat the buyers exported to Asia.

When the wheat arrived we noticed a bad smell the sample hadn't had. We hoped the odor was extraneous, picked up during storage or transport. Baking might remove it. But baking did not: the bread tasted bad. We tried lengthy aerating and even washing and then solar drying/parching before grinding and baking. That lessened but did not eliminate the bad taste. Adding spices (esp basel) masked the taste. Also alarming: only a third of the kernels sprouted. A few were brown and soft, obviously rotten. Those we could pick out before grinding. But many more kernels had brown tips. The grower offered to refund if we returned the wheat. But we had already backpacked it to our storage. Nor did we have much else to eat.

What may have happened. The wheat had been in the grower's silo several years. (He didn't grow wheat every year.) During summers, most of the wheat gradually warmed. But wheat close to the concrete foundation remained cool. Moisture migrated from warm wheat to cool wheat on the bottom - which became damp enough to start rotting. (Either that, or the silo had not been cleared out between harvests, and the bottom wheat was very old.) When we bought, not much wheat remained in the silo. The sample wheat had been barely high enough to remain dry. But the 400 pounds included much low-down rotting wheat.

Some advocacy groups claim they encourage and have info about local food growers. Most such groups did not respond to our quiries. Ten Rivers Food Web did. They suggested only one grower. He was experimenting with organic red wheat. He asked $1/pound !! Xanthippe Augerot of Ten Rivers, in Feb09 Sentient Times (Ashland), said that grains are no longer grown in the Willamette Valley (± between Portland and Eugene), partly because "food system infrastructure" had been lost. Did she not know that much white wheat is still grown here ? Or did she not know that wheat direct from combine is edible after grinding and baking ? ("Infrastructure" not needed.) Or does Ten Rivers shun non-organic growers ?

Local animal-feed dealers were asking 20¢ to 34¢/pound for white wheat. One said, their wheat was not for human consumption but didn't say why.

We told everyone we knew that we wanted to buy up to 1500 pounds of white wheat (we eat ± 500 pounds/year) and would pay 50% more than the Portland price. Via word of mouth we finally learned of and contacted a large-scale white-wheat grower who was selling some locally to poultry raisers. (Saved him hauling the wheat to Portland.) This year's harvest. When tested, 97% sprouted. He had one silo not treated with an insecticide after harvest. (Most wheat is treated. The insecticide is short lived, but we haven't learned what it turns into and if that might be toxic.) He asked 8¢/pound, the Portland price then, but we payed him 12¢ because we had widely offered 50% more than Portland and we didn't want to stint him. Also, the extra 4¢ seemed trivial, compared to prices asked by stores and feed dealers. I assume the wheat is direct from combine. (Most growers don't have cleaners.) No rye-grass seeds but quite a few tiny black seeds, angular. (Might be a buckwheat relative.) If the dough is risen long or solar baked (slow) the bread tastes sweet, almost like cake. We don't know why. No other wheat we've used, produced sweet-tasting bread.

(We bartered the remaining 300 pounds of deteriorated wheat to a chicken grower. The chickens eat it.)

We haven't yet found good sources of other dry foods. Two Ab/DP readers in nw OR separately suggested Azure Standard. I quiried by mail. No response. A friend found them on www. They don't divulge prices to non-members. Another Mtn People ?

Winco's lowest-priced legume has been split peas, 52¢. Lentils, our taste favorite, also more protein than peas and pintos, 70¢+. So, this autumn we are eating much bread, not much legumes. We are foraging much gosmore (a lettuce/dandelion kin) and chantrelles. Hopefully they balance aminos.

Regarding "organic". Pesticides migrate. All foods have some, org hopefully less. Fruits and vegies are the crops most pesticided. The fruits and vegies we eat are mostly wild. So, despite eating non-org grains, we probably ingest less toxins than does someone who eats only org but spends much time in cities or on roads. Our incomes are each around $400/year. (We don't keep records.) We spend over half for food. To buy org staples, we'd have to spend more time commuting through and working in environments that are more polluted or stressful or dangerous than the woods where we usually live.

Tips to buyers. Many newspapers print prices paid growers, both for white wheat in Portland and for high-protein red wheat in Mpls. Price is per 60-pound bushel. Eg, $6/bu = 10¢/pound. Oat prices are printed too. But, unlike wheat hulls which are removed by combines, oat hulls require steaming. To make oatmeal, the oats are then rolled and dried. Ie, oatmeal sold for human consumption is NOT raw. So, expect to pay more for oatmeal than what growers are paid for oats. Unlike whole wheat flour and wheat germ, which soon get rancid unless refrigerated or vacuum packed, oatmeal keeps a year or longer if cool.

Capital Press, a weekly ag paper (Salem), covers Northwest. Some libraries get it. (Similar pubs elsewhere ?) For legumes, it reports both prices paid growers and prices asked by big dealers which are ± 50% higher. Do beans (etc) direct from combines still have pods/stems/dirt and require further cleaning ? Even cleaned beans may include a few pebbles.

To buy direct from growers, best be flexible. Find out what is grown locally in COMMERCIAL quantity and learn to make use of that. West of Cascades, white wheat. In interior West, red wheat. In east-central areas, corn. In parts of Northeast, buckwheat. Expect to buy at harvest time or soon after. (Most growers don't retain harvests long.) To interest commercial growers, be prepared to buy hundreds of pounds and to pay cash, and to buy at their farm at a time convenient for them.

Bring your own containers unless told otherwise. For grain from a silo that had a ± 1½ ft sq door at the bottom, pails were easier to load than were big sacks. The farmer scoop-shoveled the wheat into our pails (4 gal, held ± 25 lbs).

For storage, if concerned about infestation, instead of an insecticide I'd use dry ice (solid CO_2). Approx 2 ounces CO_2 per gallon storage. Eg, ½ pound per 4 or 5 gal pail; 6 pounds per 55 gal barrel. Put CO_2 in bottom, fill with grain, place lid on LOOSELY (else may explode). CO_2 is heavier than air so, as it evaporates, it will seep up through the grain and push the air out. AFTER the CO_2 evaporates (bottom no longer cold), put lid on tightly. If dry ice not available, if container is air tight, any insects will consume the oxygen (producing CO_2) and die before eating more than a 1000th of the grain. Cooking will sterilize their remains. In a cool dry air-tight container, wheat will keep 15+ years; likewise lentils. Other grains and beans not as long (but some short-grain rice good at 5 yrs)

Advice for touring musicians, esp any who may perform in hotels.

I spent 15 years on the road as singer and guitarist, mostly at hotels and clubs. I've performed in 40 states and Canada, but mainly in Midwest where most of the opportunities were. Most Midwest hotels want country music. Hard rock and rap won't work in hotels - you must keep the volume down. Long hair and beards are taboo: look like a businessman.. Never say anything on the mic that could be taken two ways. Comedy is hard to pull off: most listeners will think you mean it.

If possible I would not use agents for road tours. They send you long distances for little money and don't care if you lose; and you must go where they send you if you want to call yourself a professional musician. If a hotel fires you during a gig and won't let you finish, the agent always has a replacement ready to go who has been out of work; a hazard in an over-crowded field. Sometimes non-union local acts will steal a gig from a touring performer by going in cheaper, esp if a club has been unhappy with the acts the agent has sent them.

Pay your agent even if he strands you. Agents are in touch with each other via computer; word gets around about who stiffed one out of a comission or booked a room without paying.

Always go meet your boss before you start work. Rules vary with the hotel. They won't tell you the rules, even if you ask - until you violate one. Some like you to mix with the guests, but may want you to be discrete if you date any. Others forbid mixing. If you date your boss, be nice - and realize the power structure. One manager fired me for dating lower-class girls from a local honky tonk. She did not want that kind in her hotel. Another manager accused me of pimping and fired me - because I let my date go into the bar and talk to men. Always stay with whoever you pick up for as long as you are there. Do not put anyone down; they will go to your boss or call your agent with lies about how you abused them.

If you dress below the hotel's standards when not on stage, that can get you fired. Always wear a shirt when room service brings a meal, and always tip them. Never forget to pay your room tab; they can arrest you. Never ask for or offer dope. Hotels are extremely straight-laced; they tend to suspect that all performers are dopers or boozers. Never forget that you are a hotel employee and part of a corporation. You are expendable and easily replaced. Hotel law is fairly complicated, and in most cases they got you because the touring performer does not know the law. Hotels never cheated me out of the dollars I sang for, but may not let one finish their gig.

While touring I usually earned $400-$500/week plus my room. When a room was not provided, I often considered moving into a van for that gig. But usually I was in the Midwest when it was way too cold. If I could have stayed in warm climates on tour, and fixed my own cars, I would have cleared much more money.

If you hit the road, be sure to have reserve cash. I've had engines blow up and had to buy the first car I could afford. I sold a really good guitar for $25 to get bus fare home. I sold blood to get home. A country band in Colorado fired me one cold December without paying me what I'd earned. With only $100 I went on to Los Angeles. A relative had to Western-Union me money to get home from there. At age 22, I did not know about missions, street people, or Travelers Aid.

I might have been happier playing taverns and rock clubs for younger people when I was their age. Rock clubs were much more fun. But hotels paid more. I missed the wild women of rock; though in hotels you can meet classier women.

I'm from Nashville. When my agent didn't have a gig for me, I'd visit Nashville, just to be around people I knew - after being a stranger in every town. At age 35, my agent finally stranded me in Nashville, and I had to make a living where there is little if any pay for live music. I really did not want to perform here. But, having long hair and a rock-n-roll attitude, I could not easily get regular work. The only singing job I could find quickly was on lower Broadway, a block of country-music dives famous to tourists. Pay: $20 for 5 hrs.

In Nashville the older country fans hate the recent rockin country, and the rockers think country is watered-down rock. When I play bars, I have to sing both country and rock.

If you come to Nashville and try to make it in music, be prepared to work a day job for many years as the song writers do. Music Row hires only young people to go on the road as stars. The music biz is winner take all. A very few make millions; many has-been stars end up bankrupt. Playing here is not much fun; people do not respect musicians. Karaoke has replaced live bands in many clubs. (Drunks singing off-key and out-of-time made me hate karaoke.) As of 2009, 50,000 people were out of work here. Marty Brown (Marty's report about trailer living was in March09 DP; and a report about car camping in Nashville will be in spring 2010 DP.)

Beg Big Bully ? Or shun Big Bully ?

Governments have various programs called "welfare". They are actually make-work programs. The work consists of learning the rules and keeping the records needed to fill out forms. This is work that lawyers and accountants are PAID to do. Like most dealings with governments, such work is RISKY. If you err, you may be fined or locked up. Ie, the hoops to jump through are razor sharp and red hot !

Someone (not in Ab/DP) disagreed, saying ±: "I have obtained several kinds of welfare and I've never been prosecut-ed. Bureaucrats are lazy. Unless you try to con them out of big money, you are unlikely to be prosecuted. Of course they publicize the few cases they do prosecute. Media give a distorted picture of what is happening. Ignore scare stories."

I agree that big media distort; we seldom read or hear them. But when something bad happens to one of the ±50 people we know personally, we pay attention. Eg, Pluma's ordeal.

Pluma lives in Tennessee, in a small cabin she rebuilt. It has a wood stove and running cold water and grid electricity. Comfortable and affordable - but not up to code: no frig, and the only hot water is from a kettle on the stove. After giving birth, Pluma's sister stayed with Pluma. The sister applied for "welfare" and gave Pluma's address. "Social" workers came to check, pretended to be friendly, and left. Two hours later they returned WITH COPS and snatched the 2-day-old baby from the arms of its mother who was breast-feeding it ! Reason given: the baby's surroundings. (More in April 2000 DP)

The most wide-spread "welfare" program may be food stamps. Years ago, Holly tried to obtain them, unsuccessfully. Recently, when food prices soared, Holly tried again. With the help of a librarian, she went as far as looking at the applica-tion form on internet. No further. The form required that all income be listed. We have very low incomes by U.S. standards (a bit below average by world standards). Most years, under $500 each, we think. (At that level, record keeping is not worth the time.) Money comes from many sources. If Holly estimated income and offered no proof, the well-paid food-stamp bureaucrat, who can't imagine anyone living so cheaply, would likely assume Holly was lying and refuse her. Holly might also be one of the relatively few charged with fraud.

Even people who do manage to obtain food stamps, may gain only slightly more than the value of their time spent keeping records, etc. The big beneficiaries of that and other gov "welfare" programs, are the well-paid administrators.

Obtaining "welfare" may be worthwhile for people who have appropriate talents and situations, and who enjoy lawyering. Sadly, the people most in need of welfare are generally the people least able to jump through the hoops !

RIDDLE. Believe it or not, one gov program really does help many low-income people including us. No hoops to jump through. Curiously, "welfare" is not its announced or main purpose. Oregon was maybe the first state to enact it. Many states now have it. What is it ? Answer at end of next item.

Political slysense. When be daring ? When be steadfast ?

I can think of 3 reasons to vote. I. You live in a small town with only ±20 voters, where one vote is quite likely to decide a local issue. II. You need to pacify nasty neighbors who insist that everyone vote. III. You are often stopped by cops; and when you fish out your drivers license, if the cop also sees your voter card, he might treat you better - else you will vote against more money for police.

None apply to us. And, to register, we'd have to lie about where we actually live. And we'd get put on a gov list.

I confess: I sometimes hope that a political candidate or party will lose. That is like hoping for no rain tomorrow. But I don't spend time praying to Mother Nature - or voting.

In U.S., two political parties, Democrats (D) and Republicans (R) share a duopoly of power. Though each is worse on some issues, overall I rate them equally evil. D pretend to help low-income people. At the city/county level, D may be not quite as bad as R on average. But at state and federal levels, D are worse. D not only try to tax low-incomers directly ("Social Security", compulsory medical insurance, sales taxes✻); but D put high taxes and myriad regulations on high-middle incomers (small/mid-size food wholesalers; specialty stores selling tents, pv, led lights, bike parts, etc; dentists, doctors, etc) that increase their costs and reduces their competition - which results in them raising their prices.

Least evil ? Generally a D president or governor (G) with an R-majority congress or legislature (L). Oregon had that for a while. L refused to pass most laws that G wanted, and G vetoed most laws that L did pass. In a lobocracy (rule by big lobbies), that may be the best that can be hoped for.

This can affect what I do, because disputes on top can trickle down and result in less enforcement of contraversial laws. That may be a good time to undertake major dwellingway changes; because, while learning a new way, goofs are likely that may attract Big Bully's thugs. Bert & Holly, Oct 09

✻ Oregon 1990s. The teachers union wanted more tax money. In L, only 1/3rd of R but 2/3rds of D voted for a sales tax. (L barely passed it but voters rejected it 3 to 1.) Sales taxes penalize low-incomers more than high-incomers. Evidence (Sci Am, July 2004): WA gets most revenue via a sales tax. It robs low-incomers THE MOST. AK, DE, MT, without state sales taxes,

rob low-incomers least.   NH and OR, too, are lesser robbers.
      Answer to riddle.   Payments for empty drink containers.
Simply collect them and take them to a store that sells those
brands. No records to keep. No hoops to jump through.

Is the U.S jumping out of the emergency room into the morgue ?
      Most Democrats in Congress support a law that requires
everyone to buy medical insurance, even healthy young people
who are unlikely to need medical care and who usually have low
incomes. Their payments would subsidize insurance of people
who are sicklier - often because of unhealthy behavior;   eg,
having consumed much junk foods, alcohol, tobacco, etc.
      Such a requirement is in essence a head tax: robbing from
everyone the same amount regardless of income. A head tax
penalizes low-income people even more than does a sales tax.
So, again, Democrats, who pretend to help "the little guys",
are trying to ROB the little guys. (Yeah, gov might give
insurance to very low incomers. But, as with other "welfare",
you must prove you have low income. Risky work !)
      The federal system would be like what Massachusetts has
had, which copied the German system (originally enacted by the
Nazis ?).   In a radio interview, a doctor who works in a MA
hospital serving low-income people, said that those laws were
originated by insurance executives. She also said: the MA
law has been a disaster - and the federal law would be worse.
      If the law passes, Holly and I will ignore it.   In MA, 5%
of residents are known to still lack med insurance. The actual
percent may be much higher, because the people missed by
counts are also the people most likely to lack insurance.
      Politicians pushing the German system on the U.S., call it
"health insurance". That label is FRAUDULANT. NO WAY can you
insure HEALTH. You can't even insure that you will receive med
treatment. The insurer, whether corporate or governmental, may
refuse to provide it for various reasons - and often does.
      Pushers of the German system claim: everyone is morally
obligated to buy med insurance because, regardless of present
health and healthy practices, a freak accident or illness might
cause them to be taken to an emergency room and, if they lack
insurance or sufficient savings, someone else must pay.
      But it is the GOVERNMENT that requires public hospitals to
treat all comers. So, any moral obligation is the GOVERNMENT's.
The gov should pay, and pay out of general revenues, NOT with
an unfair tax on low-income people who are living healthily.✱
      Furthermore, I doubt that hauling people to emergency
rooms helps much. Many die before arriving, or despite treatments - or from infections acquired in hospitals. Three of
many ways to save MORE lives and health, and save money too:
      I.   Vehicle accidents are the biggest killers and maimers,
counting YEARS of life and health lost. So, reduce use of cars
for commuting (which, per mile, may be the most dangerous
travel because drivers are often rushed, or tired, or bored, or
distracted by cell phones, etc). Reduce commuting by encouraging camping at or near work places on work-week nights, and
rescheduling work to provide longer weekends.✱
      II.   Soft drinks (cola, pop) may be the single biggest
cause of degenerative diseases, not only because they lack
vitamins etc, but because their sugars are absorbed too fast
for bodies to cope with well. So, reduce consumption of them.✱
      ✱ If the gov needs more taxes to reimburse doctors and
hospitals for unpaid services, fairest would be taxes on soft

drinks and higher taxes on car fuels and alcoholic beverages.

III. Public schools may be the biggest spreaders of infectious diseases, not only to pupils, but brought home to babies whose immune systems are not yet potent. So, abolish those day-jails, and offer more learning via web, TV, books.

A radio program we happened to hear, described the high administrative costs of med insurance presently - but made no mention of other enormous cost raisers such as:

Malpractice lawsuits cause care-providers' liability insurance to be very costly. Mexico's different legal system may be the biggest reason why costs there are much lower. (Dental work I've had in Mex seemed as good as in U.S.)

High-middle-income people, including doctors and dentists, pay high taxes. (They are the main tax cows. Big corporations and the very rich largely avoid taxes by setting up elaborate tax shelters that others can't afford.)

The medical mafia restricts the supply of MDs by limiting admissions to medical schools, and by requiring pre-med training that is padded with "liberal arts" courses (no more useful to a doctor than to a sales clerk, waitress, barber, etc).

The med mafia and subservient officials prosecute non-MD care providers or unreasonably restrict what they can do.

Many surgeons perform unnecessary and risky operations. Likewise, many chiropracters perform unnecessary manipulations.

Pharmaceutical companies promote pricy patented drugs with doubtful benefits and harmful side effects.

Med researchers paid by those companies, and the med mafia, bad-mouth (and, in Europe, outlaw) low-cost herbs that are often as effective as prescription drugs and less harmful.

The med mafia and subservient media emphasize MEDICAL care. That is one reason why many people neglect diet and lifestyle changes that could prevent or cure degenerative diseases.

Myriad gov regulations and taxes greatly increase costs of almost everything. That prompts most people to work long hours at high-stress jobs, and to not get enough sleep, etc.

That, in turn, causes many people to perpetually postpone doing the things they want. Then, when their health finally fails, they desperately try to prolong life. (I've read, on average, 3/4ths of a person's life-time medical expenses occur during their last year of life, and half during last month !)

Real reforms would greatly lower medical costs AND increase health. But don!t.expect them from Big Bully.

Insurance is the flip side of gambling. The difference: instead of hoping to win big, the insurer hopes to not lose big. Like gambling, insurance can be addicting. The addict craves more and more security. But complete security is impossible.

Insurance is least costly to administer, and claims are most likely to be paid, if the insurance is for happenings not arguable. Before planting a crop, a grower may sell the harvest for a set price per pound. The grower thereby insures receiving that price (unless buyer goes bankrupt). But most other kinds of insurance are rife with arguable uncertainties. For medical insurance: pre-existing conditions, present condition, age, occupation, hobbies, suitability of treatments, etc, etc !

Canada's system is supposedly not as bad as the German system or the present U.S. system. Yet, many Cdns are refused effective treatment in Cda. (Some go to U.S. and pay for it.)

I doubt that any med-insurance system could work well.

Many critics of the German system think it would function so badly in U.S. (because of cultural differences; eg less obedience) that it would be replaced by the Canadian system where the gov pays for all treatments out of general revenues.

Pushers of the German system may say: "Young people should not object to subsidizing old folks, because the young will someday be old. They will then be subsidized."

That is unlikely. The system will almost certainly change before then. Regardless of who then pays and how, fewer treatments will become affordable as real incomes in U.S. continue their decline toward world levels. (This assumes that, as in the past and now, little or nothing is done that actually reduces medical costs.) Effective treatments will be reserved for people who are likely to continue living (and paying taxes) for many years. Even wealthy retirees who can personally pay for treatments, may have to go abroad to get them - if allowed to. Some sociologists have advocated killing everyone at age 80. That may become the policy in some nations. In the U.S., more likely, the med system will dispense sedatives and pain-killers to ailing seniors. If you want something more when you get old, prepare to do it yourself or with friends. B&H, Oct 09

How Lauran cured or alleviated various health problems.

After reading some health and fitness books, I decided I needed to find out how many calories per day I was eating. Without changing my eating, for ten days I recorded my food intake. I was shocked to discover that I was eating only 700 to 900 calories most days; occasionally 1000 or more. That was far too little for my activity level, which included much biking and walking and an exercise regime. Seemingly my metabolism had dropped into a "low" state to accomodate my habits. As a result, I had only moderate energy and, believe it or not, I had bulges of fat I was battling.

I started eating more food. That was difficult: took me ten days to raise my intake to 1500 calories consistently. (For my energy expenditure, 200-400 MORE calories/day recommended.)

Within two weeks I began losing weight. And it was FAT I lost. Two pounds per week for several weeks until I stabilized. I had more energy than I'd had for years, and felt great.

Many Americans have the opposite problem. But for the few who may be undereating, I mention my experience.

My food costs almost doubled. I live on $5000 per year. $3000 of that is spent on food. (Yes, I keep a budget. Numbers are becoming good friends of mine.) I'd like to spend less for food. I'm experimenting with approaches that cost less yet provide enough calories. A difficulty: I had to quit eating grains and beans because they raise my blood sugar. I did just discover that if I soak spelt until it sprouts a tail about $\frac{1}{4}$" long, I can eat that grain with no rise of blood sugar. It tastes great to me, and is opening up possibilities.

Some years ago I read about a 14-year-old boy with a split personality. In one personality he is physically normal and healthy. In the other personality he has diabetes-1, requiring insulin injections to stay alive. Recently I read of a 30-year-old woman who had that same split. These stories fascinate me from the perspective of personality/moods affecting physiology.

Some books coming out talk about the personality types of people prone to some diseases. Years ago at a function in Atlanta, the woman sitting next to me was a nurse. I asked if she had observed any patterns of personality and disease. She almost popped out of her chair with a bright "Oh my yes !" At her hospital, for efficiency, they put all cancer patients on one floor and all patients with digestive problems (liver, gall bladder, etc) on another. None of the nurses wanted to work on that floor because the patients were angry or bitter or loud or opinionated, and generally difficult. She said, there seemed to be truth in the saying, "He has a lot of gall." Whereas the cancer patients were all very "NICE". Easy to please, never rocking the boat, "sacrificing themselves for others" types.

Our culture puts much emphasis on external variables with respect to health and disease. Only recently are we looking more closely at inner variables, like stress, attitude, personality; variables we can personally influence more.

I suffered a herniated disk two years ago that was very painful. I went to a chiropractor. She recommended all sorts of expensive things for me to do - which I could not afford. I just needed to know what was wrong. She diagnosed it based on my symptoms and was very concerned for me. I asked lots of questions so I could pursue my own approach - and get my money's worth. Chiropractors are cheaper than doctors but still too pricy for me to consider for long-term care. But they can be a good source for muscular-skeletal diagnosis.

She mentioned that some people with my condition show damage on xrays yet suffer no pain; while others show no damage to the body but suffer terrible pain. A baffling situation. But maybe not in light of the power of consciousness.

One of my symptoms was losing feeling in my left arm and some fingers. The supposed cause: a nerve pinched by the herniated disk. That causes the arm to feel weak, you then use it less, you then lose muscle and ARE weaker.

After that visit I came home and tried to hoist myself between two countertops in the kitchen. The lack of feeling in my left arm made it crumple under my weight. I told myself, this was an illusion. I KNEW I was still strong; I still had muscle. Only the feeling of strength was gone. I tried for three days until I could support my weight between the countertops. I also started hanging from the clothesline cross-piece to stretch the muscles of my arm, neck and back.

The pain was terrible in my neck. But if I continued to think I was weak because I felt that way, I would become weak from inactivity. Took me four months to become totally without pain and to have full range of motion. For most people in our culture, surgery plus years of pain killers are the options.

I have read that some people who have a painful inflamed tooth-root (for which dentists recommend a root-canal) can instead use their mind to deaden the infected root. The body then absorbs the dead tissue, leaving the tooth without pain, infection, or any root tissue. I wonder if you may have done this to that molar you wrote about in DP. Lauran, AZ 857, Mar

(Comments) Diet and weight. Strange ! We've read of people whose digestive systems were unusual in various ways. But we have not heard of anyone with experiences similar to yours.

Blood sugar. Adding vegetable oil to grains/beans may slow digestion. (To not degrade oil, apply after cooking.) Have you tried that ? Have you tried sprouting wheat ?

Personality and diabetes. Was personality affecting pancreas ? Or was pancreas affecting personality ? Or was something else affecting both ? Possibly the pancreas was episodic: putting out enough insulin for a while; getting exhausted; shutting down for a while to recuperate; etc. If so, the effect on the brain was probably not as simple as

the blood level of insulin determining personality; else an
insulin injection would switch personality. The endocrine
system is complex: many hormones interact with each other and
interact with the nervous system.
     Variables. Some externals (people dealt with, stressful
work, food obtained, home environment) may be easier to change
than are some internals (feeling stressed, personality, etc);
depending on the individual and their situation.
     Xrays and pain. Xrays are blurry (dental xrays I've seen).
They don't show fine detail. So, no big surprise if painful
damage does not show, or if damage that does show doesn't hurt.
     Infected tooth root. Mine, an upper molar, resulted in a
boil on the gum through which pus (?) oozed occasionally.
Tooth usually not painful unless chewed on hard. But one week
it became painful. We deadened the pain by liberally and
repeatedly applying clove oil diluted with veg oil, and by
massaging the gum and wiggling the tooth to hopefully work the
oil down to the root. (A friend who had a dentist, asked him
to prescribe penicillan over the phone, but he wouldn't.)
I decided to remove the tooth. Holly tied a strong string
around it. I spent a whole day vigorously wiggling the tooth
to loosen it, and repeatedly tugging hard on the string. The
tooth didn't come out. But the pain went away. And gradually
so did the gum boil. Maybe the clove oil killed the microbes.
     Now, years later, the tooth is still there and is function-
al. I chew on it. No pain. The dental mafia's line seems to
be: a root infection cannot be cured except by removal or root
canal, and, if left, may have serious consequences such as
heart infection or jaw cancer. But, though the body's disposal
of microbes and removal of dead tissue may be slow, apparantly
that can happen. Tooth removal may often be a good idea. But
dental advice should be tempered with the realization that the
dental schools and organizations have a vested interest in
encouraging people to frequent dentists. An individual dentist
may be sincere, but merely parrot what s/he learned in dental
school. (The same is true for MDs and other professionals.)
     Tooth removal is safer than root canals, according to a
root-canal pioneer who later changed his mind. Replacement of
a tooth may become simpler, better, cheaper. Meanwhile, if you
lose many teeth, buy a food grinder.
     Do most U.S. dentists now push root canals instead of
removals ? Root canals cost much more than removals (esp if
people remove their own teeth, which many do, though I wasn't
able to). Coincidence ? Mexican dentists, after drilling out
as much decay as they can easily, may try to sterilize any that
remains and then fill or cap the tooth. Sometimes that fixes
the tooth; sometimes it doesn't. If not, remove the tooth.

Allergies are often mis-diagnosed on basis of blood tests only.
     Half of children diagnosed with allergies, didn't have
them. Wrong diagnoses prompt families to needlessly buy
special foods that are costly. (from NPR, March 09)

I live near a National Forest in Japan. I eat dandelions.
     Which dandelion relatives are best to eat ? Misa, Nov 09
(Reply) Of plants with dandelion-type flowers, hairy leaves
usually less bitter than smooth leaves, at least to Bert
(tastes vary). None of that Tribe known to be poisonous. (But
beware tansy ragwort, yellow flowers but different shape.)

Ab

c/o Lisa Ahne, POB 181, Alsea OR 97324. #10, May 2010
$2 for big-print copy until all sold; $1 for tiny
print. Ab discusses how and where to live better for
less. Ab, an ab-apa, encourages readers to send
pages ready to copy (text 16x25cm or 6.3x10", black on white,
on one side of paper, COMPACT). Usually published unedited.

Small plastic storage bin converted to experimental cold-frame.
        I cut the bottom off at a slight angle with a hacksaw. I
planted lettuce seedlings in a flower bed outside my apartment
(in Idaho) and placed the "cold-frame" around them, angling the
top towards the sun. At first, I left the top open. When the
weather cooled, I placed fabric row-cover over the top. When
snow and cold began, I put on the bin's transparent lid. The
lettuce grew really well; I harvested it before extreme cold
came. In its place, I planted mâche seedlings. Mâche is cold-
hardy; it should
survive the winter
fine and provide
fresh salad greens
by early spring.
Dan Murphy (from
Juniper #11 wnt09;
gardening reports
& environmnt thots.)
www.juniperbug.
blogspot.com

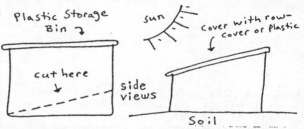

(Comment) Sometimes we find discarded plastic bins which we
salvage. Some have cracks. So, with luck, a cold-frame can be
made without cutting up a bin still good for storage. H & B

Long-time southern Ohio gardener copes with Oklahoma climate.
        (April 09) I have worked myself to exhaustion in my
garden (near Oklahoma City). But I'll get food from it.
        (June) I'm back (after a month away). Weeding and weeding
and weeding. I'm planting more vegetables. They grow fast
here. Two zucchinis are about ready to pick. Been hot and not
much rain - I have to water. I fear the water bill.
        I am ordering Skyfire garden seeds to try myself and to
share. Mom in Las Vegas likes tomatos, but too hot there for
standard varieties. And my neighbors across the street love
tomatos, but their backyard has a 6-ft privacy fence that makes
it too hot. Skyfire has 20+ varieties that are drought and heat
tolerant. Tomatos don't have to be staked. One year I let them
run and put straw under them. I lost some but got more fruit.
        (July) My bean vines are lush and have many blooms but no
pods, because no bees. Wasps fertilize the squashes; all of
the cucurbit family are doing great here. (Never in Ohio) The
tomatos and carrots are not doing well. But I've learned what
to get in early and what to plant in the shade of taller plants.
I've had to water some, but now we are getting rain. Hail
twice. No tornados nearby, but I make good use of my shelter.
        I walked around the neighborhood with chard, collards,
kale, squash. I gave them away and made new acquaintances.
        Potatos and sunflowers put unfriendly stuff into the soil,
so don't plant them near other vegies. (Black walnuts do, too.)
        Carrot seed is viable for approx 10 years, lettuce seed
for 2 or 3, onion seed for only one. Bean seeds will survive
many years if kept cool and dry. (Beans are grown in north/

central states. I doubt that any are hybrids.)

In a Russian documentary I saw, women stuck small seeds on narrow strips of toilet paper with flour-and-water paste. An easy way to plant tiny seeds and not waste any. Suzanne

(Comment) The pasting can be done during winter when gardeners are not as busy as in spring. Here (w OR), humidity usually high, winters esp. If seeds PASTED on, I fear they will absorb enough moisture to rot - before paste dries. Instead, I tried: cut strip of newsprint ±3" wide; prefold it to crease;   open it;   put thin streaks of white glue* _____ at ±1" intervals; fold, thus forming small pockets;   let dry THOROLY; insert a seed into each pocket (tweezers helped); fold flap over ⟨═•═⟩ . That held seeds adequately. I ⟨⌢⌢⟩ planted during late-Feb showers. 4 of 11 wheat seeds grew. ⟨⌣⟩
* Home-made flour-water paste cheaper. May be strong enough.

Some of the ways that Suzanne earns money and cuts costs.

I have relatives and friends nearby. All of us shop yard sales and buy things for ourselves and each other. We give WHEN we get; NOT on birthdays and holidays. My extended family frequently swaps furniture: "musical chairs".

My son teaches at a college. They give or throw away what they no longer use. He got me a folding table, 2½ by 9 feet. I set it against the wall in a bedroom and, for once in my life, I have a sewing room. (Formerly I used the dining room table. That messed up the whole house.)

My daughter-in-law phoned in a panic: her friend needed a skirt for her daughter. I whipped out two skirts, matching, for both daughters out of material I already had. I didn't ask for money but she insisted on giving me $20. So my sewing room is paying off. And I'll probably get spin-off referrals.

I love pants made of sweaters (on front of Ab#8). I made myself one four years ago. I used all black sweaters; even so it looks funny. I made another for my son-in-law who is seriously crippled with arthritis, but my daughter informed me that he would never wear anything that looks funny. So I gave it to a tall friend. She, like me, is trying to save money.

I made a down comforter (quilt) for my bed out of coats I got for a few dollars at the Salvation Army. They came apart with seams intact, so no down leaked out.

I'm trying to get more (music performance) jobs. Some nursing homes have cut their activity budgets: I've lost two jobs, but I'm finding others here and there. My jobs are closer to home than when I lived (in a small city) in Ohio. Most are 5 miles or less, one way. That saves time and gas, so I can charge less. I play free for the Salvation Army senior center, and they give me fresh produce that is donated to them. I am amazed at what many people don't want.

I turned off the hot-water heater, because I got a free membership at a nearby YMCA I often go by on my way to stores and jobs. There, I have a warm shower and a pleasant swim.

Reducing cooling costs. I brought my sheets of styrofoam out here, cut them to fit these windows, and glued aluminum foil on the pieces for the south and west windows. I open windows after dark; close them when the sun rises. I run the air conditioner for myself only if 100°F+ forecast; only for an hour in the morning while the attic is still cool, then turn it off. When more than four poeple are here, I use it plus a box fan which, with the dry air here, boosts the cooling effect. If alone, I use only the fan.   Ab #10   May 2010   Page 2

The Barefoot Architect: for building with what is available.
     This 710-page-5x8 handbook, by Johan van Longen, has
thousands of drawings that show how to build houses, bridges,
windmills, water heaters, pumps, stoves, silos, lathes, solar
driers, distillers, and much else; mostly out of natural and
recycled materials. The title honors ancient builders who
"mixed adobe by treading mud with their bare feet." "This
manual does not propose rigid rules for building, but instead
shows many ways", thus offering many choices. Excerpts:
     "When using alternative, non-conventional building tech-
niques, you should employ quality-control testing, especially
when fabricating critical structural elements." (from intro.)
     "Locate the bedrooms more or less towards the east side
so that the occupants wake up with the rising sun." p.24
     "Immigrants often build in their new homeland the same
type of house they had before ... a common mistake. Before
designing, observe how local people build their homes." p.38
     "Often large windows or glass walls are used to frame
scenic views. However, sooner or later the pleasure of looking
out of them is exhausted and the view is ignored." p.61 (Big
windows are structurally demanding, and can lose much heat.)
     Because "hot air always rises ... ceilings in cold regions
should be lower than in hot regions" for comfort. p.273
     "A quick way to protect the underground bases of wood
posts is to scorch their outer surfaces in a mild fire until
they are blackened." p.339
     "A wooden house with well-crafted joints can be built
loosely connected to the ground. During earthquakes, this type
of house 'dances' over the ground but does not collapse. All
the joints must be braced." p.362
     "Doors and windows should not be close to each other nor
to corners", to not weaken walls. "During earthquakes the
walls crack and the corners are the first parts to fall." p.399
(I wonder if this applies mostly/esp to heavy walls that don't
much resist pulling apart, such as walls built of stones or
adobe bricks.) "It is worth building strong corners and walls
to strengthen the house in case there is no time to exit in an
emergency." (Various ways to reinforce corners are shown.) "In
a disaster situation such as flooding or landslide or earthquake, inhabitants are often trapped while attempting to save
their valuables." To avoid this, "build a small secure area"
strong enough to survive a disaster, and keep valuables there.
"Usually houses do not collapse with the first tremor, but the
door is often unopenable since its frame is bent. In unstable
zones", make the door frame of thicker wood. (Or ? Make door
flimsy enough to push through - and burglar-proof the yard ?)
"Many people do not wake up at night to leave. Hang a bell in
the bedroom that rings at the very first tremor." p.401
     "A shingle roof must have a slope greater than 15° to
prevent winds from lifting up the shingles." p.455
     "Part of the floor can be built to absorb and store heat"
of sun coming through a window. Use materials that absorb heat,
such as dark-colored "stones or ceramic tile. Prevent heat
from escaping through the ground" by insulating floor from the
ground. p.276 (Is an insulated floor better than using ground
as floor ? Depends on climate. Discussed in spring2010 DP.)
     A round-bottom pot heats water more efficiently than a
flat-bottom pot. p.570 (Seems to me, best shape depends on
amount of water, area of flame, shroud on pot if any, etc.)

"In areas where water is scarce, for bathing use a vapor-izer: a container with pump that sprays water out like a cloud of fine drops. These drops penetrate the surface of the skin. This cleans the skin very well and soap is not necessary." p.639 (Shown is what I call a "spray bottle". The fine drops may penetrate and loosen DIRT on skin. If they penetrated the SKIN, that could cause infections. A translation error ?)

A section is devoted to each of 3 climates: humid tropics, 82 pages; dry tropics, 46pgs; "temperate" (cold winters, hot summers), 26pgs. However, most of the other 547 pages (design, materials, construction, water, etc) are climate-related or seem to be; requiring me to often shift focus and sometimes guess re climate. I'd prefer 3 smaller books, each about a single climate, despite duplicating info (±50pgs ?) useful anywhere. Smaller books would also be handier HANDbooks when building.

The houses suggested are quite big: eg, 6x8m(19½x26¼ft) with 5 rooms. In U.S., they'd be priced at $100,000 or more. Not for purchase by the 80% of earth's people (including us) who have incomes under $2 a day. Could they be home-built in the time remaining after growing food or earning the money to buy food ? Construction seems complicated and labor intensive. Eg, notching posts, beams, rafters where they join, p.451 and 479. But I am accustomed to the abundances here of used hay twine and various kinds of wire, free at recycles. They may be scarce in some countries. (2 pages about processing sisal fiber, which can be used to tie parts together. p.340)

Several home-made machines are described, which were actually built and used by some people, somewhere, some era. Eg, the "monjolo", a water-powered see-saw grain mill, p.544. But, recalling problems I've had with devices that SEEMED simple, I suspect monjolos were built and maintained by semi-specialists. If I built one, I'd expect to do MUCH tinkering.

Inaccuracies: "Angles" p.692. The "30º" layout actually yields 26½º. May not matter much if inclining a roof or solar heater, but could if other uses. INSTEAD use a 4-to-7 ratio which yields 29.7º or 15-to-26 which yields 29.98º. "Maps", for solar-heater slopes, p.697. Eg, Dublin shown at same latitude as Seattle. Dublin is actually ±5½º (480 miles) farther north.

Some info is not as extensive as I'd like. Eg, insulation values, p.681. A single layer of 4mm-thick glass is valued at 1; 200mm of earth at 40; etc. But not listed: TWO layers of glass (or transparent plastic) with an air space between.

I noticed a description that is not complete: a home-made battery for welding, p.534. Doesn't say what metals are put in salt water to yield electricity. (I recall reading: any two different metals may yield some elec, but some combos yield more, or higher voltage, than do others.)

Despite these complaints, we do much appreciate this book. It contains a great wealth of ideas and info that can inspire and inform do-it-yourselfers. Review by Bert & Holly

Translated from Brazilian edition by Carina Rose, 2008, $18 cover price, Shelter Publications Inc, POB 279, Bolinas CA 94924; http://www.shelterpub.com. A Spanish edition, Cantos del Arquitecto Descalzo, 1991, in Mexican libraries. Portugese (Brazilian) editions, Manual de Arquiteto Descalço, 1997-2004; for sources of it, and workshops: http://www.tibarose.com

Shelter Publ also has: HomeWork, Handbuilt Shelters: yurts, caves, tree houses, tents, thatched houses, glass houses, nomadic homes, river boats, and more. 256 pages, 1000+ photos, 300+ line drawings; 9x12", 2004, $27. Ab #10 May 2010 Page 4

Responses by Andrew to topics in Ab #9.

Re: Finding WHERE to build. Here in Maine you can build under 100 sf (eg, 10x10 or 12x8) without any paperwork. BUT, if you want grid electric, phone, etc, you have to file 'intent to build' so town can tax. But I know of a few landowners who have unreported buildings, in the woods. Tax assessors here-and-now generally don't snoop but assume that what they see is what there is. I wonder if there are any outlaw builders in the northeast who have done partially-earth-sheltered, rot-resistant-wood buildings (as in Shelter, p.151) - which would seem necessary during our cold winters. Semi-hidden, too.

I, too, have junk piles; can't hurt, might help. As for investing in tools and materials for the future, I don't. I only have those tools I know how to use, and a few spares. Buying high tech stuff or highly visible items could make you more prone to being robbed. Best to look poor and broke so as to not attract unwanted attention. I favor being aware that the future may well be rough, but obsessing over it is probably counter productive. Enjoying life, eating well, keeping in shape, and developing skills are what I try to keep foremost.

Good piece on wheat. In summer I eat grains; in winter, potatoes plus more fats and some meat when weather is cold enough to seriously sap strength and energy. This works for me; maybe not for all, or for warm-climate dwellers.

Tribode. After re-reading all ten pages, I still have serious misgivings. I. Carbon fiber is strong but it does not bend - it breaks. Ie, not resiliant. I've seen big thick-walled CF masts on sailboats destroyed by storms off Maine coast. CF bike frames must be junked if 'laid down' in a wreck, whereas steel frames can still be ridden. Reason: damage to CF may be imperceptible. CF is used much for making things lightweight to race with; not for long-term durability. II. Tribode hulls are very slender; waves will likely break THROUGH the tribode structure. Whereas a boat will ride atop waves (usually - though even big sailboats can 'pitchpole', ie, go end over end.) III. Few ocean areas are: free of storms and traffic, AND mostly warm, AND free of threats by govt & pirates.

(Comments by Bert) Earth sheltering will reduce wind chill. But, other than that, I doubt that PARTIAL earth sheltering will reduce chill much in cold climates, because the ground near the surface will get almost as cold as the average outside temperature. For earth to insulate much, I think you need to build COMPLETELY underground, with the ceiling well below the depth to which the ground freezes. Soil is a poor insulator PER INCH, but effective if MANY FEET are between the interior and the cold. Reports about two underground homes in: Buffalo NY, 6 ft under, Mar09DP; Nantucket MA, Sep04DP. The Buffalo home had earth walls; only the roof needed carpentry. That simplified construction. But unless soil is tough or reinforced by many roots, an earthquake could collapse the shelter. A fault-zone map shows one near Montreal. How far away are you ?

Re future. Yes, obsessing over it is probably counter productive, partly because the future can NOT be forecast well. It may NOT be much like the recent past, or trending the same way - or much resemble any other specific prediction.

Re investing. We try to maintain a several-year supply of those dry foods that store well, and some materials (esp those now free in recycles/dumpsters; eg, used hay twine, plastic wrappings, clothes) for personal use (tho might trade).

Re appearance. Looking poor and broke seems wise if seen by robbers, but maybe not if seen by cops. When police want to arrest "suspects" to gain favorable publicity, poor people are prime targets because they can't afford lawyers. When going into public, Holly and I try to look "ordinary": clean and neat (but not stylish; here, many people aren't). I walk briskly as if going to work. I wear a SMALL knapsack (common here). If acquiring more than fits into it plus one quite-big shopping bag, I try to arrange pickup by someone who has a car.

Re dry foods (update to Ab#9). Jim in nw OR sent Azure Standard (A) prices (THANKS) of some foods I'd bought at Winco (W) in Jan 2010. Price per pound of non-org; A, 25-pound bag; W, bin or bag: split green peas A36¢ W56¢; (whole green peas A31¢); lentils A51¢ W77¢; oatmeal A39¢ W42¢. (Organic, A: split green peas 104¢; lentils 129¢; oatmeal 67¢. A org, W non: flax A138¢ W56¢.) Thus, for non-org, A prices ± 2/3rds of W except for oatmeal. (Oatmeal seems to be one of Winco's lures to attract shoppers who, W hopes, will also buy pricy items. Most of W's lures are name-brand junk-foods which W brags about pricing lower than do other stores. But I praise Winco for NOT accepting credit cards (which not only include fees that raise prices, but forbid the giving of discount for cash). Whereas the co-op, which claims to promote the best interests of members and community, DOES.) We will try A. But, when A receives our order for ±500 pounds of low-price staples and NO pricy items, will A be "out of stock" (as was Mtn People) ? I don't know A's range. But if you are in mainland U.S. and paying much more than the price above, you can probably do better.

Re carbon fiber. Much thanks for your report. CF's limitation seems important, not only for boat builders, but for anyone thinking of building or buying anything that uses CF.

Re tribode. I reread description. Ave Dave (AD) seems aware of CF's characteristics. On p.4: "The boom sections must be straight and stiff and must be mounted so that they take mainly compressive force. The less bending force the better. They are probably formed with carbon fiber or other very strong, stiff synthetic.... I use wood in the floats and cabin because they are necessarily subject to bending stresses."

(To AD) Have you considered the force of a wave breaking against the lower portion of a boom ? Seems to me, that would tend to bend it. On p.8, "Limits", you specified max wind speed and tilt by waves that a tribode could withstand, but did not mention waves BREAKING against sections of a tribode.

(To Andrew) Does "break THROUGH" mean that the waves would go above the floats ? If so, waves would impact the booms and cables but then move into empty space (unless the waves were tall enough to hit the cabin 32 feet up).

(To Andrew and AD) Is pitch-poling a threat to a boat that is sea-anchored ? Or only for a boat moving against waves ? I assume, if a storm came, a tribode (or boat) would sea-anchor and remove sails. But might waves get both steep enough and have a length that wrenched a tribode's 32-ft-long float off of its boom ? If so, ? better if the float penetrates waves instead of riding atop them ? Would it ?

In Ab#9, AD wrote: "Before offering plans I would build a tribode and rigorously test it, and live in it on stormier waters than I recommend frequenting with it." I think that is wise with ANYTHING, on sea or land, that is new/different and big or powerful or sharp enough to be dangerous.

If you want to do something on the sea, do it pronto.

Pierre of The Connection spoke at a recent "seasteading" conference. Some of his comments (from TC#314 Dec 09):

"... Events adverse to the seasteading concept have been happening for the last forty years and are continuing.... So in my opinion it's important to get as much activity going out at sea as soon as possible, the better to weather whatever comes along.... At the conference, it seemed that most of the good ideas were centered around medical facilities of some kind or other. But whatever the best opportunities turn out to be now, it's important to get going pronto. Eg, if Paddy Roy Bates hadn't been successful as a radio pirate, he wouldn't have been in position to establish Sealand.

"With that in mind, I was particularly impressed by Mikolaj Habryn's presentation on "shipsteading." He had a lot of hard numbers, missing from most of the other talks - and on brief reflection, the reason is obvious: ships are actually out at sea operating every day, while the other concepts are only ideas. He said a cruise ship could be had for under ten million. Allowing $10M for the ship, $10M to repurpose it, $5M for incidentals, and the usual start-up fudge factor of two, a shipstead venture could probably get going for about $50M - a lot less than any realistic figure for alternatives.

"Another talk that impressed me was that of Jorge Schmidt on the legal aspects. A ship in motion enjoys a much more permissive legal regime than a stationary ship, or any kind of platform, floating or anchored to the bottom...."

(Comments by Bert of Ab/DP) Repurposing. Holly and I have not lived on the ocean. But we and other Ab/Dwelling-Portably participants often use things for tasks other than what they were built for. Some vehicle dwellers advise: Don't modify a van much. Only put in things (bed, stove, sink, table, whatever) that you can remove easily. That minimizes initial cost and labor. That also leaves both the vehicle and its furnishings more versatile/valuable for other uses.

This may apply to a cruise ship. Modify it as little as possible. That minimizes start-up costs, and gets you on the sea sooner. That also leaves the ship easiest to resell if/ when you need to change strategy.

What can you do with a cruise ship without modifying it much ? Do cruises - but of kinds and in ways different from cruises offered by others. My impression from ads seen: Most cruises are luxury vacations for rich folks who want to visit world-famous resorts without much effort or hassle. Such people are accustomed to being waited on. Consequently the ships carry nearly as many paid servants as paying vacationers. Such cruises are PRICY. Instead ? A few ideas - combinable:

Cut costs by hiring only a few pro ship commanders. Other work is done by many of the passengers. Shifts are short (not onerous): clean-up, food service, lookouts, and (?). Being at sea, the management can be more creative than can land-based competitors who are constrained by Big Bully's myriad regulations. Prices can be lower, and appeal to the many people who can't afford luxurious living on sea OR land.

Shun resort cities where, along with exotic foods and entertainments, passengers may get exotic diseases and exotic hassles (eg, be jailed with serious charges trumped up - and ransomed !). Instead, anchor off uninhabited islands and visit them with suitable small boats. Or rendezvous in mid ocean with other cruise ships that have different ethnics, foods, entertainments. Let passengers switch ships if desired.

Become a cruise college. Make use of the environments (ocean, ship) by offering training in oceanography, marine biology, navigation, ship design, etc. Traditional universities are riddled with pressure groups that not only demand high pay, but require courses not relevant to the skills that students are trying to learn. A ship-borne college might hire only a few top facilitators and let most of the teaching be done by the students themselves. A student may take a course one year and teach it the next, thus refreshing/reinforcing learning.

Pierre mentioned medical facilities. How about cruises for people needing lengthy recuperation. Eg, people with diabetes-2 who want to ameliorate it through diet and exercise (instead of insulin injections which can worsen it), and who DON'T want to be tempted by the junk foods pervasive on land.

Sizes. Regardless of founders' hopes and words, if "sea-steading" is done on a ship or big structure, I expect the resulting community will more resemble the remote company towns than the homesteads of two centuries ago. Though most company towns may not have been as bad as union organizers portrayed them, they didn't offer very much freedom.

So, a case can be made for having family-size residences and businesses. Easier to change neighbors or move to a different floating community; thus less social friction and less agitating for restrictions/regulations.

But what about shelter costs ? A big ship provides more space per hull surface than can anything smaller. However, smaller sea-shelters could be mass produced, reducing construction labor. What are the numbers ? How much space does a $10M cruise ship provide, and how much time and money is needed to repurpose it ? What are production costs of smaller shelters with equivalent space, and how quickly could they be built ? I suggest that proponents of various alternatives provide realistic detailed estimates.

(Pierre commented in The Connection #315, Jan 2010. Excerpts:)
The Seasteading Institute (830 Williams Way #3, MtnView CA 94040) ... sees seasteads as "beacons to the world", spreading across the ocean, and similar things ultimately happening on land, as the number of nations in the world proliferates, and competition between them forces them to loosen their grip....

Operating an ocean-going cruise ship is inherently a high-overhead operation.... My gut feeling: the least that a stripped-down cruise could charge would be about half of what conventional cruises cost. This is still too expensive for most people, and too spartan for those who could afford it....

"Smaller sea shelters." People have been working to build the cheapest seaworthy vessels they can for millenia. I am skeptical that any great cost breakthroughs are imminent. It's easy to project low-ball cost estimates; but any boat owner can tell you, they always cost way more than you first think...

(Response by Bert) Many kinds of vessels have been built for many different purposes. A traditional type (eg, canoe) usually gets better or cheaper only when a new material comes along. But new purposes arise, for which new types are invented. Have any vessels been designed and built primarily for DWELLING in mid ocean ? Though I (personally) am not fond of some of the tribode's features, I think the overall concept has merit.

Slavery then - and now.   How to cope ?

America has had many forms of slavery. Slaves in the South of African descent have been publicized the most, not because they were always treated the worst, but because the Union won the Civil War and victors write history (at least until it is revised).   Abolitionist and Union propaganda featured dire abuses and atrocities.   They did occur but were not very common. Southern slaves were generally treated better than were military conscripts of that period - because they cost much more.   The price of an obedient healthy adult slave was around $1000 in 1850 dollars ($40,000 in today's dollars ?).   Or, if raised, costs included: less work by women while pregnant or caring for infants, and no work by young children.   Whereas the only cost of acquiring military conscripts was rounding them up.   Because slaves were valuable, plantations often hired free laborers for dangerous tasks.   (That was before employers were often held liable for employees' injuries.)   Whereas the military reckless-ly expended soldiers' lives and limbs in the Civil War.

Competent plantation owners/managers (and incompetents often went bankrupt or got fired) tried to keep their slaves content so they would be less likely to shirk work or run away. In some regions, running away was quite easy.   Owners allowed holidays, held parties, bestowed gifts.   (Some owners gave hunting rifles.   Apparantly they trusted their slaves more than many officials today trust their "citizens".)   Owners paid slaves for extra work or for implements crafted during the slaves' free time - but delayed part of the pay, which was forfeit if a slave ran away or was fined for disobedience. (Notice any similarity to "Social Security" ?)

By the way, slavery was no more a cause of the Union's war on the Confederacy, than were German atrocities against Belgium civilians in World War I a cause of the U.S. joining that war. Both were merely fodder for pro-war propaganda.   Lincoln had not been an abolitionist.   His famous declaration that freed slaves, applied only to Confederate-held areas, and was motivated by hopes that slave rebellions or fear of them would tie down Confederate forces.   Slaves in states that stayed in the Union, remained slaves until after the war.

Some of the other forms of slavery in America, along with conscription: indentured servants, Amerinds forced onto reser-vations, children forced to attend schools, people jailed or put in mad-houses for non-violent acts, people forced to pay taxes.   To anyone who claims that taxes on low-or-middle-income people* are not slavery, consider this: In the Old South, some slaves who had valuable skills they could sell, were allowed considerable freedom to live wherever and do whatever they wanted - provided they paid their owners a portion of their earnings.   Were those slaves not really "slaves" ?

For a slave in the Old South, the best alternatives were the extremes.   Either be exceptionally obedient, productive, diligent, loyal - and hope to be rewarded with better treatment, perhaps including special privileges.   Or else, run away;   and try to make a living in some wilderness, or reach a territory that did not have slavery (at least not of that kind).   There were NO good intermediate ways.   A slave who remained but was perceived to be disobedient or surly or lazy, could expect punishment or, if troublesome enough, to be sold to (eg) a prison-like sugar-mill where slaves could be closely supervised and severely punished if they malingered.   To replace slaves who died, the mills could buy troublesome slaves cheap - so mill slaves, often over-worked and underfed, rarely lived long.

Though the details are different, the extremes are still generally the best alternatives. People who 'stay in the middle of the road get run over.' **

Both then and now, for most people freeing themselves, the biggest challenge is usually, not how to leave nor how to elude hostiles, but how to maintain themselves. Eg, how to produce everything needed or else replenish initial supplies.

Those people that Holly and I know fairly well, are free in many ways but remain vulnerable in some ways. (Eg, for us, resupply uncertainties.) How to become more broadly free ? Though no sure way, some attitudes that may help: Don't get hung up on one or a few alternatives. Be imaginative, but focus on changes do-able. (Very unlikely that, during this century, we could move to another planet or vastly change this planet.) These topics deserve more pondering in Ab and DP. B&H

* Giant organizations of all kinds, and billionaires, have government-like powers or influence. So, taxes on them can be thought of as transfers from one government to another.

** When young, Holly and I had independently concluded that middle-income people were foolish. Most of my older relatives worked themselves into early disabilities or graves, to buy stuff they didn't even have time to use much. One exception: an uncle who mostly did his own things but occasionally went to distant places where/when temp labor was in demand. He seemed to enjoy life. He was also my only old relative who remained healthy into his 60s (at least; we lost contact then). I decided: unless someone could quickly become rich (and I did not think I could), better to learn to live well on little.

My mother's several sibs and their offspring formed an extended family - though a marginally functional one. At get-togethers, their favorite pastime was dissing those relatives (esp in-laws) who weren't there. But they did pass on out-grown clothes and toys and books. An aunt who sometimes fed me, helped me learn to read. But I didn't much appreciate her, maybe because she pushed bible stories. (Even as a child I was a firm non-believer: Jehovah was too much like Santa Claus to be credible.) Reading became my favorite winter-time activity, in the inland northeast where daily highs were seldom above freezing. (The books passed on to me were mostly 'girls' stories. Apparantly, only female relatives had learned to read. Yeah, I got a crush on one FICTIONAL protagonist.)

The relatives who fed me, were usually too busy working or recuperating from work to bother with vegies other than what came in TV dinners. Consequently I often craved greens, even grass (which I chewed and chewed for the juice, then spit out the residual tough fibers). The itinerant uncle showed me some edible wild plants. I often nibbled on them, raw. One was purslane. (Holly and I have found it in gardens here, but not in the wild.) Though edible wild plants were quite common in that area during summers, I do not recall any other relative utilizing them, except for black-caps (raspberries) which, along with plenty of sugar, was sometimes made into jam. Strangely, I liked ragweed pollen, to which many people are allergic; to me, it smelled and tasted much like orange peel. When very young, I feared all mushrooms and umbelliferae (which include poison hemlock). I think I inherited those fears - I don't recall any warnings. (Yeah, these food memories are semi-digressions - to fill the page, and lead in to next article)

Some beliefs about the Stone Age are ROCKY.

Summary: During the past ± 10,000 years, most of our ancestors ate much UNrefined grains. Before that, during a SHORT part of the Stone Age, most of our ancestors ate much meat. Consequently, because the high-grain period was more recent than the high-meat period, it probably had more genetic effects on the nutritional needs of most people today.

Elaboration: Some nutrition writers favor high-protein diets. Their arguments go: Our Stone-Age ancestors ate much meat. They did not eat much grain until they developed agriculture ± 10,000 years ago. So, our genes haven't had time to evolve adaptation to grains. They remain adapted to meats.

Most such writers do not define what they mean by "Stone Age". However, one writer was more specific.* "20,000 years ago, people hunted and foraged for their food, eating lean meats, seafoods, and organic (pesticide-free) vegetables and fruits that resemble our modern kale, rose hips, and crab-apples. The diet" was "high in protein, relatively low in saturated fat, and high in non-starchy (low carbohydrate) vegetables and fruits." p.32 "The relative percentages of animal foods vs vegetable foods varied from culture to culture, but, interestingly, no society was entirely vegetarian."

HOW ancient ? Food-remains decay so, presumably, most that were studied were fairly recent. 20,000 years ago may be average. The author seems to assume that what humans ate then, was what they ate AT ALL TIMES prior to agriculture. Really ?

What were our ancestors eating ± 8 MILLION years ago when proto-humans diverged from chimpanzees ? Studies indicate that human genes differ more than do chimp genes from genes of our common ancestors. So, those ancestors probably ate more like how chimps eat now, than like how humans ate 20,000 years ago. Chimps eat mostly fruit when available. But they sometimes hunt: females and adolescents more than adult males; appropriately, they need more protein.   They make crude spears from branches, sharpening them with their teeth. (Sci News 3mar07) But they don't secure much meat. They eat the meat raw.

Gorillas genetically diverged a few million years before the chimp-human split. They usually eat mostly foliage. But when fruit is abundant, they eat mostly fruit.

What were our ancestors eating ± 100 million years ago when primates diverged from other mammals ? They ate much fruit and/or foliage. Evidence: those ancestors lost the ability (which most mammals have) to form vitamin C.

RAW meat was/is a risky food for humans, and probably for chimps and most primates; because we lack the strong stomach acids of carnivores; and because we have longer life spans - and thus more time to accumulate and be harmed by parasites.

Fire was domesticated ± 500,000 years ago. How much meat were those proto-humans eating then ? Their brain size was mid-way between chimps and modern humans. Their weapons were superior to chimps' crude spears, but inferior to humans' weapons of 20,000 years ago. So, they likely ate more meat than do chimps, but less than did late-Stone-Age humans.

Our ancestors' diets began to change greatly ±30,000 years ago, after modern humans evolved and developed (eg) accurate arrows (NOT easy to make) and sophisticated traps and fishing gear, along with language able to coordinate complex endeavors. That enabled modern humans to proliferate, spread out, and interbreed with or displace proto-humans.

When humans first arrived in an area, most animals did not fear DISTANT humans, because those animals can run faster than can a human for a short distance. Even today, in areas where humans rarely go, animals don't flee until a human gets very close. Yes, in open country during hot weather, a naked human could sometimes chase a fur-covered animal until it collapsed from heat exhaustion. But often, the animal, faster at first, would get far enough ahead to hide successfully. Did such chases usually burn more calories than they yielded ?

When humans first arrived, they were few and the animals plentiful. And the animals, fearless of a human at arrow range, were easy to kill. Thus, ± 20,000 years ago (earlier in some places, later in others) began a PEAK era of hunting, trapping, fishing - and meat consumption. As big animals were hunted to extinction or evolved fear of distant humans, humans did more hunting/trapping of small animals and foraging of wild vegetables. But meat continued to be a major source of calories in many cultures until agriculture developed.

Prior to agriculture, how much grain was eaten ? Our ancestors probably preferred fruit and meat and succulent vegies when available. But often they were scarce. Wild grass seeds were sometimes abundant, and some can be harvested and prepared with Stone-Age tools. Certainly, grass seeds were utilized; else domestic grains would not have evolved.

Mature grass seeds are one of the few foods easy to store in savanna/semi-desert areas where modern humans are thought to have evolved. So, grass seeds may have first been emergency rations, eaten during famines. Then, as harvest techniques improved, grass seeds were utilized more. Then, maybe one spring after a benign winter, someone tried sprinkling left-over seeds on bare earth deposited by a flood. Then, grass seeds began to evolve that were easier to harvest. At first, horticulture was probably only an occasional diversion. (Seems unlikely that large-scale agriculture began suddenly.)

High-protein advocators argue that ± 10,000 years has not been long enough for humans to evolve the genes needed to thrive on high-grain diets. If true, the period of high meat consumption was probably not long enough either. And the high-grain period is more recent, so its effects are probably greater

Another argument of high-protein advocates: Thousands of years ago, two "genes, which predispose a person toward celiac disease, were relatively common among humans."

HOW common and among WHICH humans ? Were most of the tested remains from people who had inhabited Europe during the ice ages and who, like arctic peoples recently, of necessity hunted and fished much more than they gathered plants ?

"During most of human evolution, these genes posed no disadvantage, because people rarely consumed grains."

During most of human evolution, EVERY type of food was probably scarce in most places much of the time. Most of our ancestors got enough to eat only by consuming MANY types.

"The situation changed about 10,000 years ago when people began cultivating gluten-containing grains.... The incidence of many diseases skyrocketed.... Archeological evidence indicates significant post-gluten increase in birth defects, osteoporosis, arthritis, rickets, dental enamel defects, infertility, child mortality, and disease and death at all ages."

Due mainly to gluten intolerance ? Or due to various adverse effects of increasingly dense populations in grain-cultivating areas ? Eg: more spread of infectious diseases;

more famines because of dependence on fewer foods; less food
variety for most of the people as gatherer-hunter bands of a
few dozen were displaced by nations of many thousands. In them,
the rulers likely hogged most of the fruits and meats and
favorite vegies, while the peasants ate mostly grain.

Furthermore, each ancient ag society was at first limited
to the FEW grains and beans (etc) native to its area. Whereas
N Americans today enjoy MANY kinds that originated all over the
world. And, we know more about nutrition. Eg, grains need
sprouting to yield vit C, and fermentation (yeasting) to yield
absorbable vit B3. So, the deficiencies of ANCIENT high-grain
diets, are not necessarily reasons to shun grains now.

(To learn gluten-intolerance's importance: In ancient ag
societies, were diseases less where the main grain was gluten-
free (eg, rice) than where the main grain contained gluten (eg,
wheat) ? Or were diseases about as common ?)

Each human alive today is carrying a unique mixture of
genes from thousands of different ancestors living in different
environments and eating many different diets. So tolerances
vary. Eg, gluten-containing grains cause serious digestive
problems (celiac) in approx 1% of people. Eg, a high animal-
protein diet, increases cancer risk in many people (Sci News
25oct08; book "China Study" summarized in Ab#6). But, considering our ENTIRE evolutionary past, I think that, for MOST
adult humans, a high-grain diet is healthier than a high-meat
diet. H&B

* Feed Your Genes Right, Jack Challem, 2005. I chose this book
to quote because it seems BETTER researched and more specific
than other pro-high-protein books I've seen. Of course, the
sources are early 2000s or older and do not report discoveries
since then. The only two Stone-Age refs to sci journals: Am J
Clin Nutr, 2000, 71:682-92; Euro J Nutr, 2000, 39:67-70.

I've also read three 2008 issues of Challem's newsletter.
(Recommended. www.nutritionreporter.com Ask a library to
subscribe. $33/yr/ten in 08. POB 30246, Tucson AZ 85751.) It
did not promote particular diets other than reporting on the
effects of vitamins, etc. Did Challem change his mind ? Or,
did publisher slant book to obtain meat-industry support ? Eg:
"Vegetarian foods, like beans and nuts, provide incomplete
proteins in that they lack one or more of the essential amino
acids. For this reason vegetarians must eat complementary
proteins, such as legumes and brown rice...." p.66. WRONG.
All beans and nuts and grains (that I know about) contain ALL
essential amino acids. Some do not contain optimum ratios. Eg,
corn, the least-balanced common grain, contains (as I recall)
30% less lysine than optimum. Consequently, more of corn's
other amino acids can be utilized as protein (rather than like
carbs) if (eg) a lysine-rich legume is eaten within few hours.
"Celiac disease is an inherited intolerance of gluten, a
family of related proteins found in wheat, rye, barley, and
many other grains." p.180. BIASED. No mention there of rice
and other grains that do NOT contain gluten.

Finally, advocating ANY specific diet for EVERYONE, contra-
dicts the book's title and theme: "Feed Your Genes Right."

Bert and I eat mostly plants - for convenience, not ideol-
ogy. We also kill and eat animals that become nuisances.
Recently, a pack rat that invaded our storage tent. Young,
tender, tasty. (Some are not as tasty. A possum - yuck !)
(For rodents, taste depends more on feed than on species.)

To breed or not to breed ? Broad eugenic policies harmful.

Some diseases are often inherited. Ie, an illness may be much more common in an extended family than among the general population. This has long been known. Recently discovered: the genes whose variants cause or contribute to some diseases.

With many of these diseases, someone will develop it only if BOTH parents provide the variant gene. If only one parent does, the variant may be advantageous - which explains why the variant is not weeded out by evolution. Eg, sickle-cell anemia. If one parent provides the variant, the child's red-blood-cells have normal shape - and are more resistant to malaria than if neither parent provides the variant. But if both parents provide the variant, the red-blood-cells are sickle shaped and and do not flow well through narrow blood vessels.

A genetic disease may be caused by a variant gene forming an enzyme that does its job less well. Eg, if its job is transforming molecules of a proto-vitamin into the active form, the enzyme might not grab onto as many of those molecules as they pass by. Such a disease may be ameliorated by ingesting more of that proto-vitamin. The book, <u>Feed Your Genes Right</u> (Jack Challem, Wiley, 2005), has quite a few case histories of inherited diseases ameliorated by appropriate nutrition.

If/when genetic determinations become inexpensive, a prospective parant can learn which potentially-harmful gene variants s/he has (most/all people probably have some) and choose a mate who does not have those variants.

Most traits result from MANY genes PLUS environmental factors. Some outstanding individuals had parents who were similarly outstanding. But many had parents who were ordinary or even "inferior" by contemporary standards. Similarly for plants. To breed a superior (in some way) variety, one method: work with open-pollinated plants, select a few with the trait desired, propagate them, select among their offspring, etc. Another method: hybrids. A superior plant may result from cross-breeding parents BOTH of which are inferior.

Broad eugenics, whether due to government decrees or conformist fashions, would produce a quite uniform population. Expect fewer morons but also fewer geniuses; and, most important, fewer individuals with freaky talents that may be vital in the decades ahead. Also, there's an advantage of a large population: the more people, the more freaks. Holly & Bert

If you would like to give birth, don't be quick to assume you are genetically unfit merely because some people disapprove of some of your traits. Be esp wary of psychiatrists (many of whom are appropriately called "shrinks": their treatments kill neurons - shrink brains). They are prone to label someone "mentally ill" merely because s/he doesn't conform.

I heard a radio interview with Temple Grandin. When young, shrinks said she had "autism". Though less capable some ways than most other people, she was superb at learning what animals felt/needed and designing/building compatable equipment. She also wrote books and became quite famous. Thereupon, shrinks said, she had "high-functioning autism". (Were those shrinks "high-functioning idiots" ?)   Holly

Soon after we met, Holly served notice that she didn't wan children. Her reasons: taking care of babies is much work; compatability of parents and kids is a gamble; and, regardless of parents' hopes and plans, the end products, adults, will likely be much like most of the people already on earth.

Valid reasons. But I was surprised. Every other woman I'd
tten to know quite well (not many), either wanted a child (or
) or already had a child. Ie, despite all the work and
oblems of gestating, birthing, feeding, tending babies, most
men wanted babies. Not surprising, considering evolution:
ose women would likely pass on their baby-loving genes.*

Holly liked kids. She sometimes baby sat. She sometimes
ayed with kids we encountered. But she didn't want any of
r own. I wondered if there might be additional reasons why.

Holly and her mother were not compatable. Their times
gether had been stormy. She left at age 13. She then stayed
iefly with her divorced dad and step-mom and their kids.
ey weren't compatable either. Did Holly subconsciously fear
at a motherhood would be a repeat of her childhood ?

Holly's birth had been difficult. Her mother had had to
 to a hospital and have Holly dragged out with forceps (which
formed one ear - externally, Holly can hear okay). Not
rprisingly, Holly was an only child. Though Holly has no
nscious memory of birth, her subconscious probably recorded
e event - and may warn: DON'T GET PREGNANT. Because, until
50 years ago, difficult births were often fatal for the
ther. If the baby survived, she often inherited the traits
at had handicapped her mother. Her best bet for propagating
r genes: become a maiden aunt and help care for relatives'
bies - who would have many of the same genes she had.

Holly hikes long distances. She also runs: if loads light,
often lope down gradually-descending parts of logging roads.

Before meeting Holly, I dated a 25-year-old woman, Amy, who
d a 7-year-old daughter, Bea. (pen names) Both seemed strong-
 than most women and girls. Amy's job included lifting boxes
d crates. Bea liked playgrounds with trapeses and monkey-bars
which she was quite acrobatic. But neither liked to walk
ch. And neither could run effectively. When (at my request)
y tried to run, I easily WALKED faster. Apparantly their
lvises or hips were not well shaped for running. One day, Amy
ntioned that her sister-in-law, Sil, bemoaned the agonies of
ildbirth. Amy believed Sil was exaggerating, maybe to guilt-
ip her husband. I asked if Bea's birth had been easy. Amy
plied, "A piece of cake." (Amy expressed interest in having
re kids. But my itinerant ways and ambitions worried her.
so my being 5 years younger (maybe because, when a woman
aches menopause and her sex interest wanes, a younger man is
re likely than an older man to seek other women - though, on
e other hand, a younger man is less likely to die before her
ds are grown.) Amy met a somewhat-older man who had had
llege training, and had a steady job and upper-middle-class
bitions. That ended our relationship.)

Tentative conclusion: Human pelvises well-shaped for
rthing are not well-shaped for running. Not surprising: we
ve had our huge brains (compared to other animals our size),
d skulls to contain them, for only ±100,000 years - not long
olutionarily. So, our bodies have not had time to evolve
mpatability with BOTH birthing and running. Bert

I wanted either no kids or many kids. I planned to largely
oid most people (who seemed demented). So, an only child
uld likely be lonely. Whereas multiple kids would have each
her for company, and hopefully would develop a well-functioning
tended family. I now think I underrated some dificulties, esp
ose caused by governments; and the time and labor needed to
velop a home in which we would not be molested. Bert

Some slightly sensational sobering safe sex suggestions.

Sex is easier to do safely than is soccer, skating, biking, eating, and many other activities.   There is LESS reason to postpone sex until age 18, than to postpone engaging in competitive sports, or traveling on wheels, or choosing foods.

As for the claim that sex is risky because of the intense emotions involved: True.   But so are competitive sports.

As for the claim that a sexually-experienced older person might seduce and possibly harm a sexually-naive younger person: True.   But advertisers persuade nutritionally-naive young people to buy and eat junk foods.   So, should the advertising and selling and serving   of colas, pop, candy bars, cakes, sugary cereals, etc, to anyone under 18 - be outlawed ?

To bike safely, you need avoid many hazards.   To have sex safely, you need avoid mainly one: DON'T TRANSFER BODY FLUIDS.

Saliva is a body fluid.   Bare-faced mouth-to-mouth kissing is risky.   Saliva may not transmit HIV very often but it sure can transmit flu.   (Bert and I tried mouth-to-mouth kissing through the two surfaces of a plastic produce bag.   Felt fine.)

For contraception, use only condoms, NOT birth-control drugs or vaginal inserts - which may have harmful side effects not discovered for decades.   Use TWO condoms: one might break or be defective.   The woman should furnish at least one of the condoms and put it on the man: it is SHE who can get pregnant. (If a man fears child-support entrapment by a woman trying to get pregnant, he may furnish one condom.   He puts his on first.) We re-use condoms: wash well, dry, then coat with corn starch to prevent condom sticking to self. (Details in Apr/Oct 1981 DP)

If you are a heterosexual woman, take command of your sex life.   Have only the kinds of sex you want and only when you want them.   Usually you can find a man or men eager to please you.   "Beauty is in the eye of the beholder."   If you don't resemble the current glamour star, not as many people may be attracted to you, but quite a few probably will be.

If you may be in private with a man you don't know well, consider taking along a few women friends as chaperones, not to prevent sex but to limit sex to what you want.

Sex is often bonding.   "The fastest way to someone's heart" is usually NOT through their stomach.   So, may be wise to get to know someone well enough to feel compatable in other ways before engaging in sex with that person.

Trying to keep children ignorant of sex, is CRAZY.   That's a good way to INTEREST kids in sex. Anything mysterious attracts kids.   Consider the many childrens books with titles like: the hidden valley, the secret garden, the locked room.   Likewise, concealing genitals, makes kids curious about them.*

Limiting children's knowledge of sex to what they may hear from other kids, increases the odds that, when they do become interested, their sex will NOT be safe.   Blame ills and unwanted pregnancies, not on pornographers as much as on puritans.

People who want to prohibit sex, may claim that health is the reason.   But, unless they also want to prohibit competitive sports (etc), they are either ignorant or LYING.   Most likely, the truth is: they want to force their religious beliefs or personal tastes on others.   Holly and Bert
* Most vicious of all: laws or customs banning bare breasts (even if breast-feeding allowed).   That prompts many mothers who would otherwise breast-feed exclusively, to bottle-feed when in public - to avoid being stared at.   Non-human milk fed to infants (esp < 3 mo) is the chief cause of diabetes-1 !

Supplement to Ab and Dwelling Portably, March 2010.

June 87 MP(DP) is enclosed (if that doesn't increase postage).
FREE, because some portions are blurry. Thrifty Prints
(Baraboo WI) goofed, but then made better copies. We seek a
low-price printer with reliable quality, the closer the better.

I attribute my dental health mostly to diet.
I had my teeth examined and cleaned for the first time in
13 years. I had much tartar but no cavities. The dentists
were amazed. I eat well - very little sugar and NO SODA DRINKS
(which contain phosphoric acid). Andrew in Maine, Feb 2010

Iodine and Chlorine only kill Giardia, not Cryptosporidium.
I read that about the water-disinfecting tablets. So
unless you are absolutely certain that your drinking water
source is safe, boil, filter, or use a new UV-light gadget.
If you filter, beware cross contamination: don't touch pickup
and discharge hoses together, or touch both with same hand.
(Comment) If you are in an area for a while,   David in MI, 09
you can probably find or develop a safe source. (Suggestions
in May 08 DP.) If you must sterilize, heat is more reliable
than filtering or UV. You don't need to boil, 170°F suffices -
obtainable if sun, with reflectors and transparent shroud - but,
to be sure water is hot enough, you'll need cooking thermometer.

Pure magnesium chloride is available from Get Tanked acquariums.
gettankedaquariums.com   Bill in cyberspace, 2009

I believe: feet must be able to flex around in the cold.
So I wear good sox and put wool insoles in boots, but buy
boots a bit big. Works good. I rotate footwear, though not as
often as you recommend (in Ab#9). I have 3 pairs of rubber
boots for winter (needed here), and many cheap sneakers for
                                          summer. Andrew, Feb
My chosen vehicle is a 2001 Dodge minivan.
I removed all the rear seats. A great way to haul - whatever. I'm not wealthy but my modest pension lets me camp in
wonderful places. I moved from Michigan to Oregon 5 years ago
and will never go back. I've grandchildren here - retirement
is terrif for me. Years ago I was a DP subscriber but let it
lapse when I moved abroad for 3 years. Recently I came across
your book at Powells in Portland. What a blast from the past.
I have always agreed with your lifestyle. Joe, OR 971, 2009

Years ago, old step-vans and buses were great units to convert.
But now they are conspicuous and 'targeted'. Clean-looking
small vans and motorhomes aren't hard to find. The big rigs
can be found in the Sun Belt when spring comes and widows want
to head home - minus rig and memories. But vans and smaller
less-conspicuous motorhomes have advantages. Few people with
the big rigs ever travel as much because of poor mileage and
lack of suitable squat spots. Al Fry (More by Al about RVs
and his experiences with them in Living Mobile. Availability?)

My dog and I are house/property sitting long-term.
We are in southeast Tennessee on a chilly plateau. The
house must be occupied for insurance coverage. It is lonely
up here but the furnished house is warm and comfortable. I must
climb a tall oak tree for a cell-phone signal. The owner pays
all utilities. Everyone except 4-wheelers respects the private-
road/no-trespassing sign at the turnoff. For food money, I
help a friend maintain his rental properties. Jimmy in TN, 09

Should Ab/DP include only well-proven devices and techniques ?

Your pole/plastic shelter designs are tried and proven. And other unconventional LAND-based dwellings/dwellingways written about in DP are generally things people have tried or currently practice. And being on the ocean in a decent boat with a good crew, is as safe or risky as any other undertaking one is prepared for and/or skilled at. But I get a sense that some suggestions in Ab/DP for OCEAN-based dwellings are by people with only theoretical knowledge who do not understand and appreciate the realities of living on the ocean.

On land I've survived for days virtually naked. Whereas the ocean is inherently hostile to humans. Without a boat you will soon die from drowning or exposure. Also, the ocean plays havoc with gear, structures, metals of all kinds. Eg, plastic wrap on a float will wear off quickly. Andrew in Maine, Feb 2010

(Response) No human will survive for days virtually naked - in Maine IN WINTER. Most of N Am is, at times, inherently hostile to humans who lack shelter (clothes being portable shelter). Our long-ago ancestors were tropical. We lack thick fur.

Each pole/plastic shelter we build is UNTRIED - because it is different from every other shelter we've built - because each is tailored to the site and every site is different.

After having built many shelters, variously configured for various purposes and sites, we do have a sense of what is likely to endure long enough to achieve what we want. But almost all have been west of Cascades - relatively mild. We've little or no experience building shelters in the inland north, desert south-west, etc. Nor, usually, do we put many details in DP, because they would not much help anyone else - because their resources and needs and site will differ from ours.

A Metronome group experimentally built a "Hillodge" during winter, inspired by our write-up in Apr92 DP. Its roof was not steep enough. Snow accumulated, sagged the roof, and had to be repeatedly cleared off during the night. Our write-up had not sufficiently emphasized the importance of roof slope: possibly because, the year or two we'd used a Hillodge, no snow.

For Metronome, the snow accumulation was merely a nuisance. Also, their motorhome parked nearby was backup. (In Metn#10, $2)

Repeatedly, we and others in DP caution: if trying anything new/different, have a backup easily accessible. (Eg, Sep04 DP, p.3) This applies to the ocean, too. Ships carry lifeboats. Sailboats heading for the same area often travel in groups.

I'm not convinced that a somewhat-different kind of ocean shelter is inherently much more dangerous than a somewhat-different kind of land shelter. With EITHER, builders would be foolish if, immediately upon completion, they headed alone, with no backup, to a remote land wilderness OR remote OCEAN area.

Holly and I know very little about the backgrounds of most Ab/DP authors. We prefer articles by people who have consider-able experience doing what they write about. But we take what we can get. With ANY info from ANYone, USER BE WARY ! The author may omit an important detail (especially if writing from memory), or the reader may misinterpret something, etc.

Re ocean vessels, at least those of family or small-group size, my impression is: most designers/builders are experienced only with traditional types, because such boats sell the most. Reason: presently, most moderate-size boats are used for sport (racing) and recreation and status; not for dwelling long on the ocean. And most buyers value tradition. Eg, in most boat races, an odd configuration would be as unwelcome as would be a

cheetah in a dog race. So, any break-through likely will come
from someone outside the field. And, yeah, the prototype likely
will need changes before it performs reliably - if it does.
    Holly and I much appreciate the specific doubts about
specific equipment/techniques/proposals that you and others
have expressed, because they may lead to improvement or
replacement, or avert disasterous consequences. But Ab/DP/LLL
will continue to publish some untested ideas, as well as
widely-verified info and long-followed instructions. B & H

I plan to leave my job and squat on some family-owned land.
    It is in nearby mountains. I am building a small cabin,
and planting a garden, and raising some capons and rabbits.
My present job (sales) is ridiculous and awful. I welcome the
advice of stressless individuals and free thinkers.
    Tom Hodgekinson, a Brit, offers some good advice, I think.
He has several books, his own magazine "The Idler", and hosts a
a website: http://idler.co.uk/   Brian, PA 185, Feb09

(Addendum) A friend looked at site briefly and reported: Tom
advises: don't seek status. He also believes most Europeans
lived better during medieval times (±475-1450) than recently.

Google "Jeff Jonas". His thinking may help DP readers.
    Re "recession": Where we are, the people are used to hard
times. However, number of food boxes distributed around here
is up 50% as of last month. Michael, AZ 853, March 09

I came across a huge database of do-it-yourself information.
    13 gig file size. Google cd3wd.com   D.S., FL 322, Jan2010

Tennessee now requires gov photo ID from EVERYONE buying beer.
    Luckily I found a store that ignores this bad law. Jimmy

A copy-ready page for Ab can also go into The Connection.
    We are previewing in TC some of our Ab pages to get
additional/quicker comments. (TC publishes 8 times a year.)
If you'd like us to put your Ab page in TC: to get in quickest
send us TWO copies. Ab's format (text 16x25cm or 6.3x10") is
okay for TC if on 8½x11 paper with at least ½" margins left and
right and ¼" top and bottom. But, unlike Ab, no cut-and-pastes.
    Our current subscription to TC (extends through Jan 2011)
lets us put in 4 pages per issue. We seldom have 4 of our own.

Wanted: clippings and net-printouts with info for Ab and DP.
    The only periodicals we have recently received regularly:
American Survivor, CD Summary, Living Free, The Connection,
Wild Foods Forum, Zine World. No big-circulation publications.
    For several years we got Science News. But we let our
subscription expire in late 08 because SN had changed. SN no
longer prints much health info do-able yourself. Instead, SN
now mostly features elaborate procedures that will become
available (if at all) only after many more years of development.
Ie, medical pie in the sky, by and by, priced very high.

Items I saw ads for that might be useful:
    Woodburning Trail-stove, mass produced version of the old
coffee-can stove, sometimes called rocket stove. $25, 2 pounds,
burns sticks and twigs. trail-stove.com
    Udap's Bear Shock, portable electric fence encloses 30x30-
foot area, 4 pounds, 6000-volt shock, runs 6 weeks on two D-cells.
$300. udap.com Expensive. Instead you could run a standard
elec fence off a car battery (indefinitely with pv tricklecharge)
    Trick birthday candles, won't blow out. David in MI, 2009

Is vitamin D from sunshine healthier than vit D from pills ?
Michael Mogadon, MD, thought so in 2001 when he wrote a
book. Though the vitamin may be the same, its transport by
blood differs. From skin, it is carried by protein. From gut,
it is carried by fat - which may contribute to artery clogging.

What percent of ultraviolet-B is absorbed by the atmosphere ?
On a typical early-summer day near noon when sun is very
high in sky (except in/near arctic) ? Knowing that, absorption
on other dates at any latitude is easy to calculate.

Source for acrylic (or?) FILM that resists UV yet passes UVB ?
Use film for winter-sunning mini-shelter. (On internet, .
a friend found only sellers of thick acrylic SHEETS.)

Do MDs and millionaires die younger, on average, than others ?
I read that years ago, but seek confirmation. Info very
pertinent re effectiveness and advisability of most med care !

What care do Nimh batteries need that NiCd don't need ?
A clerk at Radio Shack (which sold BOTH) said: unlike
NiCd, Nimh deteriorate if left discharged. Garrity recommends
cranking their light at least monthly. Also heard: a fully-
charged Nimh can't tolerate a continuing trickle charge.

How much more energy-per-weight does Li-ion store than Nimh ?
Than lead-acid ? What special care does Li-ion need ?

What simple vessels may be good for mid-ocean dwelling ?
A few years ago, Zalia sent a photo and a note about a
small boat she'd designed, built, used. (We put it into a
Supplement, but not DP then, hoping for more details.) Simple
to build. 3 sections bolted together. Mid section rectangular,
open, held 2 people. Front and back sections
tapered in depth, foam filled so unsinkable.
Could an ocean abode be built that way ?
Eg, ± six 8-foot-cube mid-sections, identical
except for deck fittings; tapered front and back sections,
identical except fittings. It'd be simpler to build than any
ocean-going craft I've seen or read of, including tribode. It
would roll more than a tribode, but could contain a pivoted
flywheel-stabilized inner room. Info/ideas welcome for other
fairly-simple mobile craft for DWELLING long on deep water.

What ocean areas far from land are usually quite placid ?
Ie, rarely have violent storms, at least some seasons ?
Usual weather ? What months ? Approx latitude/longditude
extent ? Or, what book has this info ? (This question is
especially to anyone who proposes an ocean dwelling.)

How durable/reliable are pepper-spray bear-deterrants ?
Supposedly more effective than guns for stopping charges.
But a gun can be test-fired occasionally to verify it works.

CHORD EASY, short version (12p.5x8) is FREE to any library.
IF ordered BY LIBRARIAN. (Else $1.) If public access is
doubtable, tell location, and hours, and who can simply walk in.
(Of course, we hope readers will then order the full version:
5th edition, 60 songs, 64p.5x8, $6.) In a Zine World review,
Clint said, "This is AWESOME. If more artists were familiar
with what Chord Easy is teaching, popular music would be a lot
more interesting." CE c/o Lisa Ahne, POB 181, Alsea OR 97324

Each float is kept upright by stays from its outrig to its boom mid joint or (on lead float) to a spar directly above its center. (If the bottom end of a boom kept a float upright, that boom section would get bending force whereas the stays exert only compression.)

Boat hulls are painted with toxic chemicals to keep barnicles from growing on them. Tribode floats can be protected by wrapping plastic film around them. They have shapes easy to wrap, unlike most boats. If barnicles adhere to the plastic, hot water will detach.

ACCESS.

ACCESS. If the cabin will be only a residence and light work place, I'd build the aft room's bottom to also be the hatch. (The bottom instead of deck so what when open the hatch is near level for easy passage and is somewhat sheltered from rain.) The hatch's inner end is hinged to the bottom frame. The outer end is supported, when open, by two stays to the deck above and, when closed, by latches.

Extending out and up from the room's aft corners are two spars. Their upper ends join and are braced by a stay. They hold a hoist. Safety netting extends from hatch's sides to the deck frame and from hatch's outer end to the hoist spars. A rope ladder goes to the deck.

To go from the cabin to the deck, open the hatch, walk out onto it, twist the ladder a half turn, step onto it and climb to the deck.

To haul up supplies or to descend, don a safety harness, open hatch, and unclip ladder and outer safety net to put them out of the way. If electric, the hoist can be operated either from the aft room or by remote control while riding it. If manual, I'd mount it so that the rider operates it. When the load comes up, swing it over the hatch (or deck if wanted there) and slacken the hoist.

I'd use a hoist mounted aft only for loads under 400#. For a heavier object I'd put a hoist under the center room and operate it from a net beneath cabin. I'd work on object there (not inside).

STOCAT is an open catamaran, 32' long, width optional. Its two floats are identical to the tribode's floats. It is often tethered to the tribode's booms' mid joints. It can carry supplies that exceed the cabin's capacity. To access them, position the stocat beneath the cabin's hoist. Most supplies may be in watertight containers on top of the stocat's floats. To avoid rain or sea spray, hoist a container up and into the cabin and open it there. Supplies can also be carried on top of the tribode's floats but access is not as easy. Only liquids could be carried inside floats and be easily accessed.

I'd join the floats with stretchy stays forward and aft plus a cylindrical beam that inserts into sockets on the outrigs. Unlike the tribode's booms, the beam's ends keep the stocat's floats upright which imposes bending force. The outrigs bolt to the floats, same as the tribode's floats' outrigs, but the sockets are horizontal instead of angled up. This way of joining the floats allows them to pitch independently and to a lesser extent yaw independently. This way they are stressed less than they would be if rigidly connected.

A hoist on the stocat can raise any of the tribode's or stocat's floats for maintenance. (A stocat float is raised by trying to lift a heavy bag of sea water on the opposite side. That tips the stocat.) I'd mount the hoist on the beam so that it can be slid over to either float. The hoist is braced by two stays to that float, one forward, one aft, and by a stay to the opposite outrig.

A stocat also provides space for activities that are best done close to the water. Netting extends between the floats.

If not burdened with supplies, the stocat can be used separately as a boat propelled by outboard motor or sail. To not need a mast or rigging, use a triangular sail. Attach each bottom corner to a float and hold up the top corner with the hoist.

SAIL. For sailing the tribode down wind or cross wind I'd use a
single triangular sail as big as 30x30x30'. It is curved to better
catch the wind. Its top corner is fastened to the high forward joint.
From each bottom corner two guys go, one aft, one forward, to sheaves
mounted on low joints and from there to control. I'd usually control
from a net between cabin and high forward joint. (Control from inside
requires more sheaves plus holes for the guys.) The four guys angle
the sail to make best use of the wind. To deflate sail, the control
person slacks guys and bundles sail into a pack bag. The guys remain
threaded through the sheaves for easy respreading of the sail.

To travel upwind I'd use electric outboard motors on the aft
floats, powered by wind generators mounted on the aft mid joints, and
by photovoltaics on the floats. Though probably not as fast upwind
as a sloop rig, that provides easier control and enables travel
directly into a wind whereas a sailboat must tack from side to side.

AEROCABIN. More streamlined than the view-cabin described on page 3,
it is for a tribode that remains where hurricane winds may occur. The
top view and center room (drawings 3, 5, and 6) are like the view-
cabin's, but the outer rooms' decks slope at the same angle as the
outer rooms' bottoms and the joints are more rounded.

A tailplane keeps the aerocabin's front slightly lower than its
rear so that any lift is negative. (Otherwise, swells would sometimes raise the front and a 100 mph gust then may create enough lift
to raise a near-empty tribode and tumble it.) A 100 mph wind's drag
on aerocabin will be $\sim$ 300 pounds and on the booms, spars and stays
$\sim$ 500, not enough to seriously affect a tribode's stability.

For a tribode unlikely to encounter winds over 70 mph, I prefer
a view-cabin. Better vision ahead and toward sides. (The aerocabin
may need mirrors outside.) Simpler structure because joints are not
rounded. Simpler hoist. (On aerocabin I'd want the hoist streamlined or retractable, to not mess up the cabin's air flow.) Outer
decks are nearly level and thus easier to walk on. When the cabin is
floating (not yet on tribode), outer decks are farther above water.

Either cabin is for activities needing only light equipment.

LIMITS. When the wind is fierce, open the hatch a little to reduce
pressure inside the cabin and thus reduce outward stress on deck and
bottom. (Hurricanes rip off the roofs of tightly closed houses.)

For least stress, keep the tribode and its floats parallel to the
motion of the biggest waves, using a small quickly-deployable sea
anchor on leading float's bow or wave rectifiers (hinged flaps that
resist motion one way) on the trailing floats' sterns. The stays that
position the floats are stretchy which lets the floats wiggle in
response to waves instead of rigidly resisting.

For stability, keep the center of gravity (CG) low by storing
most supplies on a stocat tethered to the tribode or on the tribode's
floats. Unless the cabin is heavy loaded, CG is highest (16' above
sea level) when the tribode is empty. For waves alone to capsize an
empty tribode, they must tilt it up to 55° (steep). That would
require a wave over 50' high that also has a length that puts the
trailing floats in a trough when the leading float rides a crest. If
simultaneously hit by a 100 mph gust, the critical tilt is $\sim$ 34°.
A 153 mph gust alone may capsize an empty tribode that lacks a sea
anchor or tethered stocat.

Structurally I'm designing for a 115 mph wind with a safety
factor of 3. (Wind force $\propto$ V^2, so 200 mph may cause damage.) I would
not keep any tribode where/when the wind might exceed 115 mph.

Stability can be increased by attaching a big deeply submerged
sea anchor to leading float. For least stress use a stretchy cable.